Ways of Voice

Matthew Rahaim

WAYS OF VOICE

Vocal Striving and Moral Contestation in North India and Beyond

Wesleyan University Press   Middletown, Connecticut

Wesleyan University Press
Middletown CT 06459
www.wesleyan.edu/wespress

Manufactured in the United States of America
Designed by Mindy Basinger Hill
Typeset in Minion Pro

Library of Congress Cataloging-in-Publication Data

Names: Rahaim, Matthew, author.

Title: Ways of voice : vocal striving and moral contestation in North India and beyond / Matthew Rahaim.

Description: [First.] | Middletown : Wesleyan University Press, 2021. | Series: Music/culture | Includes bibliographical references and index. | Description based on print version record and CIP data provided by publisher; resource not viewed.

Identifiers: LCCN 2021029474 (print) | LCCN 2021029475 (ebook) | ISBN 9780819579393 (cloth) | ISBN 9780819579386 (trade paperback) | ISBN 9780819579409(ebook)

Subjects: LCSH: Singing—India, North. | Vocal music—India, North—Analysis, appreciation.

Classification: LCC ML2551.I5 (ebook) | LCC ML2551.I5 R353 2021 (print) | DDC 782.20954—dc23

LC record available at https://lccn.loc.gov/2021029474

5 4 3 2 1

CONTENTS

ILLUSTRATIONS

ACKNOWLEDGMENTS

The first *pranam* must go to Laxman Krishnarao Pandit, my guru in vocal music. His patient, steady guidance has been my *adhara* in the course of this book project. To Meeta Pandit, I'm grateful for innumerable musical insights; and to Srimati Abha Pandit, for always making me feel at home.

In Delhi, I'm grateful to Vidya Rao for her poetic wisdom, unfailing kindness, and extraordinary hospitality. To Irfan Zuberi, for inviting me to share this work publicly and for opening my heart to Delhi in the first place. To Pratyush Pushkar and Riya Raagini for teaching me so tenderly about poetry and friendship. To Arman Ali Dehlvi, Maliha Khan, Arif Hussain Khan, Ashique Kumar, Arvind Kumar, Prateek Narsimha, and Geetanjali Roy, for their musical companionship and support. At Nizamuddin, I am grateful to Pir Syed Salmi Nizami, Mohammad Shamsad, and the family of Chand Nizami for their guidance. And to the Naqvis—Naveena, Neha, Savita, and Jawed—for all kinds of sustenance, from Delhi to Dakar. In Pune, I am forever grateful to Vikas Kashalkar, a model in music and much more. To Chandrashekhar Mahajan for his sustained, nuanced melodic guidance. To the Bapat-Scarimbolo family—Justin, Radhika, and Neel—for the warmth of a second home. To Mukul Kulkarni, Chintan Upadhyay, and Pavan Naik for teaching me through example what musical friendship looks like. I also thank Pavan, Baba Qadri, and Sultan Nizami for generously introducing me to the vast world of qawwali in Maharashtra. In Mumbai, I am grateful to Dr. Sadhana Nayak for inviting me to observe her dynamic and multidisciplinary vocal medicine practice; Anuraag Dhoundeyal, Samantha Edwards, and Marianne D'Cruz for allowing me to observe their transformative vocal pedagogies; and Apoorva Gajjala for so generously sharing her own stories of vocal resilience and growth in the face of adversity. In Ajmer, I thank Sadique Hussain and family for their assistance, on many levels. In Lunyakhedi, I'm grateful to Kabir singer Prahlad Singh Tipanya and his family for their hospitality and musical generosity, and for bringing to life a form of Selfhood that extends within and beyond the individual body. Also to those friends who did so much to open the world of Kabir to me: Linda Hess, Bindhu Narayanaswamy, Shabnam Virmani, Vipul Rikhi, and Vivek Virani. I thank the many other singers, from Karachi to Mountainview, who took the time to sit with me and share their voices: Fareed Ayaz, Abu Mohammad Khan, Shamim Bano, Chandana Dixit, Nupur Joshi, Mahesh Kale, Pushkar Lele, Sharukh Shabab Niyazi, Amjad Nizami, Khalil Ahmed Nizami, Shailaja Pandit, Vidyadhar Pandit, Rujul Pathak, Ragini Rainu, Rita Sahai, Heloise Saldanha, Warren Senders, Bhajan Sopori, and Shireesh Thakur.

This project has been shaped by the insights of many colleagues who listened generously to early versions of this research: Marië Abe, Chloë Alaghband-Zadeh, Shalini Ayyagari, Shahzad Bashir, Robbie Beahrs, Harry Berger, Brian Bond, Nadia Chana, Martin Daughtry, Anaar Desai-Stevens, Beverly Diamond, Nina Eidsheim, Jeffers Engelhardt, Carl Ernst, James Faubion, Gautam Tejas Ganeshan, Tomie Hahn, Harriotte Hurie, Deborah Kapchan, Inderjit Kaur, Thanmayee Krishnamurthy, Gregory Lipton, Tanya Luhrmann, Scott Marcus, Peter Manuel, Mark Mazullo, Kathy Meizel, Nipa Nag, Dan Neuman, Dard Neuman, Lalita du Perron, Regula Qureshi, Sumitra Ranganathan, Friedlind Riedel, Anna Schultz, Katherine Schofield, Simona Sawhney, Ryan Skinner, Stephen Slawek, Julia Ulehla, Vivek Virani, Bonnie Wade, Ellen Waterman, Richard Wolf, and Homayra Ziad. Many thanks to my colleagues at UMN who have taken the time to discuss parts of this book with me—especially Bill Beeman, Giancarlo Casale, Scott Currie, Mike Gallope, Aisha Ghani, Sumanth Gopinath, Diyah Larasati, Guerino Mazzola, Stuart McLean, Peter Mercer-Taylor, Anaïs Nony, Gloria Raheja, Arun Saldanha, Ajay Skaria, and Valerie Tiberius. And to the students who have taught me so much about my own work, particularly Maria Arriola, Anya Badaldavood, Colleen Bertsch, Anne Briggs, Lars Christensen, Sravanthi Kollu, Corey Lohman, Katelyn Medic, Tricia Morgan, Vinay Thomas, and Nyagua Tut. I'm grateful to my musical companions in Minneapolis who have kept the flame alive on the coldest days: Pooja Goswami, A. Pavan, Abhinav Sharma, Omkar Joshi, Abhijit Kshirsagar, Tanushree Naik—and Emel Sherzad, a true *rasika* and patron of music. I'm grateful to Suhail Yusuf Khan for his graceful musical and intellectual *sangat* and to Essam Rafea, beloved companion in music and spirit, to Srinivas Reddy, *knowledgeable in the essence of theory and practice*, a steadfast friend who has kept me grounded in raga throughout this process. A special thank you goes to my incomparable friends and colleagues Max Katz and

Justin Scarimbolo, who read through so much of this material, sometimes more than once, offering generous, loving critique. And nothing I say could suffice to thank my parents and older brother, who were nurturing this project long before it was conceived. Despite all this help, of course, I alone am responsible for the shortcomings of this book. I thank in advance the critical readers who will find ways to expand this work beyond its limitations.

I honor the memory of three beloved teachers who passed away while this project was underway: Jon K. Barlow, Johnny (Way-Sa-Quo-Nabe) Smith, and Veena Sahasrabuddhe. Each in their own way has expanded my understanding of the ethical powers of listening and voice. May their spirit live on in their many students.

The research and writing for this project were made possible by a Fulbright-Nehru Award, a UMN Grant-in-Aid, a UMN Imagine Fund Grant, a UMN Institute of Advanced Studies fellowship, and a Talle Faculty Research Award.

Wesleyan University Press has been a pleasure to work with. I'm grateful to Suzanna Tamminen, Deborah Wong, Sherrie Tucker, and Jeremy Wallach for believing in this project, and to Ann Brash and Natalie Jones for attending to so many crucial details. Many thanks to Nooshin Hakim for the cover illustration that so beautifully illustrates the relational conditions of a *mahfil*, and to Doug Leonard, whose brilliant design of the companion website brings the theoretical work of this book so vividly to life.

Finally, I am grateful beyond words to my wife, Jenna Dawn Rice, so brilliantly alive to the world and its voices, who has taught me more than anyone about listening with the heart over the last twelve years. Every page of this book has been nourished by her support, patience, intellectual insight, and love.

Ways of Voice

ONE

Introduction

Transcription Conventions used in the book:
<Translated by the author, with original language in footnote>
{singing; numerals indicate scale degrees}

"*Daaatoon! DaaaaaaaaaatooOOOoon!*"

Kamli's voice cuts through the thrum of the crowd on a Bombay[1] local train, advertising the neem-twig toothbrushes (*dātun*) she has for sale. The camera fixes on the face of the male lead, Dr. Pratap, a pipe-smoking voice scientist in a cardigan. He winces at the brash vocal intrusion into his personal space. But then we see his eyes narrow; he listens closely to Kamli's voice and draws thoughtfully on his pipe. He turns to his traveling companion, a musicologist named Kashinath, and remarks that although the toothbrush hawker seems uncivilized (*janglī*), her throat (*galā*) has sweetness (*miṭhās*) and flexibility (*lacak*). Dr. Pratap then utters the challenge that gives shape to the whole film: he wagers that he can make a proper singer out of her—and, thus, a proper lady—by training her voice. A few scenes later, we see Kamli sitting down for her first voice lesson. At first, blissfully ignorant, she sings out of tune (a striking transgression in Bollywood's otherwise rigorously tuneful vocal universe). But Dr. Pratap has a remedy. He sits her down in front of a refrigerator-sized machine (the "scalograph"), and guides her up the scale (*sā, re, ga, ma, pa* {1, 2, 3, 4, 5}. . .) as her voice lights up a sequence of bulbs on the device. Thus begins a long period of hard work as Kamli's voice is radically remade by the daily application of various vocal

1. Now officially called "Mumbai" since 1995; the film is shot in 1980.

techniques. Months later, she emerges transformed. The climax of the film is her vocal debut (singing "Suman Sudha Rajni Chanda" to a glittering gathering of Bombay intelligentsia). The street pedlar's sharp cry has been replaced by the sweet tones of a genteel maiden (dubbed in the light, tuneful voice of Lata Mangeshkar, the quintessential voice of twentieth-century Bollywood song). Kamli accepts the praise of the audience graciously, lowering her eyes and joining her palms in humble, pious salutation. In sonority, bearing, poise, and relational attunement, she has mastered a new way of voice. She no longer hawks her wares in crowded public trains, but croons sweetly at private gatherings; at home, she hums to herself as she fixes tea, butters toast, and fetches Dr. Pratap's slippers. Kamli realizes too late that Dr. Pratap's project has reduced her own ambitions to an experimental case study, swapping her out from one servile subject position to another. Yet Dr. Pratap celebrates this transformation as a moral triumph. Rebuking a conservative naysayer who claims that Kamli's vocal graces must have been in her blood, the doctor lays bare his scheme, proclaiming before his astonished audience—and Kamli herself, watching in horror—that even an ignorant and boorish (*jāhil aur gaṃwār*) toothbrush seller can be made human (*insān*) through "voice culture."

At the heart of this film, *Man Pasand* (1980), is a parallel transformation of voice and self. It tells a story about the cultivation of one very particular sort of vocal "humanity": bourgeois, domestic, soft-spoken. But it also draws out the ways in which this vocal work can be "dehumanizing" in a classical liberal sense: Dr. Pratap imposes patriarchal strictures on Kamli's vocal expression, muting her "own" voice and replacing it with one imposed from the outside, undermining her sovereignty, her independence, her self-determination. This moral dissonance is strongest precisely at those moments when voice and self detatch from each other and slip apart: when singing and being come mutually into play.

This book, too, is about the dynamic play of vocal work. It is driven by a curiosity about the ways in which we not only *have* a voice, but also actively acquire, cultivate, and contest vocal sensibilities. To work on one's voice is not only to strive after a sound, but also to strive after a *disposition*—of the tongue, lips, throat, nose, and chest; of attention, temporal sense, and relational comportment. These ways of voice come alive in relation to others, in a mutual attunement to enculturated listeners. They thus invite ethical, political, and relational resonances that reach far beyond the individual sounding body.

Voice Culture(s)

Man Pasand (like the many other cinematic adaptations of George Bernard Shaw's *Pygmalion*[2]) depicts a living practical tradition in India and throughout the anglophone world: *voice culture*. During its heyday in the late nineteenth and early twentieth century, from Melbourne to London to New York to Bombay, voice culture was a thriving industry, offering a repertoire of techniques for speaking and singing that cultivated desirable forms of personhood. Techniques of voice culture promised multitudes of ambitious voice students vocal and ethical upliftment, class elevation, and even a chance to remake oneself racially.[3] A vast vocal literature outlined a range of techniques, often clothed in highly fanciful accounts of vocal physiology.[4] Voice culture projects construed vocal comportment as a direct window into personal character—a character that could, in principle, be improved by changing one's voice.[5] Most aimed to produce one very particular kind of voice: round, sweet, posh, and effortless, suited for bourgeois sociality in parlors and other private, acoustically insulated spaces.[6]

Many European travelers to colonial Bombay and Calcutta were shocked by the brash voices of the singers they encountered in public spaces (devotional singers processing through the streets, courtesans singing and dancing boldly at "nautch parties," qawwals belting out praise for Sufi saints in shrine courtyards[7]).

---

2. The introductory film titles announce that *Man Pasand* is "dedicated to the genius of George Bernard Shaw," and the tunes of several of the songs in *Man Pasand* are taken directly from the musical adaptation *My Fair Lady* (1964). The first Hindi adaptation of *Pygmalion*, however (*Nili*, 1950, also starring Dev Anand), predated *My Fair Lady*. Other Indian adaptations include: *Manam Oru Kurangu* (Tamil, 1967), *Tee Phulrani* (Marathi, 1975, remade in 2016), and *Santu Rangili* (Gujarati, 1976). Despite its sugarcoated patch ending, in which Kamli abruptly returns to Dr. Pratap, *Man Pasand* did not do well at the box office, though many of its individual songs were quite popular; see Sharma 2017 for speculation about why this may have been.

3. Olwage 2004, 207.

4. See Kimber 2017 and Yahav 2018 on elocutionist precedents for voice culture.

5. Carter 2013, 11. See also Davies in Feldman 2019, 153–157; McCracken 1999, 369; and Olwage 2004.

6. For parallel vocal reform projects in France and Colombia, see Bergeron 2010 and Ochoa Gautier 2014.

7. See Basu 2011, 314.

One nineteenth-century British commentator described these loud, open voices as "all lungs and no heart, all sound and no sentiment," and hoped that vocal reform would inculcate feelings of tenderness and love adequate to an affective economy of courtship and companionate marriage.[8] Nationalist Indian music reformers often prescribed the improvement of the singing voice in the belief that the soul of India could thereby be uplifted.[9] This commitment to vocal mutability rang out in contrast to the claims of vocal racialists who maintained that each race had a fixed, immutable vocality—like laryngologist George Duncan Gibb, who claimed that there was a single racially essential Indian voice, and comparative musicologist Erich von Hornbostel, who construed vocal sonority to be a "racial characteristic . . . deeply rooted in physiological functions."[10] Voice culturists—like their physical culturist contemporaries who put calisthenics, wrestling, and modern yoga to work transforming bourgeois bodies around the world[11]—treated singing and speaking precisely as a matter of *culture*: cultivation, training, and discipline. Working on one's vocal disposition (colorless, infinitely malleable, linked to the soul, and yet subject to change through technical practice) became a common ground of moral discourse even when there was no common language. British protestants brought this vocal optimism to their Indian missions, founding choirs in which vocal timbre became a field for ethical transformation.[12]

But India was no blank slate. These zealous vocal proselytizers were surprised to find themselves in numerous vocal situations where voice was *already* an organ of ethics, and where any purportedly universal system of "voice culture" was just one among many.[13] Many missionaries found that the Indians they hoped to convert were already possessed of extraordinary voices—some sweet, some powerful, some seductive, some passionately devotional.[14] Some wrote of the impressive moral character of mendicant *bhajan*-singers, maintaining their single-pointed faith against the oppression of upper-caste ritual, living simple

8. Allen 1847, 131–132.

9. Bakhle 2005, 64, 199.

10. Gibb 1870; Hornbostel 1928, 32.

11. Alter 2004, Martschukat 2011.

12. Olwage 2004, 217.

13. Indeed, the Macaulayist idea that a British aesthetic education was the royal road to moral upliftment inspired a widespread nationalist rebuke (Bellenoit 2007, 142).

14. Harrison 1893, 97, 184; Basu 2011, 261; Bakhle 2005.

lives of extraordinary piety and devotion; some even construed *bhakti* in general as a "movement" spiritually akin to the Protestant Reformation, sustained and amplified through collective, vernacular hymn-singing.[15] One missionary account describes an Indian singer's rebuke to the near-universal injunction to sing softly: "You tell us to whisper the praises of Jesus? No sir, we cannot; we must express in loud tones our gratitude to Him who loved us and died for us."[16] Nor was this a matter of a single "British voice" coming into conflict with a single "Indian voice." While it may have been obvious to voice culturists what a "cultured" voice should sound like, this has never been quite so simple for actual singers. There were (and are) not just one or two, but innumerable distinctive vocal dispositions in North India. The earliest systematic surveys of singing voices across the cities and villages of the Hindustani vocal ecumene (Arthur Bake's survey in 1938, Nazir Ali Jairazbhoy's in 1963) affirmed a dazzling variety of vocal practices, "from the intense shouting of Haryanvi men's song, to the nasal timbre of Garhwali singing . . . the rippling, lavishly ornamented Punjabi *Hir-Ranjha* . . . plain, straightforward women's work songs . . . the tense projection of Bhojpuri *khari birha*."[17] A wide range of voices ring out in Sufi shrines and temples, in theaters and concert halls, private homes and palaces. Accordingly, there have long been multiple dimensions of ethical-vocal excellence: voices that are calm, voices that are pious, voices that are seductive, voices that are open, voices that strike you like an arrow and convert you.

Singers are keenly aware of the differences between these voices, and most have cultivated several. Qawwal Sharukh Shabab Niyazi once, as a demonstration of his own wide vocal spectrum, showed me the contrast between two widely known vocal dispositions: *filmī* voice (the sweet voice that dominated film music of the twentieth century) and *buland* voice (the high, bright, "lofty" voice so strongly associated with qawwali). He did so by singing the same words (*jān-e tamannā*, "heart full of longing") in two different dispositions. Figure 1.1 shows spectrograms of Shahrukh's demonstrations. Note that the *ā* of *tamannā* contains most of the action in each case.

Buland voice is obviously higher pitched and louder than *filmi* voice; the filmi voice is obviously breathier. *Buland* voice has a distinctive bright ring (the so-called "singer's formant") discernible in the intensity of the harmonics around

15. Bellenoit 2007, 127–130.

16. Olwage 2004, 217.

17. Manuel 1993, 52.

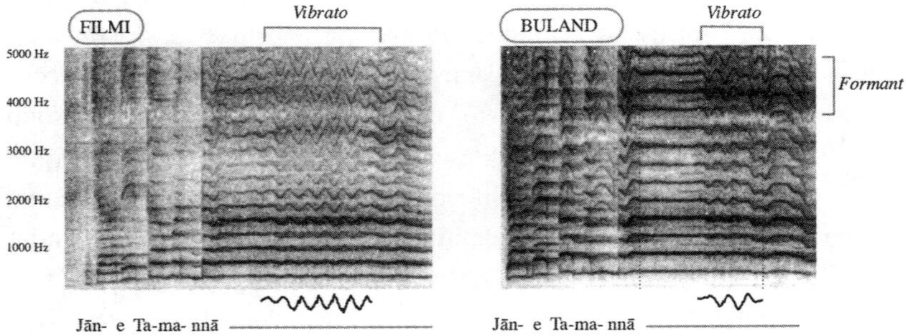

FIGURE 1.1 Spectrograms of filmi and buland āwāz

4000 Hz, whereas *filmi* voice is mellower, with its peak intensity around 1500 Hz. The *filmi* voice begins its vibrato almost immediately upon landing on the ā (lasting for seven cycles of vibrato), whereas the *buland* voice begins a brief vibrato only just before descending (and lasting for only three cycles). There are other conventional differences as well: for example, in singing *filmi*, singers often sustain /r/ melismatically, whereas this is almost unheard of in heavier vocal dispositions; *filmi* ornaments tend to be light and subtle (see chapter 2), with almost nothing of *gamak*, *mīṇḍ*, or *andolan*.

These are not merely genre-bound acoustical *traits*, but cultivated vocal *dispositions*—built, felt, heard, and amplified in and between bodies. As is widely attested by many singers, *buland* voice requires you to sing from your chest (*sīnā*), whereas *filmi* voice requires you to sing from your throat (*galā*). But they also are implicated in relational circuits beyond the individual. Whereas *filmi* voice is murmured intimately into a microphone mere inches from the mouth, projected into the virtual ear of an intimate listener, *buland* voice is tuned for the wide, outdoor spaces of Sufi shrine courtyards, audible even without a microphone to gathered devout listeners. Sharukh explained to me that maintaining the power of *buland* voice requires you to dwell on your devotional relationship with a Sufi saint. Indeed, many Sufi singers attest that the power of this voice is a blessing received in devotion, rather than an inherent quality of voice. *Filmi* voice requires a radically different, interiorly focused orientation. As Sharukh himself put it, you sing from an inner "*feel*" for the emotional content of the song. As we will see in chapter 5, *feel*—a technical term, one of many English loan words circulating in the Hindi film music industry—is not just a generalized human capacity for emotion, but a specific, hard-won attunement to particular sentiments. Neither devotion nor *feel* are natural or universal vocal capabilities. Like all vocal dispositions, they are achievements, the fruits of discipline and practice. No less cultivated are the vocal subject positions that they enable: an ecstatic devotee in relationship to a beloved saint, singing from the heart; or a sensitive, introspective crooner singing from the throat.

These ways of voice do not spring out of the soil fully formed. Singers undergo years of grueling training and practice, sometimes stretching over decades, shaping the musicking body, reinforcing specific vocal dispositions: strength or gentleness, steadiness or nimbleness, heaviness or lightness. Later in life, many singers change path, reshaping their voices in a radically different direction. Courtesans (*tawāifs*) were, through the nineteenth century, highly sought after both as singers *and* as tutors in moral refinement (*akhlāq*), their salons regarded as "finishing schools" for aristocratic young men.[18] And yet, between the revolt of 1857 and independence in 1947, an emerging middle-class public reconstrued the vocal bearing of courtesans as an object of moral disdain. Many elite courtesans thus reconfigured their vocal disposition to suit public performance in bourgeois concert halls or film studios. The new "finishing schools" for middle-class children in Pune, Bombay, and Delhi are not salons, but tidy modern music classrooms for teaching devotional repertoire, with standard syllabuses and exams, inculcating a plain, pious, restrained vocal disposition.[19] The Victorian contours of voice culture live on in these spaces, encouraging young singers to sing softly, gently, and sweetly. From the beginning, musical training at these schools has been carried out as a form of ethical and spiritual training. Women, in particular, were laden with a heavy moral burden at these schools, trained "not as performing or professional musicians, but as the carriers of religious ideology and the upholders of truth."[20] By the twenty-first century, more schools have appeared, training aspiring singers brought up with this pious vocal restraint to embody new forms of highly sought-after vocal expressiveness, inflected by R&B, rock, and pop. Disciplined female singers, trained from youth to sing demurely, now turn to a canon of vocal exemplars (such as Mariah Carey, Celine Dion,

---

18. Waheed 2014, 7–8, 12, and passim. Waheed notes that the very first appearance of the word *tawāif* is accompanied by a couplet about virtue: "The whole world is aware of my virtues [*akhlāq*]/Yet somehow you still have your doubts." [*Akhlāq se to apne vāqif jahān hogā/par āp ko g͟halat kuch ab tak gumān hogā.*]

19. See Pradhan 2014, 62–63.

20. Bakhle 2005, 171.

and Alanis Morissette) for the moral courage to sing brashly and to make public vocal demands for personal freedom. Other vocalists commit themselves to acquiring a high, bright, *buland* (lofty) voice—or, as outsiders often call it, "Sufi" voice. Meanwhile, many ambitious professional qawwals, with powerful voices already shaped for high, bright, *buland* public projection, have learned to soften and polish their tone for glossy, highly produced pop versions of Sufi songs. As groups of village devotional singers tour in cosmopolitan networks, they begin expanding their own vocal possibilities, learning to break away from their usual vocal disposition to sing qawwali and ghazal and film songs.[21] Meanwhile, urban cosmopolitans head out to remote villages for workshops in "folk" song, to *undo* the sedimented work of Victorian voice culture: to open their voices, to sing raw and authentic and *sahaj* (straightforward), to free themselves of their polite bourgeois fetters.[22] These ways of voice stand in uneasy relationship to each other, often requiring unlearning as well as re-learning. Their ecumenical plurality offers more than a buffet of aesthetic delights. It offers a spectrum of comportmental possibilities for vocal being. To inhabit one or another vocal subject position—to vocally *be* a devotee, a transgressive rebel, an authoritative master, or a self-expressive artiste—is an ethical, not merely an aesthetic, matter.

Ways of Voice

The frictions between these vastly different ways of voice, their cultivation, the contrasting possibilities for relational sociality that they offer, the forms of ethical being they announce to various publics: these are the principal concerns of this book.

These are also personal concerns. I myself have spent much of the last twenty years learning to sing the "classical" raga music known as *khyāl* in Pune and Delhi, striving after a vocal discipline (*Gwalior gāyakī*) passed through generations of masters and disciples. The heart of this training has been long-term discipular relationships with two masters (Vikas Kashalkar from 2000–2012, then L. K. Pandit from 2012 to present), numerous elder guides, and dozens of fellow students. Many of the guiding problematics of this project (self-work, reflection, conflicting forms of vocal selfhood) emerged from conversations, lessons, practice, and performance with these mentors, masters, and friends. But

21. Cf. Hess 2015, 69–70.

22. See Virani 2016, 198; Chakrabarti 2016, 110–111.

just as important has been encountering singers who are striving after altogether *different* vocal results. During my first year of vocal study in Pune in 2000–2001, I was puzzled to find that few of my fellow students actually aspired to careers performing raga music. Most were preparing their voice and tuning their sensibilities for singing devotional bhajans or stage songs. Like my guru-brothers and -sisters who were privileged to dedicate themselves single-mindedly (single-voicedly) to the arcane arts of raga, I initially dismissed these song forms as "light" music: simple, popular dilutions of what I took to be an originary, essential "classical" music. But as I got to know these students, I came to see that these singers had full-fledged vocal ambitions in their own right: affective, devotional, relational, and, above all, ethical. I began to see that these vocal practices are not mere halfway points on the royal road to raga, but parallel paths of their own, with their own exemplars, their own hard-won techniques, their own practices of listening, their own publics.

I began seeking out opportunities to explore these contrasting vocal worlds. In 2006, I went to visit Prahlad Tipanya and his family in rural Malwa, singers of the poet-saint Kabir (often referred to in cosmopolitan spaces as "folk" singers). I was immediately struck by a radically different way of voice. Among these singers, Kabir's *shabd*—his "word," his all-consuming poetic flame, is paramount.[23] Though these singers openly professed admiration of classical vocalists (for their tonal clarity, theoretical knowledge, and virtuosity), they nonetheless regarded the scant poetic content of classical music with puzzlement and even amusement—they often would mimic classical singers, spinning out endless melodic variations on a single word. At one *satsang* (a "truth-gathering" for singing Kabir's songs), I was invited to sing a khyal, an extended exploration of a single raga, drawing only on a short fragment of poetry. I was in reasonably good practice at the time: my *sur* (intonation) was accurate, my *harkat* (ornaments) were passably fluent, my voice that night was strong enough to sing without a mic. And this was a sympathetic audience—they were leaning forward, listening closely and generously, offering sincere gestures of welcome and support. But after so many hours immersed in the flow of Kabir bhajans, my own singing struck me as abstract, excessively florid, and poetically vapid. In this *satsang*, even my cleverest melodic flourishes felt empty of poetic resonance. No less striking to me, in conversations after the fact, was the difference in where vocal power was felt to reside. Whereas classical singers tend to stress the special, unique

23. Hess 2015, 266.

qualities of ancestral singers from their inherited lineage, citing and praising great exemplars from centuries past, these singers were always telling me that "anyone could sing Kabir," seldom if ever referencing great vocal heroes, locating vocal power instead in the present flow of *shabd* from body to body, cultivating and sustaining the "formless" states so central to Kabir's poetics. Indeed, this principled anyone-and-everyone universalism is crucial to the political power of Kabir song. These singers, too (despite essentialist construals of "folk" music as static expressions of fixed culture) were engaged in striving and contestation. One Kabir singer who had learned a sweet, gentle vocal comportment suited for urbane film song, found himself in conflict with the usual bright, open, vigorous mode of Kabir singing. He was directed again and again, sometimes even in the middle of performance, to open his mouth, to sing out in bright, coarse tones, to announce Kabir's word boldly and publicly into the world with his fellows rather than crooning privately.

As my vocal network expanded in the coming years, I met dozens of qawwals, kirtankars, film singers, bhajan singers, and practitioners of the emerging vocal world of pop "sufi." Spending more time in Sufi shrines, temples, recording studios, and private homes further provincialized my training in raga music, throwing familiar daily practices into strange relief. Moving between vocal worlds like this over the last decade has humbled me, honed my political sensibilities, and made me acutely aware of ways in which my own previous scholarly work had implicitly placed elite Sanskritic and Persianate traditions at the center of the Hindustani songworld. As a singer, though my passion for raga music has only intensified, encountering so many different ways of voice has thrown me again and again into the role of student. In doing so, I discovered that I was in good company—nearly all singers go through disorienting periods of changing course, starting over, unlearning old habits, and building new dispositions. These struggles, successes, and crises are at the center of this book. I thus have adopted a set of analytics that foreground the ways in which singers actively strive after, cultivate, and contest particular vocal dispositions among particular listeners (rather than simply *expressing* a fixed and inherent voice). This will, I hope, cast light not only on the dynamic conditions of voicing in North India, but also on the various forms of personhood that voices enunciate, shape, and transform.

The Hindustani Vocal Ecumene

In order to account for these varied forms of vocal contestation and striving, we need a sociological frame that offers a view beyond—and between—fixed boundaries of conventional genre and identity. The boundaries of any one nation-state will not do, nor any one religious, caste, or class formation; the singers I have worked with train themselves to traverse such boundaries with ease. Nor can we simply say that these voices are "global": there are a great many places that these voices do not reach. Instead, we are faced with a field of distinct but mutually influential forms of vocal technique, action, and being—what I am calling the "Hindustani vocal ecumene."[24] The vocal traditions at issue here stretch far beyond the time-honored, elitist usage of the term *Hindustani music* to refer exclusively to the "classical" music of North India and Pakistan (*khyal, dhrupad, tarana*, etc.). Vocal aspirants, even when trained in austere raga music, develop other ways of voice as well: suited for florid, affect-laden, "light" art song (*ghazal, thumri, hori*); for the devotional songs of Sufi shrines, Krishna temples, and Gurdwaras (*qawwali, bhajan, kirtan*); and for the vast canon of theater and film songs (*nautanki, natyasangit, filmi git*) that draw on all of these song forms.[25] Though these latter

---

24. In order to conceive of such transnational spaces of exchange and contestation—stretching far across the world, but not uniformly global, distinct from other overlapping spaces—scholars have long posited various "ecumenes" that constitute "overlapping congeries" rather than neatly delimited nations or culture areas (Appadurai 1996, 28). The Hindustani vocal ecumene thus stands alongside the Ottoman ecumene (Buchanan 2007), the Carribean ecumene (Mintz 1996), and the Victorian ecumene (Breckenridge 1989). Donna Buchanan's figuration of the Ottoman ecumene comes closest to what is intended here: marked out and cultivated in prior imperial centers, now practically inhabited in a world divided into various nation-states. She emphasizes a characteristic "tension between inhabiting a world only to push at its boundaries, the sounding of places known and unknown" that characterizes a vocal ecumene in which no one can hear or know every voice, in which there are always more possibilities just out of earshot. Some historians have spoken of a Mughal ecumene (Padamsee 2018, Green 2004) with a geographic span nearly congruent with the heartland of the Hindustani vocal ecumene. The latter, however, is not grounded exclusively in Mughal practice, but also in colonial, paracolonial, Hindu-nationalist, Islamicate-cosmopolitan, and neoliberal currents, among others.

25. See Beaster-Jones 2015 on mediation. See also Manuel 2015 on the "intermediate realm."

are often depicted as diluted "semi-classical" variations on a putative "classical" original, these vocal worlds each have their own center of gravity. A common poetic canon draws from Urdu ghazals, Braj devotional hymns, Malvi Kabir bhajans, and more—all circulating within a linguistic space of mutual intelligibility that can loosely (if controversially) be called "Hindi" or "Hindustani" language.[26] Poetic formulae of longing ("*Kala nahi āve*" [rest won't come to me], "*Nīsa dina*" [night and day], "*ras ke bhare tore nainā*" [your liquor-filled eyes]) reverberate and feed back through *bhajans* of yearning for Krishna, *qawwalis* of devotion to Chishti saints, sentimental Bollywood songs of doomed love, and elite, raga-ornamented *khyals*.[27] The distinctive *ʿayins* and *saṃyuktākśars* of highfalutin Arabic and Sanskrit are conspicuously absent, though vernacularized loan words thereof abound (e.g., Arabic *taʿlīm* [instruction] becomes *tālīm*; Sanskrit *mitr* [friend] becomes *mīt*[28]). Perhaps most importantly, this is principally a canon of song rather than literature. The great singer-saints of Hindustan (Vaishnavas, Sufis, Nath Yogis) are remembered in consocial vocal action, rather than in literary solitude: mouth open, holding a tanpura rather than a pen, inviting others to listen or even to join in the refrain.

Figure 1.2 offers a rough sketch of some of the best-known genres in this ecumene, grouped loosely into what are sometimes called *duniyās*, or "worlds" of voice: classical, light, Sufi, and so on. This diagram hints at the variegated shades of familiarity and distance between a few major song-types rather than an exhaustive categorical accounting.

This figure should be held lightly; any claim to a complete taxonomy of these vocal worlds would be misleading. For one thing, the ethnographic archive of vocal worlds I draw on here is inevitably uneven and incomplete (for more thorough surveys of individual Hindustani song genres, there is already a vast and excellent literature[29]). No doubt I have missed many important connections with Carnatic

26. On the contentious history of naming and defining Hindustani, Hindi, and Urdu, see Rai 2002 and Trivedi 2004. There are certainly also adjacent song corpuses that are intelligible only to elites (like Persian) and/or to speakers of major regional languages (such as Marathi).

27. On feedback, see Novak 2013.

28. These loan words often pass through dialectal variations in Braj (as does *mīt*) and Persian (as does *tālīm*).

29. For khyal, see Wade 1984 and Bagchee 1998. For dhrupad, see Sanyal and Widdess 2004. For haveli sangeet, see Ho 2013. For thumri, see Manuel 1989 and Zadeh

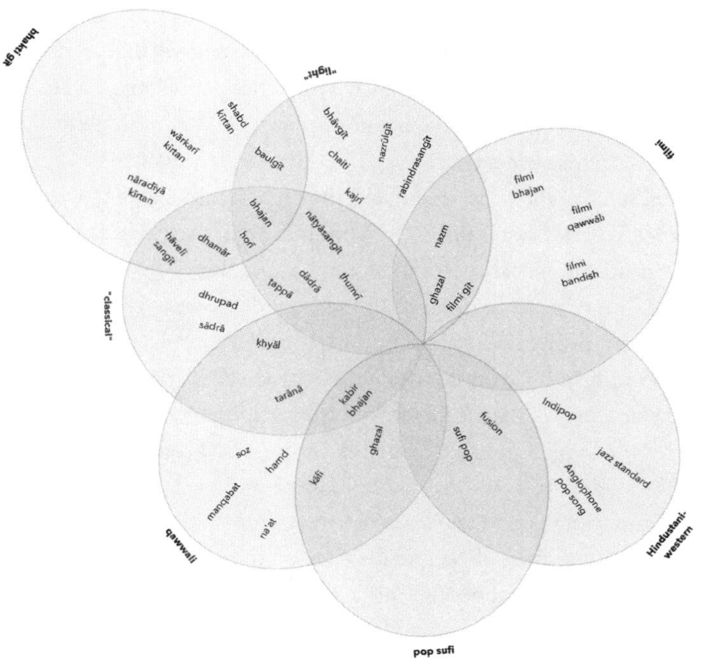

FIGURE 1.2 Sketch of several overlapping worlds (duniyas) of vocal genres

music by focusing on sites in the north; I have spent a disproportionate amount of time in cities, and thus have missed out on a great deal of village-based song; my access to female spaces (for example, the vast and largely unstudied world of women's qawwali in Maharashtra) was limited. I had virtually no ethnographic access to what Anna Morcom aptly calls the "illicit worlds" of performance in dance bars and kothas (which have their own distinctive publics, and their own

2012. For Baul geet, see Capwell 1986. For ghazal, see Manuel 1988 and Qureshi 1990. For qawwali, see Qureshi 1995 and Weston 2013; for other devotional Indo-Muslim song practices, see Wolf 2014, Manuel 2015, and Bond 2020. For kirtan and bhajan, see Slawek 1986, Schultz 2013 and 2014, and Hess 2015; for Sikh kirtan, see Kaur 2016. For film music, see Morcom 2007 and Beaster-Jones 2015. For a survey of what Peter Manuel calls the "intermediate sphere," including light-classical music, sophisticated professional folksong, dhrupad-related devotional genres, sophisticated prosody-driven genres, see Manuel 2015.

characteristic ethical projects).[30] Though I've been privileged to spend time with and conduct interviews in qawwal lineages connected with elite Sufi spiritual institutions (which overlap significantly with lineages of raga music in which I already had connections), I have had only informal contact with heterodox Sufi singers. The picture that emerges here, then, is significantly more male, elite, urban, public, and mass-mediated than a carefully balanced vocal survey might reveal. To draw generalizations from this limited archive about a singular, essential Hindustani vocality would blot out a great many divergent local voice-worlds, and thus reproduce many of the same elitist biases evident in nationalist music scholarship. The goal here is not to generalize about substance, but about relations; to shine a light on the dynamism of vocal encounters rather than to draw a comprehensive map. I know well from experience how much the omission of a beloved voice, genre, or place can sting, and I hope that this will impel imaginative readers to carry this work forward into neglected vocal territories.

To sort voices into generic boxes is also to obscure their dynamism. These neat boundaries emerge, crystallize, and dissolve on the scale of decades; reconfigurations can sometimes happen on the scale of years. More importantly, ways of voice float across genres. For example, any of these song types can now be sung recognizably well with sweet, gentle *filmi* voice—much to the dismay of purists. There are still ghazal singers who sing as openly as Begum Akhtar—but there are many more who sing gently as Noor Jehan. Some qawwals have cultivated a gentle microphonic croon for stage singing—but others drill their students hard to keep their voices bright and open. When Pandit Jasraj and Kishori Amonkar began introducing a "lighter" vocal disposition into khyal, it was immensely popular with an expanding bourgeois audience—and a matter of pointed moral disdain among orthodox connoisseurs. Controversies like these are enabled by a remarkable superficial legibility among these diverse voices, even across genres and regions. When a teacher of khyal castigates their student for singing too *light*, both teacher and student understand what is at issue: high pitch, low volume, rapid ornamental *harkat* (movements) characteristic of microphonic voices seasoned for thumri, ghazal, and film song. The severe vocal disposition of a masterful, dignified *ustad* is quite rare to encounter (in public or in media), but it has a vernacular quotability (deep *gamak*, dramatic hand gestures) akin to the comportment of a Wagnerian soprano singing with deep vibrato in a horned

30. Morcom 2014. See also Roy 2017 on sites for hijra performance and Ajotikar 2019 on caste and gender politics in Western India.

Viking hat; for many, it carries similar implications of elite classicism out of touch with popular concerns. Singers of pop sufi study and imitate qawwali recordings, even if they don't have the skills (or authorization) to bring a spiritually elite Sufi into ecstasy. When Indo-Trinidadian singers debate the relative merits of singing bhajans in "filmi air" and "Bhojpuri air," they are referring to vocal practices that are legible precisely by virtue of their mutual contrast.[31] Anna Schultz describes the meaningful distinction among Maharashtrian kirtankars between a high, tense, bright vocality (indexing a lower-caste, ecstatic *warkari* kirtankar) and a lower-pitched, mellower, florid vocality (indexing a high-caste, didactic, contemplative *Naradiya* kirtankar).[32] When the same kirtankar switches suddenly into a *bhangra* disposition, their listeners know that they are now taking on the role of a Panjabi character.[33] Accordingly, characteristic modes of voice have long been linked to types of persons with distinctive character—sometimes in explicitly named castes or *qaums* (Dhadhi, Mirasi, Kalawantin); sometimes as professions (kirtankar, qawwal, tawa'if); sometimes as persons possessed of individual virtues (sweet, devout, sincere).

Particular voices normatively address particular kinds of listeners, who in turn shape vocalization—and are shaped by their own attunements to voice. There is thus a parallel variety in listening practices (discerning the subtleties of raga, for example, or allowing Sufi secrets of love to penetrate the heart, immersing oneself in the divine nectar of Hari's name, or listening for modal "architectures" at an aesthetic distance) reciprocally implicated with ways of voice. As practices of listening produce distinctive forms of selfhood, listening well is an ethical matter. These habits of listening are linked to characteristic subject positions: *rasikas* are those able to discern *ras* (essential juice) in performance; *guṇījan* are those with the *guṇa* (virtue) of properly apprehending rāga music. It likewise takes a special kind of spiritually elite listener (*samī*) to access the hidden, esoteric kernel of a mystical ghazal sung by a qawwal at a Chishti Sufi gathering-for-listening; a deficient listener, distracted by the sensual beauty of

---

31. Schultz 2014.

32. Schultz 2013. See also Amanda Weidman's (2012) account of the hypersalient distinction between Brahmin and non-Brahmin lifeways extends to a distinction between two vocal dispositions: a Brahmin voice that is quiet, subtle, full of nasal resonance, and a Tamil (male) voice that is loud, aggressive, and full.

33. Schultz 2013, 184–185. See also Revathy Sankaran's famous "Twinkle Twinkle" episode of the Tamil sitcom *Kasalavu Nesam*.

the singer's lavishly ornamented improvisations, in contrast, is not just missing out on further aesthetic delights, but also on an order of reality, precisely because they lack a crucial virtue of spiritual discernment. At the height of the Mughal Empire, the moral danger of a seductive voice offered a sort of testing ground for the moral fortitude of aristocratic gentlemen—the subtle form of aristocratic character known as *Mirzā'ī*.[34] The practice of music-theoretic listening that discloses a sung phrase as a tone sequence (and its concomitant mode of singing in which individual tones are starkly enunciated) likewise is invoked by music reformers as a key distinguishing factor between refined, tasteful connoisseurs and "mere" unschooled hereditary technicians. These practices not only disclose different ontologies of voice, but also serve as key ethical practices in the formation of various kinds of self.

Before turning to forms of selfhood, we will briefly surrender to the cartographic impulse to ask *where* this ecumene is. As a rough orientation, we can start from a traditional heartland in the Krishna temples of Vrindavan, Mathura, and Nathdwara, the Sufi shrines of Ajmer, Delhi, and Pakpattan, the aristocratic courts and salons of Lahore, Agra, Varanasi, and Lucknow—the area once, before its radical colonial remapping, known as "Hindustan."[35] Geographically, this internally heterogenous vocal field has feathered edges; sociologically, it is less a bounded region than a network of vocal sites (dargah courtyards and recording studios, private music rooms and public concert halls). For centuries, singers, songs, and voices have circulated freely among these sites, following the winds of patronage and politics, attuned to situated practices of listening, but largely unrestrained by linguistic and regional boundaries.[36] In the eighteenth and nineteenth centuries, mendicant singer-saints, traveling theater troupes,

---

34. Brown 2006.

35. "Hindustan," unmodified, is of ambiguous reference. Its etymology does not refer to any religious community in particular, but to the land (Persian: *stān*) beyond the Indus river (Persian via Arabic via Greek: *Hindu*). By the seventeenth century, "Hindustan" was used to refer to the territory of the Mughal Empire. By the twenty-first century, it has been twice reconstrued: in reference to the Indian nation-state, and by Hindu nationalists in reference to national-religious identity, as the "land of the Hindu people."

36. Even in distant imperial outposts (such as Kabul, Khuldabad, and Dacca), the Mughal court was the central point of reference, marking a strategic vocal hegemony far beyond the imperial court (Williams 2014, 42).

and Islamicate-cosmopolitan court musicians traced out the first suggestions of a public song sphere, later re-activated, re-framed, and solidified by the vast output of the film industry in the 1950s and '60s. These "evergreen" film songs (including reworkings of classic ghazals, bhajans, and thumris) circulated widely during the "cassette revolution" of the '80s, forming a durable public song canon in Hindustani language. Crucially, this was a canon not only of songs, but also of voices—the widely-beloved voices of Lata, of Asha, of Rafi Sahab, and their latter-day imitators—sung with a light, *filmi* touch. Over the course of the twentieth century, dozens of singers shifted from courts, temples, and salons to Bombay, Calcutta, and other urban centers, drawn by newly built concert halls, radio, and bourgeois patronage, and, above all, by the nascent Bollywood film industry. Though cities remain at the center of recording, production, and distribution, India's economic liberalization in 1991 produced a market demand for a wider range of voices, notably regional "folk" and sufi song, drawing reality TV stars and local talent from across the subcontinent.[37]

And further still: the shifting spaces of the Hindustani vocal ecumene overflow the bounded regions of nation-states, and now stretch far beyond the Mughal imperial crucible. Labor migration, colonial education, and commercial ambition have produced resilient diasporic Hindustani song communities in East Africa, the Gulf, the Caribbean, Silicon Valley, and beyond. Bollywood attracts aspiring singers from all over this diaspora, and distributes thousands of songs each year to hundreds of millions of fans around the world.[38] The voices of Hindi film song resound even in South India and the North Eastern Region (much to the chagrin of regional language activists, to whom Hindi can sound distinctively imperialist). Indeed, these songs circulate untranslated among Arabic, Persian, Indonesian, and Swahili speakers; fans croon along even when the meaning of the words is lexically obscure to them. Others change the lyrics or translate them into different languages, but borrow melodies or train their voices into the ornamental contours of *filmi* voice.[39] West African singers of the controversial vocal practice known as *bandiri* mold Hausa Sufi poetry to the tunes of sentimental Bollywood love songs—even imaginatively laying claim to

---

37. For example, *Indian Idol* winners Sourabhee Debbarma (2007) and Prashant Tamang (2008).

38. Novak 2010.

39. Gopal and Moorti 2008, 28–38.

a Islamicate common root of practice for Hausa and Hindustani poetics.[40] East African singers of *Hindi taarab* sing Bollywood melodies to Swahili lyrics, and more importantly, "train [their] vocal apparatus to for the task," building what is understood to be an "Indian voice" modeled on a *filmi* disposition.[41] Voices of Sufi stars like Abida Parveen and Nusrat Fateh Ali Khan have long circulated on bourgeois cosmopolitan "spiritual" playlists and soundtracks, and even in the vocal technique of pop stars like Björk, Eddie Vedder, and Jeff Buckley (who claimed that Nusrat Fateh Ali Khan was his "Elvis"[42]). Thus, to refer to this vocal ecumene as "Hindustani" is not to imply the priority of some central organizing Hindustani essence—poetic, relational, sonorous, or otherwise. Comportmental resonances (quasi-courtly concert hall etiquette, recording studio practices, conventional Islamicate gestures of humility and goodwill) make possible a range of cosmopolitan vocal spaces (loosely glossed as "global" or "sufi" or "artistic") offering ontological grounds for mutual striving, contestation, imitation, and delight that reach across linguistic and national borders.[43]

And yet, of all the borders traversed by the Hindustani vocal ecumene, none is more controversial than the one drawn across its erstwhile heartland in 1947, at the moment of independence from Britain: the India–Pakistan border, marked not only by territorial, but also vocal rivalries. The "winning back" of Bade Ghulam Ali from Pakistan after partition is still a source of pride for Indian connoisseurs, as is Salamat and Nazakat Ali's choice to settle in Lahore for Pakistani connoisseurs. Construals of one or another singular "national voice" tend to distract from the dynamic diversity of this vocal ecumene. As an Indian cultural nationalist ideology slowly crystallized in the decades leading up to independence, the plurality of Hindustani voices and vocal sensibilities was often construed negatively, invoked as a distressing *lack* of normative national coherence. If Italian, German, and British nationalists could lay claim to distinctive (albeit fictional) national voices, where was India's? Thus the *idea* of a singular national voice has long served as a powerful discursive nationalist resource—

40. Larkin 2004.

41. Eisenberg 2017, 344.

42. See Iqbal 2013, Buckley's essay on,Nusrat Fateh Ali Khan (n.d.) and Buckley's live performance of "Yeh jo Halka Halka Suroor Hai" on YouTube.

43. See Rahaim 2019a, 29–30 on the difficulty of locating vocal-ontological formations.

"the nation singing one song," in Bhatkhande's oft-cited phrase.[44] Charu Gupta points out that early twentieth-century male publicists "inserted themselves into the public domain as the very voice of the Hindu, as representing the popular objectives of all Hindus," claiming authority to regulate divergent voices—particularly those of women.[45] Indeed, the cause for wonder is that a rich diversity of voices has flourished despite the extensive record of nationalist reform projects aimed at standardizing away vocal diversity.[46] Lata Mangeshkar (upon whom the state title "Daughter of the Nation" was recently and uniquely conferred) is often construed as the "voice of India."[47] Her nationalist credentials have been confirmed again and again, most spectacularly by her classic "*Aye mere vatan ke logon*" ("O people of my nation"). But as we will see in chapter 4, Lata's voice was not simply an *expression* of a prior national soul. She developed her signature vocality gradually, over several years, drawing inspiration from predecessors like Noor Jehan and K. L. Saigal, for a film industry that only later served as the de facto Indian popular national soundscape. Just as importantly, Lata's was not the only possible contender for the national voice; indeed, this was and is a fiercely contested question. For many elite state functionaries of the Nehru era (like B. V. Keskar, Union Minister for Information and Broadcasting from 1952–1962), the treacly surface and erotic undertones of film song seemed to threaten the development of a radically different national voice: austere, intellectual, rooted in the Sanskrit classics, adhering to the grammatical canons of rāga theory.[48] More recently, folk singers have been marketed as the true, supposedly unchanging voices of India, presented as an honest, unspoilt alternative to mass-mediated film music and cultivated raga music.[49] In Pakistan, *qawwālī*, *ghazal*, and regional folk songs such as *ṭappā* and *dholā* have all been candidates for a distinctively national song tradition. In other cases, Islam itself was asserted to be the common

---

44. Bhatkhande in Bakhle 2005, 161.

45. Gupta 2002, 11.

46. There are competing formulations of regional vocal essences—such as the *guldastā* (bouquet) model of Pakistani nationalism, or touristic arrays of variegated regional song styles in India—which turn on discourses of local authenticity and diversity rather than unity.

47. See also Sundar 2007.

48. Lelyveld 1994, 120.

49. Virani 2016.

source from which this variegated *guldastā* ("bouquet") of song had sprung.[50] The various national-vocal essences thus invoked are no more or less fictional than elite national-essentialist construals of French *mélodie française*.[51] So too with the ascription of singular voices to entire castes, religions, or other groupist macrosocial figments. A problem-space oriented around vocal identity tends to generate a closed set of groupist questions about what the (one) voice-of-the-group *is*, and thus to analytically obscure the profound disjunctures *between* coeval voices.

But for singers, these vocal disjunctures are precisely where the action is. The voices of Bollywood, once uniformly oriented around a light, gentle, vocal-dispositional complex, have exploded into a striking new vocal diversity, from the brash, self-assured vocal comportment of singers trained in "Western Contemporary" to the high, bright *buland* voice of what is now generically called "Sufi." Many of the biggest pop sufi singers are neither Sufis nor even Muslims; many of the renowned lineages of classical singers originate from sarangiyas who developed new vocal techniques for khyal. This vocal diversity is no pathology or fallen state; it is the very condition of ethical ferment (without the hegemonic foil of sweet, gentle *filmi* voice, for example, in what sense could the coarser voices of pop sufi be heard as ethically restorative?[52]). And it is likewise implicit in any practice of vocal striving (how else could a vocal aspirant work to change their own voice, to work toward a voice that is not yet their own?).

Voices and Selves

Here we encounter some conceptual friction. The very fact of this concerted vocal work on a seemingly natural vocal habit rubs against what I call an *individualist-expressivist* sense of voice: the sense in which voice is supposed to express the singular, essential character of an individual.[53] This common vocal figuration is evident in everyday language about "finding one's voice" or "letting one's voice be heard." Laura Kunreuther, in her study of public voices in Nepal, notes a common, politically potent figuration of voice as an audible marker of "personhood and individuality . . . considered to be as natural in its relationship to identity

---

50. Hemani 2011, 30–39, 59–60.

51. Bergeron 2010.

52. See Beaster-Jones 2014: *filmi* is the "other" for Indipop and Sufi.

53. See also Davies in Feldman 2019.

as the fingerprint or signature." She assigns this particular figuration of voice to the historical and political moment following Nepal's liberalization in 1990, producing those "modes of selfhood central to democratic political agency."[54] Anaar Desai-Stevens has demonstrated that these discourses are alive and well in the vast vocal world of Indian reality TV, where aspiring singers are urged to find and develop their authentic, unique voice, distinct from the widely known *filmi* voices that dominated the first decades after Indian independence.[55] She charts out the development of what she calls the "aspirational subject": a specifically neoliberal, anglophone subject striving for upward social mobility paired with an entirely revised habitus. Peter Kvetko identifies the first blossoming of this expressivist vocal figuration in the 1990s, in which Indipop singers were expected to give voice to an authentic private interiority, in contrast to the supposedly fake, public voices of Bollywood singers (see chapter 4).[56] Here, we confront an ethics of voice in which one may *fail* to sound like oneself—one's *true* self. Katherine Meizel identifies this notion of "finding a voice" as a specifically neoliberal notion, drawing its key discursive resources from the various civil rights and feminist movements of the '60s and '70s, in which the struggle for self-determination was often described as a process of obtaining political voice.[57]

And yet, in practice, a direct, expressive vocal ray from a sovereign interior to a public exterior is a special case, one among many other ways of voice in the Hindustani vocal ecumene. Take a breath and hum a fragment of a beloved melody; this by no means proceeds self-evidently from a radical subjectivity of "inner" feeling to an evident objectivity of "outer" expression. When you're in the groove of a familiar song, it can be equally convincing to say that this voice is flowing *through* you. Singing often frustrates the sharp distinctions between private selfhood and public sounding, ringing out simultaneously inside and outside, apparently both subjective and objective. At other times, singing in a particular way draws you into a particular relational subject position—one that may be at odds with the one you occupied at breakfast. The process of

54. Kunreuther 2014, 3–4.

55. Desai-Stevens 2018.

56. Kvetko 2005.

57. Meizel 2020, 25 and passim. But see Taylor 1989 on an antecedent Protestant theological construct of a true "inner voice"—in contrast to the social cacophony of others' voices—a personal covenant between each individual and God; see Luhrmann 2012 for a contrasting Protestant figuration of inner voices as polyphony.

mastering such a voice often requires a reflexive distance from oneself—a process that poet Ross Gay calls "self-weirding," by which "I does not equal me": generating a split between voice and self.[58] As we will see, there are ways of voice rooted in non-individual selves: dual selves, collective selves, embodiments of moral exemplars, relational circuits, ritual technicians, conduits for a divine agency that is precisely *trans*personal. When singing *does* function as a vector of individual expression, it stands out as ethically proper only against a perilous (and discursively constructed) background of ethical hazard: imitation, pandering, repressive sociality. Chapter 6 loops back around to reconsider what I call individual-expressivist and groupist-expressivist figurations of voice, in light of the historical and ethnographic particulars that form the core of this book.

To provincialize this individualist-expressive vocal figuration is not to deny its discursive power, or that voices are ever personal, or ever expressive. Rather, I aim to foreground the work it takes to construct a voice as an expression of a sovereign individual. The disclosure of personal, expressive voices is a very particular ontological result, produced by situated attunements, practices, and infrastructures.[59] Indeed, as we will see in chapter 5, it is often the shifting destination of an endless road. As Anaar Desai-Stevens has shown, recent projects of "aspirational" vocal self-transformation, in pursuit of the skills that allow singers to find and express a unique, inner voice, often take years. "Aspiration" in Desai-Stevens's technical sense takes place in a collective, post-liberalization "aspirational economy," in which aspiration is not only a desire to change one's voice, but an ever-present affect as well, directed toward very specific mass-mediated subject positions.[60] Of course, not all vocal striving, and indeed not all directed work on the self, is "aspirational" in this specific sense. As we have already seen, a great many projects of vocal striving predate the post-liberalization "aspirational economy" (and other projects will no doubt continue long after this particular economic formation has passed). Bhakti hagiographies tell story after story of ethical transformation through song, and accounts of hereditary musical families are filled with stories of the self-reconfiguring ascetic work of intensive practice (*rīyāz*). Projects of "voice culture," as we have seen, are and were predicated

58. Gay 2019, 109.

59. Rahaim 2019.

60. Desai-Stevens 2017, 6–8.

precisely on self-transformation, decades before neoliberal projects of the self were said to have begun.[61] The earliest sound recordings reveal a vocal ecumene with shifting contours; Lata Mangeshkar, whose sweet, high vocality is so often construed as the "evergreen," unchanging voice of India, didn't always sing *that unmistakable way*—she had to work for it over years of rigorous training. And over the course of the 1940s, her recordings show a slow shift from a relatively open, bright sonority to the relatively gentle, mellow, close-miked, more lavishly ornamented voice that she now is remembered for. Nor is this dynamism specific to urbane cultivated musics; as Pei-Ling Huang has shown, Sindhi faqīrs, singing the devotional songs of Shah Abdul Latif Bhittai, have shifted their vocal dispositions dramatically over the past century or so in response to new exemplars and shifting circumstances.[62]

Furthermore, nearly all the singers I have worked with are, to use Katherine Meizel's eloquent term, *multivocal*.[63] That is to say, they have access to several voices, singing heavy in one situation and light in another; in a Sufi lodge for spiritual elites one day and at a wedding for industrial elites the next. Which of these voices is the true self? Psychoanalysts have long considered the movement of the "I" among a spatialized field of possible voices as a form of dialogic interplay between multiple subject positions.[64] And as linguistic anthropologist Jane Hill long ago demonstrated, these plural voices enact contestation between conflict-

61. Saba Mahmood (2004, 10–11) neatly provincializes the modern link between self-realization and individual sovereignty, distinguishing this from other forms of self-realization.

62. In the nineteenth century, it seems that faqirs sang this repertoire in a very strong, moderately pitched voice called *las*. There are now two registers that they switch between: a relatively low, recitative voice called *girām*, and a strikingly high, melismatic voice, produced on the edge of falsetto, called *sanhī* āvāz (thin voice). This change is largely attributed to the singer Ibrahim Faqir, but Pei-Ling Huang also links this change to the appearance of strong steel strings for their everpresent tonal companions, their *danbūro* (cogn. w. tānpurā), allowing them to tune their instruments higher (Huang 2019).

63. Meizel 2020, 5. See also Harri Englund's work on the political efficacy of multivocal public speech that works to "assemble mutually independent voices" (2015, 252).

64. Bertau 2008.

ing social and economic positionings.[65] Nicholas Harkness's work among Korean Christian singers, for example, highlights a moral world scaffolded by the mutual contrast between two crystallized vocal dispositions: an older, rougher, shamanistic "*p'ansori* voice" and a cleaner, Christian, forward-looking "*sŏngak* voice"—each rooted in a radically different form of training and self-cultivation, each invoking a distinctive form of subjectivity in contrast to the other, invoked chronotopically as emblems of a troubled past and a shining future.[66] Moral anthropologist Webb Keane goes so far as to suggest that this multiplicity of voices—and, indeed, the elusiveness of a single voicely "point of view"—is essential to any moral self-consciousness.[67] Voice cultivation does not (*pace* Dr. Pratap, Henry Higgins, and other progressive voice culturists) follow a single linear vector from low to high; it traces multiple trajectories, rubbing against, contesting, and reconstituting what otherwise might seem to be fixed moral codes.

Seen from such a vantage, the Hindustani vocal ecumene is neither a homogeneous space of fixed vocal identity, nor a lawless land of neoliberal vocal freedom, but rather a dynamic space of contestation, striving, and friction *between* sedimented, shifting vocal dispositions. What kinds of ethical selves may emerge from this friction? How might singing and listening be implicated in projects of self-making—and devotional self-abnegation?

Ethical Traditions

These vocal projects are also *ethical* projects: projects of cultivating, sustaining, performing, and contesting proper forms of vocal selfhood.[68] The ethical char-

---

65. Hill 1995. In her case, a single speaker stakes out a position in a moral field by switches among two *voices*, differing not only in language, but in *ethos*: one grounded in an indigenous communal-agricultural tradition of reciprocal relations, and another grounded in urban-cosmopolitan individual. See also Englund 2015 on "multivocal morality."

66. Harkness 2013, 130–133 and passim. In Harkness's milieu, however, few singers have mastered both voices.

67. Keane 2010, 77–78.

68. I tend to prefer "moral" for public, deliberative practices and "ethics" for the cultivation of bodily comportment, but the two terms are nearly interchangeable in practice and mark no essential analytic distinction in the present work. See Faubion 2011, 20–22 for a survey of the terminological problem.

acter of vocal life is analytically obscured by the default register of public music criticism, which tends toward the resolutely *aesthetic*, concerned principally with abstract melodic form, temporal structure, and sonorous pleasure.[69] But under the glossy aesthetical veneer of concert reviews is a vast landscape of ethical contestation about voices and their virtues. Revered singers are often remembered as persons of extraordinary, and often unorthodox, character: generous, cruel, vain, pious, restrained, with great carnal or spiritual appetites.[70] We hear of Faiyaz Khan's "noble bearing, generous and full of life in all things," of Lata Mangeshkar's "simplicity and grace," of Amir Khan's "dignity" and "serenity."[71] Singing is furthermore widely acknowledged to be a key site of personal transformation—through the ethics of listening, through the cultivation of relational virtue in mutually implicated subject positions, and through the ascetic practices of vocal striving.[72]

Hindustani literature offers a range of conceptual resources for reflecting on the ethics of vocal life. One classic term of normative ethical evaluation is *guṇa*—a word that spans virtue and vocal skill.[73] Treatises on music often enu-

---

69. This is in accordance with the Enlightenment-based split between disinterested taste and the putatively rational spheres of ethics and politics (cf. Overing in Ingold 1996, 210–214). As we will see in chapter 3, the "aesthetic attitude"—in which one listens at a distance to abstract sound-forms, systematically bracketing out lived sociality, constituting the singer as a solitary and independent *artiste*—is but one possibility among many.

70. See Neuman 2004 for ways in which these virtues shape the construal of a musician as the "biographical figure of the nation."

71. Misra 1981. See also Bailur 1955 for a general discussion of music and character.

72. The ethical practices described here span the usual tripartite anglophone philosophical schema of ethical theories (virtue/deontic/consequentialist), but don't always sit neatly in a single category. This ranges in turn from reflection about cultivated vocal dispositions (what philosophers call "virtue ethics"); to discerning righteous vocal action ("deontic ethics"); to the good and bad societal results of voicing in particular ways ("consequentialist ethics"). But musicians and commentators move freely among these, drawing on practices, theories, and terminology (often rooted in elite Persianate and Sanskritic literature) that don't always fit these neat disciplinary categories.

73. Both Orsini (2015) and Busch (2010) translate *guṇa* as "musical talent," and this works well enough for the passages that are principally concerned with distinguishing those with *guṇa* from those without *guṇa*. "Talent," however, implies a bit too much about inborn skill. The word, like "quality," has several overlapping usages: Sanskritic

merate individual *guṇas* of a good singer: practical virtues such as *sāvdhāna* (attentive),[74] *sukhāvaha* (mind-comforting),[75] and *karuṇa* (invoking pathos in a listener).[76] These same treatises often describe *doṣas*, or unwanted dispositional faults: for example, timidity, tension, or charmlessness.[77] *Guṇa* may also be treated as a single ethical substance; those possessed of great *guṇa* are generically called *guṇī*. *Guṇa* figures in the titles of many great musicians, from Khushhal Khan "*Guṇa-samudra*" ("ocean of *guṇa*," mid-seventeenth century) to Jagannath Buwa Purohit "*Guṇī-dās*" ("servant of the one who has *guṇa*," mid-twentieth century), and the celebration of *guṇa* is the topic of numerous khyals and dhrupads.[78] Significantly, connoisseurs may also be considered *guṇī*, by virtue of their discerning sensibilities. One classical statement of the ethical breadth of *guṇa* is found in the *Mādhavānal Kāmkandalā*: "guna always bestows happiness . . . without guna one's mouth utters lowly words. Without guna one is like a blind man, without guna one is a bird without wings."[79] To invoke *guṇa* in the twenty-first century is to risk sounding a bit archaic; it sounds faintly Mughal the way that *virtue* sounds faintly Victorian. It is still a term in circulation, particularly in hereditary families, but it evokes a courtly ethical regime; it rarely comes up in discussions of Bollywood song or pop sufi. A related term is *rūh* (spirit), often narrated as a blessing that some singers have and others don't. Another domain of normative ethics is *dharma*, or the various forms of duty assigned to various castes—developed in exacting detail in the *Dharmaśāstras*, the *Bhagvād Gīta*, and vast lineage of commentaries thereof, and sometimes applied creatively to music.[80] And yet, these normative models rarely offer clean-cut ethical an-

metaphysicians often distinguish between three fundamental *guṇas*, or essential tendencies (passion, inertia, and balance), or phonological intensity; it is also sometimes used as a term of distinction between *sa-guṇ* and *nir-guṇ* devotion (focusing one's devotion on divine attributes vs. pointing beyond attributes).

74. Bhatkhande 1954, 88.

75. Shringy and Sharma 2007, 166–167 (72cd).

76. Shringy and Sharma 2007, 166–167 (74cd).

77. Bhatkhande 1954, 89.

78. For example, *Avaguna Na Kījie* in Rag Yaman and *O Gunijana Mil* in Rag Marwa.

79. Orsini 2016, 350.

80. See Vajpayi 2012 for more on the reworking of these ethical resources in modern Indian political life. For its creative adaptation to musical ethics, see Parrikar 2001 and 2002.

swers; more often, they simply offer a common discursive ground for ethical contestation. As anthropologist Leela Prasad demonstrates, even in a highly stable institutional setting organized around a single moral tradition, a variety of apparently fixed codes come flexibly into mutual interaction. Ethical life is pursued not in a straight line from maxim to action, but in the "labyrinthine relationships *between* canons." The ethical dimensions of vocal life, subject to plural, contested canons of propriety, rarely hew to an overarching "grammar of the normative"; we are faced instead with a complex vocal "poetics of conduct."[81]

One widespread model for Hindustani vocal conduct hinges on *bhakti*, or the active performance of devotion. The canonical Hindustani paragons of bhakti are the singer-saints of the fifteenth through eighteenth centuries, such as Tulsidas, Surdas, Mirabai, and Kabir. The great virtues of these saints—Mirabai's fearlessness, Narasi Mehta's generosity, Pipa Das's dedication to community—are not only narrated in legend, but are also lived, celebrated, and amplified in participatory group song.[82] Indeed, as the corpus of songs and deeds attributed to each singer-saint has grown over time, so too has the ethical span of these saints. They have become not so much historical persons as ever-ready moral and spiritual resources, "bodies of song" that are brought into being in the moment of performance.[83] In these traditions, still alive today, *bhajan* itself—collective devotional singing—is the paradigmatic act of devotion. To sing along, to join in, is a key practical injunction of bhakti; it is the practice, more than any other, that produces extraordinary absorption and grants extraordinary forms of being. As the Surdas bhajan goes, "Songs to Hari work great wonders. They elevate the lowly of the world . . . to come to the feet of the Lord in song is enough to make stones float on the sea."[84] Collective singing (*samāj-gīt*) is often used as a model for vividly imagining mind-bogglingly large social formations. Indeed, *samāj* (like English "society") has taken on a dual meaning in the age of nations: it can refer equally to a small, room-sized gathering, *and* to a vast, state-shaped social imaginary. *Bhakti* may take the form of solitary praise of a beloved divinity; sometimes it is simply repeating a string of divine names (*jap*), akin to *zikr*; but in all cases, the ideal-typical mode of bhakti "remembrance," whether collective or individual, is vocal.

---

81. Prasad 2014, 12, 118.

82. Hawley 1984.

83. Hess 2015. See also Virani 2016, 66.

84. Hawley, 248–249.

Practical ethics in Hindustani Sufi[85] traditions is paradigmatically situated in gatherings of spiritual aspirants seated around a beloved Sufi master: for instruction, for the chanting of devotional formulas, and, above all, for the citation and recitation of poetry.[86] Each such master (*murshīd*, *pīr*) bears esoteric knowledge and virtue, indescribable in conventional discourse, but passed from heart to heart in a discipular lineage that reaches back, in principle, to the Prophet himself. Some gatherings are for *zikr*, "remembrance," enacted through the repetition of sacred formulas dozens or hundreds of times, coordinating breath, physical movement, and utterance in a steady flow, evoking a distinctive form of all-consuming devotional temporality, purifying the heart by pulling it into a one-pointed vector of devotion to God.[87] Indeed, the heart is the principal organ of Sufi practices of ethical refinement. The most morally controversial of these practices is the gathering for listening (*samā*), where *qawwāls* bring poetry to life, couplet by couplet, repeating and melodically elaborating lines for the contemplation, wonder, and upliftment of their spiritually elite patrons, who are trained to listen with the heart. In *samā*, an elaborate code of etiquette, or *adab*, prevails, for singers and listeners alike. The spiritual master, firmly in charge, oversees the proceedings, drawing above all on their own training by a master, trained in turn by theirs. A centuries-old literary tradition prescribes exactly how one is to comport oneself at a samā, which serves both as an occasion for ecstasy and as a mark of one's spiritual station, marking out a trajectory of personal refinement, striving against one's current state, each stage marked in turn by the achievement of stable disposition. The Sufi "ethics of listening," developed most famously and elaborately in the literature on the seductions and spiritual poten-

85. The principal Sufi orders of the Hindustani ecumene are the Chishtiyya, Qadiriyya, Naqshbandiyya, and Suhrawadiyya. The Chishti order, distinguished by a canon of poets and popular pilgrimage sites at the shrines of Nizamuddin Auliya in Delhi and Moinuddin Chishti in Ajmer, is the principal traditional patron of qawwals, and thus hold particular influence in the Hindustani vocal ecumene. Naqshbandi Sufis, ever suspicious of music's allure, often prefer "silent zikr," recited inwardly without sound. At the other end of the spectrum is a great range of pious, mystically inclined Muslim singers (sometimes called *faqīr* or *darvish*) who wander freely, publicly singing songs of ecstatic devotion, unaffiliated with any particular order.

86. See Ajmal in Metcalf 1984.

87. Qureshi 1994.

tials of listening to music, takes place against this discursive backdrop.[88] This literature is continuous with a body of Indo-Persian courtly literature focused on the cultivation of *akhlāq* (virtue). Grounded in a parallel relational account of vocal action, in which the heart is the preeminent organ of listening, elite Mughal writers described in particular detail the ethical daredevilry of listening to enchanting songs—while *resisting* falling in love with the singer.[89] Unlike the literature on *guṇa*, *akhlāq* literature often focuses on the practical training (rather than simply prescription) of virtuous character, drawing its conceptual resources from Islamicate philosophers of ethics (such as Miskawayh, al-Tusi, and Dawwani) who drew in turn upon Aristotelian models for the cultivation of proper dispositional acquisition.

Another branch of the Aristotelian tree has flowered more recently, in what has come to be called the "anthropology of ethics," focusing on diverse practices of virtue and morality, from exercises of self-observation to comportmental training to ethical deliberation, in India and elsewhere.[90] Aristotelian *habitus* and *hexis* have found new life in this literature, largely filtered through the sociological reconstruals of Marcel Mauss and Pierre Bourdieu.[91] Bourdieu's own work is empirically rich with examples of class-based *hexis* (comparing, for example, the seemingly inevitable distinctions between bourgeois and working-class table manners or vocal accent), but peculiarly thin in dealing with competing comportmental possibilities available to the same subject. It thus offers little in the way of understanding the reflective work done by a subject to cultivate themselves along one or another ethical path. The model cases for Bourdieu's largely deterministic scheme tend to be those in which each subject is offered precisely one comportmental possibility.[92] Taken too far, Bourdieu's scheme leads to a strangely amoral realm in which ethical automata helplessly play out the dispositions that have been stamped upon them by their structural positioning, powerless to change, escape, revolt, or retrain themselves. The singers I have worked with, in contrast, are nearly always faced with clashes between

---

88. al-Ghazali 2010; Hirschkind 2006; Ziad 2007.

89. Brown 2006.

90. Mahmood 2004; Pandian 2009; Ali and Pandian 2010; Lambek 2010; Faubion 2011; Laidlaw 2014; Keane 2017; Das 2018.

91. Mauss 1973; Bourdieu 1997.

92. Noland 2009, 7.

voices, moments of disjuncture between voice and self, and necessary reflection on their own situation, sometimes changing course and undergoing a process of vocal remaking. For ethical dynamism, anthropologists of ethics have thus also drawn inspiration from Michel Foucault's late sketches of ethical self-work, in which ethical actors work to cultivate their own faculties, reflecting on their own conduct at a critical distance even as they fit themselves into a limited set of possible subject positions. In other words, voice qualifies as what Foucault called "ethical substance": a pliable object of moral striving, neither good nor evil in itself, like carnal desire or emotional sensitivity, but improvable through self-work.[93] And yet, to focus on substance alone can be misleading. Saba Mahmood, by focusing on practices of subject formation in the Egyptian Islamic revival, brought performative dynamism back to the center of the ethical domain, foregrounding the repeated acts by which humilty, sincerity, shyness, and other pious virtues can be inculcated as stable dispositions through rote, bodily practice.[94] James Faubion's rich programmatic account of voice is particularly apt for the ethical situation we face in the Hindustani vocal ecumene: "Voice is malleable. Proper voicing—whether aesthetically or oratorically or ethically proper—demands training and practice. It demands coaching and pedagogy." But it also often includes "the further directives and refinements of reflexive technologies."[95] Though the finite set of prior subject positions available to any particular subject is relatively stable, we are also faced with the extraordinary ethical possibilities and dangers offered by the exercise of reflexive freedom, yielding unprecedented new voices and, concomitantly, new vocal subject positions.[96] By explicitly thematizing practice, pedagogy, and reflexive techniques, this turn in the anthropology of ethics moves us toward a relational and dynamic (rather than substantivist and structurally conservative) analytic of voice.

93. Foucault 2012b, 26, 91; Foucault 2012c, 67, 239; Faubion 2011, 3.

94. Mahmood 2004, 156–157, 164.

95. Ibid., 259.

96. On the malleability and contestation of subject positions, see Faubion 2011, 4; see also James Laidlaw's sophisticated rereading of Foucault on freedom (2014).

An Ethics of Disposition and Relationality

Accordingly, the vocal ethics I develop here is grounded in the dynamics of cultivated, malleable vocal *disposition*[97] rather than in moral axioms or ahistorical traits of genre, caste, religious identity, etc. A disciplined voice, I argue, is not so much characterized by a set of acoustical traits or generic forms, but by a characteristic vocal gait, sonority, and poetic attunement; a posture of the tongue and pharynx, neck, back, belly, and arms; habits of listening, temporality, and—crucially—modes of performed social relation with others. Like an upright posture or a swaggering gait, these dispositions of voice connect local forms of propriety, grace, righteousness, and beauty; they bridge body and soul, singer and listener, ethics and aesthetics. A cultivated voice is neither carved irrevocably in solid flesh, nor conjured freely in a vaporous fantasy, but shaped over time: a stiff but workable sensorimotor clay.

An extensive ethnographic literature has attested to the dispositional training that underlies the public enunciation of poetry, often contrasting the apparent textuality of the words on the page to the remarkable vocal capabilities of singers and bards, reciters and griots.[98] As Rudolf Ware says about figure of the Senegambian *hafiz*, vocally assimilating a vast recitational repertoire serves "not simply to transmit discursive knowledge but rather to remold the body into a living vehicle" for the sounding word.[99] In the Hindustani vocal ecumene, devotional singers are "enveloped" in Kabir's word, "drenched" in poetic waters, or taken over by a "storm of songs," bringing the singing self into communion with a sea of poetry much bigger than any one singer.[100] The rushing flow of sung poetry becomes a crucible for ethical self-refinement, an ethical field that reaches far beyond the body, that individuals do not so much *have*, but come, over time, to *participate in*. To live with poetry in the heart or on the tip of the tongue, to be a *khazāna* (treasury) of memorized songs, to be saturated with poetry, is not so much to own a thing, but *to be* in a certain way. To sing thumri is not merely to affix words

97. See Faubion 2011, 37 and Laidlaw 2014, 73. Note that this is distinct from the use of the word *disposition* in psychological theory to mean *predisposition*—a temperament that is precisely independent of training.

98. See, for example, Caton 1990; Lord, et al. 2000; Hoffman 2001; Lutgendorf 1991; Hess 2015; Virani 2016.

99. Ware 2014, 111.

100. See Hess 2015, 273; Hawley 2015, 1.

arbitrarily to melodies, but to actively have the capability for *bol banāo*: "making the words come to life . . . endeavoring to bring out all possible nuances of emotion latent in a simple line."[101] *Kahen*, or "saying," indicates a cultivated subtlety of pronunciation that goes beyond the phonetics of any particular phrase. Lata Mangeshkar famously retrained her own elocutional disposition after receiving criticism about her bland pronunciation of Urdu—as she tells it, the accusation was that her bookish Maharashtrian recitational hexis had the aroma of plain dāl and rice.[102] A qawwal who knows how to artfully repeat a short word or phrase (*takrār*) to elevate their Sufi patrons is not merely following grammatical rules. Such a poetic disposition is entrained through years of experience, bringing together a poetic canon assimilated into the *self* with a profound relational sensitivity to *others*: one's listeners, their predilections, what they respond to.[103]

For the Hindustani singers I have worked with, the cultivation of what I call *kinetic* and *sonorous* dispositions of voice is central to *āvāz banānā*, or "voice-making." To fill a space with bright, high, ringing, *buland* voice, to "fly" through rapid *tāns* on a long vowel, to adorn a poem with fluttering, shivering *harkat*—these are all disciplined ways of comporting the vocal apparatus. The ethnographic literature on voice cultivation, from South Asia and beyond, documents a vast archive of techniques of the body that shape vocal quality: Chinese treatises on voice cultivation that prescribe specific actions of the mouth and lips; techniques of Korean *p'ansori* singers who belt out song in the face of roaring waterfalls; Balinese *dalangs* who allow cold spring water to stream over their throat as they sing; Arab singers who spend years learning Qur'anic recitation to shape the vocal apparatus for art song.[104] These dispositions are located not only in the larynx, tongue, or teeth, but also throughout the body—and beyond, coming to life in social relations with others. Such a dispositional training is not only a matter of sounding right, but of *being* right among others, building, as Ryan Skinner eloquently puts it, "local moorings and social imperatives that locate and orient [one's] being-in-the-world."[105] These dispositions may be impressed on more-or-less passive bodies—especially when training children. But

101. Manuel 1986, 480.

102. Kabir 2009, 67.

103. Viitamäkii 2008, 110.

104. Harkness 2013, 130; Herbst 1997, 25; Meizel 2020, 43–44; Zeitlin in Feldman 2019, 66–70.

105. Skinner 2015, 4.

they are also undertaken reflexively by self-aware subjects who have a definite goal in mind. And crucially, these projects of cultivated vocal disposition are often undertaken in relation to listeners.

The ethical analytic I favor here thus moves from a substantivist sociality of individual vocal quality or homogenous group identity to a sociality of dynamic vocal *relations*. Though a commonsense account of voice, rooted in recordings, often begins with a prior sound-text later placed "in context" among others, I suggest the inverse. Singing is normatively and foundationally relational, produced and performed in social relation with particular listeners. This relational ethics of voice already has ethnomusicological precedent in Timothy Rommen's conception of the "ethics of style" in Trinidadian Gospel song (which is founded on the reciprocal obligations of singers and listeners[106]) and Jeffers Engelhardt's conception of "singing the right way" (which hinges not only on canonical injunctions, but also on interpersonal practices of joining voices, festivity, enchantment, and active commemoration.[107]) These relations are primary, not contexts around individual voicing bodies. Indeed, the figure of the expressive individual emerges (if it does at all) only as a specialized construal after the fact.

Though isolated claims about vocal propriety often invoke a single imaginary ethical yardstick ("respectability," "purity," "authenticity," etc.), in practice there are multiple orthogonal axes of vocal propriety that obtain for different sites and different forms of social rapport. A qawwal who sings with excessive ornament, distracting their audience with their virtuosity, may fail in their spiritual duty to an elite audience of Chishti Sufis; and yet the same florid ornamentation, in the same *ghazal*, may be precisely what is called for on a stage, at a pop sufi concert—for authenticity, for expressiveness, for customer satisfaction. Just as one might disparage a puritanical uncle as *sanctimonious*, *uptight*, *or pious*—terms of unmistakable ethical disparagement—so too can an excessively pure vocal ethos register as deviant. In one common term of vocal critique, singers may be accused of being "too veg[etarian]": too straight, too clean, too tonally correct to reach a listener. A concert hall typically calls for silent, focused listening, not singing along; and yet things are nearly reversed at a Varkari kirtan procession, where it is ethically praiseworthy for bystanders to join in. These are traditions of relational practice, not freestanding virtues that inhere in a heroic individual

106. Rommen 2007.

107. Engelhardt 2015.

or homogeneous group.[108] Despite conventional sectarian discourse, there is no one predetermined "Hindu voice," "Muslim voice," or "Sikh voice"; despite common regional stereotypes about the "strident" Panjabi voice, "sweet" Bengali voice, or "thin, nasal" Maharashtrian voice,[109] there is a wide range of competing vocal dispositions in each of these regions. Indeed, these dispositional differences are often produced quite deliberately, by systematically retraining one's vocal proclivities. Most singers move easily between several vocal dispositions, sometimes in the same day, in accordance with different vocal sites. These sites vary widely: an intimate gathering (*mahfil*), a public temple courtyard, a private lodge (*ḳhānqāh*) for spiritually elite Sufis, a concert hall—each of these invites its own distinctive forms of vocal relationality.

To focus on relational voicing is to foreground the various kinds of situated interplay between singer and listener, producing responses which in turn feed back upon the singer.[110] From these reciprocally entangled acts of voicing and listening emerge *circuits of voice*. These circuits are not mere abstract "contexts" for given texts, but are directly *constitutive* of voice.[111] As Jody Kreiman puts it, "without a listener, vocal folds may oscillate and articulators may vary the vocal tract shape . . . but the output of this process is vibration, and not the sound of a voice *per se*."[112] We tend to imagine that vocalization is fundamentally solitary precisely when we rely on analytics that generate images of vocal solitude: transcriptions of vocal sound objects, anatomical illustrations that begin at the diaphragm and end at the lips, individualist discourses of subjectivity that assume a one-to-one correlation of voice and subject—and, above all, sound recordings that promise a stable sound item "unmoored" from the relational practices of listening

---

108. See Brubaker 2002 on groupism, and Novetzke 2007 on bhakti sociality as operating through "publics of reception" (grounded in performance) rather than prior, given homogenous groups or communities.

109. For a critical summary of these stereotypes, see, for example, Desai-Stevens 2018, 143.

110. This in contrast to the atemporal, qualitative "relations" (such as relative status) that appear to metaphorically to obtain between genres, social formations, groups, or institutions—cf. Born 2010, Feldman 2015.

111. See Clayton 2007 for an analytic approach that considers listeners as participants in a performance rather than a mere "context."

112. Kreiman in Eidsheim and Meizel 2019. Also see Abbate 1996; Eidsheim 2015; Rahaim 2018.

that make it available to experience.[113] Such an individual-centered analytic orientation can indeed reveal important things, and often serves as provisional scaffolding on the way to a broader understanding of vocal sociality. But a construal of a voice as an object or a self-identical substance implicitly relegates listeners to the outside, as incidental accessories to vocalization, an optional social "aspect" of singing, or a social *context* around an independent vocal *text*—obscuring the circuits of listening and voice, of consocial "communities of time,"[114] so crucial to the action of singing. In critic Sanjay Srivastava's terms, the difference between a voice that simply falls on generic boundaries and a voice that is socially open to relation is the difference between a textual figure instantiating a script and a relational figure of voicing in which "the listener may talk back, interrupt, and re-interpret."[115] When we speak of a voice that "cuts" you like a sword, stabs you in the heart, gives you chills, we are already speaking in relational terms. Dwelling on practices of listening and vocal infrastructures such as microphones, sound systems, and cultivated relational attunements, the aim is to foreground these circuits between singers and listeners, as a rich affective and ethical traffic between specially tuned bodies.

This analytic focus on relationality has a long lineage—several, in fact. Feminist relational ethics has long emphasized what Carol Gilligan calls the "relational resonance" between persons, in which "voices are resonant with or resounded by others," offering a sense of voicing that "depends on listening and being heard" and thus is "an intensely *relational act*."[116] Judith Butler's sustained engagement with the everyday *performativity* of such relational acts has refined and expanded this analytic, drawing small-scale relationality together with the

113. Zuberi and Sarrazin 2017, 168. See also Rahaim 2012, 4–5 on the analytic limits of individual musicking bodies.

114. Schutz 1996, 63.

115. Srivastava 2004, p. 2021.

116. Gilligan 1993, xvi. The thematic emphasis on relational voicing is explicitly developed in her introduction to the 1993 edition of *In A Different Voice*. Though Gilligan originally made the case that an ethics grounded in interpersonal empathy was specifically female (and neglected in a male regime of moral psychology that foregrounds individual duty and virtue), this model of relationality applies to men no less than women. See also bell hooks's account of a "will to connect," available equally to men and women, in tension with a masculinist, Nietzschean "will to dominate" (2000, 235; 2004, 117).

large-scale structures that form its sedimented traces and its guiding infrastructure.[117] Dell Hymes's foundational "Ways of Speaking," in its focus on relational *modes* of voice, undertaken in relation to others, has placed relationality at the center of sociolinguistics.[118] Nina Eidsheim's nuanced construal of voices as essentially linked to listening[119] and Katherine Meizel's focus on relationality in vocal-spiritual experiences have likewise helped to shape voice studies into a field grounded in sociality.[120] Harris Berger's fine-grained account of stance has opened a space for a phenomenology of performance that is rooted in social relations.[121] Edward Herbst's detailed account of Balinese voice cultivation grounds performance not just in sound, but also in the mutual interweaving of co-presence and place.[122] Steven Feld's rich and varied account of Kaluli acoustemology likewise foregrounds relations as essential to voice, though it's worth pointing out that these relations vary widely from situation to situation. Vocal relationality in the Hindustani ecumene, to be sure, is not always as acoustemologically egalitarian as it seems to be among the Kaluli. Though some forms of participatory group song (such as *gali*, *bhajan*, and *shabd kirtan*) often do proceed in spaces of common sonic sensibility, listeners and singers just as often live in radically different worlds, with different aural attunements and vocal capabilities, in accord with their mutually interwoven, interdependent, but nonetheless distinct subject positions. Indeed, the comportmental (and acoustemological) distance between singer and listener (between qawwal and Sufi listener, between courtesan and patron, between khyaliya and rasika) is often at the very heart of vocal ethics.[123] The metaphysical impulse to dissolve the alterity of vocal relations into the totality of shared acoustemological Being has been tempered, for me, by Emmanuel Levinas's insistence on ongoing *rapport*, across a distance, irreducible to comprehensive economic, cultural, or acoustemological totalities,

---

117. Butler 2004, 19.

118. Hynes in Bauman and Sherzer 1989.

119. Eidsheim 2008, 118; 2019, 10–13.

120. Meizel 2020.

121. Berger 2010, 97.

122. Herbst 1997, 5. The technical term, constructed from Indic cognates, is *deśa-kala-patra*.

123. See also Hoffman 2001 on the asymmetrical but interdependent relations between griots and their noble patrons.

as a basic condition for ethics.[124] There are uneasy echoes of this Levinasian rapport discernible throughout this book, particularly in the account of irreducible relationality in chapter 3, competing patterns of Sufi vocal metaphysics in chapter 4, and face-to-face tālīm in chapter 5.

A focus on dynamic relationality rather than fixed identity furthermore affords the analytic flexibility to survey *change*, to make sense of singers who move from one site to another, who gradually retrain their voices, over time, into new ethical dispositions tuned for different relations, different circuits of listening. It also throws into relief the various construals of the voice as *irrelational*—not just solitary, but designedly oblivious to relational connection. Whether conceived as sovereign self-expression, forming an aesthetic sound object, or indifference in principle to social feedback, figurations of irrelational vocal expression stand out as extraordinary exceptions to a normative relationality—rather than as natural, ontically given traits of the-voice-as-such, in a vacuum.

There is a risk in an appeal to *ethics* in making sense of these vocal projects. The very word may seem to suggest the inherent righteousness of the practice at hand (in contrast, perhaps, to some putatively evil, "unethical" practice). And yet, not all—or even most—ethical practices are simply good, right, and true. The rigorous *askesis* that cultivates a bright, rich vocal disposition is no guarantee against personal demons, flaws, or transgressions of respectable public morality. The brutal methods and destructive results of the anti-nautch campaign, which violently cut off the traditions of courtesan communities across South Asia, were, nonetheless, part of a clearly articulated *ethical project* in the anthropological sense. The vocal disciplines zealously imposed by missionaries, the exclusionary practices of vocal reformers, the authority wielded (and, too often, abused) in master-disciple relationships, the individualist ethos of reality TV—these all are practices that, at minimum, sit uneasily with commitments to inclusion, community, relational connection, and care. Indeed, the fact that projects of ethical reform have long been part of, as Arjun Appadurai puts it, "patently violent, brutal and exploitative regimes and practices" is an important caution for those of us with well-intentioned moral commitments of our own.[125]

124. Levinas 2012 [1971]. See Rahaim 2017 for somewhat longer meditations on what a Levinasian ethnomusicology of relations might look like and Rahaim 2020 for the possibilities offered by "voices in relation" that escape the "metaphysical box" of paradigmatic vocal solitude offered by the Husserl-Derrida tradition.

125. Appadurai n.d.

Critical attention to practices of vocal self-formation critically highlights rather than takes for granted the ethical contours of these projects, and denaturalizes what otherwise might appear to be their universal moral righteousness.

Gender and Vocal Subject Position

Close attention to the cultivation of vocal disposition also tends to denaturalize the substantivist assignment of voices to gendered subject positions. Rather than hearing voice as consubstantial with a true inner gender, disposition orients us to vocal *performativity*. In Judith Butler's classic analytic, vocality is "a set of repeated acts . . . that congeal over time to produce the [superficial] appearance of substance, of a natural sort of being."[126] Chloë Alaghband-Zadeh has argued that conventional Hindustani wisdom is loosely in agreement about the relative masculinity and femininity of individual vocal qualities in isolation (sweetness is feminine, restraint is masculine, and so forth), and it is clear that, in some cases at least, female singers consciously avoid masculine vocal action (for example, singing "from the stomach" or "open") in gender-performative principle.[127] As we will see in chapter 4, much of the public critical controversy over Lata Mangeshkar's voice hinges on whether or not it is to be heard as an expression of a monolithic—and oppressive—Indian femininity. And yet, masculinity and femininity operate somewhat more complexly in practice. Indeed, Alaghband-Zadeh's productive analytic commitment to performativity sheds light on the complex dynamics of masculine and feminine vocal action—which, in the Hindustani ecumene as elsewhere, lines up only partially and contingently with male and female subject positions. Ghazal singer Mehdi Hassan is beloved for his vocal sweetness; Abida Parveen, for her vocal strength. (Parveen herself says, "The concept of being a man or a woman doesn't cross my mind. I'm neither on stage; I'm a vehicle on stage for passion."[128]) Among current khyaliyas, masculinities and femininities are normatively *balanced* in a singer; in the canon of great recorded voices, male singers (such as Yashwantbuwa Joshi and Sharafat Hussain Khan) are sometimes criticized in retrospect for singing with a lack

126. Butler 2011, 45.

127. Zadeh 2013, 182; Alaghband-Zadeh 2015; Rahaim 2012, 25; Desai-Stevens 2018, 205; Ajotikar 2019, 339–340.

128. Iqbal 2013.

of ("feminine") tenderness, and many female singers (such as Kesarbai Kerkar and Mogubai Kurdikar) are praised for their ("masculine") openness. When Bal Gandharva, the great diva of Marathi opera, sang his famous female roles onstage, the effect was not gender-bending transgression, but gender-affirming popular entertainment: a depiction of femininity so conventional that his on-stage wardrobe shaped trends in Maharashtrian women's fashion.[129] On the other hand, vocal performance may also actively destabilize gender norms. For example, Jeff Roy has described ways in which the song practices of *hījṛā jalsās* ("third-gender" ritual gatherings) reinforce normative marriage practices even as they performatively disrupt conventional gender roles.[130]

Despite these complex performative dynamics of masculinity and femininity, most vocal institutions remain structurally patriarchal. Even the most extraordinary female qawwals are not ordinarily invited to perform for spiritually elite males, and do not ordinarily enjoy official shrine patronage. Though there is near parity in numbers of male and female performing singers in the world of raga music, female khyaliyas are nonetheless bound by a range of stringent, and largely invisible, structural constraints. As Kesarbai Kerkar, who blazed a trail of public bourgeois respectability for female singers in the years around independence, bluntly put it: "It would have been better if God had made me a man. I would not have been bothered by the obstacles that often came into the path of my music study. I would have gone anywhere on the Earth to learn to sing."[131] Gynecic khyal lineages are never granted the authority of the term *gharana*, which are exclusively identified with their male progenitors.[132] Though there are widely recognized khyal gharanas traced to gifted male singers from structurally marginalized sarangi and tabla lineages, no widely recognized gharanas are named after women, even for singers such as Kishori Amonkar and Savita Devi, each of whom developed a unique, and now widely dispersed, way of voice. This institutional disenfranchisement has subtle but important consequences for how female voices are heard. As we will see in chapter 4, dispositional distinctiveness construed as gharana gayaki suggests a traditional coherence and integrity;

---

129. Hansen 1998, 2296; Kosambi 2017, 275.

130. Roy 2017, 415.

131. In Post Quinn 1986, viii.

132. Maciszewski 2001a. On *hijra gharanas*, see Roy 2017. On patriarchal structures in guru-shishya parampara, see Ajotikar 2019, 340 and passim.

without that stamp of authority, such a voice can only hope to be construed as an idiosyncratic "style" (*śāilī*). Bollywood music directors have almost invariably been men, and gatekeepers such as managers, producers, and shrine custodians tend overwhelmingly to be male as well.[133]

There is furthermore a structural tension between being a wife (tied to private, domestic responsibilities) and being a professional singer (with her own public)—a tension that does not ordinarily constrain male householders. Many young women with promising singing careers find themselves, once married, suddenly forbidden to sing in public by their husband's family. The women who have shared stories with me of exclusion and sexual violence, who have been forced to choose between domestic life and public vocal life, have made clear just how much is at stake here; most have asked me to turn the camera off at one time or another, and nearly all have asked that certain stories not be included in this book. Those female singers I've interviewed who have *not* been hindered by these obstacles—whose careers have been actively supported by male relatives in the face of structural pressure—are fully aware of how statistically rare their situation is. Even in the absence of explicit prohibition, women singers face other structural constraints. The time and focus required for talim, riyaz, and performance is often at odds with the overwhelming burden of responsibility that so many married women are implicitly expected to carry: the daily unpaid labor of raising children, tending the home, and—in many cases—also earning a salary.[134] Some stop singing for decades until their children are settled, and pick up their career again later in life. But many—perhaps even the majority—never sing in public again.[135]

The separation of these subject positions (domestic mother and public singer) has a long genealogy throughout the Hindustani ecumene. Until independence

---

133. Three notable female music directors are Saraswati Devi (active 1935–1955), Usha Khanna (active 1959–2003), and Sneha Khanwalkar (2004–present).

134. There certainly have been exceptions—Jaddanbai, for example, had a very active career after marriage; Begum Akhtar famously stopped singing (as Akhtaribai) for the first five years of her marriage, but later returned to the stage with a glittering new name and to great acclaim.

135. To give a few examples: Tarabai Shirodkar, Chammubai of Delhi, Bindijan and Husseinijan of Rampur, and Kamleshwari Devi all gave up singing after marriage. See the corresponding biographical articles in *The Oxford Encyclopaedia of the Music of India*.

(and even well after), a woman singing for men on a public stage risked being seen as a public "singing girl" (*gānewālī*): she risked, in other words, the inference of sexual availability outside of marriage. This is partially due to the ambiguous discursive afterlife of courtesanry. For centuries, courtesans (*tawāifs, bāījīs, kalāwantīn*) had been bearers of elite traditions of poetry, song, dance, etiquette, and dress in Indo-Persian Hindustan. Many of the most celebrated singers and poets of Lucknow, Delhi, and other centers of elite Mughal culture were courtesans; they seem to have constituted the vast majority of literate, propertied women. And yet, though a courtesan might well entertain numerous married male clients, she herself would not marry. Marriage would ordinarily mark a shift in subject position: the end of public singing and the beginning of domestic life. The courtesan thus occupied a parallel world of ethical possibility, cordoned off from the patriarchal moral regime of domestic motherhood, with precious little gray area between.[136] The world of the salons, already weakened by the ascendent bourgeois Victorian norms of companionate marriage, largely collapsed in the 1950s, battered by raids and other state-sanctioned violence against courtesans. The decline of aristocratic patronage and a series of increasingly prohibitive laws throughout South Asia had already induced many trained courtesans to find other forms of livelihood in the decades following independence. Promoters in Bombay around the turn of the twentieth century presented concerts by former courtesans, now called "songstresses," who, increasingly sitting still while singing rather than dancing, would sing to entertain and uplift rather than seduce.[137] Others recast themselves as modern artistes, focusing on raga music, distancing themselves from thumri, ghazal, and the seductive perils of their prior voice. But even now, women singing in public who wish to remain "respectable" (a euphemism for upper-caste, middle-class, monogamous domestic life that is subject to patriarchal norms) are still haunted by the perilous subject position of the courtesan, the woman who reaches out to men dangerously with her voice. They therefore are under a special pressure, which largely does not apply to men, to perform a decisive respectability: singing austere raga music and devotional bhajans, in modest bourgeois dress, with a still, placid comportment and a rela-

136. Histories and ethnographies of courtesan life attest to the inversion of patriarchal norms; the birth of a female child in a courtesan community, for example, seems to have been celebrated far more than that of a male child. Oldenburg 1990; Maciszewski 2001; Waheed 2014; Dewan 2019.

137. Pradhan 2014, 342. See also Rahaim 2012 and Weidman 2006, 132.

tively plain, pious, aloof vocal delivery, avoiding direct eye contact with male listeners. This obligatory demarcation of subject position forms one of the most intractable conventional structures within which, in Judith Butler's classic turn of phrase, vocal acts "not only become possible but become conceivable as acts at all."[138] The relatively flexible performativity of masculine and feminine ways of voice, then, unfolds over a relatively stable and restrictive—but nonetheless slowly shifting—terrain of gendered subject position.

Speaking of Voice

Conceptually, *voice* seems to encompass an impossibly wide conceptual domain. Speaking, singing, and vocal attunements are everywhere, from chant to chitchat to political slogans, with a somewhat wider ambit than the boundaries of *music* in its usual aesthetical sense (as one art among many, dedicated to sonic beauty, to be pursued for its own sake). In general, the Hindustani word *āvāz* (via Persian, cognate with Sanskrit *vāk* and Latin *vox*) functions much as the English word *voice* does, and with the same dazzling ontological range: subtending individual and collective, silence and sound, body and soul.[139] A singer's *āvāz* is not only a particular sonic phenomenon at a particular moment. Flexible and malleable enough to maintain its training over months or years, we can speak of an open voice (*khulī āvāz*), a sweet voice (*mīṭhī āvāz*), or a filmy voice (*filmī āvāz*). *Āvāz*, like *voice*, may refer to something that *belongs to* an individual person ("that's Begum Akhtar's voice on the radio") or to something that is precisely supraindividual, available to innumerable individual persons ("tonight he is singing in Sufi voice; tomorrow, he will sing in Western voice"). Conversely, it may also refer to the sound of someone singing or speaking at a particular occasion ("your voice is hoarse tonight")—in *contrast* to their personal voice ("she doesn't sound like herself today"). *Āvāz* is sometimes contrasted with *galā* ("throat," which refers specifically to an individual vocal mechanism).[140] Thus,

---

138. Butler 1988, 525.

139. As Laura Kunreuther (2014) points out, *āvāz* may also imply "noise" or "sound" in a way that English voice ordinarily does not—but see Ihde ([1976] 2012) for a sense of voice that specifically does include the telltale sounds of objects.

140. The belly, chest, and nose serve equally as vocal loci along with the throat (see chapter 2). But *galā* bears special ontological weight in locating a durable vocal mechanism impervious to mere willpower. It is common, for example, for a singer whose

one could praise a young singer with a sweet voice for having a good *galā* even if they haven't yet developed their *āvāz* (indeed, this is precisely what compels Dr. Pratap to transform Kamli's voice the beginning of *Man Pasand*). Politically, we can speak of a voice of the people (*āvām kī āvāz*), which, like its modern English equivalent, implies a unanimous, collective political will, even when its expression is acoustically silent (e.g., voting). Psychologically, we can speak of a person's *āvāz* as a metonym for their individual agency as distinct from others. And, crucially, *āvāz*, like *voice*, can also be used as an icon of a dispositional complex in the moment of singing—one's ethical comportment, spiritual states, relational orientations; open, ecstatic, sweet, gentle.

This sometimes can lead to a baffling richness of meaning. For example, one khyaliya once described a certain vocal transformation to me like this, in English: "It needed a lot of surrender for the voice to open up. To realize that it's actually not about the voice." Though this utterance may appear paradoxical on a close reading that tries to pin down what The Voice is ("the *voice* is not actually about the *voice*"), the narrative logic was in fact perfectly clear. She had just been describing the process of learning to vocally open herself up over many months: to relax, to stop willfully gripping and pushing, to slow down, to allow there to be silences, to let herself be guided by a will outside of herself. Thus, as she says, this was not just about making different vocal *sounds*, but about reconfiguring her vocal *disposition*. I've thus chosen to foreground the practical-ontological particularity of *what* vocal phenomenon we are faced with in each situation, holding lightly general claims about The Voice as such, whether made by singers or scholars.[141] This is partially in service of exposing various kinds of totalizing ideologies of voice—which, in Amanda Weidman's elegant terms, "determine how and where we locate subjectivity and agency, [giving] sung or spoken utterances their power or constrain their potential effects."[142] Weidman's own virtuosic analysis of vocal ideology in Karnatak music lays bare at least one such monolithic ideology, in which The Voice came to be understood as "a realm of pure Indianness, untouched by colonialism or worldly concerns."[143] As we will see in chapters 3 and 4, there are many other figurations as well, hinging on the

---

voice cracks or warbles to touch their throat, ascribing the sonic failure to a malfunction of the flesh rather than the *āvāz*.

141. For more on practical ontologies of voice, see Rahaim 2019.

142. Weidman 2014, 45.

143. Weidman 2006, 287.

cultivation and contestation of various forms of public voicing, playing with the slippages and dynamic co-mappings between individual and collective selfhoods, between sound, feeling, ethical disposition, and imagination.

By centering plural *ways* (rather than The Voice as such), I hope to open a space of possibility for attending to dispositions of voice that are constituted by relations with others, that move between bodies, that are neither uniformly individual nor unanimously collective, and which project worlds of possibility larger than any one singer.

Chapter Summaries

Chapter 2 grounds vocal striving and contestation in cultivated vocal dispositions, demonstrating that what otherwise might appear to be vocal traits rooted in genre, caste, or ideology are in fact cultivated comportments of voice. Tunefulness, openness, ornamentation, spontaneous improvisation—these are neither random, isolated vocal actions nor permanently fixed features of an identity, but embodied dispositions of voice built through years of practice. This chapter is divided roughly into two sections: kinetic dispositions (gait, carriage, ways of motion and stillness) and sonorous dispositions (*sur*, bodily resonance, openness, sweetness).

Chapter 3 thematizes practices of listening, grounding vocal dispositions in relationality. It foregrounds the characteristic, mutually constitutive circuits of voicing and listening that afford voices their ethical and affective power. This chapter surveys several practices of listening and relation: from the esoteric techniques of Sufi *samā*, to the cultivated practices of tonal discernment that allow listeners to identify ragas, to the apparently unconscious attunements that afford chills, heart-aching, and other affective responses. It also surveys the forms of participatory vocal sociality common in bhakti practice, and the extraordinary forms of relation that emerge from singing to a divine listener. This leads to an exploration of the heady moral terrain opened by *irrelational* practices: turning away from, or deliberately ignoring, relations with listeners—in the name of art, freedom, or radical individuality.

Having marked out a territory of voice that is already inherently social, chapter 4 focuses on the moral controversies surrounding the formation of several widely legible public voices. It surveys the ethical stakes of contrasting vocal gharanas, the emergence and spread of Amir Khan's controversial introspective vocal disposition in the 1950s, the popular embrace and critical contestation of *filmi* voice, the contested femininity of Lata Mangeshkar's voice, and the contentious pop sufi song movement of the 2000s and 2010s. It also examines the emergence of charts the rise in Hindustani "Western-voice": the pop and R&B-inflected vocal dispositions that have become legible and highly lucrative since liberalization, along with their own distinctive pedagogies.

Chapter 5 addresses itself to the ongoing cultivation of vocal dispositions. Starting from two case studies of voice-making, it surveys the many techniques of vocal cultivation that make possible traffic between voices: from the ascetic practices of riyaz, to handbooks of "scientific" voice culture, to "Western-voice" pedagogy, to the metaphysical conditions of relationship between master and disciple. The study of vocal striving reveals vocal disciplines not as strictures upon an infinite field of potential vocal action but as specific techniques that *afford* power and freedom—albeit contingent and limited—already situated within relational circuits. It then turns to reflexivity: stepping back from one's own voice and contemplating it at a distance, opening up key ontological questions about voice, forms of selfhood, and relational attunements.

Chapter 6 takes up these broader questions. In contrast to the usual figuration of voice as an expression of a static individual subject or a univocal collectivity, an analytic tuned to ways of voice locates the ethical stakes of singing in the friction between sedimented dispositions learned and inhabited by singers attuned to particular relational situations. Finally, it points to vocal ways beyond the expression of fixed individual or collective character, and toward the contested dynamism of voice, affording relations among others: ways not only of singing-together, but also of being-together.

TWO

Gāyakī

Vocal Dispositions

In a way, singing is easy as walking. Just as a sprinter can dash across a field without having to fire individual muscles one by one, so too can a trained singer sing spontaneously, in tune, in a proper gait, without attending to every laryngeal twitch. Florid vocal runs (which, for a beginner, may seem to require cognitive focus on a complex sequence of notes) flow easily from a singer who has dispositionally acquired the proper gait. A bright, steady, open /a/ can seem to be a singer's own "natural" voice pouring out of them. These dispositions are so durable that aspiring singers are sometimes advised that they need more lightness "in" their voice, more gamak "in" their voice, more *tān* "in" their voice. Thus a voice (like a subject position) may seem to take on the quality of a timeless, self-identical essence. But in fact, vocal agility and weight, brightness and depth, are all molded by years of observation, imitation, correction, and repetition. It is only through years of training, listening, and vocalization among others that a singer comes to "have" sweetness or loftiness or openness as a bodily *hexis*. Even these seemingly essential vocal qualities are in fact acquired, disciplined, malleable dispositions of voice.

This chapter surveys a range of these vocal dispositions, laying the analytic groundwork for a conception of voice rooted in disciplined action rather than fixed traits. The analyses are split neatly into two sections (*kinetic* and *sonorous* dispositions) but the corporeal practices of kinetics and sonority are neither mutually exclusive nor exhaustive. As we will see in later chapters, singers actively strive after ways of voice that include poetic, relational, and temporal dispositions (among others). Though a particular vocal disposition may appear to be fixed in an individual body, we will see in chapter 3 that vocal action comes alive in relation to cultivated listeners, who both shape and are shaped by disciplined vocal action. As we will see in chapter 4, these dispositions are publicly amplified, reproduced, and contested as coherent vocal formations, shifting on the scale of years and decades, so that individual singers thus find dispositional possibilities waiting, as it were, to be acquired as bodily *hexis*. And as we will see in chapter 5, the cultivation of any such vocal disposition involves training and discipline, over the course of many years, and even consciously working for a new disposition at a distance from one's "own" voice. Thus, a disciplined way of voice, so thoroughly implicated in the dynamics of social relations, could never be fully diagrammed in the still, flat spectrograms and pitch traces that follow. These serve merely as heuristics for the dynamism of vocal action (rather than the fixity of vocal traits). To speak of dispositions in the plural is already to open the possibility of contestation, reflection, and striving.

KINETIC DISPOSITIONS

Nusrat Fateh Ali Khan's voice soars upward; Malini Rajurkar comes in for a landing at the end of a metric cycle; Asha Bhosle lightly touches high *sā* but flutters down before coming to rest on *ga*. These are more than fanciful turns of phrase: voices move.[1] Hindustani vocalists routinely use technical terms to describe vocal action in kinetic terms—*aroh* (ascent), *avaroh* (descent), *harkat* (movement), *sapāṭ* (straight) *vs. vakr* (meandering) trajectories, *ṭhaharāv* (stillness), *calan* (gait), and so on.[2]

Vocal motion is obvious enough in everyday speech: we hear rising, falling, landing on accents, and coming to stillness in the flow of words and sentences.[3] Consider figure 2.1, a pitch trace of a vocal utterance in which Qawwal Fareed Ayaz says (in Hindustani), "*har insān kī* āvāz *gāne ke qābil hotī hai*" ("every hu-

1. Cf. Rahaim 2012, 34; Van der Meer and Rao 2006.

2. A very thorough treatment of the challenges of transcribing these various forms of motion as notes can be found in Magriel and du Perron 2013, 328.

3. The literature on speech melody in linguistics is vast; see Ladd 1996 for a solid overview. Though contemporary music theorists rarely consider the melodic patterns of speech, the first-millenium Sanskrit dramaturgical manual *Natyasastra* does in its sections on declamation (XIX.60 and passim).

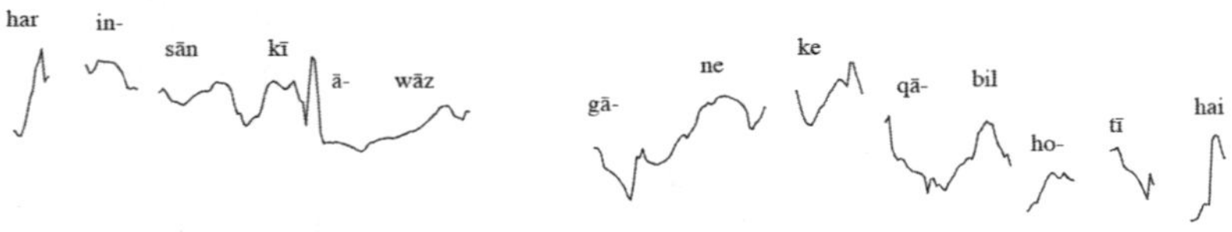

FIGURE 2.1 Pitch trace of "*har insān kī āvāz gāne ke qābil hotī hai*"

te-	**re**	**bi-**	**nā**	**ji-**	**yā**	**jā-**				**ye**		**nā**
R	RM	R	SRSN	N	SM	R	M	M	P	R	M	S
2	24	2	12 17	7	1 4	2	4	4	5	2	4	1

FIGURE 2.2 "*Tere bina*" transcribed in tones

man voice has the ability to sing"). This phrase is uttered emphatically, slowly, with a stylized, exaggerated, homiletic clarity of phrasing, heightened by the isochronous melodic rhyme between *gāne*, *qābil*, and *hotī*. Its aphoristic power—instantly memorizable, in a way that I myself have repeated—comes precisely from how it moves.

Singing, too, is kinetic. Though a tuneful voice may briefly and contingently perch upon tones, sung syllables are normatively in motion; holding steady on a specific tone across many syllables is a special declamatory effect in contrast to this norm. From film music to qawwali to khyal, each syllable is enunciated not so much on a tone as on a neumatic arc between tones. Consider the following phrase from the song "Tere Binā Jiyā Jāye Nā" ("Without You, My Heart Can't Go On"), sung by Lata Mangeshkar.[4] Her singing is exquisitely in tune, and clearly marks out a modal region between komal *ni* and *ma* {♭7 1 2 4}. A trained ear could easily analyze this phrase as a sequence of discrete, modally consistent tones notated in sargam (in figure 2.2). (Note that this is the second "tere bina" of the phrase; the first ends on re.)

And yet, a pitch trace (figure 2.3) reveals that her voice never comes entirely to rest on any one tone; she is constantly in motion.

Her voice flutters briefly on "te-," flits upwards from *re* {2} up to *ma* {4} at the end of "-re"; turns on "nā" to reach down to *komal ni* {♭7}; leaps up to gently touch *ma* {4} on "yā", perches briefly at "jā" before entering a wide pulse between

4. From the movie *Ghar*. The segment shown here comes at 3:13, the second half of the "*tere binā jiyā jāye nā*" refrain.

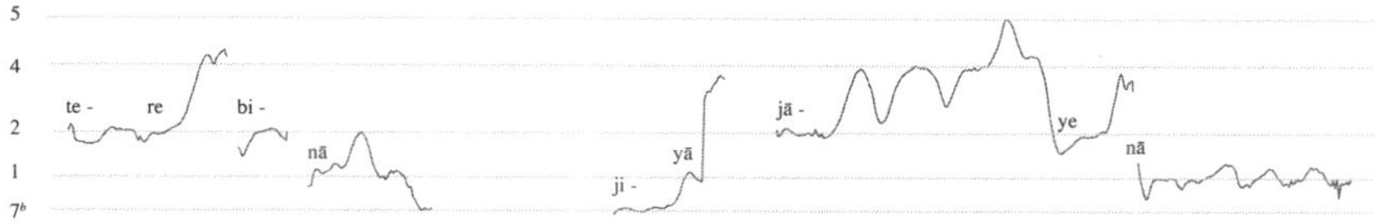

FIGURE 2.3 "*Tere bina*" pitch trace

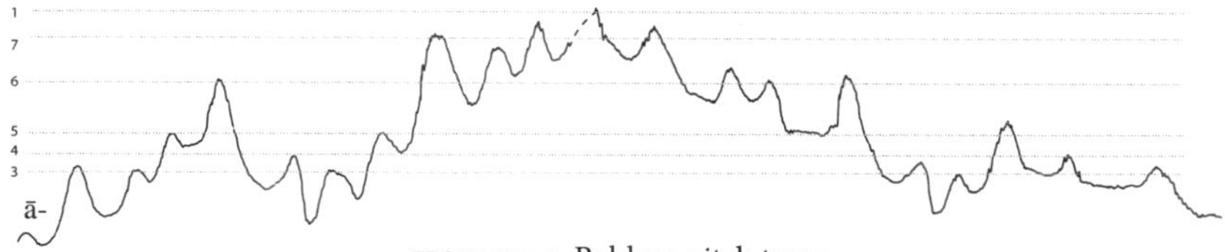

FIGURE 2.4 Bahlava pitch trace

re {2} and *ma* {4}, reaching up to *pa* {5} before stepping down on "ye" and then returning to *sā* {1} on "nā." Notice that the final "nā" sung on *sā* {1}, the only tone sustained for a full second, is sung with a slow, wide vibrato (of about 6 cycles per second). This last can be heard as a steady tone despite the fact that it is evidently in motion—it is said to be *kāmpit*, "trembling." Those that don't are typically marked by trembling. The virtuosic, florid, delicate style of melodic motion in figure 2.1 is commonly called *filmī* (i.e., characteristic of film), and Lata Mangeshkar's voice is its best-known exemplar (see chapter 1). Over the past six decades, this vocal disposition has become common even in thumri, ghazal, and bhajan, displacing older sedimented dispositions (see chapter 4).

But there are many other kinetic dispositions. For example, the steady, flowing vocal movement called *bahlavā* in khyal is also "melismatic," but could never be mistaken for *filmi* singing. In the following excerpt, Mukul Kulkarni sings *bahlavā* wordlessly on "ā," tracing a complex meandering path through raga Alhaiyyā Bilāwal. Figure 2.4 shows a pitch trace.

The undulation of bahlavā is utterly different from the delicate, trembling vibrato of *filmī* singing. Each of the peaks on the graph in figure 2.4 might register to a note-oriented, analytic ear (see chapter 3) after the fact as a discrete note (*ga ga pa dha ma ga pa ni ni sā sā ni dha dha pa dha ga ga pa ma ga* {3 3 5 6 4 3 5 7 7 1 1 7 6 6 5 6 3 3 5 4 3}). But this is not merely a sequence, and merely reproducing those tones in a *filmī* voice would not produce the same effect. This is, after all, a *way* of going before it is notes. More specifically, it is a relatively *heavy* way of going, generally at kinetic odds with light music. It is deeper and wider and slower; like an Olympic hammer throw, it is laden with weight and momentum.

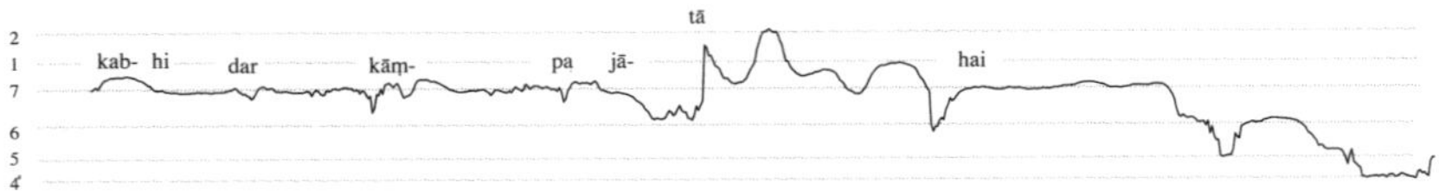

FIGURE 2.5 Pitch trace of "*kabhī dar kāṃpa jātā hai*"

To take a third example, consider Qawwal Mahmud Nizami's rendering of the line "*kabhi dar kāmpa jātā hai*" in the introduction to the widely known Manqabat "*Man Kunto Maulā*" (figure 2.5).

The steady declamation of the phrase "kabhī dar kāmpa *jā-*" only on *ni* {7}, in the upper part of his range, is a striking special effect, marking it off from the usual ups and downs of both speech and of strophic melody. This striking stability is not given, but is *achieved* through actively holding steady; note the brief, quickly corrected dips as Mahmud Sahab navigates the inevitable dips in subglottal pressure as he enunciates various stops (/k/, /d/, /k/, /p/). The closing melismata on *tā* and *hai* trace out an elegant, florid descent, first surging up to the *re* {2} and *sā* {1}, alighting again on *ni* {7} for a moment, and finally descending to the *tivra ma* {♯4} in preparation for the next line.

These kinetic descriptions may at first appear to be mere metaphoric descriptions of a primary reality made of notes. Taking notes as the a priori stuff of music, we might suppose that the most natural thing a voice can do is to produce a single, steady, eternal tone, and that melodic motion is a secondary modification of this natural state. But in practice, the inverse is true: from the steep descent of a baby's first wail, to the gentle rise of a toddler's first question, through a lifetime of meandering songs and sentences—in all of this, the laryngeal muscles, tongue, jaw, velum, and even the hands are in motion. It is only with deliberate training and effort that singers manage to hold still, forming long, steady, measurable tones.

We can hear a melody rising or falling, turning or meandering, before we discern which notes are in it.[5] Singers move their bodies and sing as one action, not two actions done simultaneously.[6] This motion, typically obscured by traditional models of note-based analysis, does not reduce to the visible, moving *flesh*

5. Hatten 2006; Van der Meer and Rao 2006; Godøy, et al. 2016.

6. Clayton 2007; Leante 2007; Moran 2008; Clayton, et al. 2011; Rahaim 2012; Weidman 2012; Pearson 2013; Paschalidou 2017.

of the arms and hands; nor does it reduce to discrete note sequences. Although ragas surely can be described analytically as grammars, scales, or patterns, to *sing* in a raga is a matter of melodic motion—less like carrying out grammatical transformations, more like finding one's way in a space. Practical fluency in a raga is a process of acquiring a repertoire of dispositional, near-habitual melodic acts—which is to say, acquiring a *hexis*. Indeed, ragas with identical scales often feel radically different, distinguished by characteristic melodic moves (*calan*) that instantly give the feeling of a raga (the measured *dha pa* {6 5} step to the quick *ma re* {4 2} fall in Nand, the slanted (*ma*)*ga re* {(4)♭3 2} cadence in Kafi, the slow *komal re—pa* {♭2–5} glide in Shree, etc.). Ragas with similar scales are likewise distinguished by their overall kinetic qualities—for example, Sohini's *cancal* (vibrant) motion vs. Puriya's *gambhīr* (heavy) motion, or Marwa's "direct and unwavering" gait.[7] In preparing to sing in a certain raga, musicians often hum a phrase or two to themselves, to get themselves into a particular way of maneuvering in this space.[8] Indeed, even in a single performance, a singer will typically move from slow gliding meend to rapid quick-moving tāns in the space of an hour or less. Individual singers, furthermore, often adopt different kinetic dispositions in singing the same raga. And different renderings of raga by different singers often vary so widely that their idiosyncratic kinetic rendering becomes the focus of critical appraisal.

None of this is to say that notes and other melodic objects are illusory, unimportant, or uninteresting. On the contrary, thinking in notes, while not universal, is an indispensible part of nearly every vocal world we survey here. As we will see in chapter 3, constituting and attending to stable objects in the midst of all kinds of ephemeral sonic dynamism is by no means obvious or trivial; on the contrary, it requires a great deal of discipline. To hold the vocal apparatus sufficiently steady to afford a note-object is a remarkable achievement; to hear a melodic gesture as a sequence of notes is not only a practice of listening that is quite difficult to achieve, but one which discloses a world of analytic possibility (see *svar-jnan*, see chapter 3). Nonetheless, notes in themselves are not sufficient to constitute a voice. For that, a singer must learn a kinetic disposition of voice characteristic of a particular way of being.

7. Parrikar 2002.

8. Rahaim 2012, 53.

Kinetic Ethics

To see a vocal discipline of performed movement as a field of practical virtue does not require any radical theoretical backflips. Kinetic dispositions are already relational, already ethical. A languorous, aristocratic promenade or a harried, urban trot already show up as conventional *ways of being* that indicate conventionally legible subject positions. To speak of someone's *regal bearing* or *upright carriage*, or of someone *strutting like a rooster*, *slinking away*, or *flouncing about* all indicate ways of moving already suffused with various kinds of ethical character.[9] Marcel Mauss's "education in walking," inculcated as various "techniques of the body" in convent schools and military parade grounds, is fundamentally an education in practical reason—in *habitus*, in practical virtue.[10] Kathryn Linn Geurts describes several ways of describing ethical virtue (*zɔzɔme*) in terms of gait (*a zɔlizɔzɔ*) among the Anlo-Ewe, including walking "like a lion" (*zɔ kazakaza*, implying dignity), walking backwards (*zɔ megbemegbe*, implying deception), or *lugulugu*, a person who moves "in a tarrying or dawdling fashion . . . a person who was not serious—an aimless, irresponsible fellow."[11] The first-millenium Sanskrit dramaturgical treatise *Natyasastra* (foundational for courtly music and theater traditions) prescribes specific ways of motion for characters of particular social standings, and Aristotle's *Nicomachean Ethics* (foundational for later manuals of courtly comportment) links gait, voice, and character: "A slow step is thought proper to the proud man, a deep voice, and a level utterance, for the man who takes few things seriously is not likely to be hurried, nor the man who thinks nothing great to be excited," while, on the other hand, "a shrill voice and a rapid gait are the results of hurry and excitement."[12]

Vocal gaits, too, show up as inherently ethical. A person who is a *chatterbox* in English, or a *tharthar* in Arabic, isn't just merely uttering a particular quantity of words, but rather is disposed in a certain way, speaking over others, rapidly, without pause. The difference between someone "prattling" and "droning on" is immediately evident from their manner of speaking. And speech often models gait. Isidore Okpewho gives numerous examples from songs and stories in various

9. Vergunst and Ingold 2016, 13, 69, 127–130. See Ingold 2008, 2 for an introduction to "thinking and feeling [as] ways of walking."

10. Mauss 1973 [1934], 72.

11. Geurts 2003, 75.

12. Aristotle 1125a: 13–16.

African languages: *suyosuyo* for a hunter stalking an antelope; *tekie tekie tekie tekie* for a clumsy gait; *shojim* for rapidly lifting a child upwards.[13] Among Hindustani musicians, distinctions between vocal dispositions are sometimes explicitly made in terms of *cāl*, or gait: the "elephant's gait (*hāthi ka cāl*)" ("ponderous yet dignified, slow but sensuous") of *dhrupad*, the faster, irregular "camel's gait (*umt ki cāl*)" of *dhamar*, and the "horse's gait (*ghoṛe ki cāl*)" of *khyal*.[14] Pooja Goswami once described to me the characteristic kinetic orientation of thumri as akin to the graceful, swaying gait required to walk on the narrow boundary-mounds (*meṇḍ*) between fields on a farm. More broadly, the term *cāl* indicates a way of going about things, the means—admirable or otherwise—that one uses to obtain an end. The compound *cāl-calan* often has a clear ethical valuation: one's *cāl-calan* may be straightforward or sneaky; *su-cāl* indicates both a lovely gait *and* ethical virtue. *Calan* (a term already absorbed into Hindustani music theory in reference to characteristic melodic moves within a raga space) can indicate a literal gait, but also, more broadly, a bearing, a manner.

At times, vocal motion seems effortless, as though a voice were soaring on its own, and the singing subject is, as Mukul Kulkarni once put it, simply "flying a kite." At other times, singing seems quite forceful, as though propelled by the impetus of the subject's will. When singers speak of *phenk* (what is called vocal "throw") or *ḍhākā* (vocal "punch"), they are describing a disciplined vocal forcefulness often applied for special impact on a listener. On the other hand, too much forcefulness can shatter a delicate vocal gait (for example, the urbane gentleness required for *filmi* voice). More broadly, to speak of effort highlights the presence of a particular musicking body rather than a free-floating voice; it is a sign of willfulness rather than surrender, of "weightlifting" rather than "swimming."[15] Some singers insist that singing should not be physical at all—that, as Pushkar Lele once told me, the body should be "not something that produces things, but just a medium . . . [if] you feel yourself allowing things to pass through you, you are not using any energy." Part of this, to be sure, is ergonomic; one can sing longer by conserving energy.[16] As we will see in chapter 4, the formation of sweet, mellow voices in the twentieth century was, in part, a reaction against the

---

13. See Okpewho 1992, 92 and passim. See also Finnegan 2014, 69.

14. Widdess 1994a, p 101. Among some percussionists, *cāl* implies a rhythmic groove at a characteristic speed. See Wolf 2014, 99.

15. Rahaim 2012, 105. See also Paschalidou 2017.

16. See Scott 1997, 456.

harsh, urgent temporality of modernity. Both forcefulness and gentleness exceed mechanics; they are dispositions cultivated through practice.

A kinetic ethics of voice, then, would not designate *particular* steps, paths, pitches, or destinations, but rather *ways* of going that are linked to proper and improper ways of being. Nor do they serve as kinetic "fingerprints," with precisely one per person, one per genre, one per gender, etc. The various forms of ethical propriety that accrue to these kinetic ways of being, as we will see in chapter 3, are not inherent, but emerge relationally among others with particular attunements to voice.

*Ornamental Movement (*Harkat*)*

Harkat[17]—literally "movements"—are part of the kinetic repertoire of every Hindustani way of voice. Flowing swiftly by, *harkat* can feel almost involuntary, and it is often difficult to explain exactly what you've just done after the fact. The quickest vocal *harkats* can give the impression of shivering, shuddering, and other involuntary physiological responses to emotional arousal.[18] In Sufi devotional settings, *harkat* is one word for the slight involuntary physical twitches that accompany the first stages of emotional arousal in an expert listener.[19] *Harkats* are often points of maximal affective power over a listener—though as we will see, this very power makes them ethically suspect and subject to various kinds of discipline.

Evanescent, ornamental movements are named variously in various lineages

---

17. The term *harkat*, despite its general meaning as "movement," also tends to connote the light, quick ornamental movement of thumri and other "semi-classical" genres. Though its Arabic cognate, simply means "movement" in Hindustani, *harkat* also has a moral connotation of sexual mischief. It also has a technical usage in Qur'anic recitation and Urdu poetics: in reference to the diacritical specifications of short vowels in script, and as part of the complementary prosodic principles of *sukūn* and *harkat*, or rest and motion. Another widely used term is *alankara*, which suggests ornamental jewelry and makeup—analytically centering objects rather than action. For our current purposes centered around *cāl*, I prefer to generalize *harkat* instead (with its rather open-ended implications of action and kinesis).

18. Most harkats (and tāns) do come around 300–600 notes per minute (5–10 Hz), approximating the frequency of human shuddering (Jessen 2012, 33).

19. Qureshi 1995, 121.

(*murki, alankara, gamak, khaṭka, kan, fandā, zamzam*, etc.).[20] Though individual singers often use consistent, idiosyncratic images with their own students—for example, Veena Sahasrabuddhe's image of "tying a knot" with *khaṭkās*[21]—there is no universally agreed upon taxonomy. Relatively slow and deep ornaments are sometimes called *khaṭka* in distinction to a quicker, lighter *murkhi*. In practice, there is a recognizable repertoire of Hindustani ornamental moves, with extremely fuzzy edges. For example, the movement usually notated as *pa dha pa pa* {5655} (taken to be an elaboration on *pa* {5}) and *sā re sā sā* {1211} (taken to be an elaboration on *sā* {1}) are found widely across genres.[22] The English loan word *māḍyuleśan* (modulation) is likewise used broadly to describe any sort of fine vocal nuance, from fine ornamental movement, to subtle swelling and retreating of volume, to vibrato—but almost always a nuance suited for a microphone. Singers distinguish between stable *svaras* and evanescent *harkats*, though there is no acoustical rule about how many milliseconds qualifies a tone as a fully manifested *svara*.

Continuity of motion—sustaining a coherent vowel in the course of a phrase without an abrupt jerk or break in phonation—is especially salient across movements that otherwise would seem to invite breaks into separate notes. One technical term that points toward this continuity is *ās* (also used for resonant sustain, and, among instrumentalists, for extended melismata from bending a

20. Nicolas Magriel and Lalita du Perron have provided the most thorough note-based analysis of Hindustani melodic "nuances" thus far (2013 (I), 291–353), as well as a survey of the various and divergent systems of notating and categorizing them (47–97). The thirteenth-century encyclopedic music treatise *Sangitaratnakara* lists 15 types of *alankāra* (*SR* 87–97b) described in terms of note sequences. It is unclear from the rhythmic notation in the SR whether these are analogous to ornaments on steady notes or instead patterns of ascent and descent, as in tāns. Singers in the twentieth century often describe melodic sequences (123, 234, 345, etc.) as *alankāras*, even when there is no clear distinction between ornament and svara. The Sangeet Research Academy maintains another such list with recorded examples: http://www.itcsra.org/alankar. See also Miner 2004, 170–173 for ornament in instrumental traditions.

21. Clayton, et al. 2011, 211.

22. And yet, even these ornaments are notated in various ways—for example, in Omkarnath Thakur's *Sangitanjali*, what I am calling SRSS or PDPP is notated as SRSNS or PDPMP; Abdul Karim Khan calls SRSS *murkhi* and PDPP *fandā* (Magriel and du Perron 2013, 61).

string after a pluck). Another is the quality of vocal "suppleness" (*loc* or *lacak*) by which a single vocal gesture moves fluidly and uninterruptedly through tonal space. The limit case of this kind of continuity is *mīṇḍ*, long, sliding portamenti across a third, fourth, fifth, or even octave.[23] Musicologist B. C. Deva evokes the image of a bird in motion, alternately perching (on svaras) and flying (through ornamental connections).[24] The systems of notation in currency in the north (staff notation, sargam/solfege for most singers) likewise affirm a distinction between these levels of organization, usually setting off brief ornamental motion in smaller characters or grace notes. As one singer once instructed me: "*Kaṇ* has to remain *kaṇ*, and *svara* has to remain *svara*." Commentators on Indian vocal music have long commented on the ubiquity of these "graces," often in stark nationalist terms. "The Indian song without grace," Ananda Coomaraswamy tells us, "would seem to Indian ears as bald as the European art song without the accompaniment which it presupposes." The distinction is not, in fact, nearly so sharp: singing any of the styles now called "Western" requires ornamental enculturation; inversely, as we shall see, ornamental restraint shows up as a positive virtue in khyal, ghazal, bhajan, qawwali, filmi gīt, among others.

And yet, distinctive kinetic patterns of ornamentation—fluid, sharp, heavy, light, quick, languorous—are among the most telling features of a vocal disposition. And rendering harkat is not so much founded on analytic acuity as kinetic enculturation. Even novices who stumble over discrete note sequences may have a keen sense of *how* harkats should *go*. It is no more obvious for an untrained voice how to render the *pa dha pa pa* {5655} harkat in practice than it is for a spectator at a cricket match to get up from their seat and simply "bowl a yorker." The *cāl* of any such movement is learned through years of listening, training, and practice. Just as a trained footballer has developed the habits of kinetic reckoning necessary for a "lead pass" (to place the ball on the foot of a running teammate), a trained Hindustani vocalist has developed habits of kinetic reckoning necessary to hear and reproduce harkats as *moves* rather than

23. These may be likely modeled on a style of bīn playing that developed around the turn of the nineteenth century. Allyn Miner notes that nothing like *mīṇḍ* is mentioned in Sanskrit treatises before the *Saṅgīt Sār* (c. 1800), and that it likely is derived from bīn playing (1993, 162).

24. Deva 1959, 176. The image of a bird perching and flying is drawn from William James's account of "substantive" and "transitive" modes of consciousness, respectively—see James 1950 [1890], 243.

FIGURE 2.6 Notes vs. curves

simply pitches. Like many musicians who learned to play the keyboard from an early age, I was fixated on note sequences, and had developed a keen ability to translate between tones and note-names—the very specific note-centric aural sense called *svar-jnan* in Hindustan (see chapter 3). Sometimes, in the course of a vocal lesson, my fingers would press down on a phantom keyboard, translating vocal motion into notes the way a court stenographer transcribes the wild vocal and rhetorical action of a courtroom into discrete characters. My teachers were sometimes impressed by what at first appeared to be a very accurate ear. But the intricate motion of *harkats* dazzled this analytic sensibility, making it clear that I had a good deal more to learn than simply identifying notes. My first teacher, Vikas Kashalkar, reoriented me toward the shapes of phrases rather than just notes. He drew the following picture (figure 2.6) in my notebook—suggesting a path of kinetic progress from my note-sequential way of voice (on the left) to the proper, curvaceous way (on the right).

As a corrective, I tried turning my attention toward willfully sliding *between* notes, but this only reinforced the basic model of starting from a string of notes that had to be "connected." Watching me struggle, he diagnosed my inability to produce proper harkat as a symptom of a dispositional lack. He told me that I needed to develop a *gol galā* ("round throat"), a phrase with wide currency among singers. This was not a suggestion that I should surgically alter the shape of my pharynx, but that I should acquire a new disposition—but one so durable that it seems to reconfigure the throat itself. What was required was not individual kinetic actions, but a way of voice. He thus counseled patience, and he was, in the end, certainly correct about this. It took several years of intensive practice before my *galā* got appreciably "rounder."

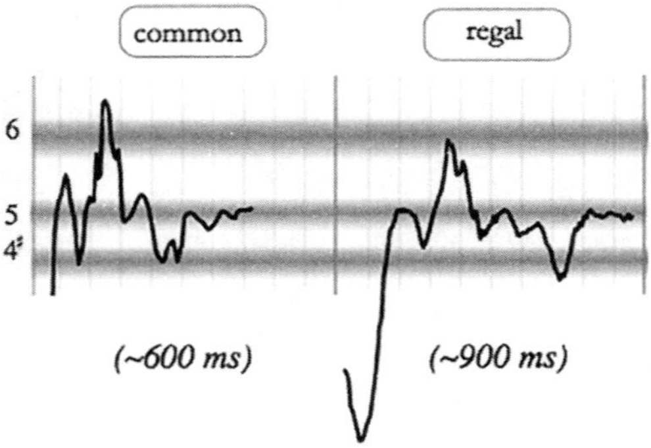

FIGURE 2.7 "Common" vs. "regal" harkat

Moving Heavy and Light

A *harkat* is given a unity of texture by an overall kinetic disposition rather than simply a sequence of notes. As a person walking may steer right and left while effortlessly maintaining the integrity of a particular gait, so too does vocal action emerge from a unified vocal hexis.

This became clear to me once when I was singing for Chandrashekhar Mahajan, who insisted that I was singing a particular *harkat* too quickly. He imitated my way of singing, and then demonstrated the correct way (see figure 2.7).

Measured in seconds, the "regal" harkat[25] is longer than the common harkat; measured in pitch, it has a slightly lower range overall. But Chandrashekharji explained that more was at stake than a mere aesthetic predilection for a particular acoustic result.

> What happens if we take faster melodies? There is a difference between common and regal people. How [do] regal people present themselves? They never haste. . . . Slowly. <[ordinary] people like us—the way we catch a train.> (*Aisā ham log—jaisā kuch gāḍi pakaḍegā.*) . . . We have to catch a train, then we run if we are late. They [i.e., regal people] never will do that. The train will halt for them. Unless they get on the train, the train will not leave. Like that. So they don't have to haste. [And] the way we are singing should be a regal way.

25. Taken at this speed, it is typically called a *khatkā*.

His prescription was not simply that my vocal gait should slow down for technical reasons (so that, for example, the objective clock-time of the meter comes out right), nor for aesthetic reasons (so that the sound was more pleasant). He prescribed a certain *disposition*, a way of vocally being-regal as opposed to being-common. I was vocally rushing as though I had to meet an external schedule; a regal disposition proceeds at a measured pace, as though others would wait.[26] This was an issue of temporal relations, of rhythmic comportment, not metrical behavior. And accordingly, learning to dispose myself in order to sing this harkat more led me into an awkward phase when I felt myself, as though watching at a distance, to be singing too *arrogantly*. Particularly in the presence of a mentor, to sing in this way felt rather like speaking slowly, with long gaps, in public. I felt the urge to speed up, to sing quickly and glibly so as not to waste his time, so as not to make him wait for me. The long process of acquiring this heavier disposition required me to willfully train my own temporal sense—to not only sing heavy, but to *become* heavy.

The quintessential heavy vocal gait is *gamak*.[27] *Gamak* is a way of moving in a series of dramatic upward swoops, typically ranging between a major second and a full octave. As with *bahlavā*, *kāmpit*, and *andolan*, a single peak-and-trough cycle is insufficient to qualify as *gamak*; *gamak* emerges as a groove, flowing from one peak to another, at a consistent speed, and at a consistent depth. The deeper such a gamak groove is, and the more consistently maintained, the heavier it is felt to be. It is perhaps the mark of heaviness par excellence, and is the near-exclusive preserve of khyaliyas and dhrupadiyas singing raga music. A conventional association of heavy *gamak* with a masculine, regal, serious, and pious comportment is widely legible. A few singers, particularly dhrupadiyas, report that each sweep (in principle) proceeds from consciously chosen lower notes; most khyaliyas, on the other hand, name each gamak in turn for the note that is swept up to. Whether the melodic path as a whole is ascending or descending, heaviness is not a single isolated action, but a groove of repeated movements, a gait that is established in the course of singing.

---

26. As Italo Calvino puts it, "Kings do not have watches: it is assumed that they are the ones who govern the flow of time; submission to the rules of a mechanical device would be incompatible with regal majesty" (2012, 36).

27. Though many Carnatic vocalists consider gamak to be a generic term for ornamentation, including meend, Hindustani vocalists typically reserve the term for this particular, heavy, swooping movement.

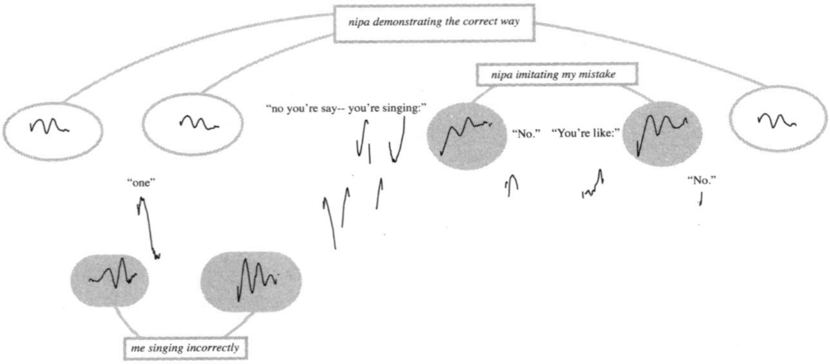

FIGURE 2.8 Heavy vs. light harkat

To sing lightly requires a rather different disposition, one suitable for the emotional subtleties of delicate song forms that can be crushed under the weight of a heavy disposition. I discovered this only after spending a decade or so working to develop slower and deeper harkat. I was visiting Calcutta, sitting with Nipa Nag, a versatile singer of many vocal genres, who was showing me a well-known ghazal (*Ishq Mein Ghairat-e Jazbāt*). She emphasized the vocal lightness, sharpness, and subtlety that give this ghazal its characteristic feeling—as Nipa put it, "a lot of poise and a lot of *chanchal* [playfulness, volatility, trembling] at the same time." Among the many points I struggled with was a sharp, precise harkat leading from the 5 to the ♯4. I kept hearing and performing it with deep gamak leading to each note. My manner in this case—rather than being too fast—was too slow and heavy. But Nipa told me that in order to sing *ghazal*, "you have to fly like a feather. It has to be so light, your voice." We worked on this one harkat, which lasts less than half a second, for nearly ten minutes. Nipa would sing the harkat, and I would imitate it. She repeated it dozens of times, occasionally pointing out what I was doing wrong. At first, I couldn't hear a difference, though it is quite visible in a melograph after the fact. Figure 2.8 shows pitch traces from the lesson.

Wrongly assuming that the problem was the sequence of notes I was singing, I asked, "*pa pa ma ma* {5 5 4 ♯4}?" She shrugged. The problem was *not* with a sequence of stopping points, nor even the absolute tempo of a sequence of notes—both were nearly the same. The problem was my manner of moving among them. I was swooping up from below and transforming her subtle turn into a sequence of wide, deep gamaks. The deep, slow, "regal" technique that I

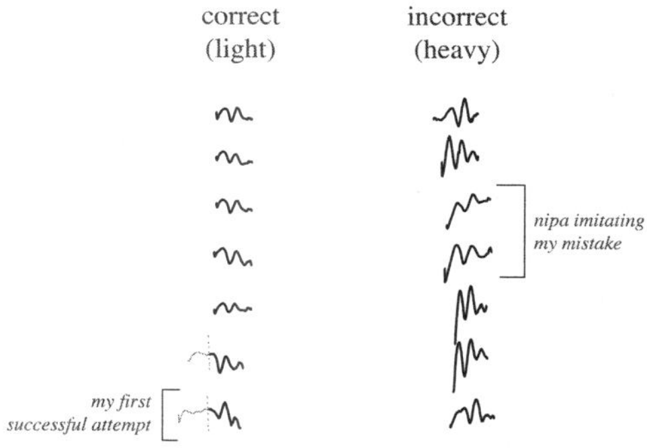

FIGURE 2.9 Harkat comparison

had worked to develop registered to Nipa as too dull, too heavy, and too masculine for singing *ghazal*. Figure 2.9 places the proper and improper movements side by side.

I finally was able to discern the difference when she extended the first section of the harkat—a steady tone on 5—before proceeding. (The last two entries in the "correct" column in figure 2.9 show first Nipa's, then mine.) By extending the initial portion, she demonstrated to me that there was no swoop from deep below to the first svara. This felt very awkward to me after years of training in articulating harkats with deliberate depth and slowness, but I was able to do it quite deliberately once or twice in a row. And yet, heaviness was still too deeply dispositionally engrained to allow me to freely "fly like a feather." Even after grasping what she wanted me to do once or twice, I could not spontaneously render sharp harkats with the proper ease and flow in the middle of a poetic line. It would be another two years before I would be able to fluently sing "light" in concert.

Lightness and heaviness alike are thus vocal dispositions, not merely individual melodic gestures to be performed one by one. "Light," quick melodic action tends to be produced gesturally with quick movements of the fingertips or a rotating wrist joint. Heavy harkat (deep *gamak*, very slow *tāns*, and *mīṇḍs*), on the other hand, often involves movement of the whole arms, working with a virtual object[28] that is much heavier and thicker. Just as, for example, certain

28. Rahaim 2012, 92.

kinetic dispositions in Nihon-buyō training have come to be felt as dispositions of "spiritual strength,"[29] some singers of raga hear heaviness as ethically proper. Veena Sahasrabuddhe, for example, describes a spectrum of kinetic disposition from weightiness (*vazan-dār-paṇ*) to *lightness* (*halkā-paṇ*). She says that while *mīṇḍ* (clean glides), gamak (deep scooping articulation), and *ās*[30] (distinctive ways of sustaining and closing off a svara) are "dignified," others (such as *harkat*) "are to be used with caution."[31] On the other hand, for partisans of sweet, light voices, heavy *gamak* is often a point of mimicry and ridicule, implying an arrogant, heartless elitism out of touch with popular sentimentalism. Though lightness tends to be gendered feminine and heaviness masculine, women are often criticized for singing too lightly in khyal (Kishori Amonkar is a famous example), and men for singing too heavy. Thus, even where the ethical implications of these vocal dispositions are fairly consistent, they do not cleave to a monolithic moral code.

Tāns

A *tān* is a melismatic phrase, usually on a single vowel, but the word most often denotes extended, rapid vocal runs on the scale of ~3–6 seconds. These virtuosic moments, the fruit of rigorous vocal training, can be (and often are) analyzed as a sequence of several dozen tones. But tāns are first and foremost *actions*: astonishing public deeds akin to feats of strength or magic. Legends abound about the power of these vocal feats. Mubarak Ali, a great nineteenth-century Jaipur court singer, was said to have sung such a forceful tān that it rocked his tanpura accompanist "as if he was struck by lightning," knocking the tanpura from his grip.[32] Neela Bhagwat reports that "the lamps used to blink and flicker" when Krishna Rao Shankar Pandit "sang a tān in his full-throated, deep voice."[33] In extreme cases, taking an extraordinary tān seems to require a superhuman effort that mortifies the flesh. According to legend, the fabled *kaḍak bijlī kī tān* ("thunderclap tān"), for example, was so powerful that it ruptured the lungs of

29. Hahn 2007, 42–43.

30. See Miner 1993, 172.

31. Sahasrabuddhe 1999, 13.

32. Haldankar 2001, 17.

33. Bhagwat 1992, 36.

Bade Mohammad Khan.[34] Empirically verifiable or no, these legends remind us that a tān is a coherent *act* with a coherent texture and a clear trajectory. To be sure, tāns can be picked apart for analysis as a sequence of rapid, evenly spaced, clearly audible individual svaras—just as, in swimming, a butterfly stroke could be analyzed into individual muscular contractions. But in practice, once a tān pattern is mastered, to sing a tān is to enter into a field of action enabled by a particular vocal disposition. A successful tān has a coherent arc and texture, and shows up as a single coherent entity like a *melisma*, a *church run*, or a *lick*. A legend comes down to us of a young hereditary singer who paused for breath in the middle of the tān—his master scolded him, saying, "It would not matter if it kills you, but complete the tān . . . and then die. Do not die in the middle of the tān."[35] Connoisseurs, for their part, may praise or criticize a specific tān in terms of note content or internal patterning, but just as often, in practice, make note of how it moves ("that one landed well," or "that tān lacked propulsive force").

Tāns also have a distinctive speed. Two *svaras* per second is the approximate bottom limit of what registers as a coherent *tān* (below this threshold, tones begin to stand out as independent items), and twelve per second appears to be the approximate upper limit of physiological possibility.[36] Approaching this limit, of course, takes years of practice; but so too does singing slowly. In fact, most singers find that singing slow tāns with consistently deep gamak is, in many ways, more difficult than singing at top speed—requiring a delicate balance, "like riding a bike slowly," as one singer put it. Physiologically, faster tāns tend to take relatively shallower *gamak*; slower tāns likewise take deeper gamak.[37] *Dānā* (fleck, grain) is a technical term for a single melodic pulse within a tān, a single gamak at the very edge of salience that marks each svara as a discrete melodic item, just as a slight flick of the wrist might appear a discrete gestural "item" in the midst of connected motion. Just so, a *dānedār tān* is one in which each note stands out distinctly as a *dānā*. As L. K. Pandit once aphoristically put it to me, "the essence of *tāna* is *dānā*." *Dānedār* (having distinct grains) is likewise a culinary term—a properly prepared biryānī, for example, should be *dānedār* rather than mushy.

---

34. Wade 1984, 40. Other oral accounts suggest that the singer was Hassu Khan.

35. Deodhar 1993, 59.

36. Among the very fastest tāns that I have measured on record are found in Salamat and Nazakat Ali's *drut khyals* and Malini Rajurkar's *ṭappās*, all hovering around 700 svaras per minute.

37. Radhakrishnan 2010.

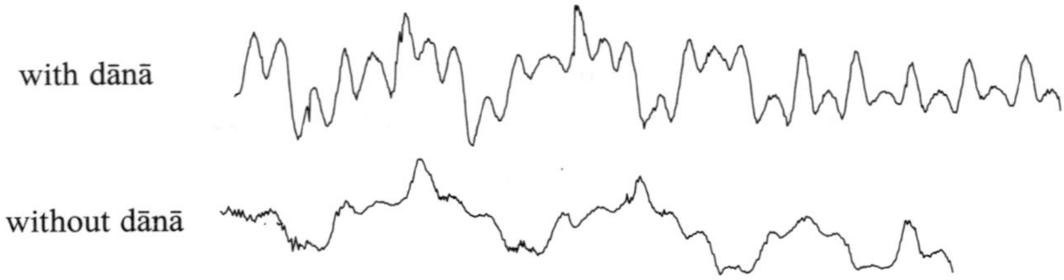

FIGURE 2.10 Tāns with and without dānā

Tāns too, can be mushy. In figure 2.10, Apoorva Gajjala demonstrates the difference between a tān with dānā and without (a "failed tān").

Phonologists studying tān production note that tāns are "voluntarily controlled, in contrast to vibrato productions."[38] This is surely the case when one is first learning a particular tān, when one's teacher may insist on going very slowly, separating each pitch from the others. But once a tān gait is mastered and one is singing it at speed, it would be impossible to make individual choices for each note separated by 100 milliseconds of deliberation. Maintaining the momentum of a tān requires continuous force: sublaryngeal pressure, diaphragmatic support, a balanced tension of the laryngeal muscles to preserve regular turbulence. Just as a fabric is identified by its weave (twill, canvas, etc.) rather than by the absolute locations of its individual threads; just as a sprint is identified by its speed, direction, and gait rather than by the geographical coordinates of its footprints—so a tān is identified (and heard, and felt, and practiced, and performed) principally according to its gait rather than the frequencies of its tones. A *sapāṭ* ("flat") tān moves in a straight line; a *vakr* ("meandering") tān moves in zigzags; a *khaḍḍā-dār* tān slips downward repeatedly, as though sliding into a ditch (*khaḍḍā*); a *maṭṭhā* ("slow, sluggish") tān is undertaken very slowly, with deep gamak, toward the bottom of one's range.[39] In singing a tān, you must put yourself in motion, not simply arrange notes together. The gait of a new *tān* must be undertaken deliberately, like skipping or breaking into a sprint, rather than accidentally emerging from individual sounded notes. Singers' hand and arm movements often are linked to such a tān gait rather than to any particular sequence of notes.[40]

38. Radhakrishnan, et al. 2010.

39. Another folk etymology holds that *maṭṭī* is derived from the circular motion of a marble rolling around the bottom of a clay (*miṭṭī*) pot.

40. Rahaim 2012, 116.

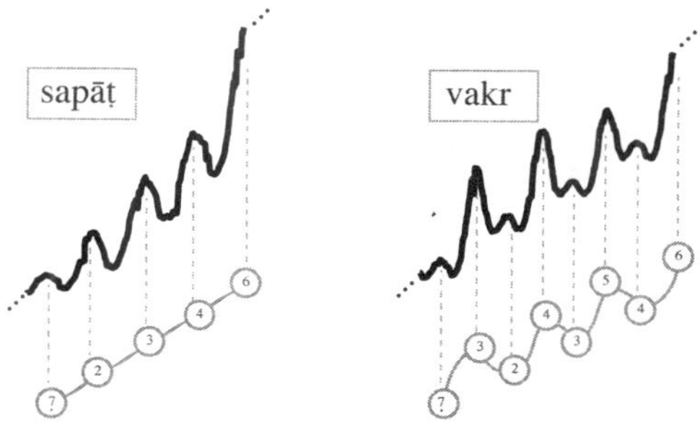

FIGURE 2.11 *Sapāṭ* and *vakr* tāns

For example, figure 2.11 illustrates two distinctive tān gaits: *sapāṭ* (straight) and *vakr* (meandering).

Both tāns include articulations of each *svara* by gamak, and the pitch trace renders these *visible* as apparent zigzags. And yet the *sapāṭ* tān nonetheless *feels* straight—the gamaks articulating each note are not apperceived as zigzagging but rather as a straight path with second-order, constant motion, a *manner* of movement rather than a *direction*. The vakr ("meandering") tān, on the other hand, proceeds through a palpably twisted path. Thus, when one throws oneself into the *vakr* tān pattern in figure 2.11—*ni ga re ma* {7324 . . .}, the *ga pa ma dha* {. . . 3546}—what follows is not a willful compositional "choice," but a kinetic continuation of the snaking groove. One knows the space of the rāga,[41] one has learned the gait with which one navigates this space, and one simply falls into step.

Different species of tān also afford different temporalities. A *sapāṭ* (plain, flat) tān, which runs straight up or down without any zigging or zagging, is immediately recognizable by its shape, even if you don't notice what note it started on. More importantly, launching into a sapāṭ tān gives a palpable feeling of its inevitable ending, like throwing a ball in the air. Once you begin a sapāṭ tān, you can feelingly protend (anticipate) where it will fall on the scale of seconds, even without counting beats or doing arithmetic. An *alankarik* tān, on the other hand (which follows a melodic sequence upward—for example, {1323 2434 3545}, etc.), is more open-ended. One can extend it as far as one wants, turning back again, ambling about the melodic space, filling as much metrical room as is required by the metric cycle (*tāl*). And thus you may move into an *alankarik* melodic gait at any point, finding your way through the metric cycle as you go.

41. Rahaim 2012, 53.

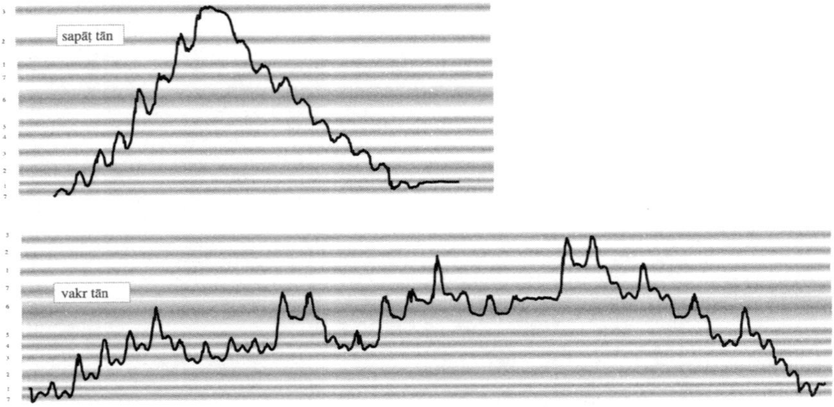

FIGURE 2.12 Full sapāṭ and vakr tāns

Figure 2.12 depicts the full tāns that these gaits were excerpted from. Each tān has the same basic trajectory: an arching ascent and descent. But their *cāls*, their gaits, the way they proceed along this arching path, are palpably different. When I began my training, I was fixated on the individual svaras that make up a tān, thinking of these as kinds of improvisations in which a singer has the freedom in principle to arrange svaras however one chooses. I thought that naming and assigning species of tāns was a mere taxonomic exercise. I thought, since we were, *in principle*, free to improvise combinations of notes in a tān, that to prescribe fixed patterns was to shackle free artistic expression. I was puzzled by my guru's insistence that I should write down and practice fixed tān patterns. But I was also frustrated by just how difficult it can be to land a tān gracefully, even if you know the sequence of notes. With practice, however, it gradually became clear that tān patterns are first and foremost actions to be *done*, not lists of individual notes. To sing a *sapāṭ* tān with constant flow, clear intonation, and confidence across an octave may be boringly simple to *understand* in terms of note sequences. But it is among the most difficult tāns to *do*. As Arun Kashalkar eloquently puts it: "It's like ascending or descending the steps. So you need not think of each and every step . . . You can just climb up or climb down. It happens like that, not thinking of each and every note."[42] There are many gaits available for these paths, as we have seen. But keeping these gaits clear and distinct from each other is itself a matter of clarity and discipline: an ethical matter. Music

42. Kashalkar in Rahaim 2012, 35.

reformer V. N. Bhatkhande castigated singers who sang their tāns *veḍyā-vākḍyā*, a term used in Marathi to describe a disorderly mess.[43] In lessons, my guru L. K. Pandit will often suggest a particular gait with a single tān and then gesture to me to sing more like it, expanding further across the space of the raga in the same way of motion.

These tān types are not merely names for sequential patterns, but for disciplined gaits. Just as a trot and a gallop have characteristic speeds, so too do tāns. A *mattā* tān is usually between 200 and 300 svaras per minute; the florid tāns of *ṭappā* hardly ever fall below 300 spm. Oddly enough, singing slow, heavy tāns is generally harder than singing fast, light tāns. The difficulty is akin to the difficulty in walking slowly (say, five seconds per step), compared to walking fast (say, two steps per second). As Nipa Nag put it:

> [Singing tāns is] like riding a cycle . . . if you can ride it really really slow without falling . . . that's where the balance shows. Riding fast is always easy, and the newcomers will always tend to ride faster. . . . We always tend to sing faster because it's easier and you cannot do it the other way around when you sing slow. You need much more breath and command.

The "command" and "balance" required to ride an extended, slow tān requires a great deal of practice, both learning and unlearning. One common habit is to move the jaw along with the pulsing of the tān—never an issue at faster speeds, when the jaw muscle can't keep up. Another is to merely jerk upwards to each svara, interrupting the easy serpentine flow of *gamak*. Like any kinetic disposition, it is a cultivated habit, not a mere compositional choice.

Moving Simply

In the first several years of my voice training, learning to fluidly produce harkat and tāns was such an intoxicating pleasure that I wanted to do nothing else. Vocal progress seemed to me to consist in progress from straight, plain singing to increasingly florid ornamentation. I got in the habit of fluttering about whenever I had a chance. But, as my teachers pointed out (to me and to other beginners), this was not the proper way to go. Vikas Kashalkar, my teacher during this early phase, pushed me again and again toward simplicity: slow, gradual movement from resting place to resting place. The idiom "*digambar svara rakh re*" (keep the

43. Bhatkhande 1954, 92.

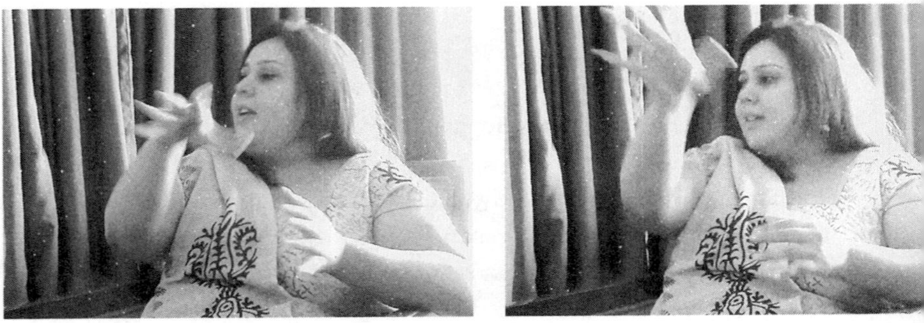

"Lulululu" [miming aimless, automatic harket-s]

FIGURE 2.13 Controlling harkats

svara "sky-clad," i.e., bare) is sometimes used to discourage excessive ornamentation (in reference to the virtue of unclothed ascetics).[44] Qawwals, particularly at gatherings for spiritual elites with the strictest decorum, are discouraged from overly sophisticated vocal elaboration that distract the listeners from the mystical poetry at hand.[45] Ragini Rainu, a singer of Sufiana Kalam in Bombay, described her own struggle with over-ornamentation: "I think too quickly. So if you give me an opportunity, I end my performance *lulululululu* {traces elaborate but aimless melodic trajectories}: full of harkats. Give me a chance, I'll do it all . . . But [you have] to actually *control* that {grips the moving virtual objects and holds them still with both hands}."

Here, as in figure 2.13, to sing quick, ornate *harkats*—no easy feat for a beginner—arises as an easy, automatic mode of comportment for a technically accomplished singer. Constraint, on the other hand—singing more simply—is what requires the active grip of control. Just as important, the ethical force of this active control is performed in relation to a listener (see chapter 3). As Ragini puts it, "[Otherwise] it won't come across as anything to people. They won't get it. . . . You have to give them the wordings, give them whatever you are there to give them. Else they won't, they won't even get it." This same relational criterion is sometimes applied to singing bhajans, which should not "seek to dazzle" with "ingenuity or cleverness [or] too many melodic variations" but rather achieve

44. Cf. Saxena 1976, 39.

45. Qureshi 1995, 118.

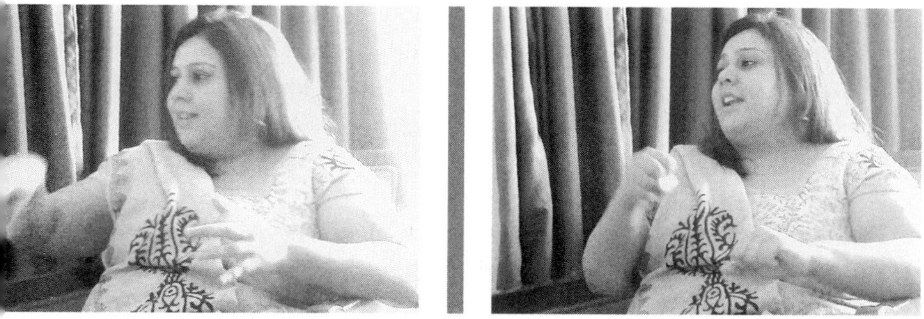

But to actually *control* that.

an "immediate and favourable impact on listeners" with "straight and simple" rendering.[46] Thus, singing simply and straightforwardly often shows up as a matter of disciplined kinetic *restraint* rather than as a failure or a lack. Conversely, singing with extensive ornamentation often shows up as a failure to restrain oneself from the charms of easy sweetness rather than something one is actively choosing to do.

The high ethical stakes of excessive ornamentation became clear to me many years ago as I sang a composition for a khyal singer who is exceptionally fastidious about maintaining the form of canonical bandishes. At that moment, I was eager to impress upon him that I had developed a round throat, and that I was capable of ornamenting fluently. I overdid it; he shook his head. He admonished me for singing like a courtesan rather than a khandani singer:

> Respect goes down if you add something [of your own]. You have to be . . . *khāndānī* [maintaining the strictures of a high-status musical family] . . . It is related to ethics only, ethics of an ancient family, like that. . . . [The *khāndānī* way is] to restrict yourself to only one companion of yours . . . keeping relations only with each other . . . But prostitutes [i.e., singing courtesans] . . . cannot do this, otherwise they will not survive! So their *manner* is different. <The thing that is in *thumri*, and *adā* [genres of courtesan performance] and so forth, no? Doing these things {mimes dancing} while singing, no?>[47] . . . Those tricks

46. Critics Prakash Wadhera and G. N. Joshi cited in Manuel 1993, 113.

47. *Ṭhumrī mein jo hotā hai, aur adā vag͟hairah hotā na? Aisā aisā karke gāti hai na?*

are not to be practiced in khyal. . . . The <canonical bandish> [*nāyakī*] is just like a script: musical script, ancient script. . . . So you are not supposed to add anything in that. It is better if you can subtract, remove something, make it simpler. . . . <It has become a cheap manner.> [*Cīp mainar ho gaya.*] You have to control yourself.

This characterization draws on a sedimented moral discourse that distinguishes sharply between two ethical worlds: the patrilineal world of orthodox (*k͟hāndānī*) singers and the matrilineal world of courtesan singers. In this conventionally stereotyped discursive distinction, the manner of khandani singers is marked by control and restraint; the manner of courtesans is marked by charming tricks and flexible rules.[48] It turns on the linkage of textual fidelity with sexual fidelity, and elaboration with promiscuity. This characterization of the vocal comportment of courtesans did not aspire to sociological accuracy—as this singer himself knew quite well, the sophisticated socio-musical practices of courtesans do not boil down to either sexual promiscuity or economic necessity. But this intervention was nevertheless quite comportmentally precise: my excessive ornamentation of the canonical bandish was not simply a matter of extra *notes*, but a symptom of an inappropriate *manner*.

It is also, of course, possible to sing *too* simply. Singers who intone note after note without ornamentation are often accused of singing "dry," "intellectual," "veg," or "like a harmonium." What is called for is not the mechanical replication of any particular melodic squiggle, but a disposition suited to a particular kind of listener in a particular situation (see chapter 3).

SONOROUS DISPOSITIONS

To attend to Mohammad Rafi's "silken"[49] tone, to the "clarity"[50] of Kesarbai Kerkar's voice, to Asha Bhosle's "thin" melodic line,[51] or to Faiyaz Khan's "husky"[52] sound is to recognize sonority: a texture that remains steady through vocal twists

48. See also Weidman 2006, 135, on a parallel construal of elaborate *svara kalpana* in Karnatak vocal music as "cheap," like a "characterless woman."

49. Poolakkal 2014, 203–204.

50. Pradhan 2015, 1.

51. Deshpande 2004, 5181.

52. Nair 2007, 48.

and turns.[53] Critic V. H. Deshpande compared a singer's cultivated sonority to a sculptor's chosen medium: "stone, marble, or ivory."[54] Sonority is more than acoustical timbre, more than relative intensity of harmonic overtones. While *timbre* tends to put us in the place of a detached observer reflecting on a textualized voice, *sonority* focuses our attention on the action of singing: the active comportment of the vocal apparatus, producing distinctive forms of vocal resonance. A singer's voice, after all, typically retains its consistent sonority despite the dramatic overtonal variation between vowels. The instant recognizability of a familiar voice, then, hinges on dynamic disposition of voice rather than a single, unchanging arrangement of harmonics. Singing from the belly, the chest, or the nose, projecting an audible imprint of a configuration of the musicking body that can be positively contagious, even penetrating a listener's heart.

At first, sonority appears to be something like a vocal fingerprint, inscribed in the body, entirely beyond one's control.[55] Bright, smooth, and high sonorities often index youthfulness and thus innocence. Vocal hoarseness, often heard in the voices of seasoned qawwals and elderly khyal singers, is not something typically chosen for cultivation, and not easily rid of through practice; it is the inevitable consequence of decades of vocal labor. Distinctions between such seemingly transparent, sonorous dispositions have crystallized into habits liked to distinct subject positions. Among Maharashtrian kirtankars, for example, a "deep, mellow" sonority indexes a high-caste Naradiyā kirtankar, while a "high, strained, loud" sonority indexes an ecstatic wārkari kirtankar—only the latter of whom might hope to convincingly embody a great bhakti saint.[56]

And yet, sonority is no more determined by anatomy than is posture; each is situated, produced, and enculturated among others. Thinking merely in terms of a fixed timbral substance or a fixed vocal identity can obscure this fact. Sonority is actively generated through techniques of voice production: openness, power, nasality; projection from the chest, navel, or throat; and the hard-won quality of *surīlāpaṇ* (tunefulness). It is specifically in relation to sonority that singers are

53. Not to be confused with "sonority" in the phonological sense, as the relative salience of a particular speech sound. See also Nancy 2007, 39.

54. Deshpande 1989, 66.

55. As Nina Eidsheim (2008, 30 and passim) points out, timbre often reads as fixed and racialized even though it is flexible, shapable, and dependent on the listener's noetic practices.

56. Schultz 2002, 312.

most likely to apply the English term "voice culture" for long-term, disciplined practice. But whether acquired actively through deliberate practice or acquired passively through imitation and absorption, sonority is eminently a *hexis*—a vocal disposition that one comes to "have" on the scale of months or years.

Sur

Sur (tone, melody, tune) is fundamental. While it may be used narrowly in reference to the tuning of an individual note,[57] "good sur" is typically used to describe a quality that a singer *has*. Indeed, while there are seven distinct *svaras*, *sur* itself is a disposition: a luminous vocal quality underlying the superficial variegations of melody. As a coherent singularity, *sur*—rather than any note in particular—requires and invites a singer's one-pointed devotion (see chapter 5). *Having good sur* (or being-*surīl*, or having the *guṇa* of *surīlāpaṇ*) is a more or less stable disposition: once you've achieved it, you needn't re-achieve it freshly with each note. As Bade Ghulam Ali is said to have murmured admiringly about Lata Mangeshkar, "<*That wretch is never besur*!>"[58] While a teacher may from time to time encourage a student to work on the tuning of this or that particular *svara*, the *guṇa* of *surīlāpaṇ* generally applies wholesale to a singer. Music critic V. H. Deshpande described this disposition as a "total tonal vision" (*surācī nazar*), a "feeling for tonal accuracy," and a "revelation (*sākśāt*) of perfect intonation." Conversely, for the unfortunate singer who is still *besur* (without-sur), it is not one note or another in particular that eludes them; it is a *guṇa*, an overall vocal-aural disposition of reflexive attunement, that they are missing. Sur is one of the first demands of a young singer, and one of the first signs of a knack for singing. A lucky few are said to have natural *surīlāpaṇ*, picked up as it were by osmosis.

---

57. *Sur* is cognate with *svara*. In Carnatic music, *sruti* is more often used to refer to intonation in general, whereas in the north, *sruti* tends to refer either to very fine intonational nuance (like its equivalent, *darjā*, or sometimes in relation to an obsolete 22-tone gamut), or to a singer's preferred pitch of the tonic *sā*. In the north, *Sur* may refer to individual notes (interchangeably with svara), to tunes, to melody in general, or, in certain modal traditions, to a melodic mode (Ayyagari 2012). The usage I develop here replicates a fairly consistent ethnopractical triad of interrelated terms: *sur* (intonational propriety), *surīla* (tuneful), and *surīlāpaṇ* (tunefulness).

58. *Kambakht, kabhī besurī nahī hotī.* Deshpande 2004, 5184.

But for most singers, sur is acquired through years of listening, imitation, and devoted practice.

There are many kinds of sur that operate differently in different vocal worlds. Fastidious attention to intonation generally matters more in settings for bourgeois, aesthetic listening (e.g., pop sufi, or film music, or khyal) than it does in devotional settings (say, bhajans, kirtan, or qawwali). The great Bollywood vocalists of the pre-autotune era (most famously Lata Mangeshkar) are revered for their sur even when they sang with widely tuned orchestras, vibrato, and a gentle crooning sweetness that would ordinarily be inappropriate for classical music. This kind of *surīlāpaṇ* has centrally to do with what aficionados sometimes call a "tuneful" or "melodious" voice—smooth connectivity between notes, gentleness, evenness of tone. In the twenty-first century, Bollywood music producers have increasingly applied autotuning to achieve the particular kind of intonational precision so valued in anglophone cosmopolitan pop music. Shireesh Thakur, an aspiring film singer from Bombay, describes sur as a source of solidity and strength: "what Hindustani classical . . . teaches you is, the sur . . . the notes become really solid if you've done your riyaz . . . So that gives you that strength."

Though sur may certainly have a profound emotional effect, it is not typically *expressive* in and of itself. Instead, the fulfillment of sur is akin to devotion (to the steady call of the tanpura's drone, to a tonal ideal, to the deeply felt presence of an all-pervading entity (variously called *shabd*, *svara*, *music*, or *nād*) rather than as an expression of personal feeling. When singing with great attention to sur, one usually proceeds with the sense of a tonal ideal for each note, as though there actually *were* a single perfect, ideal svara out there waiting for us to try to reach it. As we will see, sometimes this ideal is imagined as a point on a vertical or horizontal line; sometimes it is felt as a bull's eye; sometimes as a kind of depth. Often, this tonal ideal is understood to be unachievable in principle. Sometimes an ideal tone is auditorily protended, or "preheard" in its "forthcomingness,"[59] either as a tone-about-to-come or as an aimed-for overtone in the drone of the tanpura; in the early stages of my own training, Vikas Kashalkar would often ask me to imaginatively hear a note in my mind before singing it. As a metaphysical matter, most singers thus agree that the path to sur is an endless road.

As an acoustical matter, sur is never perfectly achieved numerically. Consider the following pitch trace in figure 2.14, from an alap by a young dhrupadiya.

After a slow loop around the *ma* {4}, the voice settles on a *pa* {5}, which is held

59. Sudnow 1993, 62.

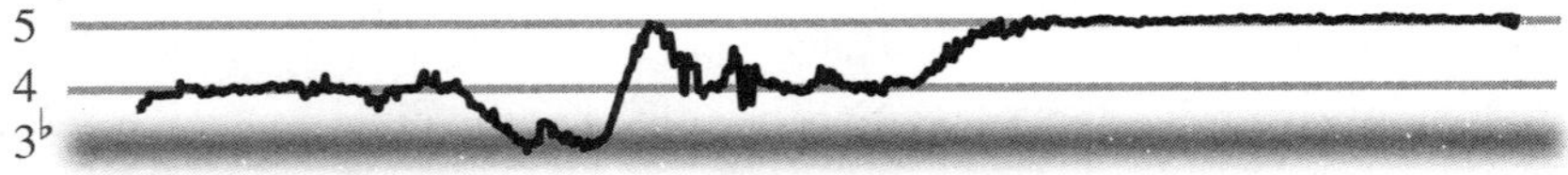

FIGURE 2.14 Tonal accuracy

steadily for nearly five seconds. This steadiness does not imply numerical fixity (it varies subtly, 3 Hz over a five-second span). But it nonetheless shows up as steady, clear sur. This sur, then, is much more than pitch.[60] If a stable, unchanging pitch were all that mattered, we could easily produce stable tones of consistent frequency from synthesizers, harmoniums, or hairdryers. Indeed, one of the early acoustical surprises about Hindustani voice revealed by oscilloscopes and melographs was the fact that "the frequency and amplitude of [vocal] tones are never perfectly steady" (Deva 1959). Even so-called "straight" tones waver, often by considerably more than 3 Hz; holding sur to a standard of absolute, acoustical stillness would leave us with no *surīl* voices at all in the recorded archive of human voices. The acoustic signal is by no means a horizontal line, yet such a voice sounds as though it has come to rest, utterly still and transparent. More to the point, singers do not arrive at sur by taking measurements or doing arithmetic; nor do listeners count hundreds of individual vibrations each second to arrive at a numerical frequency. Teachers teach sur through example, or by simply pointing out that a particular phrase or note was out of tune. In the rare cases when a teacher does suggest that a student move up or down by a *śruti* (tonal quantum), or adjust the *darjā* (level) of a tone, they are not prescribing a particular frequency or ratio. Rather, they are indicating fine shades of vocal tone, asking the student to attune their ears to tonal subtlety. One simply notices that one's voice is not blending with the tanpura, not entering the svara deeply enough, that one's sur is impure, weak, or shaky, or that one is off the mark. Two equally accomplished singers may sing a given svara consistently at rather different frequencies, and the same singer may even sing the same nominal *svara* differently in different situations.[61] For example, the lowered-7 in Rāg Malkauns, when ascending to the 1, is often sung considerably higher. Likewise, the extremely variable but relatively high lowered-3 of Bhimpalasi, the extra lowered-7 in Jaunpuri or the controversial, ambivalent 6 of Lalit, and many other cases. That these svaras vary

60. See also Van Der Meer and Rao 2006.

61. Levy 1982.

is by no means a sign of arithmetical miscalculation. On the contrary, for a singer attuned to their fine differences, the variation is a mark of exquisite sensitivity to sur. We now turn toward several common ways of hearing and achieving *sur*: steadiness, spatial accuracy, and blending.

Sur is often experienced as a practiced tonal steadiness. Holding a note exquisitely in tune for five seconds, without vibrato, with only imperceptible wavering, is an extraordinary vocal feat (try it). It stands in stark contrast to the vocal sounds we are usually surrounded by in speech and song, which are (as we saw in the last chapter) constantly moving up and down. It often sounds as though motion has stopped altogether. A voice with good sur stands out as quite distinct from other mere sounds, just as a gold-painted "human statue" performer stands out as exceptional in a way that a bronze statue does not. Even if no voice is absolutely free of wavering, hearing *steadiness* (*ṭhaharāv*) in a voice is no more of a misperception than marveling at the steadiness of a master surgeon's hand that wavers less than a centimeter. Indeed, many singers grip a virtual note with their hand while holding it very still.[62] This is a remarkable constraint of motion every bit as rigorously disciplined as the impressive (relative) stillness of an archer taking aim or a gymnast in repose on parallel bars. Good sur in this sense is a learned technique for stilling a voice that is ordinarily in constant motion; it is a learned technique of restraint, not the ground state of a mechanism.

Qawwal Fareed Ayaz once described to me three facets of *sur* in turn: the sonic quality of steadiness (*ṭhaharāv*), the aesthetic/ethical quality of a pure vocal disposition (*shuddh gāyakī*), and the disciplined action of keeping-stable (*qāym rakhnā*).

> <*The technique of cultivating our pure vocal disposition* [shuddh gāyakī] *has a fundamental, basic point, and that is keeping the sur stable* [qāym rakhnā]. . . . *it is called* shuddh gayaki, *and* [*called*] ṭhaharāv [*steadiness*]. . . . *In whatever song, or note, or poem, ṭhaharāv is required.*>[63]

Ṭhaharāv—the capacity to maintain a long, steady tone—is an entirely different skill from holding a key down on a harmonium or letting an open string ring out on a sitār. At a physiological level, it requires the restraint of motion. The

62. Rahaim 2012, 95.

63. Hamare pās shuddh gāyakī kā rīāz kā jo fanḍamenṭal hai, buniyādī poīnṭ hai voh hai sur ko qāym rakhnā . . . *shuddh gāyaki* kaha jātā hai, aur *ṭhaharāv* . . . kisi bhi chiz mein yā sur mein yā kalām mein *ṭhaharāv* chahiye hotā hai.

thin, delicate vocal folds live in a wind tunnel, with air rushing past. The sounding larynx finds a balanced poise in the midst of gravity, variable air pressure, and several different vectors of muscle tension. Some wavering is inevitable. To hear this slight motion as *ṭhaharāv* is not to find horizontal lines on the melograph that correspond to steady states of the objective vocal apparatus, but to hear relative steadiness. Sur is thus a doubly disciplined achievement: holding-steady and judging with the ear.

Sur is also often described—and felt—as a form of spatial accuracy. The practice of correct sur, from this point of view, is a matter of discernment (finding a place within a region or hitting a target) interwoven with action (getting there). This spatial conception is quite different from a numerical sense of frequency mapped onto a spatial dimension. The technical terms *maqām* (place) or *darjā* (level) are sometimes used to describe the correct position of a svara.[64] Individual svaras may at times be visualized analytically as points in tonal space, but in discussions of sur, each svara functions in turn as a space for action: a bull's eye, a zone, often with depth as well as breadth. Kumar Gandharva, for example, reportedly described a dimension of depth-of-sur orthogonal to pitch height: "You must think of a swara as though it were a fish. It can go straight ahead along the scale, or swim in the same place at various depths. If you do not go ahead [i.e., even without tonal movement], there [are] . . . plenty of places where you are on the same note at different levels."[65] Another widely cited image echoes this dimension of depth orthogonal to a surface: *svaras* are a series of doors which beginners knock on, and masters open and enter.

Other models of sur spatiality deal in zones rather than points. Shailaja Pandit, a student of Kirana gharana master Hirabai Barodekar, invokes a picture of a bull's eye, distinguishing between the "circles" of a bull's eye and its "core." This distinction entails a dimension stretching from periphery/surface to center/essence. Of course, singers are aware that a svara may be sung at a different pitch depending on melodic context. Ascending notes, as in many melodic practices, tend to be higher in pitch than descending notes. But even this (with some

64. *Maqām* in the general sense of "place" should not be confused with its older Hindustani usage to describe melodic modes, a usage that still has wide currency in Central Asia and the Middle East. *Maqām* has now largely fallen out of use in South Asia and Iran, where *rāga* and *dastgāh* (respectively) have supplanted *maqām* as the dominant term for melodic mode.

65. Quoted in Menon 2001, 97.

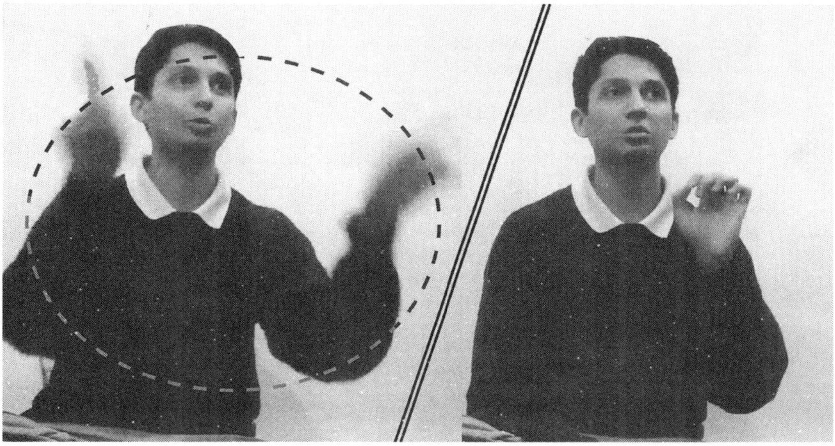

FIGURE 2.15 Bull's eye of sur

imaginative effort) can be accommodated in a vision of properly sung notes as the core of an ideal region. As Shailaja herself puts it: "Of course the core [of the note] also changes with following notes and [preceding notes]. So it changes, but automatically, your voice also attends to that. But you have to be very sensitive to get attuned to that." Note that *sensitivity*—not the absolute location of the "core" of a note—is precisely what is at issue. This noetic sensitivity—always in a loop with vocalization—is at the heart of sur.

But even among singers who think of placing notes accurately in a space, the precise center of sur is unattainable. Pushkar Lele, like Shailaja Pandit, described this to me as a bull's eye—but the center point is never reached.

> If you imagine a note to be a bull's eye {*traces ellipse with hands*}, right in the center is where the actual [i.e., ideal] note is. And we are *never* in the center. We are always somewhere {*moves hand around bull's eye*} in that territory, in that area, but never really in the center of the note.

The practical spatiality of *sur*, then, exceeds a one-dimensional spatiality of absolute points: it consists of zones and regions, spaces and subspaces.[66] And the disciplined disposition of *surīlāpaṇ* is a disposition of properly *operating* within these zones, actively and sensitively *svar lagāo*-ing within a space, rather than simply instantiating numerical relations.

66. See Rahaim 2012, 61–65 on raga spaces.

FIGURE 2.16 Tanpura spectrogram

Another practical sense of sur foregrounds the unified blend of voice and tanpura (*tānpurā*). In raga music, the drone of the tanpura is sounded continuously behind the voice. The constancy of its sound (an ongoing hum strengthened by the buzzing of a curved bridge, with minimal attack, seemingly without beginning or end) through hours of practice, study, and performance is part of the deep, sentimental bond that many singers form with their tanpuras. But to focus on its drone, its temporal constancy, obscures the dynamic texture of its sound. The curved bridge of a tanpura produces a broad buzzing as the strings are plucked. This buzz contains a vast wash of high harmonics: a constantly shifting sound, like dozens of tinkling bells. These are sometimes called *srutis* or *svayambhu* (self-originating) *svaras*.[67] Figure 2.16 renders these high tones visible in a spectrogram.

This blending is sometimes also described as a kind of unity, as, for example: “<The throat should be one with the tanpura”> (*tānpurā ke sāth tumhārā galā ek honā chāhiye*). Kumar Prasad Mukherji describes seeing Abdul Karim Khan “lingering on the sa, the tonic in the upper octave, and his voice had mingled with the finely tuned tanpuras and the shadaj of the harmonium so well that it created the illusion that he had lost his voice.”[68] This refers not simply to numeri-

67. Pandya 2005.

68. Mukherji 2006, 11.

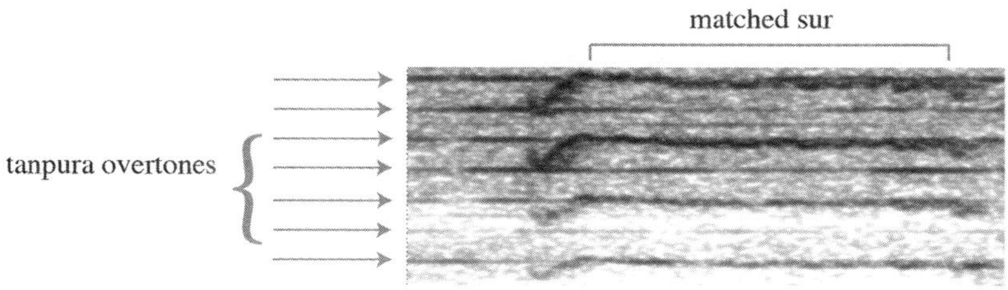

FIGURE 2.17 Matching sur

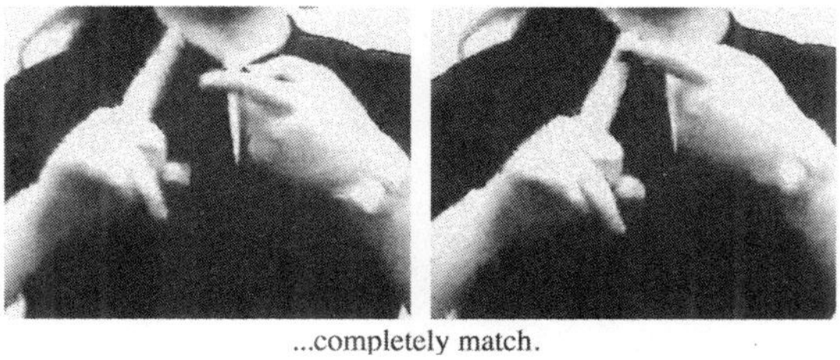

FIGURE 2.18 Matching sur gesture

cal accuracy, but also to a disciplined way of voicing-and-listening, in which the voice-and-ear complex tunes into and sounds out a particular relationship with the sound of the tanpura. V. H. Deshpande describes learning to hear sur in relation to the tanpura during his training with Sureshbabu Mane: "with a correctly [*barobar*] produced note, the tanpura in one's hand sounded intensely melodious [*sundar aikāyalā*: was heard to be beautiful] whereas the noise created by a false note [*bighaḍlelyā svarācyā goṃgaṭāt*: the noise of a corrupt note] drowned the drone of the tanpura."[69]

Singer Apoorva Gajjale once demonstrated to me how she achieves a "match," with the tanpura, singing an extended *sā* {tonic} that seemed to melt into the drone of the tanpura. This "matching" is a processual, disciplined achievement, involving a slight glide (see figure 2.17).

As she said, "It should completely like match with that sur. <Whichever note I sang>[70] . . . My sur and what the [tanpura] is playing should completely match." As she said this last phrase, she pressed her index fingers together, showing voice and tanpura becoming one (see figure 2.18).

---

69. Deshpande 1979 (Marathi version), 20; English edition 1989, 4.

70. *Jo bhi sur maine lagaaya.*

Even this much, blending the *sā* of the voice into the *sā* of the tanpura, is difficult for beginners.[71] But with training, other svaras can blend as well. Part of the key to this is attending to the many high, tinkling harmonics in the drone of the tanpura. Vikas Kashalkar once instructed me to listen to the tanpura before singing the first note of Rag Yaman, and not to make a sound until I could discern the high *ga* {3} in the tanpura. But there are so many harmonics in a tanpura texture that the ear cannot attend to them all at once. Instead, like a conversationalist in a noisy room, the ear focuses on one or two of these tones at a time. Depending on which ones the ear picks out, in fact, many singers find themselves "hearing" a raga in the tanpura, and gravitating toward what they hear.

Voices, too, are rich in harmonic overtones. As they are shaped by the mouth, throat, and tongue, alternately muting and reinforcing overtones, they ordinarily sound like unified wholes: as different vowels, rather than different harmonic complexes of multiple tones. Many singers note that the bright sound of nasal resonance enhances *sur*—as Nipa Nag put it <from [singing] nasal, *surīlapaṇ* is greatly filled out.>[72] But it is also possible, as with the tanpura, to hear individual harmonics pop out of a voice. Allowing the voice to become *one-with* the tanpura certainly has something to do with pitch, but it is equally a matter of vowel, a matter of tone, a matter of hearing one's vocal harmonics in resonance with the tanpura. Though every voice is made up of many upper partials, not every ear attunes itself relative to the partials of the tanpura. In Hazrat Inayat Khan's aphorism, "while [a singer] tunes his tanpura, he tunes his own soul."[73] Vijay Sardeshmukh demonstrates this aural discipline in the film *Koi Sunta Hai* ["Someone Is Listening"] (2008):

> <From one sound, everything comes out, the whole gamut of notes. Every sruti comes now. Consider this one kharaj [low tonic string]. *{Plays kharaj string of the tanpura.}* In this, we can hear so many svaras. *{Sings ga [3].}* We can also hear this svar, like this; this too we can hear: *{sings pa [5].}* When our [sung] svara matches [the overtones we hear], that is perfection.>[74]

---

71. See Hess 2015, 36–37.

72. *Surīlapaṇ bhī nezal se zyāda bhartā hai.*

73. Khan 1996, 63.

74. *Ek sāūnd se jo sab nikaltā hai pūrā saptak . . . sab sruti abhi ā jātī hai. Abhi ek kharaja dekho. Ismeṃ ham kitne svar sun sakte haiṃ. Yeh bhi svar sun sakte haiṃ, abhi yeh jaise. Yeh bhi sun sakte hain. Jab hamārā svar match ho jātā hai usmein, to parfekśan hai.*

As Pushkar Lele puts it: "only [at] the center of the note will you hear the exact harmonics that come from it. If you can hear the *pancham* {5} that comes from my own voice when I sing the exact *sā* {1}, *that* is the point when I will truly reach the exact *sā* {1}." A commonsense acoustical account of this might hold that an in-tune *pa* {5} sounds in tune *because* the *sā* {1} is in tune. But from the point of view of a singer, the situation is reversed: in this case, it is precisely because the harmonic *pa* {5} becomes salient, ringing out clearly above the harmonic wash of the tanpura, that the sā {1} that is sung sounds in tune. Sur, from this point of view, is achieved through a cultivated aural-vocal sensitivity to particular harmonics.

Figure 2.19 juxtaposes a range of common harmonic alignments between several shuddh (natural) svaras and a tanpura tuned to *sā* {1} and *pa* {5}. Only the first several harmonics are shown here—the ones most commonly cited. More are discernible with a carefully trained ear. It should be noted that neither the voice nor tanpura has arithmetically perfect overtones, and the frequency of both voices and strings of non-infinitesimal thickness shift slightly over the course of a single svara. *Sur* thus requires a constant, ongoing attentional presence, unlike, for example, pressing down a key on a harmonium. Nonetheless, it is possible to tune the ears to these contingent resonances. For example, in singing *ma* {4}, it is possible to focus on the high *sā* {1} that pops out (*nikaltā hai*), and to align this with the *sā* {1} that jumps out of the tanpura. Likewise with singing *re* {2}, aligning one of its high partials with the *re* {2} overtone that jumps out of the *pa* {5} string. In the moment of singing, this resonance, is not simply *there*. Nor is it ever perfectly achieved; it is actively sought by a properly disciplined ear and voice.

This sense of sur as reciprocal overtonal attunement between voice and tanpura does not require calculations of frequencies or ratios. One *can* hear it (*sun sakte hai*) but one ordinarily does not. This is why we are exhorted to attend (*dekho*[75]) to the particular harmonics, which is by no means automatic. It requires time and attention. Indeed, it is not possible to hear *all* of the harmonics disclosed by a spectrogram at the same time. This shifting fabric of aural possibility is *polystable*. Just as the eye may see a line drawing of a cube as facing up

75. As in English, both *suno* ("listen . . .") and *dekho* ("look . . .") often serve as more-or-less interchangeable rhetorical exhortations to *pay attention* (rather than to merely exercise hearing or seeing in sensorially discrete ways). See also the discussion of *sunāo* in chapter 3.

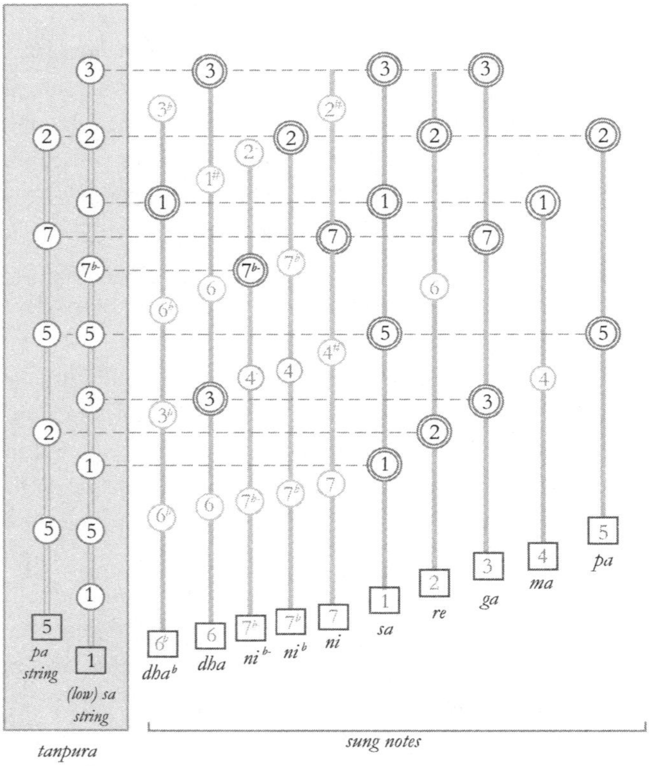

FIGURE 2.19 Tanpura harmonics diagram

or down (but not both at once, nor a tetrahedron), the ear has a range of discrete, finite possibilities for hearing harmonics, some more salient than others. While immersed in a rāg with a prominent natural-2 (such as Durga), the natural-2 may seem to pop out of the tanpura, whereas in a rāg with a lowered-2 (such as Komal Asavari), this harmonic doesn't ordinarily present itself to audition.

Bodily Sonorities

Hum the lowest and loudest note you can; then gradually slide upward, like a slow siren, to the top of your range. You may feel movement upward through the chest, the collarbone, the back of the throat, and even in the nose and face. While singing low, you may feel as though your voice is emanating from the chest or belly; while moving higher, you may feel the place of voice moving upward; the nose and face may even be felt to buzz along. This feeling of bodily placement is notoriously hard to pin down in strict physical and physiological terms,[76] yet singers from a wide range of traditions agree that one sings from the belly (*nābhī*), chest (*sīnā*), throat (*galā*), and nose (*nāk*). These places are often called *maqāms* or *sthānas*,[77] parallel to the spatial placement of sur.

Some may count only these three points of placement; others boast of having mastered five, nine, or more (such as the tongue, the head, and teeth; or corresponding to the variously numbered *cakras*; or even, as one singer attested, the uterus). Nobody, however, claims that the elbow, ear, or thigh is an stable point of articulation; nobody claims that their voice originates in the nose and proceeds downwards. Vocal production starts low—ideally, from the navel—and proceeds upward, along a one-way path through the center of the trunk, up and out of the head, gathering power and resonance along the way. This standard vocal body schema has wide currency across worlds in the Hindustani vocal ecumene (and beyond).[78]

Note that the throat (*galā*) in this body schema is not physiologically equivalent to the larynx; nor is it construed to be the exclusive acoustical origin of tone. Indeed, singers sometimes go out of their way to downplay biomedical anatomy. The story goes that Begum Akhtar was once asked how she could sing so well despite smoking and drinking; she smiled and replied, "Who sings from the throat, anyway?" This story has become a piece of folklore now deployed precisely to highlight the ontological tension between biomedical anatomy and the lived musicking body. The throat is often construed as the seat of a very particular faculty of voice: kinetic flexibility. Singing quickly and accurately is typically construed as an act of the *galā*, not the chest or navel. Preparing the throat for singing largely means cultivating flexibility, and a *gol galā* (round throat, see chapter 2) is a throat disciplined to sing curvaceous, smoothly connected vocal lines.

This is one of the few fields of voice cultivation that has a long and clear tradition in the Sanskrit literature. The dramaturgical treatise *Natyasastra* (XIX.41), for example, lists characteristic bodily loci (*sthānas*) for different kinds of speech by stage actors: the chest (*uras*), throat (*kaṇṭha*), and the head (*śiras*); grammatical

76. Kreiman and Sidtis 2011, 390.

77. Note that, like *sthāna*, *maqām* is used both for a place in the body and the location of a note.

78. Merleau-Ponty 2013, 101. See also Herbst 1997, 25 on bodily resonance.

treatises typically include the nose (*nāsikā*) as well as specific points of articulating consonants in the mouth.[79]

A separate (and, apparently, latter-day) approach recasts this schema in terms of yogic physiology. This seems to have first appeared in the influential music-theoretic treatise *Sangītaratnākara* (III.3–5), and is duplicated verbatim in the *Svaramelakalānidhi* of Rāmāmātyā (II.18–20):

> *Wishing to speak, the soul* [atman] *inspires the mind, the mind stokes the fire* [vahni] *within the body and the fire circulates the vital air* [prāṇa]. *This* [vital] *air stays in the brahma-granthi* [the "knot" comprising the lowest *cakras*] *and slowly moves into the upper body through the navel, chest, throat, head and mouth, and manifests as sound.*[80]

Though the standard vocal schema does not ordinarily imply anything about subtle energies such as *prāṇa* and *vahni*, many singers freely draw from yogic physiology to make sense of voice production.

But singers don't learn to sing "from the chest" by consulting treatises on yoga; they learn from their teachers. There are many ways to bodily emplace one's voice, all of which require training and enculturation. Students spend years striving to sing from the belly, brightening or mellowing their tone by controlling the nose, strengthening the power of a chest voice through repetitive exercises. Accordingly, maps of these vocal territories nearly always include *prescriptions* about right and wrong ways of placement. Teachers of voice workshops sometimes instruct their clients to sing the triphthongal syllable *auṃ* as a way of moving through various points of resonance, sometimes invoking a metaphysical tradition that hears *auṃ* as the originary form of all-pervading *nād*. Singer Anuraag Dhoundeyal describes a particularly elaborate training process with his teacher Ramdesh Pande:

> [He taught me that] singing is not just about the throat, it involves each and every part of your body. . . . He would say things like, "Project from your diaphragm" and "Project to your incisors" . . . he would say, "Bring more of your right side into the song" and he would say these things and really emphasize

---

79. For example, the palate (*tālu*), teeth (*danta*), lips (*oṣṭha*). Incidentally, this classification scheme served as the basis of the universal-in-principle phonetical designations of modern linguistics: "dental," "retroflex," etc.

80. Translation Srinivas Reddy. See Rahaim, et al. 2015.

> on the balance of your inner being, being in the right sort of balance and then singing, because it's not just about singing anyhow . . . he would say things like, "Now press your nose and make sure you feel your nose" . . . often times he would ask me to tap on my front teeth and then project and feel the voice hitting those teeth. And then after that he would tell me that, "OK, imagine that you're fitting a biscuit in your mouth and then open your mouth and then sing."

We see that the standard vocal body schema is not merely an anatomical description of voice in general, but a template for training oneself into a particular embodied vocal disposition—which, as always, implies a certain regime of ethical propriety. Shireesh Thakur, an aspiring film singer, speaks of singing from the chest as singing "from within, rather than just doing it for the sake of doing it." This ascription of sincerity and realness to the inside of the chest is widely legible; the expression *dil se* ("from the heart") has roughly the same ethical implication that it does in English. Mohammad Hafeez Khan Talwandiwale reports that deep *gamak* (unlike florid *harkat*) is permissible in dhrupad precisely because it "comes from the heart."[81] The distinction between heart-singing and head-singing constitutes a major structural opposition in the well-known Marathi opera *Kaṭyār Kaḷjāt Ghusalī*; where the hereditary Muslim court singer is said to sing from the head (with dazzling speed and virtuosity), and the humble Hindu *bhakt* from the heart (with devotion and sincerity).[82] The hero, Sadashiv, learns from both, and thereby reconciles head and heart in his voice by singing from the throat—while also reconciling these two contentiously counterposed dispositional traditions. Many qawwals make a parallel distinction between singing *filmi* and *Sufi* according to their bodily emplacements—the former from the throat (*galā*), the latter from the chest (*sīnā*).

Singing "from the nose" (*nāk se*) produces a bright vocal timbre. Physiologically, it seems to require opening the velum to allow resonance in the nasal cavities.[83] Hindustani language has a special phonemic distinction between nasal and non-nasal vowels;[84] and yet singing with the disposition of *nāk se* does not

---

81. Widdess 1994a, 95.

82. See also Chaubey in Dard Neuman (forthcoming) on the criticism of Abdul Wahid Khan that he sings from the head rather than the heart—the implication is strong that this is ethically improper.

83. See Sengupta, et al. 1989.

84. Ohala 1983.

blur this distinction. Its opposite (when the nasal cavities are closed off by the palate) produces a mellow, crooning sound typical of Amir Khan, Kishore Kumar, and male *filmi* voice in general. Broadly speaking, there are two kinds of nasal resonance in broad currency.[85] Among khyal singers, particularly those from Agra gharana, the buzzing resonance of the nose is sometimes called *jivārī*, the same word used for the zinging upper harmonics produced by a tanpura—and accordingly, this kind of voice blends easily with a harmonic. (Indeed, singers who teach "Western contemporary" to classically trained Hindustani vocalists often complain that this bright nasal resonance is an intonational crutch that must be abandoned.) Singers of light music, on the other hand, tend to use nasal resonance rather more sparingly to lend a certain sweetness. The absence of this latter moderate nasal sound is often described as *dry*—that is, it doesn't offer *ras* (juice) to a listener—or flat—that is, it doesn't offer *tasir* (impact) to a listener (see chapter 3). One Hindustani aphorism ("*Nāk meṃ, jo hai nakhrā dikhāte hai*") describes singing from the nose as a kind of *nakhrā*, or an artful, alluring attitude of playful disdain, traditionally cultivated by courtesans. Nearly everyone agrees that too much nasal resonance is excessive.

The "head voice" is a term loosely (and controversially) used for a smooth, high, round tone on the verge of falsetto. Indeed, it is often called "false voice" (*fāls woīs*, the usual Hindustani term for falsetto), and its falseness, in principle, lies in its mere *seeming*, floating above the throat without foundation—as opposed to the grounded realness, strength, and power of a voice projected from the navel and chest. It is used almost exclusively for light *filmi* singing, especially for singing lightly into microphones. Its ethical standing is a matter of wide debate among Hindustani vocalists. Widely associated with the West, singers of raga music consider head voice, at best, to be a special effect. Even more than singing from the nose, the head voice is a voice that one slips into occasionally as a special effect. No qawwals or khyaliyas for example, boast of singing "from the head" the way that they might sing from the navel, chest, or nose. It seems to be almost exclusively in "Western" vocal lessons that singers locate and cultivate a voice centered in the head.

85. Titze (2001) distinguishes between two types of nasality: "nasal murmur," in which acoustic energy is transmitted into the nose, and "twang," which he links instead to acoustic resonation in the epilarynx tube. Others have found that nasal resonance accomplishes more or less the same thing as the singer's formant around 3500—see Datta, et al. (1988) and Sengupta, et al. (1989).

Range

To speak of Faiyaz Khan's "deep" voice or Lata Mangeshkar's "high" voice is not to specify single, absolute frequencies; it is to speak of a range of pitch dispositionally available for vocal action. In many cases, the span of this range is a sense of great pride. When singers claim to have a "three-octave" range, they are not indicating the ability to produce an actual viable span of 36 semitones, but to sing flexibly in some each of the three octave-spans, or *saptaks*:[86] mandra (low), madhya (medium), and tār (high). These *saptaks* serve as a kind of shorthand for three vocal regions—though in practice, as we will see, vocal range may include several spaces (*jagah*) that overlap with these saptaks (distinct again from the jagahs of raga space[87] and the jagahs of individual svaras). One's vocal range, then, is more than a mere span of pitches; it contains a finite, varied set of distinctive possibilities for vocal action. Low voices are said to be "broad" and "resonating"; high ones are "thin" and "flexible."[88] As we will see, different vocal ranges call for different dispositions, and have very different affordances, as viscerally distinct as the difference between murmuring and shouting. As we will see, "shouting" is one of the terms of ethical reproach often applied to singing at the top of one's range. Conversely, as we will see in chapter 3, the power of *buland* voice is often construed as a vehicle for blessing from a Sufi saint.

Most singers choose a *sā* that comfortably accommodates their vocal range with the ambit of most songs. Music directors composing for film singers can transpose their songs to accommodate their ranges—Lata's range, for example, was at its sweetest between F♯ and C♯. On the other hand, some singers persist in singing a bit higher or lower than is comfortable in imitation of a model singer. But in most situations, singers have latitude to adjust to the capabilities of their voice. Many Hindustani vocalists vary their *sā* depending on which raga they will sing by as much as a major second (singing lower for ragas with high ambitus, and vice versa), and by time of day, when practicing, by as much as a third or fourth. When male teachers teach female students, or vice versa, it is

---

86. This term is roughly equivalent to "octave" despite the etymological difference (*saptak* implies the 7-note ambitus, whereas *octave* implies the span including the eighth step).

87. See also Rahaim 2012 for the jagah found in ragas.

88. Deshpande 1973, 13–14.

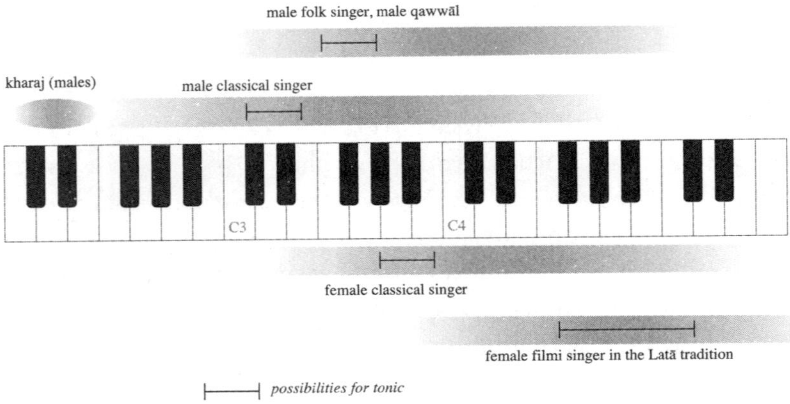

FIGURE 2.20 Typical vocal ranges

sometimes necessary for the teacher or student or both to adjust their range by a third or in order to sing a full octave apart.

With all of these qualifications in mind, and as an orienting generalization, a selection of conventional ranges is shown in figure 2.20.

The great majority of melodic action is measured relative to sā {1}, the tonic, and stretches from a fourth below the tonic to an octave to a third or fourth above, with most of the vocal action happening in the mandra saptak. However, for male classical vocalists and qawwāls in prestigious lineages, demonstrating the extremes of their range for momentary vocal feats is part of demonstrating competence and training. For example, male singers will often sing *kharaj* (a very low, sustained note an octave below their *sa*) once during the performance, even though it is not required by any raga or song. Similarly, some singers will conspicuously press their range very high, beyond the high *pa* {5}, into a thin falsetto. Only rarely do canonical compositions demand notes this high; instead, this expansion is a demonstration of unusual vocal ability. Film singers and folk singers rarely push the extremes of their range.

Qawwal Fareed Ayaz, like many singers, emphasizes the necessity of knowing the limits of one's range, so as not to push oneself too far in a performance. He calls the highest and lowest points of vocal range *top dead center* and *bottom dead center* (technical terms used by auto mechanics to mark the limits of a piston's possible motion). This metaphoric frame, among other things, implies the fixity of vocal range—the piston cannot exceed its limits without breaking. In the long term, however, the limits of vocal range are a bit more malleable than a metal piston. Most singers can physically squeak out high notes and groan out low notes that they would not attempt to produce reliably in a concert. More importantly, as we will see in chapter 5, there are techniques for expanding one's range, as well.

These ranges change over time. On the scale of hours, one tends to wake up with a low vocal range, and this is the time when many classical vocalists practice singing *kharaj*, a full octave below their sa. By mid-afternoon, one's range may shift upward by as much as a fourth. On the scale of months, adolescent singers often find their vocal range descending, and vocal prescriptions for easing this change (such as kharaj practice) are a common topic in discussions of voice culture. Elderly singers often find their range lowering or shrinking overall, especially after years of concertizing. Conventional ranges also change over the course of decades. While twenty-first-century male vocalists tend to have a *sā* {1} in the range of C♯ or D♯, early twentieth-century recordings of male classical vocalists are often pitched around E or F. Abdul Karim Khan commonly sang around F♯. This is, in part, because microphones have made it possible for men to croon in their lower ranges, whereas singers filling a room with their voice were better off singing in the higher, louder parts of their range. But it also is no doubt a result of the common practice of singing along with recordings of vocal idols (see chapter 5). Early pioneers of singing at lower ranges included Faiyaz Khan,[89] whose tonic was often as low as B, and especially the soft, gentle style of Amir Khan, whose exquisite microphone technique, velvety, closed voice, and low range has served as a model for post-independence khyal (see chapter 4).

While the farthest outer limits of vocal range possibility, like the possible tunings of a stringed instrument, are limited by the length of the vocal folds (~13–17 mm in adult women, ~17–24 mm in adult men), one's practical vocal range as

---

89. The entry about Faiyaz Khan's range in Ramanlal Mehta's 1969 *Agrā Gharānā: Paramparā, Gāyakī aur Cīzen*, 28–29, is worth quoting at length. "Most musicians in those times used to use a high pitch, either a white four, or a black two, or sometimes a white three. This sleight of hand was used to gain better control over voice throw, strength, weight, and brightness. As a result, many musicians neglected their natural sound. Ustād Faiyāz Khān's natural pitch was quite a bit lower. He would sing either from white one or the white seventh of the lower octave. His sound had such strength, weight and rounded timbre that his music stood out as unique. His slow tempo nomtom ālāp had such gravitas, that when it preceded a dhrupad dhamār, one could not find a parallel to the resulting music even among the music of the old masters." (Translation by Arijit Mahalanabis.)

an adult is achieved rather than fixed (they are stretchable through practice, by a few mm). It takes only a few weeks of kharaj practice and other vocal exercise to shift the range up and down by a whole tone or more (see chapter 5). Over the course of months, with careful practice, the range can shift considerably; indeed, it is not unusual for male classical vocalists (especially dhrupad singers) to insist on an initial six months or more of only kharaj practice from prospective disciples, both to extend their lower range and to enrich the upper ranges. L. K. Pandit, now in his eighties, has cultivated his vocal range to such an extent that he casually hums kharaj (a low C♯) with great clarity while attending to household tasks, at any time of day.

Many classical singers strive to cultivate a single sonority that stretches unbroken over the entire vocal range. And yet, such a range is by no means homogenous in practice. Nipa Nag, who grew up singing with a high, thin, *filmi* range with *sā* {1} around C♯, had to adjust her range lower in college for singing *khyal*. Singing *khyal* in a range that high "just doesn't sound like classical. In the lower pitch, *I sound like a different person* [even when I sing the] same song." As Nipa put it, "In the low pitch . . . the orientation is not Bollywood-y. Bollywood means little, high-pitched things." The inverse is true, as well. In her early twenties, Nipa used to sing high up, at C♯, even for classical bandishes, giving them a *filmi* texture. But her professors in the music program at Pune University objected. "All my examiners said '<your voice is good . . . but child, take your pitch down.'>[90] Because it just. . . it doesn't *sound* like classical."

Shireesh Thakur points out that singing in the higher range (D–G) typical of film songs requires a special vocal disposition that is generally unacceptable in khyal—what he calls "falsetto" or "head voice." He has learned this vocal disposition through "Western" voice lessons: "for me, doing Indian classical, I knew I could only go up to *pa* [{5}]. Beyond *pa*—it doesn't exist. . . . But now coming into Western, I do have at least another octave to work on where I can control and do transitions through falsetto. . . . Yeah, so most of the Hindi film songs where my interests lie are between this only, from D to your G, most of the songs will be." Small changes can make a difference as well. I vividly remember an afternoon when a guru-bhai suggested that I sing from D♯ (instead of C♯) to make my voice more nimble. The results were immediate and unmistakable—my tāns were faster and brighter, my intonation was clearer, my voice felt stronger and louder. In many ways, I felt as though I had a different voice at this higher

90. *Acchī āvāz hai . . . lekin beṭā, pic sur nīce kar lo.*

range. The problem, of course, was that singing *rāgas* with a high ambit (such as Adana or Deshkar) now put excessive tension on my voice. This voice centered at D♯ had a rather different spread of vocal regions and capabilities.

Likewise, certain harkat and fast tāns come easliy only at the middle of one's range, and it is difficult to sing fast tāns toward the very bottom or very top of one's range. Just as important, the upper range takes on a distinctive function of public proclamation. Especially among qawwals, this is their most characteristic, publicly recognizable range, singing bright, high, and open: the range of *buland* voice. As Qawwal Mahmud Nizami points out, the lower range, usually reserved for the clear, syllabic enunciation of poetry, is relatively slack (*ḍhīlā*), whereas a higher range offers a certain kind of tonal solidity (*mazbūtī*). This is why qawwals tend to set their *sā* at a higher range than classical singers: "<Because from this [high range], a solidity [*mazbūtī*] abides in the singing; slackness [*ḍhīlāpaṇ*] doesn't come into [the singing] while sustaining a note [*qāym lete*]."[91]> Vocal range in practice is by no means reducible to a homogenous, one-dimensional line segment. Modes of vocalization occur in overlapping vocal zones [*jagah*] with specific local qualities. Two ranges with the same limits may have very different internal territories. One singer may have a deep, whispery low range that fades into a bright medium range around the *ni* below *sā*, and a dull, soft high range that begins in ascents up to *sā*, reaching up to high *pa*. Another singer may have a brassy nasal range that is employed in nom-tom alap reaching from lowest sā to middle *pa*, a rounder tone for songs that mostly fall in the middle range, and a bright nasal tone reserved for high ā from middle *pa* to high *pa*.

Openness, Loftiness, Power

An open voice (*khulī āvāz* or *khulā*[92] *āvāz*), particularly in higher ranges, has a striking effect. For many singers, an open voice is cultivated even at lower ranges. Singing open requires a special cavernous disposition of the pharynx, as though a resonant space has opened in the middle of the head. Open voice tends to be quite a bit louder than closed voice—roughly twice as loud.[93] To call

---

91. *Ki isse jo gāne me jo ek mazbooti rahti. Woh qāym lete, ḍhīlāpaṇ nahi ātā usme.*

92. The –ī ending of khulī accommodates the feminine gender of āvāz in Hindi. In the Marathi-tinged register of Deccani Hindi often used in Bombay and Pune, the grammatical gender of *āvāz* is sometimes masculine, giving *khulā āvāz*.

93. My own coarse measurements of open and closed voice yield an approximately

someone *khulā*, or open, has very much the kind of ethical implications you might expect in English.[94] It implies directness, sincerity, and a lack of inhibition. An old advertisement for a bank in Bombay, for example, used to show a family man in carefree repose by a lake, exhorting its viewers to "live life *khule se*": freely, openly, without concern. One who is *khulā* is not merely truthful; it is not so much that they rigidly and fastidiously insist on bare facts, but rather that they freely "tell it like it is" without concern for the consequences. (If you cannot hear your mistakes, after all, you can't fix them.[95]) The consubstantiality of vocal quality and virtue is so smooth that it was possible, for example, for one current singer to refer quite sensibly to Rāmkrishnabuwā Vāze as "a very *khulī āvāz* type of person." Another nearly equivalent term is *khaḍī āvāz* ("upright" voice), another common term of ethical praise that translates well into anglophone comportmental ethics.

The term *buland* ("lofty") voice, has wide currency among qawwals for an extraordinarily open voice in the highest range, used for moments of maximal intensity. *Buland* voice is generally sung from the chest, with ample nasal resonance, often rendered with vibrato, and always very khula. *Buland* has connotations of piety and righteous public praise. In particular, it evokes the sound of the call to prayer and the moments of maximal affective intensity in florid Qur'anic recitation. Among non-Muslims, this voice is most famously associated with qawwal Nusrat Fateh Ali Khan, often widely employed on film soundtracks at moments of searching or personal revelation (see chapter 4). As a verb, *buland karnā* implies a grand proclamation to a public; one would never *buland karnā* an intimate secret to one other person, for example. Most professional qawwals make a living singing in wide-open outdoor courtyards in Sufi shrines, and thus a strong, high voice is necessary for the songs to be heard and understood. The strong "singer's formant," around 3500 Hz in the above—much like the famously powerful tone cultivated by opera singers to be heard above an orchestra[96]—is typical. But there also appears to be more to this than simple audibility. Several qawwals reported to me that they were able to sing in *buland* voice only with the blessings of God (or the intercession of Sufi saints on their behalf), and that

10 dB difference between them (e.g. ~70 vs. ~80 dB measured at 3 feet.) As the dB scale is logarithmic, this amounts to roughly double the physical intensity.

94. Rahaim 2012, 130.

95. Cf. Rahaim 2013, 223–224.

96. See Beeman in Hobart and Kapferer 2005 on singer's formant.

singing with *buland* voice was, conversely, a way to magnify their blessings. In this way, *buland* voice is a nexus of vocal power, audible public proclamation, and the flow of blessings.

While no one complains about a voice with too much *sur*, openness is a virtue nearly always sought in moderation. Indeed, one can be *khulā* without being very tuneful and vice versa. Many qawwals explicitly caution against "shouting" (*chillānā*), even in wide-open spaces. Years ago, after my first several months of training in the open sonority of Gwalior gayaki, I sang for a prominent singer in Pune from a different gharana, who warned me that my voice had become *so* open that it sounded *unnatural*. She demonstrated how open the mouth gets when talking (about an inch between the lips), measured it between two fingers, and reproduced it while singing. The mouth likewise can also be so open that nasal resonance gets lost.

Indeed, part of what makes an openly disposed voice so striking is that it is so different from the usual disposition of the mouth during speech. Such a voice does not murmur, does not coax, does not have delicate *kahen*. The power of an open voice is thus often contrasted with the virtue of gentleness or sweetness. The opposite of an open voice is often simply described as closed (*band*), *beḍh* (fenced-off), or—tellingly—*fāls* (i.e., false, as in "*fāls woīs*," the usual Hindustani term for *falsetto*). When I was first learning to sing, I would often close my lips or raise the back of my tongue to conceal an out-of-tune note; my teacher would scold me: "*khul ke gāo*"—sing openly.

Sweetness

Sweetness (*mīṭhās, madhuram*) is a quality long attested in the Sanskritic and Persian music-theoretic traditions, and is one of the few vocal qualities that seems to be equally evident to connoisseurs and to untrained listeners. Along with creaminess and oiliness, it seems to be universally desirable (rarely is a bitter or sour voice explicitly called for). It is unclear, of course, what a sweet voice may have sounded like in the sixteenth century. But by the middle of the twentieth century, a pattern of vocal sweetness had crystallized in the great heroes of *filmi* voice (especially Lata, Asha, Kishore, and Rafi Sahab): they tend to be high, smooth, relatively soft, with moderate nasality and relatively gentle enunciation of consonants. The dispositional domain of sweetness overlaps significantly with "thin" and "light." In contrast to the open throat and lowered tongue of *buland* voice, the back of the tongue tends to press upwards and forwards slightly. A sweet voice shows up most directly, however, as a sugary, fluid substance, a palpable enunciative flavor on the tongue and lips, as though the words themselves were sweet.

One of the most controversial features of vocal sweetness is vibrato, or *kāmpit*, which falls on the boundary between kinetics and sonority. At 5–10 cycles per second, it roughly corresponds to trembling, and indeed, *kāmpit* can refer to the trembling of a hand or a leg.[97] But ordinarily, it is heard as a textural feature of a single extended note—sweetness, liveliness, emotional intensity—and tends to be applied to long, still notes rather than as a second-order motion on top of gamaks or meends. Unlike the pitch wobble shown in figure 2.14, which inevitably applies to even very steady, sustained tones, audible vibrato is generally very even and regular. This is quite a different matter from *andolan* (a very slow undulation, usually around 1–3 cycles per second, and with a wider tonal ambit), which is often explicitly prescribed as part of the landscape of very heavy ragas, and which often are visible in singers' gesture.[98] As vibrato has long been popularly associated with opera, centrifugal-nationalist construals of Indian voice claim that it is—or should be—absent from Indian music. Renowned sarodiya and musicologist Kaukab Khan, for example, claimed that the "trembling" voice of European singers displease Indian ears, as it fails to grasp the "essence" of sur. Construing vibrato as a kind of motion, rather than as a kind of sonority, he specifically complained that the voice of popular soprano Nellie Melba "does not rest on any *sur*."[99] He may well have been correct about this particular kind of vibrato, but varieties of vibrato are found in the Hindustani vocal ecumene: from high, declamatory sections of qawwali, to low murmuring of Kabir bhajans,

---

97. Kāmpit is used for other kinds of trembling ornaments apart from what we might ordinarily think of as vibrato. See SRA. In the *Natyasastra* (XIX.45) *kāmpita* is given as a "mode of articulation" rather than an *alankara* (ornament). In later treatises (the *Sangīt Darpan*, the *Madan-e Mūsīqī*, the *Hindustānī Sangīt Paddhati*) kāmpit is listed as a *doṣa* (flaw) of singers.

98. Rahaim 2012, 101–102.

99. Kaukab Khan in Katz 2017, 94. Oddly, he claims that the harmonium also produces tremolo. This may be in reference to the tremolo stop on some models that produces an amplitude variation (like a modern tremolo pedal) but not frequency variation (like vibrato). But it also places Kaukab Khan in line with the casual discursive conflation of all things Western, typical of music writings in the decades leading up to Indian independence (cf. Rahaim 2011).

to the microphonic crooning of film songs and *filmi* renditions of ghazals.[100] The most austere genres of raga music are exceptional in this regard; they do indeed tend to cultivate long, still notes without vibrato. Conversely, even when singing with vibrato (as, for example, Lata often did), a singer may be said to have excellent sur, and indeed, to be singing with particular sweetness.

When deployed properly, sweet voice can be a powerful vehicle for a poetics of tenderness and vulnerability; it has thus, since the reign of Mehdi Hassan, become the default sonority for rendering romantic ghazals. But as we will see in chapter 4, sweetness (like sugar itself) has its ethical detractors as well, construing the sweet voice that dominated the late twentieth century as false and saccharine.

Indeed, nearly all vocal dispositions are subject to ethical contestation. As we have seen, however, these are not projections of human character onto a neutral acoustic field; they emerge from various stances on a dispositional character already heard in ways of voice.[101] As we will see in chapter 3, however, these dispositions do not simply reside in individual voices; they are developed and come to life in relation with listeners and fellow singers.

---

100. See Deva 1959.

101. Berger 2010.

THREE
Vocal Relationality

Agar naśā śarāb meṃ hotā toh bāṭaleṃ nā jhūmtī?
"If intoxication were located in the wine itself, wouldn't the bottles be swaying?"

We are packed into a comfortable living room, three dozen of us, on several rugs spread out on the floor, leaning against the walls, squeezed in between bookshelves and doorways. The singer, who until now has been carefully tuning the tanpura with his eyes closed, his attention focused entirely on the precise intonation of the strings, now opens his eyes and regards us. He greets us formally, singling out a few special connoisseurs in the audience. He addresses us as *rasikas* ("tasters," accomplished listeners) and announces the raga he will sing in the common idiom: "In front of you (*āpke sāmne*), I will present rāg . . ." He asks permission (*ijāzat*) from one of the special connoisseurs seated in front of him, who responds in turn with an open palm of invitation. A hush falls over the room; now all that is heard is the drone of the tanpura. My friend and I lean forward silently, pushing all other sounds to the periphery of our awareness. Outside, a vegetable seller sings out the litany of his wares, but it doesn't pull our attention away; for us, yearning for the *ālāp* to come, there is only one voice we are prepared to hear right now. The vocalist lets us have it; he lowers his eyes, takes a breath, opens his mouth, and fills the room with a steady, open, ringing *ā*. All other sound fades into the background, and we are utterly absorbed in his sur. He takes another breath and comes out with a sighing phrase, dropping down from above and gliding up gracefully from below before settling on the tonic. Just when the steadiness of the tone takes on the quality of a *svara*, a stable note with its own integrity, he climbs a bit higher up, building tension, before gliding down and back up to the tonic. The grace of this phrase makes my heart ache; I press my hand to my chest and my friend does the same, shaking his head slowly in stylized wonderment. We are not alone; two people in the front row simultaneously murmur *kyā bāt hai*,[1] a common formula of praise. The singer opens his eyes, gestures at his own heart in deference, and continues. As the performance proceeds, the responses from the audience become louder and clearer. Listeners call out *wāh!* at dazzling or heart-melting or unexpected phrases; they mark the culmination of metric cycles with a nod or a flick of the wrist; they extend their open hands in delighted bafflement. The singer, in turn, spurred on by their support, gives them more of what they respond to. Over the next thirty minutes, as his phrases fly faster and soar higher, the intensity increases, and so too does the praise from the audience, so that a mutual rapport emerges between singer and listener, in which the singer's voice comes alive. The room is transformed into an altogether different sort of place than what it was just a few hours ago; the singer's voice becomes an altogether different sort of entity.

This is a *mahfil*,[2] an intimate gathering-for-listening, the site for vocal relationality par excellence in the Hindustani vocal ecumene (see chapter 1). The heart of a mahfil is its relational structure. Its particular architecture or repertoire is secondary: it may happen on a train, in a bedroom, on a balcony; it might consist of five to seven friends sitting on the ground in a circle, or dozens more leaning against the walls; its songs may consist of romantic thumris, ghazals of mystical love, or didactic khyals.[3] Singing for such a gathering requires more than just speed, improvisational fluidity, and sweetness; it also requires a special mutual attunement, with the listeners seated before you. A properly attuned singer is connected to their listeners, who, in turn, are deeply attuned to the singer's voice.

We will soon return to the relational possibilities of the mahfil format. First,

---

1. Lit., "What a thing!"

2. Sometimes also called *jalsā*, *majlīs*, or *baiṭhak*.

3. See Niranjana 2020 for more on the wide range of spaces for mahfils. There also can be instrumental mahfils, though these are rarer and tend to consist exclusively of raga music.

we step back for a moment to consider Hindustani practices of listening more broadly.

Practices of Listening

Though listening to a voice is often an occasion for profound delight, active listening is about far more than personal pleasure.[4] A shared, consocial attunement is precisely what allows a voice to show up as a matter of common ethical concern. The Sufi practice of *samā* (listening with the heart to an esoteric spiritual content in qawwālī), for example, has long been at the heart of Chishti traditions of ethical self-refinement. There's a story of someone coming to the great Chishti saint Nizamuddin Auliya in the thirteenth century bemoaning the fact that "no one is capable of *samā* anymore"; Nizamuddin replied, "If no one were capable of *samā* then the world would end . . ." Public voices are disclosed, evaluated, and morally contested through disciplined, institutionally ratified practices of listening. The world-disclosing potential of listening also figures in the pedagogical desiderata of populist nationalism. It seems that when V. D. Paluskar, vocalist and "missionary" of twentieth-century Hindustani music reform, was challenged to name a great singer that his school had produced, he famously replied that his schools hadn't produced a *Tānsen* (a legendary virtuosic singer of the Mughal court)—but they had produced a great many *Kānsens* (i.e., properly enculturated listeners).[5] Teaching ordinary citizens to listen properly to this newly forming national music, training a national ear in a common aural canon, was a task that every major reformer shared. In the decades after independence, an unprecedented wave of doctors, lawyers, clerks, and middle-class children learned to become connoisseurs of raga music. This project of training listeners to listen for something other than mere pleasure is often hailed as a nationalist breakthrough whereby thousands of Indian national subjects reclaimed their musical birthright, free at last to hear what had theretofore been sealed off in palaces, salons, and hereditary households. Indeed, the success of this movement is apparent in the seemingly self-evident transparency of listening-for-tones that undergirds so much modern raga theory.

---

4. See, for example, Kapchan's vivid account of practices of listening in the Boutshishiyya Sufi order, 2009, 73–77.

5. Bakhle 2005, 191. The play on words substitutes *kāṇ* (ear) for *tān*.

There is, of course, a strange tension between the idea of a national sensibility and the fact that citizens must be *trained* into it. In the mahfil scene I sketched earlier, for example, the teenage son of our host was squirming around, fidgeting with his trouser leg, checking his phone furtively—he was tuned into something rather different than his uncles and aunts were. If he somehow develops this listening practice, it will not appear one blessed day like a moustache; he'll have to acquire it just as his aunt and uncle did. These practices of listening may seem natural and transparent once achieved, but they take years to develop: sometimes through poetic or vocal or spiritual training, sometimes through explicit instruction, sometimes by passively absorbing a poetic or melodic repertoire—but always in relationship to particular vocal exemplars. Such aural pedagogies, in turn, have their own structural and institutional conditions of possibility: *gharānās*, music schools, ashrams, temples, and Sufi shrines all offer particular regimes of aurality to some and not others. In other words, the mutually adjusted relational dispositions of listening and voicing take place *between* singers and listeners, and in fact are unthinkable without lived, situated relationships between disciplined consociates. This is not to say that the dispositions of listening and voicing are necessarily symmetrical, or that they form a single seamless acoustemology. Qawwals and their Sufi patrons have mutually constitutive, relationally attuned, but quite *different* skills and dispositions, offering radically different sorts of spiritual and social possibilities. Further, as we will see, these practices of listening—which may at first seem to be invisible, personal, and subjective—are often publicly on display and fiercely contested.

Some listeners are drawn by the intellectual challenge of discerning rare rāgas; others are drawn by the heart-aching call of poetry; still others (rarer, perhaps, in the city) by a devotional yearning for the sonic adoration of a beloved saint or divinity. Devotees of classical music often find themselves at a loss when faced by qawwali; they may awkwardly attempt to identify the raga at hand, or nod at the occasional virtuosic melisma, but entirely miss the resounding poetic resonances that draw listeners around them into tears and ecstasy. For a listener who savors and cherishes the impact of the sung word, the price paid for melodic plenitude is poetic impoverishment. Bhajan singers or qawwals who have taken hundreds or thousands of verses to heart often find a classical vocalist grinding through endless elaborations on a single word to be numbingly repetitious and dry. As one Kabir singer said: "If you know rāg and tāl, you'll say *kyā bāt hai*," but "if you're in *bhakti*, you won't understand it."[6] A great many people who come to a concert of rāga music sit restlessly through an hour or two of what to them are meaningless, interminable tones, waiting for the lyrically rich, "light" songs that resonate with their poetic attunements; many connoisseurs of rāga, for their part, have no ear for the poetics of bhajans or ghazals, and often scoff at these apparently saccharine tidbits which seem to lack the modal depth disclosed by an attunement to rāga. These practices of listening are undertaken with the whole body, including posture, movement, and even vocalization alongside attentional and temporal attunements. For a properly attuned connoisseur, listening is an active practice that tunes in to a world of vocal action—as G. N. Goswamy puts it, "perfecting the rendering of the song by the force of their own imagination and emotion."[7] Participants in devotional kirtan—from Sikhs to Varkaris to Hari Krishna—sing along with repeated refrains, joining their voices in praise; yet for a Sufi listener to do so in a *samā* would distract from the poetic force of the ritual. Likewise, the explicit gestural-vocal expressions of praise and delight expected of a connoisseur of rāga music would violate the careful etiquette of qawwali at a dargah, turning the attention of pilgrims seeking blessings to the singers rather than to the saint whose blessings are sought. These practices of listening are undertaken with the whole body, choreographed with the musicking bodies of singers, implicating posture, movement, and even vocalization alongside attentional and temporal attunements.

In cultivating a discipline of listening, a new world opens up. Powers of voice suddenly come into focus that one scarcely had access to before. It is in this sense that a skilled listener practices what Ananda Coomaraswamy called "an art of his own"[8] that not only helps him appreciate sounds, but also discloses a world of vocal possibility—a *duniyā*. Poetry may come alive, a rāga may come into focus, a message may be revealed; one may even be palpably moved to chills, goosebumps, and tears.

For a singer, enculturation into a vocal disposition requires attunement to a particular kind of listener. A singer touches the hearts of their listeners, pleasing them, winning them over, persuading them. Dhrupadiya Sadiq Ali Khan compared this art of listening to courtship; a singer "expects his listeners to seduce

6. See Shabnam Virmani's film *Koi Sunta Hai*, around 56:20, where they imitate a classical singer spinning out endless variations on the word "māyā."

7. Goswamy 1986, 18.

8. Coomaraswamy 1917, 73.

him into doing his best."[9] The relation with listeners is the very essence of many singers' vocal aspirations; as singer Nupur Joshi put it, she doesn't sing just "to sound nice," but "to touch people's hearts." During *samā*, elite Sufi listeners strive to discern a special esoteric message, heard directly by the heart, offering an ecstasy that is not even available to the qawwal who is reciting the poem. The moral authority granted by proper listening is often explicitly juxtaposed with political authority, as in the many stories of musicians correcting a nobleman's understanding of raga, or Sufi poet Mir Dard correcting the Mughal emperor's posture at a *samā*.[10]

Circuits of Voice

Think of this mutual attunement as a dynamic circuit.[11] As Kabir singer Shabnam Virmani once described it to me, the "wisdom" of Kabir's mystical songs does not simply emerge from an arrangement of words or notes on the page, but publicly, among people: "It's in a throbbing, pulsating place between listener and performer. . . . Some sort of circuitry is '*bzzzz*' because something got connected." The sonic figure of the buzzing circuit is particularly apt for a relational figuration of voice: without a relational connection between its components, there may be a latent electrical valence, but there is no continuous *bzzz*. The mutal attachment, or *lagan*, between a listener sung-to and a singer listened-to does not produce an undifferentiated oneness; singing emerges relationally, *between* singer and listener. This circuit is constitutive of—not merely a context for—voice. Hindustani vocal teachers of all kinds often give advice pitched in implicitly relational terms: singing so that it has "impact," so that it "strikes" the listeners, or, as a teacher of Rita Sahai's teachers once told her, your "voice should be such that when you open your mouth, people should be quiet." In one common formulation, a sharp (*dhār*) voice, like a sword, should "cut" listeners. Voice, in every ethically and politically meaningful sense, is fundamentally, rather than incidentally, relational. The circuit between singers and listeners, in all of the Hindustani worlds that we survey here, is mutually constitutive. Just

9. Chaubey 1958, 47–48.

10. Ziad 2010, 375.

11. Eidsheim depicts the primacy of the listener, circuitously implicated with the voice, in elegant diagrammatic form (2019, 12–13).

as listening is listening-*to*, singing is, at minimum, singing-*to*. The listener is an inseparable limb of voice.

This intuitive sense of vocal relationality is marked out in everyday speech. It is the very substance of the Hindustani aphorism, "Melody is that which spirit hears and spirit makes-heard" (*naġhmā vahī naġhmā jo rūh sune aur rūh sunāe*). The verb root of "make heard" here is *sunā-*, a modification of *sun-* "to hear." *Sunā-* is the usual Hindustani verb root used for singing-for-listeners; its implication of listeners is built-in, both grammatically and pragmatically.[12] Sitting among friends at home, in order to request a song, one is likely to say "*ek* ġazal *sunāo*" ("let us hear a ghazal"). The textbook Hindustani verb for singing is *gāo*, and certainly this is the verb you would use for singing in solitude, or when talking abstractly about an individual singer or a recording.[13] But once one is actually sitting in a musical situation—especially in an intimate gathering of connoisseurs—it would be a bit harsh to simply ask a singer to *gāo* a ghazal.[14] *Sunāo* functions as the aural equivalent of "show"[15]—a relational activity that already implies an audience. And just as one doesn't *show* something without someone to show it to, sunaoing happens only in relation to a listener: "She was sunaoing us a *thumri* at the wedding" or "Uncle used to sunao us that passage

---

12. Another common form uses the auxiliary verb *denā* ("to give")—for example, *sunā do*—to emphasize the offering of song *from* singer *to* listener. Another common relational verb used for vocal performance is *pesh karnā*—to "present," or "offer" a rāg or a song. See also Narayan 2016, 141, for a discussion of the relationality of *guānā* "to cause to sing."

13. For example, *voh bahut acche gāte haiṃ* ("he sings very well"), or *maiṃ filmī gīt gātī hūṃ* ("I sing film songs"), etc.

14. The verb stems are *gā* and *sunā*. *-o* endings are commonly used in adapting the verbs for English grammatical constructions. There certainly are situations where *gā-* is appropriate. For example, a teacher may indeed command a student to, for example, sing openly ("*khul ke gāo!*") It further is used to reference song-objects: individual songs and song genres (as distinct from other songs and song genres, without reference to listeners) are called by the noun form *gānā*. *Sunānā* also has a specialized use in one particular relational vocal scenario—virtuosic, face-to-face, verbal insult, characteristically heightened by a pair of echoing opposites depicting manner: *ulṭī-sīdhī sunānā*, ūṃcī-nīcī *sunānā*, *ainḍī-bainḍī sunānā*, *khoṭī-kharī sunānā*, etc.

15. In specific cases, singing may even be described as "showing" (*dikhānā*, lit. "causing-to-see") particular techniques or patterns. Were there a handy English form of *show* that applied to hearing, this would be the perfect translation of *sunānā*.

from the *Gita* about duty." In my early stages of learning Hindi, I was puzzled by this turn of phrase. It seemed to me that *sunao* was merely a roundabout way of describing singing or speaking. But I've now come to feel that *sunao-ing* (which always implicitly assumes a relation with a listener) is an important conceptual resource for understanding vocal socialities. The ratio between *gao* and *sunao* is the ratio between vocalizing in the abstract and situated, relational singing-for-others. To *sunao* for a room of tuned-in listeners fills you with new musical ideas, strengthens you, gives you courage and stamina to keep going for much longer than it seems like you could otherwise, supported by what G. N. Goswamy calls the *utsāha* of the audience—their enthusiasm, responsiveness, energy, and zeal.[16]

This responsive energy comes in many currencies. Vocal dispositions are tuned for *particular* circuits of voicing and listening that emerge between properly attuned listeners and properly disposed singers. As a singer, I find that different audiences call forth different vocal dispositions according to their own sensitivities. In singing for mahfils of listeners who intuitively appreciate vigorous, heavy gamak (see chapter 2), it is easy for me to get into this groove. Their heads sway subtly, they meet me gesturally at the culmination of rhythmic cycles, they utter words of support; it is as though the movements of my voice fall into resonance with the rhythm of their listening. For other listeners, heaviness doesn't register; only sweetness—light, delicate *harkat*, a crooning sonority, delicate pronunciation and clear poetic phrasing—finds its way to their heart. Still others prefer the rollercoaster thrill of fast tāns. Accompanists are often acute listeners, as well, and indeed, the *cāl* of a voice (see chapter 2) is often conditioned by the groove reciprocally established between vocalist and accompanist.[17] For a qawwal, attending to a particular listener's spiritual arousal and driving it further with just the right poetic-melodic formulae is the very essence of their skill. Mughal accounts of singers often make note of the patron *to whose pleasure* singers were especially attuned (as when, for example, Burhani Amirkhani "sings in accordance with the pleasure of Amir Khan (*Amir Khan ke zauq ke mutabiq gata hai*)."[18] Critics often report which parts of a concert resonated with an audience (as with the account of Alla Bande Khan's 1925 concert, in which gamak and

16. Goswamy 1986, 17.

17. A great deal of ethnomusicological literature has dealt with relations between singer and accompanists. Clayton and Leante 2017; Leante 2016; Napier 2007; Neuman (Dan) 1997, Neuman (Dard) 2004; Silver 1984.

18. Dargah Quli Khan in Lath 1988, 11.

nasal resonance fell flat—only when he shifted to "the style of Alapa, 'nom-tom' and 'tanas,' free from guttural explosions of gamakas, that the audience listened to them patiently"[19]). Singers often speak about the heavy responsibility for singing for learned audiences. Audiences in Pune, for example, have a reputation for evaluating raga grammar; Dehli audiences for poetic rigor. In many cases, listening to a voice thus entails ethical responsibilities complementary to the ethical responsibilities that fall to singers. Singers and connoisseurs alike often complain of audiences that only respond to fireworks precisely because it calls forth a certain disposition in vocalists. B. R. Deodhar relates a conversation with Bade Ghulam Ali Khan, in which Khansahab anticipates the disapproval of his audience if he sings in an "orderly" fashion: "*We came in the expectation of some fireworks, tans and punjabi graces and the fellow is wasting his time* [*with slow elaboration*]." Khansahab's response, for Deodhar, is tragic: "When I realize this my concentration fails me and I begin to sing the way they want"—Deodhar calls such a circuit a "vicious cycle."[20] In this light, stories of great singers who refused to perform for unprepared audiences[21] may not merely be a snobbish reticence to cast pre-made vocal pearls before swine, but rather a caution about the kind of voice that might be called forth by such listeners.

We now survey a few other different forms of vocal circuitry, proceeding from seemingly involuntary quasi-affective responses, through highly refined practices of connoisseurship, mystical attunement, and participation in collective devotion. Each habitus of listening,[22] and its concomitant form of circuitry, scaffolds, demands, and affords ethical possibilities for particular forms of vocal comportment. By the end of the chapter, I will loop around to forms of voicing that appear to be *anti*-social—for example, singing to an imagined public; to one's *self*; or even to a divine Auditor. These irrelational aspirations typically stand out as extraordinary precisely in contrast to a normative primal scene of voice: a gathering of listeners in which singer and listener are bound together in mutual vocal rapport.

---

19. Report 1925, 84.

20. Deodhar 1993, 58–59.

21. Scarimbolo 2014, 524 and passim.

22. See Becker 2004, 70–71.

Vocal Impact: Tāsīr

Late one night in Bombay, at an intimate *mahfil*, Naina Devi and Hirabai Barodekar were taking turns elaborating on the famous thumri "*Bājuband khula khula jā*." Hirabai's student, Shailaja, sitting close by, suddenly found tears flowing down her cheeks. She teared up as she told me about this powerful moment, carefully distinguishing these tears from the sobbing that accompanies sorrowful weeping:

> I started—it was not weeping—it was, you know, ā*nanda*: ecstasy! Ec-sta-*sy*! It was flowing from my eyes. It was like a—I cannot explain. I was so emotionally elevated. . . . So [Hirabai] stopped in-between and said, "Do you remember your mother? Or why you are weeping?" [I said,] "I am not weeping, please don't stop!"

Chills, tears, a "churning of the stomach,"[23] goosebumps, utter mind-halting captivation, a palpable ache in the chest—*tāsīr* ("impact," also *asar*)[24] is used broadly to refer to these irresistible responses to voice, simultaneously blissful and painful. This range of powerful responses (like voice production itself) is usually felt to occur in the central core of the body—not, crucially, in the ear itself. The heart (*dil*) is its principal receptive organ. As qawwal Sharukh Niyazi once put it to me, in order to make a listener's hair stand on end (*rom rom khaṛā*), a qawwal's voice should connect itself to their heart (*āvāz lag rahī hai dil pe*). This impact is sometimes described in terms of *dard* (pain), *ṭīs* (stabbing), *hazin* (reflective pathos), and with two nearly interchangeable words for yearning for a distant beloved, *firāq* and *viraha*, from Sufi and bhakti lineages, respectively. This yearning is often highly prized and deliberately sought after: as a contest of courtly virtue, as a way of winning patrons, or even, in devotional situations, as

---

23. Nagaraj, 2013.

24. *Tāsīr* and *asar* are both derived from the same Arabic trilateral root (a-th-r; th often becomes /s/ in Hindustani-Persianate pronunciation). Despite a clear but subtle technical distinction derived from Arabic (*tāsīr* refers to the making of an impression, while *asar* refers to the impression itself), the two terms are often used interchangeably in colloquial Hindustani. Their usage in reference to an emotional force on the edge of pleasure and pain invoked by music has much in common with what is now called *ṭarab* (ecstasy) in Arab music. See Racy 2004.

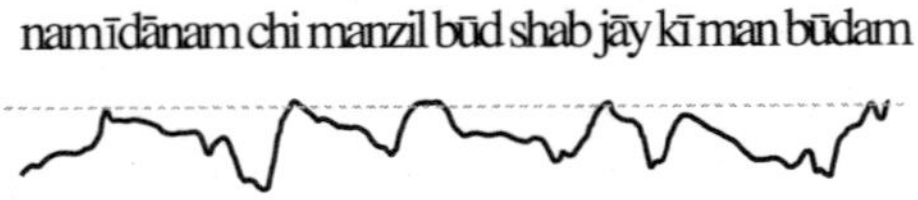

FIGURE 3.1 "*Nami dānam*" recited without asar

a way of arousing longing for spiritual union with a divine Beloved. Wajid Ali Shah, legendary nineteenth-century connoisseur and musician, describes the impact of the great courtesan Waziran's performance: "Tears from my eyes had become fixed in my pupils, until at last I was left in a stupefied state (*be ḳhwudī ke ālam meṃ*) and unable to contain myself (*mujhmeṃ ẓabṯ kī tāqat na rahī*)."[25]

Expressing emotions is neither necessary nor sufficient for these effects.[26] Though singers often speak of singing "from the heart," and are even sometimes themselves deeply moved in the course of a performance, they often actively *resist* being carried away by feeling. One may tear up between verses, but it is hard to sing between sobs; a skilled singer must thus be able to evoke tears without giving themselves over to crying. Though there is no single vocal trick to touching a listener's heart—the circuit, not the sound, is primary—there are some general tendencies: singing toward the top of one's range, in poetic rather than metrical rhythm, brightened by nasal resonance, heightened by melismata. Qawwal Chand Nizami once demonstrated for me the difference between a voice that has an effect on a listener and a voice that does not, using the first line of the famous poem by Amir Khusro, *nami dānam chi manzil būd shab jāy kī man būdam* (I wonder what [strange] place I was in last night). He first recited the line very quickly, marking the accents isochronously on a single tone, slurring the words together carelessly, as shown in figure 3.1.

The "wonder" at the "strange place," when recited in this way, sounded like someone casually remarking on a missed turn down an unknown street. He smiled, shook his head, and said of this desultory rendition, "the *taste* isn't coming" (*mazā na ā rahā hai*).[27] His sons and the others gathered in the room chuckled. But then he took a breath, closed his eyes, and sang the same line with

25. In Williams 2014, 97.

26. On the shortcomings of "expression theory" for accounting for raga music, see Saxena 2010, 8.

27. See Anjaria and Anjaria 2020 on mazā.

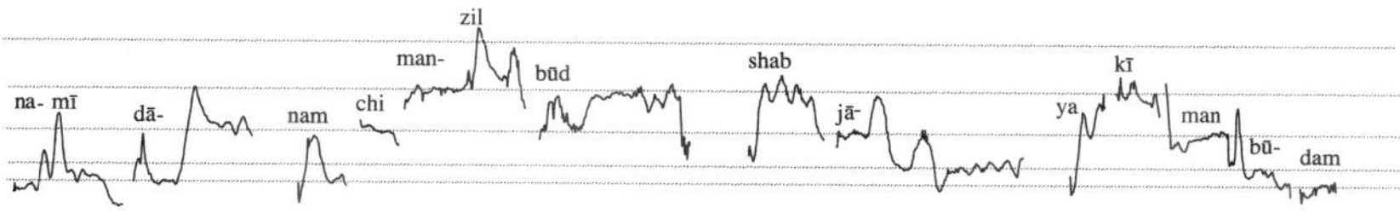

FIGURE 3.2 *"Nami dānam"* recited with asar

slow, meandering grace, exquisitely in tune, with graceful *harkat* and *kāmpit* (see figure 3.2).

By the time he reached the apex of "*manzil*," his sons joined their voices with him, swept up in the flow of a canonical line they evidently knew deeply. Opening his eyes, he said, "Thus, the effect will fall upon the listeners (*to sunewāle pe asar paḍegā*)." The comment was unnecessary. This rendering had given me chills; another connoisseur who was sitting with us and drinking tea wiped tears from his eyes. The whole room seemed to fall silent, suffused with a palpable poetic atmosphere.

Tasir in this sense seems to just come over you, whether you want it or not.[28] Accounts of great mahfils describe singers casting a spell on an unwitting audience,[29] or drenching a mahfil with tears.[30] Ghulam Haider Khan recalls feeling as though "something forceful had gripped [him]" and brought him to tears when he first heard Salamat and Nazakat Ali Khan.[31] In Imam Hakim's classic account, tasir is a spirit (*muwakkal*) conjured by a singer's magical incantation (*duā bā tarkīb*) of a raga.[32] Others report something like temporary self-annihilation: getting "lost" in notes,[33] "entrancing . . . captivating . . . pure hypnotism,"[34] a silent loss of self-consciousness,[35] or, conversely, being "lost to

28. This specific usage is like *hāl*, which can refer either to "condition" in general or specifically to the extraordinary condition of ecstatic trance.

29. Deshpande 1989, 83.

30. Haldankar 199, 59.

31. Khan (Ghulam Haider) 2010.

32. Schofield and Orsini 2016, 27.

33. See the interview with the Nizami brothers in Nicholas Magriel's video "*Dekhiye, Sikhiye, Parakhiye* (Watch, Learn, and Understand), Islamic mysticism and musical enculturation."

34. Deshpande 1989, 2.

35. See Miner 1993, 85.

the world."[36] It is in this sense that notes themselves are said to be "murderous," bringing the heart of a listener into a "fury of delight."[37] Even music theorist V. N. Bhatkhande, usually remembered as a stern grammarian of raga, attested again and again to the magical effects of singing on a listener. In his more philosophical moments, he described singing as a form of enchantment over a listener (*mohini*), and described vocal techniques that have astonishing effects (*camatkārik pariṇām, vilakṣaṇ pariṇām*), or, on the other hand, can settle the audience into calmness (śānt *hoūn basel*).[38]

The listener is typically described as utterly passive in such accounts, both gramatically and metaphysically. The ways of listening that afford these effects are not even ordinarily described as practices at all. Though musicians can demonstrate the relational vocal habits that move the listener,[39] there is no conventional name for the subtle noetic stances that produce it. It is thus tempting to consider tasir to be a kind of pure affect, perfectly coincident with the voice, independent of enculturation, refection, or training.

And yet, these profound effects do seem to depend on acquired, if unconscious, practices of listening available to some and not others. This is evidenced, in part, by the innumerable stories of listeners that just don't get it. The canonical example is provided by theologian Mohammad al-Ghazali's twelfth-century defense of *samā*, suggesting that those who oppose music are simply insensitive to it, implying that music-haters lack even the refinement of camels (who can be aroused by song). Many uninitiated nineteenth-century travelers seem to have been immune to *tasir* upon first hearing Hindustani music. Some were positively

---

36. Bhatkhande, *HSP*, Vol. 3, 244–248.

37. Ziad 2007, 555.

38. Bhatkhande, *HSP*, Vol. I, 41, 42, 224, and passim (translated from Marathi). Also *Lakṣyasaṅgīta*, Canto 2, Verses 215–221, p. 134. "It is true when they say that music is a kind of magic spell [*mohini*]. The singer should produce such an effect in the listener's mind by using these tools for his presentation—appropriate mood, gestures, language, and rāga."

39. Qureshi describes several vocal functions that yield "sadness and weeping" in *ghazal* performance: "the prolongation of notes on appropriate long syllables, often at a salient point in the rhyme syllable at the end of a verse line," and "a lyrical 'soft' voice" that evokes *dard* (Qureshi 1990, 476). She also suggests that descending melismas may "evoke the sound of weeping" and thereby "arouse grief" (480).

repulsed by "screeching notes";[40] others were simply bored, faced with vocalists who apparently "[remain] for hours together in the same attitude, singing a monotonous air."[41] Nor is this a simple matter of national sensibility. Many Hindustani connoisseurs of film music or ghazals find raga music to be dry and boring; qawwals may turn up their noses at film music; khyaliyas from different lineages often find each others' vocal dispositions dry, cheap, or empty. But the strongest evidence for the comportmental contingency of *tasir* is that one can acquire the capacity for it over time. When sufficiently preoccupied or nervous or distracted, one cannot tune in properly, and no voice seems to have any magic. *Tasir* is no mere spinal reflex; as we will see, it depends on cultivated practices of listening.

Ras *and the* Rasika

Powerful voices are said to contain flavor, or *ras*; inversely, a voice that has no effect is often called "dry." *Ras* has a venerable lineage in elite Sanskritic and Persianate literature, often placed in a canonical scheme of nine distinctive types of *ras* evoked through music, poetry, and drama.[42] But *ras* has a parallel vernacular usage among musicians in reference to a single substance of emotional intensity. In Hindustani poetics, *ras* has long served as a wine-like fluid of longing and intoxication, as in the common poetic formula "*ras ke bharī nainā*" (eyes full of *ras*), which ambiguously evokes a lover's intoxicating eyes and the "wine-filled" eyes of a charismatic Sufi shaykh or even Krishna himself. Among the *doṣas* (flaws) listed for bad singers in early modern music treatises was *virasa* (*ras*-lessness),[43] suggesting the lack of a single substance (rather than nine

---

40. Skinner in Farrell 1999, 22.

41. Solvyns in Miner 1993, 99. On the other hand, some European listeners were surprised to find themselves developing an ear for Indian music—see, for example, Bernier 1826, 296.

42. The classical scheme delineated nine (and sometimes ten) distinctive kinds of emotional *ras*—compassionate, fearful, erotic, etc.—evoked by drama or poetry. Medieval Persian and Sanskrit musical treatises often assigned specific *ras* to specific *svaras*, often as part of a totalizing scheme linking planets, humors, and affects in a closed system (Schofield 2016, 418). Modern commentators, too, often attempt to assign a ras to a raga or two, though these assignations rarely agree with each other; in any case, few if any ragas can be seen to evoke the classical ras of disgust, humor, or fear.

43. Bhatkhande 1954, 18; Imam 1959, 18.

separate ones). The *ras* that a singer either has or lacks serves as a substance of vocal character, akin to the Galenic humors of Yunani medicine, as likely to be found in their voice as in their eyes. (When we hear of voices "laden with pathos [*hazin*]," we find a similar ontology of vocal substance, albeit called by a different name, made available to sensitive listeners.[44]) At devotional sites, certain occasions of participatory singing are held to be particularly full of ras; a particularly powerful occasion of Sikh kirtan, for example, might be said to be ras-drenched (*ras-bhinna*), or to offer a "taste" of divine union.[45] Accordingly, the bhakti-inflected sense of ras is often quite distinct from the sense implied in rāga music. This became clear to me one evening in Pune when I was boring my gracious hosts with a heavy nom-top alap, hewing to the grammar of an arcane rāga, adrift in a vast but poetically arid modal space. Seeing that I was losing my audience, I switched to a Meera bhajan. As soon as I launched into the well-known refrain *pag ghunghru bānd Mīrā nācī re*, they sat up and generously offered me gestures of satisfaction and approval. The matriarch of the family even hummed along. "Ah!" she said immediately afterwards, "that one had much more *ras*." She was right; but whatever *ras* may have been there in the room with us, it was not emanating from my throat. It emerged between us in a circuit.

The circuit of ras is completed by its dyadic complement: the *rasika*, the connoisseur, the one who tastes. "Tasting" *ras* is not as simple as registering the chemical-sensorial zing of honey or pepper; on the contrary, it calls for discernment of a subtle, essential flavor often hidden by superficial features like sweetness or spiciness. A rasika acquires these capabilities of discernment through many years of listening, study, and practice.[46] Indeed, the class implications of this subject position (like a connoisseur who is said to have cultivated a "taste" in painting) are so strong that it is possible to translate *rasika* simply as "one who has good taste."[47] And yet, to be a rasika is not merely to sit in solitude and approve or disapprove of sounds according to an implicit grammar of class standards. The elevated sense of co-presence and attunement at a good mahfil rests precisely on the dispositional attunement of gathered rasikas. Indeed, the very act of tasting, like "impact," requires at least two entities, inviting a relational

44. Brown in Bor 2010.

45. Kaur 2016.

46. See Pollock 2016, 16–17 and 31–34. See also Sathaye 2010.

47. Chloë Alaghband-Zadeh (2017) has worked out this reading of rasika subjectivity quite thoroughly and systematically.

ontology, and affirming the central importance of listeners at a mahfil.[48] In this sense, ras and tasir are easily conflated: both are specific to a particular occasion, with particular singers—and, crucially, particular listeners.[49]

Mahfil Relationality

Rasikas, like all listeners, are doing far more than passively subjecting themselves to vocal effects. They are actively savoring the subtle enunciation of vocal poetics, discerning the form of a raga, following along. Such a gathering is joined not just in cognition or beliefs, but in shared spaces of mode and meter, kinetics and sonority, poetics and deep feeling. They furthermore bear a responsibility to listen properly and to praise the performer appropriately (to give *dād*) when they are touched by the tasir of the singing. Common expressions of praise include "*kyā bāt hai,*" "*subhān Allāh,*" "*bahut ḳhūb,*" or even, at times, inchoate exclamations such as "*āhā,*" "*are,*" "*vāh,*" etc. The essence of dād is not in its verbal content, but in its relationality—it performs and affirms an ongoing bond between singer and listener. Particularly in genres like *khyal* and *ṭhumri*, where singers are improvising more or less constantly, this circuit of singing and listening is essential to the unfolding of a performance, rather than an incidental tag hanging on the outside.[50] In recordings from the golden age of urban mahfils, in the 1950s and '60s, the singer's voice is often drowned out by periodic choruses of *dād* from the listeners.

---

48. See Goswamy 1986, 22 for a rendering of the classic relational figuration of ras in Bharata's *Naryasastra* (early first millenium CE): "just as well-disposed people while eating food cooked with many kinds of spices enjoy its taste . . . so the cultured people taste the durable emotional states."

49. See Dard Neuman 2004, 54.

50. Any of these phrases may be used in praise of spoken or recited utterances, in poetry recitals, or even elevated public conversation, from theological debates in a dargah to academic conferences in an auditorium. But their preeminent setting is certainly the mahfil, and especially for the performance of khyal, ghazal, thumri, and Sufi song. See Daniel Neuman (1990 [1980], 76–77). Van der Meer (2014), Brian Silver (1984) points out that mahfil etiquette evokes the prestigious adab of courts. See Dard Neuman (2004, 2012) on embodied vs. classificatory knowledge. See also Leante and Clayton (Clayton 2007, Clayton and Leante 2015); Meddegoda 2018; and Silver in Metcalf 1984, 315–329.

Part of the pleasure of giving dād at a mahfil is the pleasure of giving it together with others. A chorus of *āhā!*, responding to the same remarkable moment, both by virtue of a shared world and through a kind of relational resonance, affirms a bond between listeners as well—no less than cricket fans who respond together as one.[51] Musical connoisseurs (*rasikas*) are an irreducible part of the vocal circuit, not a mere context for the presentation of material.[52] Descriptions of great singers often are situated in a mahfil, described in inherently relational terms, according to who hears and how:

> *Dhrupad*-singers were pleased with [Bhaskarbuwa Bakhle's] *vilambit alapi* [slow expansive phrases], *khayal*-singers acclaimed the fast *tana* passages with raised hands and with cries like "*Subhan Allah*." Expert percussionists . . . excitedly applauded [his] *layakari* (rhythmic play). In short, every member of the audience had something special to admire . . .[53]

Though such accounts often come across as celebratory praise, it is important to note that *dād* is more than the empirical affirmation of objectively good singing. It is also eminently performative and aspirational. Young singers are often praised ardently by their elders in their early, shaky public performances precisely in order to encourage them to be better than they are. Conversely, a lukewarm *kyā bāt hai* muttered quickly at the right moment can put an otherwise accomplished performer in the position of a student. Giving *dād* puts the listener in an authoritative, morally prestigious subject position. As Dard Neuman points out, *dād* can also be a "form of recognition that demands a response" in negotiations of musical status, particularly when deployed by lower-status accompanists.[54] Chloë Alaghband-Zadeh goes so far as to argue that *dād* has come to be a form of

---

51. One of my own dearest musical friendships, with dhrupadiya Arman Ali Dehlvi, was forged at just such a concert where we introduced ourselves after again and again giving *dād* at the same time.

52. Katherine Schofield's vivid description of Mughal mahfil comportment (*adab*) is founded on just such a reciprocal, circuitous relation (2006, 74). Martin Clayton (2007) goes so far as to say that "performers and audience [form] one group of participants constructing the event together."

53. Deshpande 1974, 54.

54. Neuman 2004, 298.

virtue signaling, performing "old middle class"[55] virtues (publicly affirming one's own open-minded, critical stance, free of communal prejudice) in contrast to the consumerism emblematic of the "new middle-class," whose listening practices are more suited for passive listening in concert halls. Each of these relational functions derives its discursive power from a normative case in which a rasika is able to discern something special in the voice, to praise it publicly, and thus to take one's proper place in a vocal circuit. Thus, even when *dād* is socially ambitious, it cannot be merely arbitrary, in principle or in practice. Indeed, *dād* can be done wrong. A listener who remarks on the wrong things can be just as inhibiting as an unresponsive audience, and thus overexuberant audience members are quietly criticized or even publicly called out.[56] Just as Chishti Sufis are vigilant against pretenders to ecstasy in *samā*, so too does the fake, pedantic listener serve as a cautionary figure against mere shows of connoisseurship.

Hearing what virtuosic connoisseurs praise is a way of learning to listen. As they gesturally protend the metrical cycles with a singer, as their dād picks out especially subtle melodic or poetic phrases for special retention and consideration, they offer a distinctive, contagious form of presence.[57] V. H. Deshpande gives an account of one such virtuosic listener, harmoniumist Govindrao Tembe, whose role as a rasika is described on equal terms with singers:

> His arrival at a concert was indeed an event. The audience would whisper "Govindrao is here," "Govindrao is here," and when he left the *mehfil* would appear deserted . . . I had seen Govindrao at music recitals on several occasions before I was formally introduced to him. To watch him hear and appreciate classical music at a concert was itself an aesthetic experience. I can recollect an entrancing recital by Manji Khan with Govindrao in the forefront of the select audience. On such an occasion it used to be difficult to decide whether one should listen to Khan's singing or watch Govindrao's appreciative gesture and the charming responses reflected on his face.[58]

Cash donation serves an important pathway of vocal circuitry in some mahfils that cleave to Indo-Persian courtly etiquette, as well as at Sufi shrines, qawwali

55. Alaghband-Zadeh 2017. The figuration of "old" and "new" middle-class values is adapted from Dwyer 2000.

56. Silver in Metcalf 1984, 321.

57. Cf. Kalpana Ram 2011, Rahaim 2012, Clayton 2007.

58. Deshpande 1989, 26.

stage shows, and salons. Cash donations (*nazrānā*) are often offered visibly and publicly, bill by bill. (Some particularly enthusiastic donors "make money fly" [*paise uḍānā*] in a flurry of small bills, though this is sometimes regarded as excessively flamboyant.) At Sufi shrines, tourists and devotees alike offer *nazrānā* to qawwals, and these crisp bills of small denomination amount to visible, flowing blessings that do not reduce to monetary value. After all, even a full minute of ostentatiously making one-rupee notes fly amounts to a very small amount of money.[59] As Patrick Weston points out, *nazrānā* often passes from hand to hand: from listeners to spiritual elites to shrine custodians to qawwals, becoming a "limitless flow" of resources and blessings between singers, officials, and listeners.[60] *Nazrānā* also allows for immediate and conspicuous feedback, and is one of the key ways that listeners shape the course of a performance. Courtesans are known for having especially exacting standards of etiquette for the offering of *nazrānā* (sometimes called *vail* in salons). Though, as we have seen, these salons have largely been figured in moral reformist accounts as immoral spaces free of ethics, it is clear that listeners and singers there, too, are scaffolded by distinctive ethical practices. *Vail* is not merely a *wage* paid for an hour of vocal labor. Indeed, Fouzia Saeed recounts the complaint of one courtesan from Lahore that receiving a fixed fee obviates vocal circuitry:

> Who wants to perform for a dead audience who just claps after the end? . . . [When they pay in advance, they] look at us like objects, and there is hardly any interaction with the audience.
>
> *Vail* is a constant message for me from my customers that they appreciate my work, and I operate on those signals. If I don't know that I've touched their hearts, why should I continue to send messages to them? . . . It's this communication that makes the magic . . .[61]

Note that applause after the fact, though certainly a form of communication, is not sufficient to "make the magic" of ongoing circuitry. Indeed, such an ar-

---

59. To give a sense of scale: Qawwals on stage tour receive fixed fees of tens of thousands of rupees for pop sufi concerts; qawwal's nightly share of nazrana is typically under a thousand rupees.

60. Weston 2013 (151 and passim) points out that the circulation of cash serves not only, in the traditional Maussian formula, as *barakat* (blessing), but also as a medium of relation across caste, class, and gender lines.

61. Saeed 2015, 217.

rangement yields only a "dead" audience and an objectified performer, rather than living dynamic of circuitry between listener and performer.

Temporal Attunement and Empathetic Listening

In many cases, the attunement of a rasika to a singer verges on empathetic participation: following a singer where they go: soaring with them, landing with them, and even, in moments of calm, dwelling in a peaceful, expanded present. This empathy implies a reciprocal responsibility with a singer who, as khyaliya Mukul Kulkarni once told me, "takes the audience with them."[62] One salient form of this appears in listeners who move their hands or even sway along with a singer's voice, marking not only the culmination of metric cycles, but also the gaits by which the singer is moving.[63] In G. N. Goswamy's account, the "gentle movements of head and hands, the meaningful exchanges between singer and listeners signify . . . that *they are with the singer*."[64] This empathy is often quite specific, and enabled by training in a particular vocal discipline. In khyal, the temporal pleasures of following 20- to 30-second metrical cycles requires a special kind of expanded temporal presence, retaining what has come before and portending what is about to come next. This temporal attunement is not merely a matter of correctly predicting where the sam will fall, but also of intense pleasure. V. H. Deshpande describes such a scene in which "the fascinated audience acknowledged every *sam* from the innermost core of their hearts."[65]

And yet, not everyone is able to hear in this way. Uninitiated listeners who find themselves at concerts of Hindustani music often complain about vast, boring, boundless spans of time without any clear textual or rhythmic handholds, no groove, no obvious refrain, and scant poetic nourishment. Travelers' accounts often describe such temporal unmooring, in which "the ear, baffled repeatedly, soon lost any clue, and wandered in a maze of noises, none harsh or unpleasant, none intelligible."[66] Many Carnatic musicians, too, find the long spans of slow ālāp in Hindustani music to be excessive—as one South Indian connoisseur once muttered to my friend while listening to a dhrupad recording: "What is this, a

---

62. Rahaim 2012.

63. See Alaghband-Zadeh 2017, 207.

64. Goswamy 1986, 18.

65. Deshpande 1989, 45.

66. Forster quoted in Lelyveld 1994.

tanpura recital?" Just as baseball fans feel that "nothing happens" in a game of cricket, so too do the vast majority of Hindi speakers find Hindustani music to be not just boring, but empty.

To a rasika, however, a good performance of raga music is overflowing with action, with far more going on than anyone could absorb—no more "empty" than a cricket match. And, like cricket, getting into the flow of raga music—either as a performer or a spectator—requires more than simply knowing a set of rules or taking in the perceptual data. It requires the development of habits of temporality: long arcs of expectation, of tension and release, of retaining some key details and letting others recede from consciousness. Such a temporality takes time to crystallize into a durable habitus, and when it does, it is sometimes glossed as "patience." Indeed, as we will see in chapter 4, the style of calm, expanded temporality that I had learned to value is not simply natural. It too has a history, linked to the development of an inner temporal sensibility that resists, in principle, the tyranny of clocks, wage labor, and train schedules.

And yet, this empathy never achieves complete participatory closure; surprise is crucial to the excitement of a mahfil.[67] Even when elite listeners to qawwals or courtesans are profoundly affected by song, their personhood—including their ethical and spiritual possibilities—remains entirely distinct from the singer. Khyaliya Babanrao Haldankar describes this pleasurable surprise with reference to a striking temporality of breath. He says that when Kesarbai Kerkar sang tāns, "the listener was driven to hold his breath . . . as she approached the sam, the descending [tān] used to take the ascending turn unexpectedly and force the listener to hold his breath. He could breath[e] a sigh of relief only when she caught the sam like a jet."[68] Vikas Kashalkar described to me once how Gajanan Rao Joshi used to delight listeners in his mahfils not just by metrical correctness, but by making his audience "a hundred percent sure that he would not catch the mukhṛā," as though they were watching somebody trying to catch a train, "saying, *No, he cannot catch the train*—but then he gets onto the train!" Again, this is not merely a matter of formal propriety, but of deep feeling: "Everybody used to feel relaxed and relieved like *wah! kyā bāt hai*."

This profound pleasure finds its place in a temporal economy of yearning, anxiety, and relief—which is to say that the temporal attunements that disclose it are always relational. The attunement to the conventional expectations of raga

67. See Rahaim 2017.

68. Haldankar 2001, 33.

and tala enables surprise. It never produces an all-consuming oneness, either in principle or fact, that subsumes singer and listener, and thus always falls short of the participatory ethos of bhakti. This relational delight unfolds in the elite space of a mahfil, in the dyadic space between specially disposed singers and specially disposed listeners, not as an inherent acoustical feature of a voice.

Discerning Svara

One highly focused, distinct discipline of tonal discernment, known as *svar-jnan*, is less conventionally delightful: it deals in sequences of notes. With this critical ear engaged, vocal sonority, kinetic discipline, and poetic action (see chapter 2) tend to show up as mere packaging; the deep content, to such an orientation, is a complex sequence of notes.[69] One conventional name for this highly intellectual form of attunement is *noṭeśan*—derived from the English word *notation*, but in reference to an action rather than a written document: analyzing a vocal utterance into notes. Singers learning raga music will often find themselves asked by their guru, "What is the notation of this phrase?" To do so is not trivial—as we saw in chapter 2, the melodic voice is ordinarily in motion, only occasionally settling on a sustained tone. As one theorist puts it, when singers merely touch on notes or slide between them, "the listeners have to complete it as [if] it were from their own imagination."[70] This "imagination," like tasir, is no arbitrary fantasy, but is disclosed through a very particular discipline. Unlike the movement of the fingers on a sitar, sarod, harmonium, or sarangi, vocal movement has no external positional framework upon which named note sequences can be measured and verified. Thus, vocal *svar-jnan* is in large part a matter of training, convention, and tradition. There is evidence of an acoustemological precedent for svar-jnan in the Mughal courts and perhaps even in the *marg-sangeet* of the early second millenium. Both the Sanskritic tradition of *sangītśāstra* and the Persianate "systematic school" of musicology had long depended on the practice of reducing melody to note sequences, and the capacity for analytic listening had appeared in lists of the practical virtues (*guṇs*) of musicians and listeners. Elite courtly listeners held the capacity to distinguish ragas and analyze melodies as individual notes in high regard, alongside sensitivity to tasir.

---

69. This is a necessary basis of what Dard Neuman (2004) calls "the musicological ear."

70. Ray Chaudhari in Sanyal and Widdess 2004, 77.

This capacity was radically reconstrued in the early twentieth century as the ontologically fundamental form of listening, largely through the work of Vishnu Narayan Bhatkhande, the most prolific, widely read, and controversial Indian music theorist of all time. Bhatkhande named this capacity *svar-jnan*, which he explains in terms of practical ability: "if someone asks you to sing a particular svara, you should immediately be able to sing that svara; likewise, on being asked what the svara of a certain sound is, you should instantly be able to name the svara of that sound."[71] The parallel vocal practice requires a singer to make a clear imprint (*ṭhasā*) of a raga on a listener's imagination (*man*) rather than confusion (*bhrāṃtī*). V. N. Bhatkhande sought to propagate *svar-jnan* on a mass scale, as the foundation for a national ear; on the very first page of his *Hindustani Sangeet Paddhati*, he argues that without *svar-jnan*, a listener will never understand "the *śāstriya* [canonical/classical] part of music." He goes further to insist that "without *svar-jnan* one cannot understand the true secret of the system; nor can one derive real joy."[72] Dard Neuman points out that Bhatkhande's figuration of svar-jnan is implicitly graphical, presupposing a "hidden level of correspondence, that between note-name and its iconic representation, the mental visualization of the note's alphabetic grapheme."[73] He further points out that *svar-jnan* is not necessary for melodic fluency, even among highly fluent hereditary singers.[74] Indeed, Bhatkhande's complaint about musicians who "make a living through music but who do not have proper *svar-jnan*" is further evidence that svar-jnan is neither necessary nor sufficient for singing. Bhatkhande's innovation, then, was not in discovering svar-jnan, but in insisting that it should take precedence over other ways of listening—indeed, that it should be taught first—and to explicitly lay out a system founded on the practical mode of listening that discloses notes. Bhatkhande was not alone in seeking to cultivate this disposition. Most textbooks

---

71. Bhatkhande 1954, 1. Translation mine.

72. Part of this may have been a direct musicological influence from German musicologist Guido Adler, to whom Bhatkhande dedicated his *Kramik Pustak Malika*. He explicitly cites him as an influence, and there is a remarkable resemblance in Bhatkhande's work to Adler's precept that: "Musicology originated simultaneously with the art of organizing tones. As long as natural song breaks forth from the throat freely and without reflection; as long as the tonal products well up, unclear and unorganized, so long also there can be no question of tonal art." (Adler 1885 in Martinez 2001, 49.)

73. Neuman 2004, 114.

74. Neuman 2004, 174.

on Hindustani music begin with notes, and rarely get much further. This is, to be sure, a practice of listening that discloses to a listener a very particular kind of vocal *truth*: eminently testable on exams, teachable in textbooks, aspiring even to a limited, provisional sort of "objectivity" about what one's voice is doing, independent, in principle, of the specificities of gharanas. For this reason, it often serves as the basis for auditions for All India Radio and other scholarships. As we have seen, however, it is not the only (nor, surely, the richest) truth.

Samā

Samā is another elite, cultivated form of listening with particularly high spiritual and ethical stakes.[75] The word itself simply means "listening," but, like *tasir*, it refers to something rather more specific: a heightened, focused, extraordinary mode of harkening to the recitation of esoteric Sufi poetry (*kalām*). The ideal-typical case goes something like this: qawwals (hereditary professional musicians) are singing, a group of trained Sufi aspirants are in attendance, a properly trained and authorized Sufi adept hears the mystical core content in the poetry that is sung, it touches his heart, he stands and dances in ecstasy, called *wajd*—and the qawwāls, in turn, seeing signs of ecstasy, sustain it through repetition or elaboration. These gatherings are sometimes only for spiritual adepts, sometimes for only two or three or even one listener. At other times, there is a mix of spiritual elites (who might go into a state of mystical ecstasy) and a few high-status spectators, including blood descendants of a great saint or custodians of a shrine, great connoisseurs of mystical poetry (*kalām*)—and, in exceptional cases, the odd ethnographer. Such a mahfil may take place in many different kinds of places: a room in a *khānqāh* (Sufi lodge), a *hujrā* (private cell) in a shrine complex, a living room of a private home, even a secluded outdoor space. But in all cases, a *mahfil-e samā* is an exclusive gathering. A spiritual authority (*pīr*) makes sure everything goes properly; in principle, those who might go into trance are disciples of the *pīr*. Advanced Sufis[76] have access to elite *mahfil-e samā* (gatherings for listening to *qawwāli*) precisely because they have been trained to hear the

---

75. *Samā* is a term in wide circulation across the Islamicate cosmopolis. It has, for centuries, served as a general term for various musical rituals practiced by Mevlevis in Konya, Qadiris in Paris, Uighur in Western China, and many others.

76. Most typically, Chishtis, but also Naqshbandi, Suhrawardi, and Qadiri—often South Indian Sufis are initiated into more than one, or all four orders.

inner content of the songs sung, opening the door for mystical states available in principle not to the singers, but only to specially attuned listeners.[77]

Though easily confused with the pleasurable relish of Sufi pop music, *wajd* (like *tasir*) is only rarely joyful or pleasurable.[78] Samā is typically prescribed only for morally developed Sufis, who have purified themselves of desire for pleasure in favor of (in principle, unquenchable) spiritual yearning for God. Allowing the sound of mystical poetry, declaimed in a clear, beautiful voice, to reach the heart, can lead a sensitive listener into various forms of spiritual arousal: first *tasir* (chills, tears, aching), then visible as rocking or shaking or nodding, and often described as the outward signs of an "opening" of the heart. In the most powerful cases, the arousal blooms into a trance-like state called *wajd*,[79] in which the listener stands and spins or thrashes about in a mode of spiritual ecstasy, often requiring others to step forward to protect the listener from injury while in the state. Some faint, and in a few legendary cases, listeners have been known to die in the course of *wajd*.[80]

There seems to be some evidence that the earliest traditions of listening to khyal were much like *samā* rituals, and there are even hints that these modes of listening may once have been less distinct than they are now. Since independence, at any rate, they have become quite distinct. However intense the *tasir* may be at a ghar mahfil, however astute a connoisseur may be at following the metric cycles or catching modal allusions, no one goes into a trance; no one stands up in ecstasy; no one is subject to the authority of a presiding *pīr*; no one needs spiritual authorization to attend. And yet all of this happens in *samā*. Samā thus requires a rather different ontology of voice than what obtains in a mahfil dedicated to rāga music or ghazals, a rather different temporality and style of presence, and strikingly different ethical roles.

In canonical accounts, it is the listener (*samī*), rather than the vocalist, who is the main subject. The figure of the spiritually elite Sufi at qawwali gatherings is always the listener—not the qawwal himself. Stories circulate freely about extraordinarily sensitive Sufis who are brought into *wajd* by the words of a film

77. Though this is an oft-cited state of affairs in principle, particularly in defense of qawwali, qawwals themselves often contest this, as we will see.

78. Avery 2004, 92, 98, 99.

79. Avery 2004, 94.

80. The canonical case is Khwāja Qutbuddīn, but there are others too. See Avery 2004, 89–91.

song, or even by a line of poetry misheard at a distance.[81] These stories reinforce the canonical Chishti emphasis on esoteric listening rather than genre distinctions, by which the spiritual power of samā is available in principle to some and not to others. Orthodox apologists for *wajd* are often at pains to distinguish pious, properly prepared *samā* from mere spontaneous emotional arousal, contrasting their rules for samā with the morally corrupt lovers of the world who thrash about in fake ecstasy, spurred on merely by the excitement of rhythm and melody.[82] And yet, it is equally clear that not all *wajd* is formally authorized. Wandering mystics (variously called *qalandar*, *darvesh*, *bazāri*, etc. to distinguish them from orthodox listeners) often do go quite visibly into *wajd*.[83] It is not uncommon for casual attendees of qawwali sessions in the public courtyards of dargāhs to flail about or scream; they are usually quickly brought under control by shrine custodians, their state explained away as madness or intoxication. Indeed, the strongest evidence for *wajd* among the non-elite devout is the numerous injunctions *against* it in moral literature.

A *mahfil-e samā* (a mahfil of listening) is a radically different situation from the *ghar mahfils* of urban raga music connoisseurs (see chapter 1). The arrangement of listeners in a *mahfil-e samā* (mahfil of samā) is rather different from a classical mahfil, which tends to be arranged around a singer. Ordinarily, for *samā*, pride of place is given to the *pīr* (spiritual authority), who sits directly in front of the qawwals at some distance, with the other listeners (authorized by the pīr, specially invited) gathered on either side. And despite the fact that qawwali is sung, it is also different in important ways from the performances of qawwali in the open, public courtyards of *dargāhs*.[84] A mahfil-e samā is an exclusive

81. See, for example, Qureshi 1992, 119.

82. For another example, see Qureshi 1994, 514 on "ecstasy based on sound alone."

83. See Wolf 2006. This tends to be true at some shrines more than others.

84. I follow Qureshi (1995, 112) in distinguishing *mahfil-e samā* from public qawwali in a shrine. This distinction is made so sharply in support of a larger analytical point: that situation is constitutive of relational circuits of voicing and listening. And there really is a sharp distinction to be made between, say, a private gathering for spiritual elites and a public performance of *qawwalis* in a dargah courtyard containing uninitiated tourists seeking *baraka* and colorful photographs. Qureshi further distinguishes the two by their temporality, pointing out that a *mahfil-e samā* is convened at the whim of the spiritual authority rather than the daily, weekly, or yearly cycles of shrine performance. As an empirical matter, however, there are many gatherings for qawwali

event (sometimes also called a *mahfil-e khās*, or mahfil for the elite) held in a private space, open only to specially prepared spiritual elites, and organized as a gathering for instruction with a *pīr*. In Regula Qureshi's classic account, samā is "focused on the listener . . . and on his spiritual capacity for receiving what he hears" rather than the singers who are "causing the message to be sounded."[85] Accordingly, it is best thought of as a special case of gatherings for teaching with a *pīr*[86]—one focused on listening to mystical poetry—rather than a special case of a concert, or of a mere "context" for qawwali. To be sure, a similar repertoire of qawwali may be sung at both public shrines and private mahfils. But the *adab* at a mahfil-e samā is different, the structures of authority are different, the vocal disciplines are different, the vocal ontology is different, the attendees are quite different, and the possibilities and goals are different.

As *samā* is almost exclusively practiced in a gathering (a *mahfil-e samā*), theological debates about its propriety are almost always paradigmatically situated among others. The standards of comportment for listeners at a mahfil-e samā are shaped by inculcated habit, by a centuries-old textual canon, and by the specific injunctions of spiritual authorities. These include inconspicuous dress, pious sitting posture, and restrained gestures, all in the interest of "occupy[ing] the heart and mind fully with the thought and remembrance of Allah." Likewise, listeners are instructed to resist the urge to stand up; *wajd* is permissible only to the degree that it is involuntary and irresistible. In practice, these do not always function as strict rules. Particularly in less exclusive gatherings, when someone's legs fall asleep, one may shift them to the side. Attendees certainly whisper or nod to each other in the course of the event. At one *samā* that I attended, I was permitted to take video more or less constantly, and even to make what must have been highly distracting adjustments to the camera—all of which were met

---

that fall in a wide gray area between the two. Zuberi and Sarrazin, in demonstrating the profound generic differences of *filmi* qawwali, emphasize the relative generic continuity between *khānqāhī* and *dargāhī* qawwali (2017). Furthermore, as they point out, many spaces for *mahfil-e samā* are located in and around dargahs. Listeners sometimes do go into unauthorized trance, even in public gatherings in a dargah, or in the absence of a spiritual authority.

85. Qureshi, 1986 [2006], 82–83.

86. See, for example, the accounts of gatherings with Nizamuddin Auliya recorded in the *Fawā'id al-Fu'ād* of Ziya-Ul-Hasan Faruqi, translated by Bruce Lawrence (1991). See especially discussions of adab in, for example, *I Assembly* 32, 120.

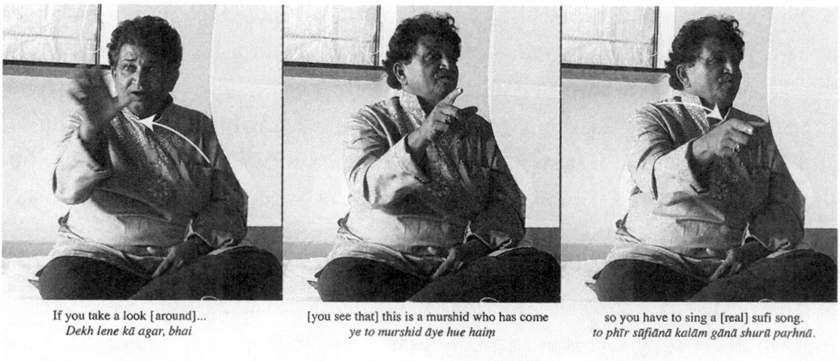

FIGURE 3.3 Vectors of samā relationality

with patient smiles and gestures of kind encouragement. To frequent attendees, one needn't painstakingly repress the urge to drink water or sing along moment by moment any more than one must suppress the urge to sit down while at bat in cricket; the *mahaul* demands a proper comportment, and a properly disciplined attendee simply falls into it.

For a qawwal, samā requires highly cultivated relational attunements to those who are listening. The *adab* they must adopt at a *mahfil-e samā* is a form of practical virtue in and of itself that allows the possibility for *wajd* to happen. This requires flexible attention to the details of a situation, rather than simply a ready-made set of conventional gestures. A qawwal must attend to his specific listeners with an "eagle eye,"[87] and aim his singing to them in particular. Mahmud Nizami describes this practiced attentiveness to the spiritual elites at a samā, specifically distinguishing it from the relatively looser standards at a dargah:

> In a dargāh . . . anyone might be there. You start singing, this guy comes, that guy comes, common people, elites, everyone is there. At those times, you sing common songs, the sort of thing that anyone can understand. [But] in a *mahfil-e-samā*, only the elite people come: the holy men, the masters. If you take a look [around, you see that] this is a *murshid* [i.e., master] who has arrived, so you have to sing a [real] Sufi song.[88]

87. Qureshi 1995, 133.

88. *Dargāh mein . . . koi bhi āyā. Gānā shuru hai, yeh bhi āyā, voh bhi āyā, ām bhi āyā, khāṣṣ bhi āyā, sab āyā bhi. To us vaqt, ām gānā gānā paṛhtā. yūṃ hī sab ko*

Mahmud Sahāb describes this virtual mahfil from the viewpoint of a singer already situated among listeners. He takes a look around (his hand, in this telling, showing his gaze scanning the listeners before him), he spots a spiritual elite (*murshid*) who is sitting there (pointing at him, singling him out for attention), and sings that special sufiana kalam *to* him (extending his hand from himself to the virtual listener). Like the vector of a pointing finger, singing here is already foundationally relational, rather than simply placed in one context or another. Qawwal Chand Nizami similarly reserves certain special songs (which he calls *Sūfī* qawwalis) for exclusive gatherings, where Sufis are seated. But he also stresses that whatever song text is at hand, it must *reach* "from here to there," from qawwal to Sufi, with a *lambī* (tall, broad) voice, high and strong.[89] This circuitry operates, for the most part, through subtle, implicit signals passed back and forth between qawwal and Sufi listener, rather than requesting that a qawwal sing a particular poem. Qawwals who have had generations-long associations with Chishti lineages often know the individual listeners personally, and know what touches their hearts. Some commentators attribute this careful sensitivity to divine inspiration, received and transmitted through the heart, rather than rational deliberation.[90]

But virtuosic listeners may also intervene quite explicitly. High-status, authoritative listeners, particularly in the role of *mīr-e mahfil* (lord of the mahfil), are sometimes known to interrupt a qawwal in mid-verse.[91] I have seen this most often when a spiritual authority interrupts to comment on a verse or clarify its meaning, particularly if the verse is in Persian. At other times, an authoritative listener will correct a qawwal who gives a variant version of a canonical verse, substitutes a near-homonym, or mispronounces a word. In rare occasions, the ethical quality of a qawwal's voice may be adjudged inappropriate for samā: as when Khwaja Hasan Sani, an eminent spiritual authority in the Nizami lineage, once stopped a qawwal from singing because there was insufficient *ārzū* (long-

---

samajhte aisa . . . Mahfil mein sirf khās hi log hai. Vaise ki pir-o-murshid hai . . . To unko dekh lene ka agar bhai, yeh to murshid aye hue haiṃ, to phīr: sufiānā kalam gānā shurū paṛhnā.

89. *"yahāṃ se wahāṃ tak . . . upar jā ke . . . lambī āvāz." Lambī āvāz* is often used interchangably with *buland āvāz.*

90. Viitamäki 2008, 86.

91. Qureshi 1995, 177 and 180.

ing) in his voice.[92] Note that Qawwals themselves do not ordinarily enter deeply into *wajd* in the course of a *mahfil*. As we have seen, singing for a *mahfil-e samā* requires so much careful attention to the listeners that a qawwal could hardly afford to disappear into ecstasy. Occasionally, a qawwal *will* start to get carried away, and must be brought back to continue on performing. And certainly, qawwals go into intermediate states of openness, longing, and intense joy. Many report immediate effects on their voice when in *nisbat* (relation) to a saint, or singing *dil se* (from the heart). But as a matter of simple professionalism and respect for the Sufis they sing for, even the most spiritually sensitive qawwals manage to keep their attention on the state of their patrons. A mahfil-e samā, after all, is not principally a gathering for disclosing and appreciating vocal *art*.[93] A qawwal's skill and artistry lies in delivering spiritually elevating poetry as beautifully as possible to specific listeners. In the presence of such powerful poetry, which seems to take on a numinous substance of its own, the proper comportment of listeners is paramount; all the more so in the presence of a *pīr*. In *samā*, a qawwal becomes, in Richard Wolf's apt phrase, a "technician of emotion"[94] rather than an artist.

Listening with the heart, rather than with the ear, remains a way of figuring samā as counter-authoritative, without the requirement of authorization or special esoteric teaching. Qawwal Asrar Hussain reports that listening with the heart doesn't even require the listener to understand the language that is sung, as it entirely circumvents the *aql* (intellect).[95] And yet, the heart, no less than the intellect, requires ethical cultivation for moving beyond what Regula Qureshi calls the "immediate sensory level"[96] of *tasir* (crying, weeping, chills, etc.). What does this preparation consist of? What exactly is revealed? This is hard to say, in part because *samā* is esoteric in the sociological sense: it is the special dispositional preserve of insiders, modeled, regulated, and passed on in a relationship between a master and a disciple, and rarely (if ever) explicated to outsiders. But *samā* is also esoteric in a metaphysical sense: even to an initiated insider, samā offers a temporary glimpse of something concealed beneath the

92. Viitamäki 2008, 98.

93. See Rahaim 2019.

94. Wolf 2014, 281 f1.

95. Weston 2013, 95.

96. Qureshi 1994, 513, 524.

surface of poetry, and thus impossible to fully explain in words after the fact. We thus are left with a faint adumbration of *samā*, in large part by specifying what it is not. Even the outlines, however, suggest a discipline of listening distinct from *tasir*, *svar-jnan*, or the "aesthetic attitude."

Accounts of samā tend to be cryptic. One common figuration refers to an inner message disclosed to the heart by samā, in contrast to the conventional surface content of the text being sung. Versions of al-Ghazali's canonical twelfth-century account give examples of poetic construal, so that the Beloved is understood to be God; "dark locks" are taken to be "the darkness of unbelief"; "drunkenness" is taken to be divine ecstasy, and so on. One thus might be tempted to think of samā as a sort of *de*-poeticizing process, in which symbols are decoded into their true referents. But most accounts of samā suggest that the revelations of *samā* move the listener away from discursive meaning and *toward* ineffable poetics. This deep engagement is more often a matter of heightened poetic intensity, founded on long-cultivated resonance and connotation, drawing on a finite reservoir of allusive poetic fragments, emerging from years of association with a beloved spiritual master, or *pīr*. As Qawwal Sultan Nazan puts it, a line of poetry brings the *tasāwwur* (evocation of presence) of one's master; the one for whom the qawwal sings listens from *inside* the love of his pīr. The canon of Sufi poetry sung by qawwals is also memorized and recited by Sufis, and has a rich life in the master-disciple relationship central to Sufi initiation and instruction. Couplets circulate between teachers and students, addressing love, metaphysical yearning, death, sacrifice, and other mysteries usually impenetrable to theological interpretation. Sufi masters, no less than qawwals, practice *girah*, or the artful insertion of canonical poetic couplets into their informal sermons, teaching, and spiritual advice.[97] When a sensitive student hears these couplets recited by a qawwal, the poem is already indexically saturated with the disposition and felt moral presence of their own pīr and his teachings. In Nizamuddin Auliya's classic spiritual autobiography *Morals for the Heart*, for example, we hear again and again of his pīr answering questions with affectively saturated poetic citations, many of which evoke collective weeping. This, again, is not merely a matter of discursive comprehension, but a deep affective connection that seems to go deeper than lexical meaning. In general, these trained listeners are understood to have the strongest reactions to poetry

97. I thank Scott Kugle for this valuable insight.

that circulates in their particular lineage, and this is part of why qawwals must know their mahfil audiences intimately. While a shrine audience is likely filled with many strangers, pilgrims, and tourists, and thus calls for widely known repertoire like *Allāh Hu*, a qawwal invited to sing at a mahfil-e samā often knows the predilections of those present from long association, and will even direct particular poems to particular Sufis.[98] Some families of hereditary qawwals, for example, are linked over many generations to particular Sufi lineages, know from experience which songs the listeners are attuned to, and sing the same set of songs at mahfil after mahfil.

Another facet of *samā* is a distinctive temporality, what Regula Qureshi (following Jonathan Kramer) characterizes as a "moment" experience. The ghazal form, for example, consists of a great number of mutually substitutable, internally coherent verses, any one of which might stand on its own. Qureshi's account of this stresses the parallel progress of the listener's state and the sung form. Each verse has a regular logical rhythm of assertion and reply, and a concomitant emotional rhythm of "cathartic"[99] suspense and release. When a particular listener is touched by the *tasir* of one line in particular, the qawwal will often repeat that verse to sustain and heighten the state. As the qawwal ushers the listener through successive stages (*maqamat*) of illumination, they move toward increasingly terse repetitions (*takrār*) of a single line or phrase, dropping away from the usual dyadic flux of the ghazal. These short phrases (for example, "*merā pīyā pīyā pīyā, merā pīyā pīyā pīyā, merā pīyā pīyā pīyā*" [my beloved, beloved, beloved]) are ordinarily only a few seconds long, much shorter than full sentences, and thus floating free of the usual poetic temporality of assertion, argument, and reply. The qawwal guides the listener into the depths of *wajd* by "filling the perceptual present with nothing but the *experience of its message*."[100] They thus begin to approach something closer to *zikr*. The drumming that accompanies qawwali intensifies this temporal focus, as well. This is sometimes attributed to the raw intensity of drumming,[101] and yet there

98. See examples 3, 4, and 5 at the end of Viitamäki 2008.

99. Qureshi 2006, 510.

100. Qureshi 512. See also Viitamäki 2008, 118, "listeners merge into the metaphorical meaning of the verse."

101. Avery 97; also Inayat Khan on tāl: "the tāl intensifies the feelings as the beautiful meaning of the verses stirs the heart . . . [it] creates such an effect that the hearts

is also a discipline of listening that hears a "voice in the drum," constituting the cycles of strokes as *zikr*.[102]

Participatory Devotional Song

A radically different form of relationality emerges in participatory, devotional group song.[103] In streets, temples, Gurdwaras, and pilgrimage buses, singing becomes an "act of collective devotion," an entirely different sort of activity from individual song pitched to elite connoisseurs.[104] Indeed, the very word *bhakti* is often assigned an etymology suggesting sharing or participation.[105] *Bhajan karnā*, to "do bhajan," is ordinarily to do something *together*, to sing-with others, rather than merely to *gāo* or *sunāo* a song that happens to have devotional lyrics. Bands of singers (*maṇḍalīs*, or "circles") acquire their own collective agency, gathering, singing, and traveling as a coherent unit. Processional singing (in public Hare Krishna bhajans or the grand parades of Ganapati Chaturthi) often invites passersby to participate in *doing bhajan*—often containing repeated exhortations to say the names of a divinity—and indeed processional melodies tend to be repetitive enough to allow devout newcomers to join in.[106] Chanting *Pānḍuranga, Pānḍuranga, Pānḍuranga* . . . with dozens of devotees produces a sort of "moment temporality" akin to *takrār*, but sounded and heard together, in an immersive collectivity of notional equals (unlike in *samā*, where a clear spiritual ranking obtains). The coordination and rhythmic togetherness required for this participation thus depends on voicing and listening at once, and in much the same way for all involved—a vocal oneness sometimes called *sangat* in Sikh

---

of all, both great and humble, begin to tremble in a state of ecstasy. As the pace of the tāl grows faster, the heart is even more stirred, and each stroke of the tāl gives more impetus to the ecstasy and intoxication." (*Minqar-e Musiqi*, 78.)

102. Wolf 2014.

103. Slawek 1988; Kaur 2016; Schultz 2012.

104. Ranade 1984, 134.

105. Prentiss 2001, 24; Singh 2006, 26. On the theme of participation in ethnomusicology, see Rahaim 2019.

106. In practice, of course, such an invitation to song is rarely truly universal. Bhakti vocal participation lends itself to publicly claiming public space, and the formation of social formations with clear insides and outsides—characteristically: participants and non-participants.

congregations.[107] This is a rather different mode of reciprocal, mutually dependent relationality than that which obtains between singers and rasikas at a *mahfil*, or between qawwals and Sufis at a *samā*.[108] A single emergent voice, pouring out of innumerable mouths, often serves as a participatory icon of a unanimous collectivity.[109] The putative metaphysical unity produced by choral singing has likewise been a crucial discursive resource in imagining the nation singing in one voice, internally coherent constituencies aligned against each other, the "voice of the people" in contrast to elites.[110] Common *Nirguni* poetic motifs that affirm a common spiritual dispensation to all humanity (such as *sab ghaṭ mein* ["in every body"]) are likewise often construed as an egalitarian political logic.[111] Some commentators celebrate the experience of vocally joining-together in devotion as a morally uplifting realization of a prior metaphysical unity; Sathya Sai Baba, for example, commends the kind of occasion in which "a myriad throats join in uttering the name of God" as a "demonstration of oneness."[112] It is not clear that this felt oneness is a matter of conscious reflection (or even a matter of fact) for all singers.[113] Kabir singer Prahlad Tipanya, for example, describes doing *bhajan* in a rather more metaphysically ambiguous way: the act each of joining with (*joḍnā*) the true thing (*satya cīz*) that is inside everyone—rather than joining individual parts together into a unified whole. At any rate, bhakti singers often report pleasure, joy, and lightness (*halkāpan*) in doing *bhajan*.[114] One

107. Kaur 2020.

108. Whether in a private *samā* or a public *dargāh*, there is a clear line between the qawwali party (who sing) and the silent listeners (who listen); to sing along as a listener would be a severe breach of adab.

109. Turino 2008; Rahaim 2019.

110. Jhingan 2009; Schultz 2013.

111. Hess 2015.

112. Sathya Sai Baba 2004, 53. From a discourse given January 26, 1995.

113. Kiran Narayan's study (2016) of women's group devotional singing in Kangra virtuosically surveys a range of indigenous ontological resources for making sense of what it *is* to sing together, and a sense of metaphysical unity among singers is not among them; the closest equivalent is "bathing" in sound. Krishna Rao Shankar Pandit's *Sargam Sār* enumerates the social (*samājik*) benefits of singing (alongside spiritual, physical, and intellectual benefits); the social benefits listed are the healing of the heart and the correction of evil deeds, but social unity is nowhere mentioned.

114. Hess 2016, 428 n8.

point of ethical friction in the world of bhakti is that not all bhajans invite such participation. Naradiya kirtan and haveli sangīt, for example, typically feature a single singer who may, at moments of maximal participatory fervor, be spurred on by the audience as though singing at a mahfil, but only rarely lead the whole assembly in singing. The raga-based bhajans that end so many Maharashtrian concerts of classical music hardly ever invite singing along. And at large stage shows of bhakti music, audiences mostly sit still and listen to leading singers perform. As one sardonic pun goes, such a gathering can be called a *satsang* only in the sense that the singers "sat and sang."

As for bhakti practices of listening, first and foremost is the classic injunction to chant the names of God, to hear the names of God, to bathe in the very aural substance of God. The fruits of listening (*phal-śruti*) to these divine names are widely attested, and rely upon an ontology of voice in which the utterance of a name itself is consubstantial with the divine entity named, rather than an arbitrary symbol, and thus directly offer salvation, healing, and moral upliftment.[115] Another common report in bhakti traditions is that listening to devotional *song*, rather than bare recited words, induces absorption or even metaphysical unity.[116] There is also a well-attested mode of listening in Krishna institutions whereby a devotee steeped in song is pulled into a parallel world of intoxicating devotion and play (*līlā*), including actually *seeing* Krishna's activities.[117] The exhortation to listen (*suno*!) in the course of song is a recurring relational theme in Kabir *bhajans*. The utterance that follows is usually a memorable aphorism that aims to shake the listener out of one taken-for-granted conventional stance and realign them to another. In this sense, the form of attention called for is ethically transformative in principle, a vector between two ethical subjects separated by a gulf of wisdom and understanding. At other times, Kabir describes a way of attending to the unchanging *shabd* (unqualified eternal utterance, as opposed to a particular word), or *anahad nād* (unqualified eternal sound prior to phenomenal sound).

Maharashtrian kirtankars, serving both as professionals *and* as moral exemplars, have historically been expected to preserve the purity of their ears, avoiding any hearing of "lascivious" song.[118] Unlike qawwals, who are largely

---

115. Williams 2014, 193.

116. See Slawek 1986, 162.

117. Sanford 2008.

118. Schultz 2012, 30.

professionals at delivering poetry to their more spiritually attuned patrons, "the impact of the bhajan rests entirely on the singer's personal character and approach. 'A devil cannot cite scriptures' so far as the rendering of a bhajan is concerned."[119] But the discernment of these virtues requires attunement on the part of the listener. Vaisnava song texts, for example, are often suffused with erotic-devotional imagery, in which, for example, the devotee might stand in the position of Krishna's lover. Devotees are called to discern the hidden spiritual content of these song texts even as they partake in the love and longing for love that are the essence of these song-poems. Just such a mode of listening ultimately grants moral triumph in the legend of the great Marathi saint Tukaram's victory over a courtesan. The best-known popular version of this story is found in the 1936 Marathi film *Sant Tukaram*. A courtesan sent to tempt Tuka lures him out of his house with a song of erotic yearning for Krishna, but is bewildered to find him gazing off into space rather than at her, playing along with wooden clappers, in a trance of devotion. This stands in stark ethical contrast to an earlier scene in which Tuka's hypocritical Brahmin rival, Salo, listens to the courtesan's song in the attitude of a courtly patron, reclining, chewing pan, meeting her gaze, smiling back at her, giving *dād* in a courtly circuit of voice. Tuka, in contrast, is able to resist her charms—and, eventually, to convert her—precisely because of his devotional listening practice: in the participatory stance of a bhakt among other bhakts, rather than the reciprocating stance of a courtly rasika at a mahfil.

IRRELATIONAL PRACTICES

We have seen that particular listening practices, and particular circuits of voice, often invite radically different relational dispositions and ethical possibilities. Indeed, just as particular relational circuits afford of certain vocal potentials, so too can they restrict others. Thus, some ways of voice are founded in *irrelational* practices: turning away from, negating, or blocking normative forms of social relation. This is more than mere accidental solitude. Young singers are often insulated from the pressures of singing to audiences—subject exclusively to the exacting ear of their master, a circuit of voice with rather different contours—until they are prepared (*taiyār*). Irrelationality is a studied, practiced indifference

119. Wadhera in Manuel 1993, 113.

to relational circuitry while singing. For many post-independence music critics, classical singers are normatively construed as free artists, unswayed by the vulgar tastes of the masses, similarly insulated in principle from the demands of their less-sophisticated listeners. This sense of vocal independence is strengthened by the world-disclosing technology of the microphone, projecting voices floating free of their socially situated bodies (on recordings, through speakers, in films) isolating a singer from coeval relationships with consociates, offering listeners a disembodied, sonorous object for aesthetic contemplation.[120] Even the experience of singing "for oneself" has a peculiar relationality rather different from singing for someone else, or solitary practice. In some extreme cases, singers pursue spiritual ambitions to enter into a form of being entirely free of relations: a oneness that recognizes no boundaries, no separate listener, no Other.

A Voice Unpolluted by Human Ears

Ek kahūṃ to hai nahīṃ; do kahūṃ to gālī . . .
If I say *one*, it is not so; if I say *two*, it is abuse.
Kabir

The images of bhakti song we have considered thus far are primarily founded on participatory singing-together with others. But another form of bhakti takes place far from the crowd—out in the jungle, up in the mountains, off in a lonely, secluded shrine. This figuration of devotion situates the individual devotee alone with their divine auditor, singing a song fit only for the ear of God, free of the relational distractions of the bazaar, the palace, and the home.

Consider the oft-told tale of the great bhakti singer-saint Haridas, the legendary guru of Tansen, acclaimed court singer of the Mughal court. Akbar (emperor of the Mughal Empire and a great connoisseur of music) hears much of Swami Haridas. He hears that he sings even better than Tansen, and thus sends a messenger to invite him to sing at court. Haridas politely refuses. Akbar visits Swami Haridas himself in disguise, covertly listening in. He is awestruck at the profoundly moving effect of this voice. He later asks Tansen what it is that makes Haridas's voice so special. Tansen replies: "Tansen sings for the delight of the royal court, but Haridas sings only to God." In another variant on the same

120. See Herbst 1997, 136 on amplification and *deśa kala patra* in Balinese vocal performance.

theme, Akbar listens in on the singer-saint Govindswami singing Rag Bhairav, and is so moved that he spontaneously cries out, "*wāh*!" In doing so, he reveals himself—at which point Govindswami immediately renounces singing Bhairav ever again, claiming that it is now "polluted"—touched even for a moment by Akbar's profane courtly practice of listening.[121] In these and many other cases, an extraordinary vocal-ethical power is marked precisely by solitary vocal devotion that turns away from the mahfil, away from public delight and acclaim, away from the circuit of touching a listener's heart and receiving *dād* in return. But this ethical power is marked equally by turning *toward* a radically different Listener, unpolluted by human ears.[122] (See figure 3.4.)

Similar stories are told of many singers. The lone voice singing to God is a generative scene in many hagiographic accounts of saintly singers. Legends of the great Krishna *bhakt* Mirabai emphasize her rejection of her courtly social obligations to sing alone in a temple, for Krishna alone. Abdul Karim Khan is said to have been cured of a tumor by singing in solitude at the shrine of Shamsuddin Hussein in Miraj; his daughter Hirabai regularly sang there as well. Kumar Gandharva speaks about the great power of the voices of Nath yogis precisely because "the svaras that come out there are not the svaras that come out in the drawing room . . . [they] convey a sense of solitude."[123] Pushkar Lele, a khyaliya who has deeply imbibed Kumarji's vocal attitude, describes this solitude as precisely a commitment to self that affords indifference to one's listeners: "I am singing because I am lost in myself [so] I don't need you to listen to me. So that kind of *phakkaṛpan* [free from care], that kind of independence, that kind of confidence in you: I am my own. So *that* kind of voice should come from *this* kind of an attitude." Many dhrupadiyas eschew florid harkat in dhrupad precisely on the grounds that one is to be "singing before God" rather than the capricious

121. In the *Nijmat Siddhānt* of Kishoridas (ca. 1760), according to Delvoye's translation (in Habib 1997, 206), Tansen claims that Haridas sings only for *himself*. There have been numerous reconstruals since, including many variants on the narrative motif of Akbar confronting a bhakti saint and failing a test of listening. For another telling of this story, see Neuman 1990, 102. For more on the totalizing figure of the Royal Ear hearing song, Adriana Cavarero's rereading of Italo Calvino's "A King Listens" (2005, 5).

122. Likely painted by Nihal Chand at Kishangarh ca. 1760. Delvoye in Habib 1997; also see Pauwels 2017, 140.

123. Hess 2009, 30–31.

FIGURE 3.4 Akbar and Tansen hearing Haridas's solitary voice in his forest hermitage

sensibilities of human listeners and thus require a kinetically restrained, solemn disposition.[124]

For qawwals singing at major Chishti shrines, a similar temptation prevails to sing to the crowd—and no doubt, to earn money and acclaim, they must.[125] And yet, in principle, the single most important audience for qawwali in a shrine is the palpably felt presence of the saint presiding over its activities. Thus, gatherings in the courtyard of Nizamuddin in Delhi are sometimes called *darbār-e auliyā*—the court of the saint. This nisbat is vocally invoked by "taking" the name of saints or prophets [*nām lenā*], speaking or singing it aloud. A name thus taken is not an arbitrary semiotic index, pointing to a referent; it is a situated performative invocation that *does* something. It may simply be a claim to spiritual authority, an exemplary performance of humble piety—or in some cases, a relational

124. Widdess 1994, 95.

125. See Weston 2013, 75–77.

call for help. Qawwal Amjad Nizami, for example, once pointed out to me that taking the name of Nizamuddin had cleared up the *kharāsh* (itchy hoarseness) that had assailed his voice all afternoon, suddenly allowing him to sing high and clear.[126] Many qawwals report that their *nisbat* (relation)[127] with the saint's presence is necessary in order to sing with requisite effect. Some go so far as to say that they are only ever singing for the saint.[128] On one occasion, early in my training, I myself was invited to sing at the shrine of Moin-ud-din Chishti in Ajmer. I had been practicing with Sadique Husain (a qawwal from the hereditary qawwal family attached to the shrine) for an hour or so that afternoon, trading khyals, and he suggested that we go together to the shrine that night to sing. I protested that I didn't know any traditional qawwali repertoire, and he said it didn't matter. "You can sing alap," he assured me, "in pure raga." I briefly fretted aloud over which raga I should sing, and whether I should bring a tanpura or a harmonium—key considerations in preparing for a mahfil. But Sadique was totally unconcerned with all of this. He gave me only one instruction: sing *to* the great saint entombed at the shrine, Moinuddin Chishti (Khwāja Sāhāb, as he is called by his devotees). The substance of this devotional offering was not so much tones, but attention. I was instructed *not* to sing to (or even look at) anyone who gathered—instead, I was to keep facing toward the tomb and singing to Khwāja Sāhāb until they got the picture. When a handful of listeners did gather, Sadique deftly directed the listeners' attention, through gesture, gaze, and the direction of his voice, toward our true listener. By any classical standard, my singing that night was mediocre: plain, formulaic, coarse, even shouty. The few listeners who were drawn over to us surely did not come for the beauty of my voice, but for *nisbat* with Khwaja Sahab.

The figure of the lone voice singing to a saint or a divinity certainly is irrelational with respect to other humans; yet this remains an ethical scene of *extraordinary* relations. As Tanya Luhrmann's recent work has demonstrated, a divine voice, even if inaudible to an observing ethnographer, nonetheless can show up quite vividly as an occasion for relation for those with proper training.[129]

---

126. See also Reisnour 2017, 253 for an account of a Balinese singer whose voice was "stiff" until praying to the divinity Saraswati, who freed him.

127. Literally, *nisbat* means "ratio" in the arithmetical sense, and has Pythagorean resonances as well.

128. Weston 2013, 96.

129. Luhrmann 2012.

Microphones, Stages, and the Aesthetic Attitude

A rather different irrelational attitude constitutes the singing voice as a sort of sonorous *art object* for contemplation and delight at a distance, as one might admire architecture.[130] The singer-as-artiste is responsible only to their own genius, and is thus praised precisely for their *indifference* to relational circuitry. V. H. Deshpande, for example, contrasts the artistic disposition of "restraint" with the antiquated relational disposition of a mahfil singer directed toward evoking *tasir* in their listeners.[131] Critic S. K. Chaubey's praise for dhrupadiya Nasir ad-din Khan likewise hinges on his "supreme contempt for the visible audience" which was "part of his genius and temperament . . ."[132] Aesthetic philosopher S. K. Saxena distinguishes between between musicians who end "climactically and quite loudly at the *sam* (i.e., metrical culmination)" in order to win the applause of "the poorly trained"; and another kind who "delights in the contemplation of *lay*," who "unwind[s] a pattern that is subtly arranged . . . so softly, yet surely, that the *sam* can be sensed . . . by a genuine rasika."[133] As we will see in chapter 4, the most famous public exemplar of this detached restraint was Amir Khan, who has served as a model for irrelational, self-contained artistry for generations of khyaliyas.

The relational complement of a vocal "artiste" is an aesthetic listener who observes, silent and still, as the artiste gradually builds an edifice for their delectation. Though widely naturalized by critics as the fitting attitude for any art, this distanced aesthetic contemplation is by no means obvious or automatic. As Hindustani critic and aesthetic philosopher S. K. Saxena elegantly puts it, it "has to be brought about and carefully kept up."[134] The aesthetic attitude—by

---

130. This focus on distanced contemplation of objects is a specific (and thus narrow) use of the term "aesthetics." A much broader use of aesthetics is favored by anthropological advocates of "cultural aesthetics" such as Steven Feld and Jeremy Coote. Feld sketches out an aesthetics of Kaluli song that is not *distanced* (as it typically is in post-Romantic criticism, Indian and German alike) but directly iconic of a way of life: comportmental, relational, ethical, and participatory. See also Coote in Ingold 1996.

131. That is, "arousing passions" and "superficial emotional excitement." Deshpande 1989, 23.

132. Chaubey 1958, 47–48.

133. Saxena 2012, 73.

134. Saxena 2010, 169.

which a voice becomes an object with qualities appraised at a distance, rather than through a shared vocal circuit—relies both on technologies of vocal isolation (microphones, sound systems, hushed auditoria, radio, recordings) and on a set of listening practices.[135] An "aesthetic" experience in this sense is rather different from the chills or tears of *tasir*, which pervade one's body and thus are "underdistanced." It likewise is distinct from the "overdistanced" attitude that looks for "technical accuracy in respect of raga and tala."

One key technology for the production of the aesthetic attitude is the stillness and aural focus offered by a concert hall. Any song sung in a *mahfil*, *satsang*, *dargāh*, or *samā*, of any genre, may, in principle, be reproduced in the very different social format of a *concert stage*.[136] But in a darkened theater, projected through a large sound system, the voice that emerges is squeezed into a tightly circumscribed form of relationality: a clean, unidirectional vector of vocal transmission from artiste to aesthete. Unlike the relatively noisy ambience of a mahfil (where all are seated together in the same space and the explosive *dād* of rasikas offers an ongoing counterpoint with the sonority of the singer's voice), a dark concert hall affords quiet, focused listening in a zone utterly separate from that of the singer on stage. The audience sits still and silent before the stage, avoiding sounds or gestures that may register to the other mostly anonymous listeners, and most of all, avoiding any interference with the singer.[137] Certainly, audiences will applaud at appropriate places; some cognoscenti will mark the culmination of metrical cycles with an understated, barely visible wave of the hand; a row of noted connoisseurs in the front row or seated on the floor in the front may even try to give *dād* aloud.[138] But in general, a concert hall demands a radically,

---

135. Rahaim 2019.

136. See also Racy 2004 on the distinction between a small, private *jalsah* and a public *haflah*.

137. This is, *mutatis mutandis*, very close to Christopher Small's classic, if highly general, description of concert hall listening practice (Small 2012, 26–27).

138. Often, a public concert will include a section in front of the stage spread with clean sheets and cushions for *baiṭhak* (seated) seating—for those willing to sit on the floor, as in a ghar mahfil. Those sitting in this section move around more freely, comment on the concert, and even, sometimes, give audible dād. There is, of course, a gray area between *mahfil* and *concert* (including, for example, public recitals on the scale of one hundred people or so in a well-lit room filled with plastic chairs, where dād may certainly occur in the front rows).

palpably different comportment from a listener, and thus an irrelational, aesthetic attitude. To withhold interaction requires a disciplined bodily stillness (much like the *sitzfleisch* required for listening to absolute music in European concert halls) no more obvious or less cultivated than giving proper *dād* in a mahfil. One often sees concert hall aesthetes sitting with their eyes entirely closed, in utter silence, lost in contemplation. As musicologist Deepak Raja puts it with characteristic dialectical rigor: "nothing misses the listener—every detail is captured,"[139] and yet, "a psychological distance is created between the performer and the listener. There's a certain disconnect taking place."[140]

This attitude is further cultivated by the aural focus of an amplified, electronically enhanced microphonic voice, where every murmur is made available for contemplation, even at great distances. Live sound engineers use effects to enhance the sonority of the singer's voice. Heightening harmonics in the 3k–5k range gives an enhanced sense of sur—both in the blend with the tanpura and in smoothing out inconsistencies in vowels; reverb blurs out the wavering of the voice; compression smooths out the inevitable changes in amplitude that accompany movements up and down through the range. And a well-tuned monitor system presents to the singer an amplified, enhanced reproduction of their own voice, drowning out the voices of the audience. The process of gradually tuning the sound system (often including numerous tweaks in the first ten minutes or so of the performance) involves the singer requesting fine adjustments to monitor volume and EQ. Sound engineers are acutely aware of the "sonic placebo effect," in which you pretend to turn a knob to placate an acoustically demanding singer; the trick works precisely because something in the ear *is* turned. The sound check thus is not only an occasion for tuning acoustical levels, but also of attuning the ear to the peculiar reflexive sonic environment afforded by stage monitors. For those on the other side of the speakers, seated far away, a voice thus selectively amplified, enhanced, and re-presented to the audience stands out as a sonorous voice-object available, with immaculate clarity, for distanced, irrelational aesthetic contemplation. If all goes well, an amplified voice sounds loud, clear, rich, and bright. This voice stands out—sonically, spatially, relationally—among the unamplified, acoustically muted voices of the crowd. By selectively amplifying the voice of a singer (and not the responses of listeners) concert hall sound systems strengthen one leg of the vocal circuit at the expense of the other. Bathed in the

139. Raja 2016, 23:30.

140. Raja 2016, 35:20.

sonic output of her monitors, a singer on stage cannot hope to detect the futile attempts at unamplified *dād* offered from the middle of the audience; blinded by bright lights, she may find it difficult to see even the front row.

This relational deprivation can make singing quite difficult for singers whose vocal sensibility is tuned to the relationality of a *mahfil.* Vikas Kashalkar, for example, once told me about a particularly awkward concert early in his career. He brought a long rendition of a *raga* to a close in a dark, cavernous concert hall, and, after fifty minutes of sitting silent and still, the audience stood to give him a standing ovation. Nothing could have surprised him more. It wasn't that he sounded bad: his sur was clear, his improvisations fit elegantly into the metric cycles, everything was correct. Rather, he was surprised because he had sung for nearly an hour without receiving a single word or gesture of praise. This would have been unthinkable at the intimate gatherings that he was accustomed to. "They sat with their hands tied up, not even nodding. I could guess from their face—I could see them: no response." Feeling rather at a loss, Kashalkar had assumed early in the concert that the audience simply didn't understand what he was doing. So he simplified things somewhat, avoided "intricacies" and gave what he considered a relatively anodyne performance—not directed at anyone in particular, like a recording. After all, "if they don't give the response, what is the fun of going into the intricate part?" Though everything was sonically correct, he felt ill at ease and dissatisfied with the performance.

> [Ordinarily,] I sing something and I get the response from the audience. We are *used* to that. On the basis of the response . . . Because we get the nodding from the audience, and we get that this is liked by the audience, and so a similar type of presentation is done [i.e., we keep on with the vocal gait or sonority that evoked the response]. Suppose I don't get the nodding from the audience: then I will have to shift to something else.

This was not merely annoying; it also made it hard for him to continue to sing: "Then I thought: it is very misplaced to sing before these people . . . How to go on [singing] for one hour?"

This is something like the inverse of stage fright: rather than anxiously registering every twitch in the audience, the singer loses the will to sing precisely to the extent that there is *no* response. The problem is not how to avoid panic, nor merely intellectual "puzzlement,"[141] but how to *go on singing* at all without

141. Cf. Farrell 1999, 192.

a response? The singer without a responsive listener must learn to overcome listlessness, aimlessly shifting from one vocal disposition to another, deprived of relational bearings. Many singers echo this disconcerting sense of relational unmooring.[142] As singer and critic Sheila Dhar puts it, the concert hall audience "is no one in particular, just a vast black pit with an unknown animal in it. It might roar or pounce, purr or go back to sleep. He has no way of knowing."[143] As Kaivalya Kumar Gaurav asked in a recent concert in Minneapolis, after asking again and again for the lights to be brought up so that he could see the audience, "Without seeing the audience, what should I sing?" Obviously, it is possible to go on *making sounds*. It's a perfectly ordinary thing to hum to "oneself" with no one else around. And even in the darkest, quietest concert hall, one is, of course, in a room full of listeners, albeit of a very special kind. But to maintain a vocal disposition without resonance from listeners requires an effortful turning away from these relations.

The concert stage, however, is not nowhere. Nor must audiences always be entirely invisible to singers. Indeed, many singers took pride in "conquering" large audiences from the stage. Shailaja Pandit once told me about her guru Hirabai Barodekar's ability to size up an audience:

> She used to assess the audience within first ten minutes . . . What is the response? And accordingly she will change the duration, the choice of raga, the type of music she has to present. In Jaipur, she started some yaman-like thing . . . but I think not much of a response she was getting from them. So she cut it short, say half an hour immediately. And immediately she started Mānd (a popular light raga)—it was really popular. So the audience—I saw it, *wow!*—they gave a standing ovation immediately. So how to win the concert, it is a *knack*.

This is a different kind of relational circuit, one that works in making discrete decisions about length and repertoire rather than, as in a mahfil or a samā, repeating and developing individual phrases that connoisseurs respond to. The conventions of live qawwali stage shows likewise are directed to a generalized listener—when audience members clap along as a bloc, or stand and dance as anonymous individuals (in stark contrast to the conventional comportment at a

142. This was apparently a common complaint among the first generation of Hindustani musicians who toured in Europe. See Farrell 1999, 144.

143. Dhar 2001, 91.

mahfil-e samā), qawwals certainly respond to the energy of the room as a whole rather than particular listeners. This is precisely the kind of relation that critics bemoan when they complain about bad listeners corrupting musical standards.

Recordings, too, foster this one-way contemplation of singing as an aesthetic object. To be sure, listeners may discern svaras and ragas; they may even be deeply moved, to tears and chills—but one is not faced with a singer to encourage with *dād*; there is no circuit in the relational, interactive sense that we encounter in a mahfil, a samā, or a satsang. This sense is heightened by repeated listenings and especially by rewinding repeatedly, as when trying to reproduce a particular vocal move (see chapter 5), which affords a view of a dependable, formally consistent object. The "voice" that we tune into through headphones is reliable, rewindable, unresponsive, disembodied, abstract—the perfect aesthetic object. And yet, the production of such an object is by no means obvious or natural. It is only through meticulous microphone placement and audio engineering that recordings can give the illusion of a pure, isolated voice that may be freely resituated anywhere. For most modern studios, this requires the uncanny acoustical dryness of soundproofing (sheets of foam, in wedges or eggcrates) that aim to remove any acoustical or relational particularity of the room the singer is in. Sufi singer Mukhtiyar Ali, for example, says that he "surrenders totally" and feels "euphoric" singing for others, but becomes "fidgety" singing alone in an air-conditioned studio.[144] As Martin Stokes notes for the near-contemporaneous rise of recording practices in Egypt, the shift from small gatherings of connoisseurs to microphonic mass broadcasting marks a shift between two modes of social relation: from "respectful and knowledgeable interactions between vocalist, instrumentalists, and audience in performance" to the vocal sentimentality produced by the "abstracted and authoritarian work disciplines of the recording studio . . ."[145] It is partially for this reason that many early Hindustani recording sessions tried to make things easier on singers whose sensibilities were tuned to a mahfil by including an audience. But such listeners, too, must learn to suppress their relational habits. Ustad Ghulam Rasul Khan, for example, was once invited to such a commercial recording session as a knowledgeable listener. Though he was instructed to remain quiet, his enthusiastic *dād* interrupted the

144. Nagaraj 2010.

145. Stokes in Nooshin 2016, 64–65.

first three takes of the recording before he was persuaded to be silent for the sake of "sterility."[146]

On the other hand, even when isolated in a booth, it is exceedingly difficult to sing to *no one at all*. When faced with huge, anonymous audiences—on radio or TV, in a studio, or in a vast auditorium, with no listeners in particular—singers often find ways to pitch their songs to a virtual "audience imaginary."[147] This discipline of addressing an invisible but vividly imagined audience requires what Marié Abe calls "imaginative empathy" with unseen listeners,[148] or what Mark Katz calls an "intelligent rapport" with a virtual ear.[149] Anuraag Dhoundeyal explains this act of projection as "preempting how you would perceive this song to be, and then singing how you would want it to be sung, and then singing that way." To emphasize the "imaginary" practices that disclose such a public is not to dismiss the real power exerted by mass-mediated song; these practices may even be seen to produce, through "audiencemaking" feedback, an audience so imagined.[150] In fact, the undifferentiated "mass" audience of this imaginary maps rather neatly onto the ethical distinction outlined by Chloë Alaghband-Zadeh: whereas a true rasika, emblematic of the egalitarian "old middle class," participates knowledgeably in performance, the wealthy but uneducated "new middle class" concertgoer simply buys a ticket, sits back and consumes what is on display.[151] This distinction between the inheritors of feudal *adab* and the recent arrivals into the urban middle class is conventionally marked through the traditional binary "*ḳhās/ām*" (often rendered rhymingly into English as "classes/masses"). Whether this *ām* imaginary is understood to want widely accessible songs of universal love rather than esoteric Sufi theology, catchy dance numbers instead of contemplative mystical songs, or simply "emotion" hardly matters; such an audience is nearly always ascribed simple, vulgar tastes.[152] And yet, as we have seen, the anonymous, distanced listening of a concert hall paradoxi-

146. Silver 1976, 30–31.

147. Tejaswini Ganti 2012.

148. Abe 2018, 102–103.

149. Katz 2004, 39–40. As Steven Rings points out (in Feldman 2019, 43) recordings that imply vocal interaction with an audience can afford "slippage into real-world interaction" in concert.

150. Ettema and Whitney 1994.

151. Alaghband-Zadeh 2016, following Rachel Dwyer's distinction (2000).

152. Desai-Stevens 2017, 75.

cally also produces the radically individual aesthetic attitude that has become so central to modern music criticism—that has, along with recordings, produced a distinctively modern sense of voice as an art object.

Self as Listener

Not all figurations of solitary song explicitly call for a divine listener. In one telling of the Haridas legend cited above, his ethical power is attributed to the fact that he sings not for God, but for *himself*.[153] Many singers, in fact, will say that your principal listener is yourself, rather than those gathered in front of you. As Rajan Mishra once put it: "You should enjoy your music yourself, first . . . [the] first condition of your music is that you should yourself enjoy your music first, then the audience will be enjoying you."[154] Dhrupadiya Chintan Upadhyay once described to me an irrelational disposition that, he argued, was essential to dhrupad, expertly narrating a vividly imagined primordial past corrupted by the relational practices of early modern mahfils, when "people started proving themselves [and] showing off." Chintan pointed out that the allure of mahfil relationality is hard to resist, and thus, that the cherished irrelationality putatively adequate to dhrupad requires work: "It is very tough when you are on stage, when there are thousands of people. . . . You have to consider that actual purity of the form of dhrupad, that it is not for entertaining somebody . . . it is to make them more aware about the inner study of your *own* self that you do on stage." And, as a practical matter, most young classical singers spend much more time in solitary practice (riyaz) than singing for others.

In any case, these practices do not succeed in making an island of any singer, in fact or principle. Even when practicing alone, even with purely technical (rather than devotional) intention, singers bear the traces of their lineage in their paramparic body,[155] including the practices of listening that guide them toward vocal progress (see chapter 5). To sing for "oneself" is not to short out a circuit of voice, but to form a special circuit between two ethical faculties of self: one that sings and one that listens.[156] One learns to hear with the scrutinizing ear

153. Delvoye in Habib 1997, 207.

154. Scott 1997, 213.

155. Rahaim 2012.

156. For more nuance on this thorny question, see Macken and Jones, 1995; Tomatis

of one's guru, and learns to hear and root out one's "own" imperfections. In the Kabir tradition, a particular transcendent inner listener is often invoked, one that stands apart from the usual conditions of existence. As we will see in chapter 4, the ambiguity between singing for God and singing for Self serves to bolster the pop sufi inflections given to the figure of the singer as romantic genius. The denial of relationality, the exclusion of relations, is nonetheless a common theme in vocal ethics—always as extraordinary cases, marked ethically in contrast to a relational norm. A practical relational ontology of voice serves, in most cases, as the unmarked norm. Aesthetical, individualistic, and transcendental ontologies of voice appear to offer ghostly, extraordinary, spiritualistic possibilities in part precisely because they appear to bypass the normal singer-listener circuit. And as we will see in the following chapter, forms of relationality and irrelationality are often at the heart of vocal contestations.

2005 [1988]; and Zahavi 1999.

FOUR

Kiskī Āvāz?

Vocal Formation and Contestation

We have already seen that a way of voice—a way of bodily comportment, of temporal attunement, of relational connection to others—does not merely belong to an individual. To sing heavy or light, open or closed, to sing "in Lata's voice" or "Agra gayaki" is to vocally dispose oneself along with innumerable others. These disciplined, supraindividual voices are amplified and refracted in mass media, feeding back upon themselves, serving in turn as exemplars for young aspirants, cohering into public vocal formations that outlive individual singers. Any such vocal formation takes time to take shape, and it takes its place in a variegated, ecumenical voicescape of other, alternative formations. A voice comes to take on public ethical stakes precisely to the extent that it it is heard as a vocal subject position, sounding out not only itself, but in dispositional *contrast* to these other possibilities. This chapter surveys several of these vocal formations and the various kinds of moral contestation that they have provoked.

Gharana Gayaki: Crystallizations of Lineage

Gharānās (vocal lineages for raga music) offer the most institutionally stable and explicitly delineated vocal formations.[1] For a khyaliya, it is not enough to sing

---

1. Musical lineages founded by women are routinely denied the term *gharana*, but the term *śaili* is in currency among female singers and does much of the same conceptual work. There are also named tabla gharanas (Farrukhabad, Panjab, etc.) and instru-

with proper *sur*, nor even to have had an individual authoritative teacher; one must also have the lineage of a *gharana* discernible in one's voice. In the nineteenth century, the word *gharana* referred to a "house of music" from which a vocal tradition emanated: an extended family of singers into which one was born or married, with a distinctive, secret corpus of repertoires and techniques, with whom one would identify even when attached to courts far from home, guided by more or less explicit institutional structures of authority.[2] By 1947, this usage, linked to a family, a place, and an authoritative hierarchy, was already largely obsolete. The collapse of aristocratic patronage, the rise of the music reform movement, and expansion of new bourgeois listening publics had attracted a great many gharana-trained singers away from courtly centers to Bombay and Calcutta, where they trained thousands of non-hereditary aspirants. Thus, by the twenty-first century, to invoke a gharana is principally to invoke a *gayaki* (a coherent constellation of vocal dispositions) rather than a familial institution. The gayaki associated with each gharana is (in principle) unique, distinctive, and unmistakable. A great deal of detailed musicological work was and is committed to distinguishing between gharana gayakis in terms of structure, design, and ornamentation, enabled by comparison of recordings after the fact, foregrounding the architectural form of melodic objects.[3] For an aesthetic listening attitude attuned principally to recordings, where one rewinds and listens repeatedly to a segment of a performance over and over, a gharana may indeed show up as a kind of fixed aesthetic grammar, analyzable in terms of features, traits, tone, and form.

But for a singer, a gharana gayaki is (in B. R. Deodhar's apt phrase) a "method and discipline" before it shows up as a text for critical evaluation.[4] It is built on a foundation of hard-won, skilled vocal dispositions, rather than a set of abstract stylistic traits. To sing with the "vigour of Agra gharana" or the "*chaindar*, contemplative and restrained approach of Kirana gharana"[5] or the "serious and sombre mood"[6] of Jaipur gharana is to comport oneself vocally, charged with an evident, distinctive, recognizable form of extraordinary vocal character. As

mental gharanas (Maihar, Lucknow, etc.), as well as dhrupad *banis* (Dagar, Darbhanga, etc.), which imply much the same thing as khyal gharanas.

2. Neuman, Daniel 1990.

3. Deshpande 1989; Wade 1984; Bagchee 1998; Raja 2009.

4. B. R. Deodhar, foreword to Deshpande 1989, ix.

5. Datta, et al. 2017, 128.

6. Haldankar 2001, 26.

Babanrao Haldankar points out, each gharana gayaki requires its own "specific excercises to cultivate."[7] Accordingly, belonging to a gharana requires taking on a certain form of disciplined vocal being larger than oneself or one's teacher: to cultivate one's individual voice in accordance with a crystallized, supraindividual vocal disposition. Indeed, in intimate mahfils, singers will often take the name of a beloved master when singing in that particular gayaki. Conscious reflection on just *whose* gayaki it is typically comes after the fact, once they have already found themselves singing in a particular kinetic or sonorous disposition.

A gharana gayaki is, in principle, older than any living singer. It includes in its ambit both one's own immediate master (whom one has met again and again for instruction, face-to-face) *and* a chain of legendary masters (whom one has never met in the flesh). Yet, these legendary masters somehow seem to live on, audibly, palpably, in one's own voice. This is often expressed in grand narratives of musical skill, virtue, and public celebration—the effect a particular gayaki has on listeners, the "defeat" of a musical rival, the public blessing of a great political or spiritual figure. If these extravagant, richly embellished stories are not quite disinterested historical reportage, nor are they merely self-serving propaganda. They impart an idealized situated relationality to vocal technique. As Max Katz has shown, lineages are made affectively real and present through "embodied dispositions that connect the superiority of lineage ancestors to the value of inherited knowledge in the present."[8] My own guru, L. K. Pandit, often refers not only to the *guṇa* (quality, skill, virtue) of his own guru and father, but also to the foundational masters that imparted the secrets of Gwalior Gharana to his family—Haddu Khan, Natthu Khan, and Nissar Hussain Khan. Once, in the middle of teaching me a difficult phrase in Rag Puriya, he stopped singing, stared off into the distance with tears in his eyes, sighed, and murmured, "Haddu Khan was a great man, *bābā*." The utterance was no less poignant for the fact that Guruji was born decades *after* Haddu Khan had died. I have described elsewhere the astonished utterance of one young khyaliya to the effect that he was the "next birth" of one of his musical ancestors that he had never met, but was seeing for the first time in a video.[9] Such a *paramparic body*—an embodied vocal disposition that spans generations—is not a wholesale inheritance of muscle and bone,

7. Haldankar 2001, 114.

8. Katz 2017, 86.

9. Rahaim 2012, 132.

but a dispositional complex built, over time, from a wide range of exemplars, encountered both in face-to-face training and in vivid imagination.

A gharana gayaki is also, by necessity, *esoteric*: it consists of a corpus of techniques, songs, and lore transmitted to insiders and guarded from outsiders. While raga theory and even skeletal notations of compositions are widely published in books, videos, and speeches, the esoterica passed from master to disciple reveals secret places inside ragas, secret compositions at variance with common raga grammars, secret methods of vocal production linked to bygone masters. In this sense, the institution of a gharana is, by necessity, as structurally conservative as any orthodox Sufi order. If its windows are open, its doors are closed. Just as a great shaykh embodies spiritual secrets passed down, in principle, from masters of a prior age, so too does a gharana singer embody vocal secrets traceable to a great vocal ancestor. And as with elite Sufi institutions, gharanas tend to privilege elite men (indeed, the word *gharana* is typically reserved for lineages with male progenitors).

The vocal secrets imparted in each gharana are often dramatically at odds with other gharanas. For this reason, a great deal of vocal contestation occurs between gharanas. Partisans of Agra gharana will often disparage Kirana gayaki for being incoherent, inchoate, and merely sweet; Kirana singers in turn may regard Agra gayaki as too rigid and dry, and so on. In practice, these distinctions indicate not only an aesthetic conflict of "taste," but also a palpable and irreducible ethical friction.

This friction is well illustrated by the career of singer and critic V. H. Deshpande (1907–1990), who describes the "formidable," "painful," "shocking experience" of transitioning from Gwalior gayaki to Kirana gayaki to Jaipur gayaki over the course of his career. After his initial Gwalior training, Sureshbabu Mane gave him his first "revelation" of Kirana gayaki, which was "so entrancing and captivating" that Deshpande was "instantly enslaved by him. It was not just music but pure hypnotism."[10] But learning Kirana required loss as well as gain: Mane told Deshpande that he would have to "wipe out" all of his prior training in Gwalior gayaki.[11] Deshpande was indeed radically changed by his training with Mane; over the course of the next few years, in Pune, he was given a "divine revelation [*sākśāt*] of perfect intonation," developing a new capacity for the purity of *sur* (see chapter 2) so widely associated with Kirana gayaki. Several years later, Deshpande

10. Deshpande 1987, 2.

11. Ibid.

was won over once again, this time by Naththan Khan of Jaipur gharana. The new style was not as immediately "entrancing," but it was "lively, disciplined, refined."[12] In Naththan Khan's presence, the sonorous "Kirana" disposition that he had earlier worked so hard to acquire now appeared as a mere unreflective "habit": a "a pronounced nasal accent." It furthermore appeared as a dispositional *lack* ("not quite full-throated") in comparison to the new disposition he was now striving after.[13] Once again, he was compelled to retrain his sensibilities, to unlearn old habits. And once again, over the course of only a year, "the sweetness and artistry of this new style" became evident, "as if I had been roaming happily in a garden but there was another garden next-door, extraordinarily beautiful, differently landscaped. How was it that I had failed to see it?"[14]

In this sense, training in a gayaki is also training in micropractices of listening that give access to a particular vocal world. As Arun Kashalkar once put it to me, once you've undergone training in a particular gharana, "the whole world looks different."[15] This ontological shift often reconfigures one's sense of what is "natural." Once Deshpande was fully attuned to Jaipur gayaki, it seemed to him that Agra and Kirana had "imported artificiality into their voice-production," in contrast to the "natural, free and full-throated voice" of Jaipur gharana.[16] This naturalness and freedom, of course, is in the ear-and-voice of the beholder, shaped by and dispositionally attuned to the kinetics and sonority of its own vocal training. Kumar Prasad Mukherji charts a similar change. At first, he found Krishna Rao Shankar Pandit's voice "gruff, his mannerisms comical, and his taans verging on acrobatics. This was due to my early addiction to Kirana [gharana]." But later in life, on attuning himself to Gwalior gayaki, he found that this same voice "sounds so much more in sur than how he sounded when I was young. The change was not in him, but in me."[17] In my own case, it was only after I opened up the *jivārī* (bright, nasal resonance) in my own voice that I began to admire the vocal openness of Yashwantbuwa Joshi (who had theretofore sounded harsh to me) as a sort of steadfastness, maintaining an unwavering openness despite complicated kinetic vocal action. Conversely, less open voices began to sound

---

12. Deshpande 1987, 16.
13. Ibid.
14. Deshpande 1987, 18.
15. Rahaim 2012, 116.
16. Deshpande 1987, 16.
17. Mukherji 2006, 98–99.

artificially covered up to me. So too do sweetness, liveliness, entrancement, refinement, naturalness, freedom, openness, and other vocal *guṇas* come to life in a particular sedimented circuit of listening and singing. The transformative power of this circuitry allows us to harken in a slightly different way to the common complaint about supposedly "intransigent," "feudal," "old-fashioned" *ustads* who don't allow their disciples to listen to singers from other gharanas.[18] To the extent that listening is dispositional, to the extent that particular listening sensibilities are practiced and built, any responsible teacher attends to what (and thus *how*) their disciple is hearing. As every listening body is also a disciplined paramparic body, there is no neutral, untrained position in which to stand and evaluate a gayaki.

Gharana conservatisms thus sit uncomfortably with nationalist desires for musical unity. Though gharana singers are often publicly burdened with the custodianship of what has come to be seen as a singular, exoteric national musical heritage, they are bearers of inescapably plural, esoteric modes of vocal being. Music reformers of the early twentieth century tended to see gharanas as institutional obstacles to public music education; inasmuch as a gharana keeps its secrets to itself, it is seen to be hoarding knowledge that, in the logic of nationalism, should belong equally to all citizens.[19] In one majoritarian telling of this story, gharanas are narrated as guild-like families of Muslims, protecting their musical monopoly, keeping it locked away from a national-Hindu citizenry clamoring for knowledge.[20] A related stream of criticism tends to denigrate the very idea of comportmental boundaries implied by gharanas. The post-independence figuration of a singer as an *artiste*, and the adoption of romantic aesthetics by music critics, tends to construe gharana discipline as a restriction on a prior artistic freedom (often narrated as eminently *national* in character). There are, to be sure, sound musicological reasons to avoid "making a fetish" of gharanas (that is, to prioritize each gharana's claims to aesthetic purity above the evident vocal diversity in their performers), and sound sociological reasons to critically highlight the patriarchal elitism of gharanas.[21] Indeed, public disdain for gharana orthodoxy has never been stronger. The most conservative torchbearers of

18. Scarimbolo 2017.

19. Bakhle 2005, 6.

20. Scarimbolo surveys this narrative (2014, 275) and demonstrates its historical inadequacy.

21. Lath 1988; Scott 1997, 137; Srinivasan 2020.

nineteenth-century gharana repertoire labor largely in obscurity, and most of the most popular national superstars of khyal have broken from gharana orthodoxy. Many of the foundational national heroes (such as Bade Ghulam Ali Khan, Abdul Karim Khan, and Amir Khan) came from what Dard Neuman calls "heterodox" lineages of accompanists who transitioned to the more prestigious role of singer in the decades before independence, and only later, on receiving national public acclaim, were ascribed gharana names (Patiala, Kirana, Indore).[22] Many of the most successful hereditary singers self-consciously brought together techniques from outside of their gharana training (as Kishori Amonkar and Pandit Jasraj did with "light" harkat and Kumar Gandharv did with the *pukar* of nirgun bhajans).[23] The conflict between gharana-bound discipline and artistic innovation is often mapped onto ethical faculties (as for example, Kishori Amonkar "infusing more *emotions*" into the orthodox Jaipur framework, for which she "faced criticism from purists for distorting the set *rules*").[24]

In other words, the purported conservatism of gharana gayaki often serves as a moral backdrop to the formation and contestation of new voices. We turn now to one such vocal formation in particular: the innovative, widely influential, and highly controversial gayaki of Amir Khan.

"A Calm That Spreads": The Life of Amir Khan's Gayaki

Across gharanas, there has been one clear vocal-dispositional trend in khyal since independence: away from the open, relational, mahfil-oriented voice cultivated in orthodox gharanas, and toward a gentle, relatively closed microphonic sonority sung at dramatically slow tempi. This widespread, supraindividual voice is usually attributed to the profound influence of Amir Khan (1912–1974), whose ultra-slow metric cycles, soft voice, and calm bearing was a model for nearly all singers who followed—male and female alike.[25] Amir Khan's voice became

22. Neuman, Dard, 2004, 27.

23. Critic Deepak Raja specifically alleges that these three had led a trend among khyaliyas to "invade, and annexe, the aesthetic space being gradually vacated" by thumri.

24. Deshpande 2017.

25. Though it is widely agreed that Amir Khan adapted his ultra-slow approach (as well as the recently revived combinatoric method of merukhand [see Dard Neuman, forthcoming]) from Kirana master Abdul Wahid Khan, the few existing recordings of

nationally known when he sang in the hugely popular film *Baiju Bawra* (1952), in which his voice stood in for the voice of legendary sixteenth-century Mughal court singer, Tansen.[26] Though Amir Khan is sometimes assigned a gharana, most tend to treat him as a singular genius, developing a personal "Amirkhani" gayaki outside of an orthodox teaching lineage.[27]

Amir Khan's critical reception hinged principally on his relaxed, "unhurried," introspective vocal disposition, which he seems to have developed right around independence.[28] His very earliest 78rpm recordings (for example, Adana and

---

the latter indicate that Amir Khan took things much further, arriving at tempi nearly twice as slow, after decades of singing at more conventionally brisk tempi (Magriel and du Perron 2013, 253–254). Furthermore, Amir Khan's post-1947 vocal disposition, for which he was and is famous, was mellower, gentler, and more closed than Abdul Wahid Khan's own relatively open voice. Abdul Wahid Khan indeed is said to have mistrusted microphones. For example, see his 48-minute recording of Darbari Kanada, in which he sings bright and open on the high *sā* within a minute of beginning.

26. It is notable that, in the film, Tansen is ultimately defeated in a royal singing competition by Baijnath, voiced by D. V. Paluskar, another hugely influential singer who brought a clean, streamlined vocal sensibility to the traditional repertoire of Gwalior gharana (see Jhingan 2011). The courtly contest, however, ultimately hinges upon speed and vocal intensity, rather than the slow, gentle, introspective gayaki that Amir Khan was widely identified with.

27. Nadkarni 1999, 177. He is sometimes subsumed under Kirana gharana (due to the influence of Abdul Wahid Khan) and sometimes considered the progenitor of Indore gharana. Others consider him a unique genius with no true esoteric inheritors (only imitators), and thus not truly gharanedar. Bonnie Wade (1984) considers him an individual singer; Dard Neuman (2004) regards him as a heterodox innovator who took on many of the alap-centric reforms of Behram Khan.

28. Saxena in Wade 1984, 269. Critics also took exception to the deployment of the combinatoric technique of *merukhand* in concert. Dard Neuman demonstrates that merukhand was a twentieth-century refiguration of a thirteenth-century practice technique, largely embraced by singers outside of orthodox kalawant gharana structures, largely disdained by orthodox singers, "a form of knowledge that was exogenous to existing kalawant knowledge systems and was used therefore used by musicians who had less access to claims of traditional authority." Critic S. K. Chaubey claims that Abdul Wahid Khan "treats music as mathematics . . . Though he is clever and consistent, he sings from his head, and not from his heart." (Chaubey in Neuman, forth-

Todi, which were little noticed, then or now) were "full of vitality, keeping pace with fast movement," full of rapid tāns, with open voice and bright, ringing jivārī. Musicologist Ibrahim Ali marks the change in Amir Khan's voice at 1948, at which point he turned to the "capability to hypnotize by means of swara."[29] Many traditionalists regarded this shift as an unwelcome modern innovation. Critic V. H. Deshpande described Amir Khan's gayaki as having "the languor of unfinished sleep, ready to relapse and yet vaguely thinking thoughts of activity of the approaching day-time."[30] Gwalior master Krishna Rao Shankar Pandit warned that by singing so slowly, khyal "is bound to lose its significance and meaning [and] character."[31] Even today, many singers committed to traditional Gwalior, Agra, and Jaipur gayakis tend to regard the Amirkhani approach as a modern concession to popular taste, oblivious to the flowing temporality of metrical cycles, freely indulging in extended, ametrical alap, and listening for the last strokes of tāl to sing the *mukhṛā*.[32]

In other circles, however, Amir Khan's calm came to be regarded not as a modern innovation, but as fidelity to a vividly imaged form of traditional, premodern virtue. Though there is no evidence that vocal calm was ever a legible *guṇa* for pre-independence singers,[33] many listeners heard Amir Khan's carefully

---

coming.) Thomas Ross (1993) argues that Amir Khan did not ordinarily deploy strict merukhand in performance, deploying artful combinations of *phrases* rather than mechanical combinations of individual notes.

29. Ali n.d. Amir Khan's early recordings in Adana and Todi give a picture of this early period of influence.

30. Deshpande 1987, 64.

31. Nadkarni 1986.

32. See Morris 2004, 233 and passim, on the "slow-down." See Mukherjee interviewed in Grimes 2008 for further critique of imitators of Amir Khan. I admit to some puzzlement, however, at the charge that Amir Khan himself was quite so indifferent to the passage of tāl. On the contrary, his avartans are gracefully filled and lead very smoothly to the mukhra, evidencing a careful sense of metrical proportion.

33. Among the lists of singers' good and bad habits (*guṇa* and *doṣa*) in Sanskrit and Persian treatises, grimacing and visible physical tension appear quite commonly as *doṣas* to be avoided. (*Karabha* and *vakrī*, for example, seem to have suggested physical tension; Hakim 1959, 6 suggests that the doṣ of *kampit* is a result of nervousness.) But calm itself rarely appears as a *guṇa*, or positive virtue.

cultivated disposition as a "return to ancient music" in contrast to the bustle of modern life.[34] Sushila Mishra described "his dignity of bearing and his posture of Yogic calm," in harmony with the "serene grandeur of his music."[35] G. N Joshi described his comportment as "the posture of a yogi doing his *tapasya* [ascetic exercises], with closed eyes and deep meditation," praising the "atmosphere of solemnity and tranquility"—a welcome escape from "the noisy and sometimes un-musical gymnastic bouts" of orthodox singers.[36] This onstage persona, heightened by strikingly plain dress, worked to distance Amir Khan's voice from his background as a sarangiya (which, in popular imagination if not fact, would have suggested a life of hedonism centered on courtesans' salons). Indeed, this restrained presentation of self may even have been carefully cultivated; Amir Khan famously made it a point to never perform thumri or ghazal in public, or to be accompanied by sarangi, despite the fact that he sang these song forms quite well in private (and in a lighter, sweeter vocal disposition).

Amir Khan's public-facing vocal disposition was widely construed as a vocal icon of an older, gentler temporality, morally uncorrupted by the indignities of modernity. This became particularly salient in the decades after independence, at a time of migration to big cities and Nehruvian public works, marked out by clock and calendar time (symbolized dramatically by the eviction and flooding of medieval rural villages to build high-tech dams).[37] Invocations of "Indian time,"[38] often as light-hearted apologies for late start times or leisurely teatimes, like many postcolonial nationalist stereotypes, is pitched precisely in contrast to a particular picture of British colonial modernity—in this case, the unforgiving progress of the minute hand on the clock. Such a rhythmanalytic valorization of indistinct slowness reads slow vilambit khyal as morally uplifting precisely for resisting the temporality of industrial modernity.[39] Anthropologist Kalpana Ram describes the temporality of savoring music—emplaced, paradigmatically, in a concert hall—"slowing down the 'action' of a narrative or a text" for savoring.

34. Nadkarni 1987 in Ali n.d., section 12.

35. Mishra 1981, 170.

36. Joshi 1984, 92.

37. See Neuman 1980, 35 on music as a locus of reflective nostalgia about the leisurely pace of times past.

38. A Google Books Ngram analysis indicates no usages before 1930, with a dramatic, steady increase since independence.

39. See Lefebvre 2004, Syring 2009.

Pivoting on discourses of *ras*, she invokes the counter-modern critique of fast food, extolling a temporality of savoring, "taking time over the cuisine, preparing the ingredients, but also intervening at the right time to adjust the heat."[40] In such appraisals, Amirkhani temporality, like "slow food," serves not a *representation* of the breathless time of modernity, but a *remedy*. It opens a parallel world, free from the demands of ringing phones, honking horns, looming deadlines, and other temporal-moral privations of bourgeois urban life. Incidentally, this same affinity for a slow progression of sustained tones found traction among another set of anti-modern innovators: the West Coast minimalists, led by Terry Riley and La Monte Young, who construed Hindustani music as a Pythagorean world of droning, atemporal, rationally measured tones.[41]

Amir Khan also seems to have been the first master of a disposition toward raga music that was at once irrelationally introspective *and* available to a national listening public. Sensitive microphones allowed the distant listener (in a concert hall, or gathered around gramophone) to listen in to his extraordinarily mellow, inward-directed tone. He would often sing with his eyes closed or lowered, singing quite close to the microphone. His mouth hardly opened at all, particularly in the lower range, and there was very little nasal resonance even when he opened his mouth to sing high passages. This subdued introversion stood in stark contrast to the relational attitude of pre-independence gharanedar singers such as Yashwant Rao Joshi or Salamat-Nazakat Ali Khan, who were attuned to mahfil sociality, singing-to particular listeners, reaching out to the audience with rhythmic surprises, singing loudly and openly, and evoking *dād*. Orthodox singers trained in the pre-microphonic era had developed techniques of voice projection adequate to unamplified mahfils, where only vocal power and openness could ensure that one's voice reached a roomful of listeners.[42] Indeed, Deepak Raja attributes the decline of Agra gharana gayaki and the rise of gentler voices precisely to the rise of modern amplification techniques.[43]

Amir Khan's gayaki is frequently described in plainly irrelational terms: free

40. Ram 2011, S161–162.

41. California minimalism shares a lineage with Amir Khan's radical style, traceable to Abdul Wahid Khan, through his disciple Pran Nath, the eccentric teacher of Riley and Young who settled in the United States.

42. See, for example, the picture of Nisar Hussain Khan singing several feet away from a microphone in Magriel and du Perron, 2013, xxii.

43. Raja 2016.

of "showmanship,"[44] performed "without any desire to titillate,"[45] with "Proustian introspection."[46] By all reports, Amir Khan affected an "absolute indifference, while singing, to the reactions of the audience. He would here heed only his music, and his own conception of it. Our response, or lack of it, had just no effect on him."[47] Perhaps Amir Khan's most authoritative advocate was sitar master Nikhil Banerjee, whose own playing had been profoundly influenced by his gayaki. Banerjee paints a dismal, if familiar, picture of Hindustani music in which musicians had been compromised by the relationality of aristocratic mahfils. After so many generations of having "catered to the taste of the court," Hindustani vocalists had become dedicated only to "entertainment" and "showmanship"—that is to say, implicated in a circuit of singing and feedback. Amir Khan, by contrast, is located in a separate tradition: that of great bhakti singer-saints like Swami Haridas—"lone wanderers of life," who spent their day "absorbed in their sadhana" rather than pleasing listeners, for whom music was a medium not of relations with listeners, but of "self-realization."[48] S. K. Saxena elegantly describes this introspective attitude as "a tuning of the self," but also notes its influence on his listening public: it is "a calm that spreads."[49]

This calm did indeed spread widely among Amir Khan's vocal admirers; though he had few students of his own, a great many others studied his recordings and took on his slow tempi, gentle kinetics, mellow sonority, and irrelational introspection. This tendency has been particularly strong among Bengali khyaliyas, where orthodox gharanas made less headway—Amiyaranjan Banerjee goes so far as to simply call it the "modern Khyal style."[50] By the turn of the twenty-first century, this disposition had become the unmarked norm among khyaliyas. Orthodox gharanedar singers who maintain faster tempi, consistently open voice, and distance from the microphone in the face of the Amirkhani tide are few and far between. Relationally singing-to particular connoisseurs in

44. Atre in Ali n.d., section 15.

45. Devidayal 2019, 178.

46. Quoted in Grimes 174.

47. Saxena 1974, 6.

48. Banerjee 1975. The pun on *self* here, spanning the sovereign, individuated self of liberal modernity and the Atman-Brahman self-identity popularly identified with yogic striving, echoes the ethics of the popular Sufi revival.

49. Saxena 1974, 7.

50. Grimes 2008, 173.

a concert is now often construed as pandering and artificial, at odds with the spiritual introspection and independence expected of an artiste. Amir Khan's gayaki thus stands as a prime exemplar of the solitary, irrelational artistry that has come to dominate raga music.

Filmi *Voice and Its Discontents*

Just as Amir Khan's mellow, close-miked gayaki was sweeping through the world of raga music, a parallel, unprecedentedly popular vocal disposition was emerging in the film studios of Bombay. Over the course of the 1950s, Lata Mangeshkar, Asha Bhosle, Kishore Kumar, and Mohammad Rafi had become India's first national vocal superstars.[51] They were and are the key exemplars of what I will be calling *filmi* voice: a particular vocal disposition that dominated the Hindustani vocal ecumene in the second half of the twentieth century. Though the careers of these particular playback singers tapered off in the 1980s and '90s, *filmi* voice lives on, and not just in recordings. The *filmi* canon has taken on a life of its own beyond films, known and loved by an unprecedentedly wide listening public, across class, community, and region. Its characteristic vocal disposition has been convincingly applied to almost every Hindustani repertoire and genre, from bhajans to thumris to ghazals to sufi pop.[52] Among barbers and computer programmers, bus drivers and domestic workers, it's common to find people who can sing in rather good *filmi* voice, even without formal training. Indeed, its domain reaches far beyond India and Pakistan to coastal East and West Africa, Southeast Asia, and the Gulf. *Filmi* voice may well be the best-known and most widely disseminated voice not just in Hindustan, but also in the history of the world.

To sing *filmi* is something rather more specific than merely singing for films; it is to sing gently, softly, sweetly, and intimately at close range. Such a voice is typically directed toward a sensitive microphone mere inches away, and thus

---

51. Geeta Dutt, Mukesh, Mahendra Kapoor, and Talat Mahmood could well be included here too. On playback music in the Tamil film industry, see Weidman 2016.

52. Qureshi has demonstrated its influence—particularly through microphone technique—on contemporary ghazal singers (1990, 489). Anna Schultz has demonstrated its currency as a distinctive vocal disposition, in Indo-Trinidadian and Maharashtrian devotional music, in salient and explicit contrast to louder, more open sonorities (2013, 2014). The Indo-Trinidadian technical term is *filmi air*.

requires low volume and low pressure. As Nipa Nag once put it to me, such a voice should sound "as if you are whispering or talking very softly, [with] no sudden jerks." *Filmi* voices generally have clear, precise *sur*, with mellow to moderate nasal resonance, light *harkat*, enunciated sweetly, with soft consonants and gradual vowel onsets rather than sudden, glottal stops, and occasional, expressive vibrato on held tones. Male and female *filmi* voices have different dispositional requirements (and, as we shall see, slightly different genealogies). The female *filmi* disposition (modeled on Lata Mangeshkar or Asha Bhosle) tends to remain very soft, even when very high in its vocal range—a difficult balance to achieve—with sparing nasal resonance, moderately khula on the vowel *ā*, relatively thin and closed otherwise. The male *filmi* disposition (modeled on Kishore Kumar or Mohammad Rafi) tends to remain lower in its vocal range, with a duller, more closed tone—with notably less *jawāri*, less nasal resonance. There are, to be sure, a range of expressive techniques for heroism, romance, seduction, and melancholy—for example, at heroic moments, a male *filmi* voice may soar into high range, shifting his range a fifth or so higher, and becoming moderately open.[53] And yet, a consistent, recognizable dispositional kernel applies to the great bulk of the *filmi* canon.

Filmi voice crystallized in the 1940s as a special technique of "playback" singing: recording a song offscreen, to be dubbed over footage of an actor lip-synching. Prior to the playback era, when actors sung live on film for relatively distant microphones, films featured a rather more diverse range of bright, vigorous, and open voices, performed by singers accustomed to singing at some distance from their audience.[54] Playback singers, in contrast, tended to sing very close to the microphone, enabling them to sing quite softly.

The formation of this voice is complexly overdetermined; its myths of origin are various and overlapping. Over the course of the 1940s, the great film singer and actress Noor Jehan had mellowed her early open voice to a gentle micro-

---

53. Even now, singers and music directors often distinguish between "hero" voices and "romantic" voices, or "vamps" and "good girls." In any case, the most versatile individual singers, such as Lata herself, are flexible enough to sing for a wide range of parts.

54. Alison Arnold convincingly contrasts the earlier and later voices ("styles") according to their ranges. It is worth noting, however, that the less sensitive microphones in use in the 1920s and '30s would have required a louder tone, particularly when singing from a distance into a horn.

phonic hum.[55] The most significant *filmi* precedent in male voice was Bengali film star K. L. Saigal, whose "softly whispered" tone was already enormously popular in the 1930s.[56] Three closely related origin narratives attribute Saigal's gentle crooning tone to various constitutional afflictions. According to one story, he developed this vocal disposition while playing a character afflicted with tuberculosis. According to another, Saigal himself was stricken with a sore throat during a recording session, and sang in "soft voice" to avoid "cracking."[57] A third story credits Saigal's affinity for liquor for his "mellow" vocal disposition.[58] All of these stories center on Saigal's own individual musicking body, but Saigal was also, no doubt, tuned into the international rise of soft, crooning, microphonic voices circulating on gramophone records in the 1920s and '30s. Crooning had proven to be widely appealing in many popular music markets, from São Paulo to Cairo to Paris, and had become the most popular singing voice in American radio by the 1920s; gramophone records of "crooners" such as Vaughn De Leath and Rudy Vallee had wide circulation.[59] In fact, a crooning vocal disposition seems to have emerged in the 1930s and '40s everywhere microphones were used. No doubt this was both an influence of circulating recordings *and* an affordance of microphones.

Like these other mellow, gentle voices, *filmi* voice had a popular appeal that was also palpably *intimate*.[60] As one critic said of K. L. Saigal, his voice was "as audible as a wish in your heart."[61] The close microphone technique, the gentle diction, the soft murmur amplified into the ear of the listener gives a palpable sense of closeness—in uncanny dialectic with the fact that these voices were broadcast and distributed into tens of thousands of households at once. Martin Stokes diagnoses this binaural ontological effect as a distinctive form of "cultural intimacy" (i.e., evoking a national, collective public felt through personal, sentimental attachment) very much in tune with popular nationalisms emerging

55. Arnold 1991, 49. It's possible to argue on structural grounds that Lata filled the space left by Noor Jehan's departure to Pakistan after partition. See Jhingan 2013, 99.

56. Beaster-Jones 2014, 31–32; Menon 1967.

57. Boral 1956.

58. All three stories are reviewed in Arnold 1999, 50.

59. Douglas 1999, 87; Taylor 2002, 437; Katz 2004, 40–41.

60. Stokes in Nooshin 2016; Denning 2015, 184.

61. Menon 1967.

between the cracks of official music patronage.[62] *Filmi* voice never received the official cultural status or state patronage given to khyaliyas; it rose to unprecedented public popularity *despite* state restrictions on film song imposed by bureaucrats at All India Radio and the Ministry of Information and Broadcasting.[63] As legendary music director Naushad wrote in a polemical defense against these policies: "Film music brought a great art out of the musty halls of the Nawabs, out of the possession of the few, to the millions who were denied the privilege of enjoying it for centuries."[64]

Never before had there been such a consistent and widely beloved vocal disposition in Hindustan. It was the first voice that could be reasonably construed as a national voice, cutting across class lines—a voice that had, as Gangadhar Gadgil put it, "a unique appeal for us Indians."[65] And yet, as we will see, the very ubiquity of this appeal became a matter of ethical concern for many critics.

Contested Femininities

The first star of *filmi* voice was Lata Mangeshkar, widely known by her admirers, even now, simply as "Lata." Her voice, more than any other, is claimed to be the national voice of India.[66] And yet, like Amir Khan's voice, Lata's voice was made, not given. She sang for years in her father's Marathi stage dramas, and trained systematically with Amanat Ali Khan and Ghulam Haider.[67] Lata's voice in her early Hindi and Marathi film songs sounds quite different from the voice she later settled upon. In "Shravan Aala Taru Tarula" (*Pahili Mangalagour*, 1942) and "Door Desh Se Aane Waale" (*Gaja Bhaau*, 1944), for example, her voice sounds relatively bright and open, particularly in the upper range. By the time she recorded her hit "Dil Mera Toda" (*Majboor*, 1948), she already had learned

62. Stokes draws on Lauren Berlant and Michael Warner's concept of cultural intimacy (1998), which applies well here as well: "the mechanism by which a core national culture can be imagined as a sanitized space of sentimental feeling and immaculate behavior . . ." (549). For more on microphonic intimacy, see Weidman 2006, 126. On binaural nationalist vocal ontologies, see Rahaim 2019.

63. Lelyveld 1994; Jhingan 2011.

64. Naushad 1955 in Jhingan 2011.

65. Gadgil in Deshpande 2004, 5179.

66. Jhingan 2013, 106.

67. Beaster-Jones 2014, 60.

to soften her voice significantly for the microphone; by "Chand Maddham Hai, Aasha Chup Hai" (*Railway Platform*, 1955), the transformation of sonority was complete. Though Marathi was her mother tongue, she trained herself (after receiving early criticism) to pronounce Urdu poetry. Once crystalized, her disposition stayed remarkably consistent for decades—one of the most consistent voices on record. Soon, others began to adopt this disposition as well—most masterfully, her younger sister Asha Bhosle, who eventually went on to record more songs in *filmi* voice than Lata herself. Lata is nonetheless popularly identified with *filmi* voice, as though it were simply her own natural, individual voice.

Lata's thin, sweet, *filmi* sonority was widely associated with young, innocent female characters.[68] But equally striking was what it did *not* sound like. In the years following independence in 1947, Lata's voice rang out in salient contrast to a prior voice that was louder, thicker, brighter, more open, attuned to the relational conditions of a mahfil—and strongly associated with the voices of courtesans.[69] Indeed, many of the most successful female playback and recording artists of the pre-Lata era were renowned as courtesans before they began their studio careers.[70] By the mid-1940s, there was a rising tide of criticism against these singers. A 1945 *Filmindia* report calls courtesan singers "paan-chewing frogs" (invoking the courtly practice of chewing *pān*) who "croak with tiresome monotony."[71] This voice, attuned for the relationality of a mahfil, invoked intense *tasir*. It is far "heavier" than the *filmi* voices which later supplanted it, including in their vast dispositional repertoire danedar tān, deep zamzam, extensive meend, and a bright, open, heart-rending sonority (for example, listen to Rasoolan Bai's *Javo Javo Mat Karo* or Begum Akhtar's *Babul Mora*). Its affective intensity, its capacity to evoke the most intense *tasir*—indeed, its power to seduce and control men—was precisely its moral danger. A growing flame of outrage against courtesans and their practices was enabled by decades of discursive normalization of companionate marriage and fueled by ethico-medical anxiety about venereal

68. Beaster-Jones 2014, 59–65.

69. See Indraganti 2016, 60–62, including her citations of Seth 1980, for a survey of these early singers, and Arnold 1991, 106–113 for a full analysis of these two contrasting styles.

70. For example, see Jaddanbai, Kajjanbai, Rasoolan Bai; see also Indraganti 2016: 60–62.

71. *Filmindia* 1945 in Indraganti 2016, 61.

disease that construed sexual transgression as a kind of contagious filth.[72] By the mid-1950s, police raids had shut down many of the largest salons, and All India Radio, in addition to imposing severe restrictions on film songs in general, had banned the voices of women "whose private lives are a public scandal."[73] Some courtesans who had honed their craft in years of training with masters and long practice were able to find new careers as silent "classical" dancers or "songstresses," giving ticketed public concerts.[74] Others made a place for themselves in the emerging repertoire of urban bourgeois subject positions, becoming divas or prostitutes or bougeois housewives. A catastrophic proportion stopped performing altogether; very few carried on into independence the traditions of cultivated dance and song for which they were so renowned in the nineteenth century.[75] In any case, the effect on the Hindi film industry was clear: by the 1950s, the "*kotha* style of singing"[76] so widely associated with courtesans had largely been eclipsed by Lata's sweet, gentle *filmi* voice.

Onscreen, the disappearance of real, working courtesans in the studios did not herald the silencing of courtesan characters, but rather an amplification of their dramatic presence. Courtesans had long been stock figures in early hagiographic and "social" films, usually as an ethical foil to a plot oriented around the achievement of bourgeois marriage. During the 1930s and '40s, when salons were still functioning alongside cinema halls, cinematic courtesans had often been depicted in "social" and "saint" films as sexual predators manipulating the desires of otherwise upstanding citizens with their highly cultivated charms.[77] Other courtesans had been represented as figures in need of moral redemption.[78]

---

72. Gupta 2002.

73. Luthra 1986, 105. Anna Morcom (2013) identifies this moral regime with a pervasive discursive logic in which courtesans are understood to be prostitutes and therefore *not* performers.

74. Pradhan 2004, 341.

75. Morcom 2013, 15.

76. Srivastava 2004, 2024; Menon 1989.

77. There were, to be sure, exceptions to this, most famously Chandramukhi in the numerous productions of *Devdas*. A transitional moment is visible in *Bazooband* (1954), in which the courtesan figure is an evil seductress but is voiced by Lata.

78. In *Sant Tukaram* (1936), for example, this redemption was made saliently audible in vocal disposition, when the courtesan Sundara undergoes a radical dispositional transformation once converted to bhakti devotionalism: her sonority becomes

But by 1960, once state disenfranchisement of courtesans had done irreversible damage to their vocal traditions, a new kind of courtesan figure came sharply into focus onscreen. The new courtesan was usually an innocent victim of circumstance, singing gently in *filmi* voice. These characters were often set in the past, detached from the everyday struggles of real-life female singers. Classic figures of this period include Sahibjan (voiced by Lata in *Pakeezah* [1972]) and Umrao Jaan (voiced by Asha in *Umrao Jaan* [1981]). As Sara Waheed puts it, these new representations "heralded the prostitute-courtesan as an ethical figure struggling against an unjust social order . . . as a figure of political desire . . . an ideal citizen as imagined within a secular nationalist framework."[79] But they were more than simply glittering figures of nostalgia; they become forces of ethical instruction as well, which a significantly wider range than the cautionary figures of the earlier period.[80] Ruth Vanita identifies two distinctive stances: a "feminist woman-as-victim" stance, in which patriarchy itself is the villain, and a "voice of pleasure" stance, voicing an ethics of seizing the day rather than puritanical deferral.[81] Even in films that were not set in salons, like *Mughal-e-Azam* (1960) and *The Burning Train* (1980), we meet courageous, virtuous, self-sacrificing courtesans: fully developed moral subjects with rich inner lives, voiced in gentle microphonic *filmi* voice.

This shift may partially explain why Lata's voice in particular has become such hotly contested territory in ethical debates about Indian femininity.[82] This contestation over the ethical texture of *filmi* voice has become particularly vigorous in retrospect, in the years since Lata (and Asha) began to step away from recording in the 1980s. One critical register highlights an older set of virtues that

---

duller and softer, her posture and gestures more restrained, her eyes closed, her entire comportment turned inward rather than relationally attuned to the audience she seeks to seduce. (See Rahaim 2012, 23.)

79. Waheed 2014, 3.

80. This ethical figure was distinct, both vocally and ethically, from the figure of the *vamp*, whose voice often included breathy gasps and audible exhalations—which, too, were enabled by the intimacy of the close microphone technique.

81. Vanita 2018, 26.

82. Another part of the story is the body of rumor that circulates over Lata's own family background; her mother, Shevanti, is rumored to have had a career as a highly regarded courtesan before starting a family (Desai-Stevens 2017, 92)—though these are difficult to confirm.

filmi voice lacks, construing it as a "flattened out," "standardized," or "purified" version of an authentic original. Critic Raghava Menon mourns the loss of "the *kotha* [i.e., salon] type of singing" which has the "strange ring of truth" and celebrates a "frightening freedom."[83] Begum Akhtar's biographer Robert Ollikala notes that "*Nakhra* (coquettishness, blandishment) is missing" from *filmi* voice, "along with . . . the *bhava* (emotion, flavour, sentiment) of the olden days," and, echoing Roland Barthes, the "grain," or "the body in the voice that it sings."[84] This form of critique often dovetails with the celebration of the figure of the courtesan as an alternative form of anti-patriarchal resistance, both historically anterior to and discursively orthogonal to modern liberal feminisms.[85] In such figurations of lack, Lata's voice is often construed as negatively *dis*embodied, a voice removed from its body both by playback technology and by vocal technique.[86] Another critical register hears Lata's voice enforcing a single, hegemonic form of womanhood, what Pavitra Sundar calls "quintessential and ideal voice of Indian femininity," and what Neepa Majumdar calls "the ideal norm of aural femininity" projected consistently "across numerous female bodies."[87] As Vijay Mishra put it, "Lata prized out the female voice from its great, heterogeneous tradition."[88] Sanjay Srivastava asserts that the conventional appeal of this "shrill adolescent-girl" norm mimetically compels even grown women to sing "with all the sweetness of a girl-child."[89] He argues that Lata's thin sonority worked to "thin" the presence of women in public, vocally undermining the images of female freedom and emotional expressivity offered on the screen. Lakshmi Subrahmanian locates the dominance of this voice in a historically contingent, relational circuit of voice, adumbrating a particular "auditory habit that emerged in the late 19th and 20th centuries" which sought out a specific form of morally pure vocal "innocence."[90]

---

83. Menon 1989, 61–63.

84. Ollikala 1996, 164.

85. Oldenburg 1990; Shoaib 2014.

86. Morcom 2013; Beaster-Jones 2015, 62. "Disembodiment" here serves as a pithy pun, but the absence of a visible body in film is of a radically different ontological order than the relative floaty headiness of *filmi* voice.

87. Sundar 2007, 145; Majumdar 2010, 176.

88. Mishra 2013, 166.

89. Srivastava 2004, p. 2019, 2025.

90. Subrahmanian 2004, 1561.

Such a general diagnosis of the inherent moral texture of this voice, however, is easier to discern in the abstract than it is to hear in particular performances. For one thing, as economist Ashwini Deshpande points out, Lata sang a great many "sensual" songs that "cajole, plead, beckon and mesmerise."[91] And the light *filmi* voice developed by Lata was not only picturized upon helpless waifs, but also upon strong, independent women who stood up to patriarchal authority (as in, for example, the brave courtesan Anarkali's performance of "*Pyar Kiya to Darna Kya*?" in *Mughal-e-Azam*, performed defiantly in front of the Mughal emperor Akbar himself). Nor can the putative passivity of Lata's voice be read as a simple expression of Lata's own personal character (few singers, women or men, have exerted more control over their own career), or as a reflection of a monolithic society (Lata's career, after all, coincided with a period of "increased participation of women in politics, education, and mass struggles"[92]). In light of this slippage between voice and self, Sindhumathi Revuluri has recently suggested that Lata (like her sister Asha) was actively playing with and even critically refiguring two stereotyped and oppositional female roles: "innocent good girl" and "vampy, worldly club woman." Far from an abdication of agency, she sees this critical vocal work as a way of voicing a "humanity" that had been theretofore denied to public women under British colonialism.[93] To assign a simple meaning to the sonority of Lata's voice in absence of these critical practices of listening would be to adopt an analytic habit that hears voice as an expression of a homogenous collectivity (see chapter 6), winnowing the range of ethical potentials of this voice down to just one, critically projecting (rather than empirically demonstrating) a "single vision of 'the Indian woman.'" It is, in any case, difficult to sustain the reflectionist view that the "thin" vocal sonority in question is straightforwardly expressive of a (putatively nation-state-congruent) ubiquitous Indian femininity. On the contrary, this voice has provoked a great deal of *contestation* about varieties of feminine subject positions. That is to say, it functions not only as a themitical exemplar for other voices, but also as a dynamic field of ethical reflection.

---

91. Deshpande cites "Lag Ja Gale ke Phir Ye Hasin Raat Ho Na Ho," "Sapnon Mein Agar Mere," "Mora Gora Ang Lai Le," "Aa Jaane Ja," and "Wo Chup Rahen to Mere Dil ke Daag Jalte Hain." No relation to khyaliya Ashwini Bhide-Deshpande.

92. Deshpande 2004, 5183. See Rahaim 2021 for a critique of reflectionist models of vocal soliloquy.

93. Revuluri 2013, 848–852.

Post-Filmi *Individualist Voices*

In the decades since the economic liberalization of the 1990s, *filmi* voice has also provoked critical reflection on the very nature of selfhood and voice. It is now often heard as an icon of insincerity and conformity, in contrast to a true, authentically individual voice. A cynical ear listening for expressive personal authenticity may well hear the sweet, pristine murmurings of *filmi* voice as a vocal mask put over the self, a beguiling spell manufactured to enchant, persuade, and sell. Even before the emergence of *filmi* voice, critics had imputed inauthenticity to the practice of playback singing, calling them both "mechanical singing machines" (i.e., soulless) *and* "ghost singers" (i.e., bodiless).[94] Early articles about playback singers likened the practice to fraud, counterfeiting, and even prostitution.[95] By 1980, critics had already been grumbling that *filmi* voice had become virtually the only available voice for popular song.[96] Lata's "hegemony" over film song was often construed as a result of her own forcible domination, squeezing out rivals and granting her imprimatur to a select few. Her imitators were decried by critics as "pitiful clones."[97] The newly liberalized music market of the late 1990s and early 2000s, inviting foreign investment and courting international markets, demanded new voices.

There had, of course, always been occasional non-*filmi* voices in Hindi film, even in the era of *filmi* dominance. Music directors deliberately sought out folksy, foreign, or provincial voices for special touristic local color precisely in contrast to an unmarked *filmi* norm. For example, in order to evoke the simple, uncultivated voice of a boatman in *Sujata* (1959), music director S. D. Burman famously sang "Sun Mere Bandhu Re" himself in broad, coarse tones, at some distance from the microphone, rather than relying on a conventional playback singer with a *filmi* voice. The revolt against *filmi* voice in the 1990s and 2000s, however, was not principally concerned with cinematic *realism,* but with personal *authenticity*. The new voices that proliferated in the meantime (particularly those called "Sufi" and "Western") functioned not so much as depictions of exotic others as celebrations of selfhood, adopted by cinematic heroes rather than colorful

94. Weidman 2016, 22.

95. Ibid.

96. Jhingan 2013; Srivastava 2005.

97. Purushottam in Jhingan 2013, 103.

locals. Here, the tension between a personal, individual voice and a sedimented, supraindividual voice provoked contestation about the very nature and desirability of finding and vocally projecting a unique self.

This discursive moment was prepared in part by the "cassette revolution" of the 1980s, in which a wide range of new "copy artists" produced a wave of "version recordings" of classic film songs virtually indistinguishable from the originals.[98] As Lata, Asha, Kishore, and Rafi stepped back from recording, copy artists were also increasingly called on to sing newly composed film songs, succeeding or failing on their ability to sound like one or another classic *filmi* voice. Vandana Vajpayee, for example, built her early career by singing *in* Lata's voice; Mohammad Aziz built his on singing in Mohammad Rafi's. The packaging of these recordings typically highlighted the name of the original singer—whose voice was at issue—rather than the copy artist.[99] The essence of these original voices is referred to variously—as *bāt*, or "feel" or "magic"—but it is the job of copy artists to seek that essence, to actively recall (*yād karnā*) their vocal exemplar as they sing, not to find or express themselves.[100] Even today, when young singers are making their debut, they often explicitly do so (to cite Anaar Desai-Stevens' formula) "*X ki āvāz meṃ*"—"in X's voice."[101] Aspiring young female singers during the reign of the *filmi* voice would often be asked by music directors whether they sang in Lata's *or* Asha's voice—those being the two exhaustive alternatives. But things had changed by the mid-2000s. As music producer Clinton Cerejo put it to Jayson Beaster-Jones: "There used to be this thing, '*āp kiski āvāz mein gāte ho*?' ['whose voice do you sing in?'] . . . Nowadays, you say 'main *apnī* āvāz mein gātā hoon' [I sing in my *own* voice]."[102]

An ascendant post-liberalization vocal logic in Bollywood places a premium on this ethics of voice. Rather than fidelity to a prior original, singers are ex-

98. Manuel 1993, Jhingan 2013.

99. Jhingan 2013, 102.

100. "Mimicry artists" such as Sugandha Mishra are engaged in a rather different vocal enterprise. Their acts only make sense in stage shows, geared toward the ontological thrill of hearing a familiar voice in an unfamiliar body. This is especially so in cases like Gautam Deonani, a Lata mimic, whose startling appeal lies precisely in the virtuosic production of Lata's voice from a male apparatus.

101. Desai-Stevens 2017, 116.

102. Beaster-Jones 2015, 152.

pected to sound authentically like *themselves*—to eschew the conformity of *filmi* voice and find their own.[103] Indeed, as Desai-Stevens has shown, music directors positively demand that aspiring singers sing with their own distinctive "heart," "soul," and "vibe."[104] A plethora of newer voices, suffused with various kinds of personal sincerity, have thus appeared in mass media. Many of these voices are immediately, recognizably individual (such as Sunidhi Chauhan, Shreya Goshal, Sonu Nigam, Kailash Kher, and Lucky Ali). In other cases, critical acclaim for these new voices simply hinges on their contrast with *filmi* disposition, as, for example, praise for Sufi singer Mukhtiyar Ali's voice, described as "raw," "open," and "uncoached," or Kailash Kher's "rough and full-throated tone," heard approvingly in contrast to that of "honey-voiced" Bollywood singers.[105]

And yet, this proliferation of new voices has provoked a nostalgic backlash. *Filmi* voice is now often construed as "clean" in comparison to newer "impure" styles, its canon classicalized in retrospect as "evergreen." *Filmi* voice (and song composition) is now marketed not only as comparatively *surīl* [tuneful] and *jazbātī* [feelingful]—but also, tellingly, *Indian*.[106] The demand for fidelity to evergreen voices has not gone away; many aspiring film singers are placed in what Desai-Stevens calls a "double bind, caught between an increasing premium placed on musical innovation and an ever-present demand for fidelity to culturally nostalgic forms."[107] (She thus wisely cautions against assigning a single "neoliberal logic of voice" to this moment.[108])

After all, these new voices are not merely diverse. The Hindi film industry, following the logic of global neoliberal marketing, might well have been expected to absorb voices that sound superficially Arab, Ethiopian, or Indonesian in order to appeal to international markets—but such racially stereotyped voices appear only occasionally, applied as exotic flavor rather than alternate centers of subjectivity, gathering little sediment or momentum of their own. As we will see, two cosmopolitan vocal dispositions in particular have dominated the post-liberalization era, both of which are heard in ethical opposition to the conformity of *filmi*: "Western" and "Sufi."

---

103. These terms are borrowed from Desai-Stevens 2017.

104. Desai-Stevens 2017, 108–112.

105. Nair 2014, Virani 2017, 229.

106. Beaster-Jones 2009, 425.

107. Desai-Stevens 2017, 89–90.

108. Desai-Stevens 2017, 34.

Western-Voice

When singers and music directors refer to "Western" singing, they don't mean Italian opera, or Swedish death metal, or Irish ballads. Indeed, "Western" typically implies a set of vocal techniques that would be equally unwelcome in khyal and opera: belting, breathy gasps, creaky sonority, glottal fry, expressive scoops, yodeling jumps to head voice, straight tones swelling into vibrato. Some voice teachers thus prefer the term *Western contemporary*, an ecumenical vocal complex akin to the Hindustani vocal ecumene, drawing largely from rock, gospel, folk, jazz standards, R&B, and pop—but not ordinarily strict *bel canto* technique. As we will see in chapter 5, the process of developing such a voice often requires sophisticated techniques grounded in putatively universal, scientific vocal principles. But in practice, the disposition called "Western" in the Hindustani ecumene is grounded in a very particular milieu. The golden era seems to have been the first decade of liberalization in the 1990s; classics of the Hindustani "Western contemporary" canon include Mariah Carey, Bryan Adams, Alanis Morissette, and Celine Dion. *Western* functions as a more or less distinctive vocal disposition, with a more or less stable moral frame, fully achievable by Indian vocalists. Hindustani Western-voice singers like Meera Desai and Samantha Edwards do not perform as copy artists, but as fully developed creative singers in their own right; in the moment of singing, they fully inhabit this voice. They are not "faking it" or mimicking an alien voice; they improvise and ornament freely and idiomatically.

Prior to liberalization, there had already been at least two traditions of representing pathological "Western" vocality. One is the decades-long Bollywood tradition of "Westernized" vamps and hipsters who performed a Western mode of being "signified by whisky, bikinis . . . [and] uncontrolled sexuality."[109] But for the most part, these songs were still sung in *filmi* voice, embellished with occasional moans and sighs, marked as "Western" largely by instrumental accompaniment. This "West" was marked by free love, drug-induced ecstasy, freedom from family obligation, and other tempting—but, as the story goes, ultimately corrupting—ethical possibilities, often set in stark contrast to a morally exemplary Indian figure.[110] The second pathological "Western-voice," imagined more than heard, was a discursive cartoon of rigid, anodyne singing, an occidentalist foil

109. Thomas 1985, 126.

110. Potter and Sorrell 2012, 275.

applied by anti-colonial, nationalist musicologists who attempted to decisively distinguish between Indian and Western vocal essences. This Western-voice is not so much a disciplined vocal possibility as it is a bogeyman of moral failure. Where Indian vocality was construed as naturally continuous and connected, this Western-voice was construed as artificially disjointed, emblematic of a morally defective, characteristically Western subject position. Hemendranath Roy, for example, claimed that "the Westerner apparently never used continuous transition between two tones himself; he has failed to perceive its use by others."[111] Ananda Coomaraswamy asserted, "We [Indians] recognize accordingly a continuity of sound: by contrast with this, the European song . . . seems to unaccustomed Indian ears to be 'full of holes.'" Rabindranath Tagore mapped the "relationship between one note and another" directly onto a communitarian politics of "blood relation." Western music was and is often construed as tragically lacking in this relational virtue, "oblivious of that element of correlationship which endows music with its depth."[112] Over the course of the twentieth century, vocal continuity was often contrasted with the harmonium, a pumped reed-organ that produces a fixed tone for each key, but no curvaceous connections between notes. The harmonium was often taken to be an icon of modern "Western" musicality—the precise opposite, in romantic-nationalist principle, of a genuine Indian voice.[113]

---

111. Roy 1934, 322.

112. Tagore in Rahaim 2011, 668.

113. Weidman 2006; Rahaim 2011.This distinction, for all its efficacy in sustaining anti-colonial sentiment, is hard to sustain empirically in retrospect—particularly in light of the near-ubiquity of the harmonium. Even in singing styles where continuity is most prized (khyal, dhrupad, etc.), there are times when the continuity among resting tones needs to be clearly broken. Sometimes this is to properly highlight the structure of a phrase—to clarify the syntax of a poetic phrase or to set up the arrival of an important *svara*. At other times, discrete movement, with clear breaks between note-objects, also serves as the practical vocal correlate of note-based listening—implicated in a circuit of voice attuned to individual notes, it actively *constitutes* a given phrase as made of notes (see *svar-jnan*, chapter 3). Singing with abrupt delineations of notes is often used when explicating the "grammar" (*vyakaran*) of a rāga, much as a grammar teacher might separate out each word of a sentence in order to clearly demonstrate its syntax. This mode of singing, usually enunciated with note-names on each tone, serves much the same purpose as a demonstration on a harmonium: it affords a clear grasp of a phrase as a sequence of notes. The distinction between these two ways of articulation often stands in for a distinction of subject position: between the figure of school-

The post-liberalization development of what I call "Hindustani Western-voice" has a rather different discursive life, a third possibility apparently unmarred by these pathologies. For a liberal-individualist subject, it offers distinctive ethical possibilities: self-expression, independence, and personal empowerment—and, crucially, in counterperformative contrast to *filmi* voice. The flourishing of "Indipop" in the 1990s had already marked out a celebratory ethical position for self-expressive voicing. A generation of Indian and Pakistani rockers like Silk Route and Junoon, raised on anglophone pop music, developed ways of delivering rock vocals in vernacular Hindustani: belting, roaring, and soaring much like their counterparts in Seattle and London. (Chapter 5 will explore the dispositional contours of Western-voice, as well as its pedagogies.) More importantly, as Peter Kvetko has shown, Indipop vocalists were framed by a novel "ideology of Romantic self-expression" and "innovation," marketed as individual artists with distinctive voices.[114] In contrast to *filmi* song, where singers sweeten and soften their voices to express the feelings of fictional cinematic characters, one sings "Western" as a sovereign, highly audible individual, often explicitly sounding out against expectations and restrictions.

Singers trained in raga music and *filmi* are often drawn to Western-voice because of these ethical possibilities. Unlike a gharana-based gayaki or the drama of *filmi*, Western-voice announces individual selfhood and personal desire. Apoorva Joshi, for example, describes how she gets to be a "spoiled brat" while singing "Hand in My Pocket" by Alanis Morissette. Weaving her way through the lines of the song—which refer lyrically, reflexively, to the postural and gestural attitude of a brash, independent, self-assured woman—she places a casual hand in her pocket, flicks a virtual cigarette, and lets out a spontaneous whoop at the end of the line. The pleasure of being a "spoiled brat" is also grounded in a particular vocal setting: as she puts it, "broad" rather than "thin" (see figure 4.1).

Recall that "thin" is precisely the quality of Lata's *filmi* voice that so many feminist critics construe as a sign of self-abnegation. Broad voice—the vocal

---

educated, intellectual musicologist and the seasoned, authentic bearer of lineage who was trained in an authoritative household. Singers of rāga music are ordinarily expected to be able to perform both fluid continuity *and* unambiguous distinction. Those who are unable to separate out individual notes are often figured as craftsmanlike but uneducated; those who are unable to connect tones are often considered to be beginners, still singing like a student in a classroom.

114. Kvetko 2005, 83, 195.

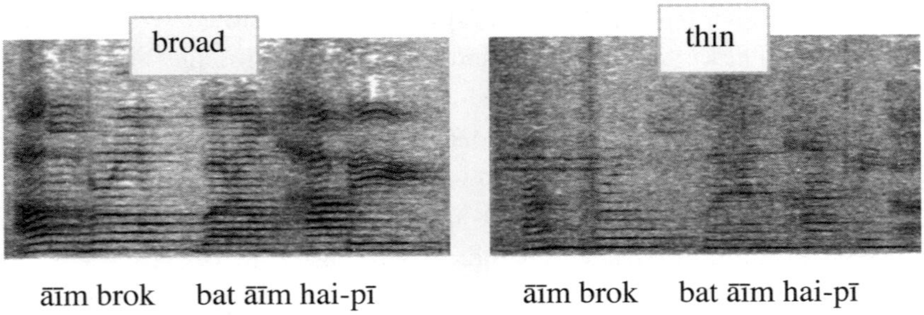

FIGURE 4.1 Broad and thin

disposition of the self-announcing, self-celebrating "spoiled brat" that Apoorva enjoys becoming—is not only louder overall, but also has more nasal resonance, as shown by the greater intensity in upper harmonics. (See fig. 4.1.) It seems to take up more space in the room.

Nupur Joshi, a longtime student of raga music, describes the disposition of irrelational freedom she hears in the voices of Mariah Carey and Celine Dion: "It's like they just *fly* . . . I mean it's like they don't care who's listening. They just *go*." Among the first songs that inspired her to develop Western-voice was Mariah Carey's "Hero." Nupur sang along with the song every night for a year, and now renders the song with ease, smoothly moving through the fine, gospel-inflected harkat in the melody. Her attraction to this voice was not so much in a distanced aesthetic appreciation of its sound, but in a yearning for empowerment and self-betterment. Mariah Carey's free, self-assured vocal disposition led her to feel that "if you believe in yourself, then you can definitely find a way and go where you want to go." The act of singing these songs, as she puts it, "brings out the light within yourself." This voice not only inspired personal virtue, but even a sort of charismatic zeal: "The same message which I personally felt that I got from Mariah Carey, I wanted to give out that same message to people."

The quasi-religious fervor associated with this voice recalls the reformist ambitions of missionary efforts and Victorian "Voice Culture" projects. But its ethical contours are radically different, directed not toward muted bourgeois conformity, but self-expression and personal agency. As we will see in chapter 5, the individualist liberatory potentials of this music require discipline and concerted effort. But first, we turn to another highly lucrative way of voice that came into vogue at nearly the same time as Hindustani Western-voice: the vocal formation that has come to be known simply as "Sufi."

Contested Sufi Voices

A high, bright, amplified *ā* spills out from the third-floor Kaffeine Bar & Grill, soaring above the domes and pillars of Firoz Shah's thirteenth-century *madrasa* in Hauz Khas Village, Delhi. Earlier that evening, the same vowel, coming from a mosque around the corner, had filled the same space: an extended melisma from a call to prayer, the ā of *Allāh*. But this *ā* is different—it is the *ā* of "*Mitwā*," one of the breakthrough pop sufi hits of the mid-2000s, from the film *Kabhi Alvida Naa Kehna* (2006). Underneath this vowel, an acoustic guitar loops its way through a cycle of chords, marking out a steady, jangly backbeat. At street level, an LED sign advertises "HAPPY HOURS + LIVE SUFI MUSIC" in bright red scrolling letters. Walking among the galleries, tattoo parlors, and boutiques of Hauz Khas Village on any night of the week, you can hear at least three such soaring voices, in three different bars, their voices weaving in and out of the chime of cocktail glasses.

Pop sufi song has spread rapidly across the Hindustani ecumene in the early years of the twenty-first century, ringing out in coffeehouses and on glittering stages, ranging from indie rock to blockbuster film soundtracks. In record stores and streaming platforms, "Sufi" takes its place generically alongside "classical" and "Bollywood" and "Western." Pop sufi superstars draw on a canon of poetic texts well-known to professional qawwals; some of these poems ("Chhaap Tilak Sab Cheeni," "Dam Mast Qalandar," "Allah Hoo," etc.) are as likely to be heard in a shrine courtyard as they are on stage at a Sufi rock concert. But the song texts that are chosen for Sufi tend to be those with broad crossover appeal rather than songs of devotion to specific Chishti saints, or songs with arcane scriptural or theological references. Pop sufi is largely de-Islamicized by design, voicing a cosmopolitan subject rather than a devout Sufi, turned inward, toward a pristine individual self, rather than outward, in self-effacing devotion. Poetically, pop sufi sounds resolutely Hindustani and folksy, shorn of the fancy *qofs* and *ghains* that mark the lofty Perso-Arabic loan words found in elite qawwali. The voices of pop sufi singers are often cultivated in much the same ways as qawwals, including both classical training in raga music and the studious adoption of sonorous and kinetic dispositions from classic recordings by Nusrat Fateh Ali Khan and the Sabri Brothers. However, unlike most shrine and khanqahi qawwali, pop *sufi* often features gentle *filmi* crooning, interspersed artfully with high, bright *buland* voice.

But singing pop sufi is more than a distinctive sound. Its appeal lies above all in a way of *being*, in a distinctive form of selfhood heard in the voice: free, open, unhindered by boundaries. This ethical aspiration is quite distinct from the forms of ascetic self-work undertaken by formally initiated Chishtis, Qadiris, or Naqshbandis under the guidance of a *pīr*—the practices of which, though various, nearly always include behavioral strictures, obedience to authority, and clear boundaries between initiates and outsiders. The idealized ethical models for its savvy, cosmopolitan stars tend to be heterodox, solitary wanderers—faqirs, bauls, dervishes—rather than qawwals linked to orthodox sufi institutions. In the world of pop sufi, even the uninitiated can choose from a wide range of products for ethical self-fashioning: Sufi song, Sufi self-help books, Sufi workshops that promise extraordinary experiences and personal transformation. Pop sufi has spawned a range of designer clothing, ranging from elegant flowing robes to *sherwani* jackets, to fur caps and beards, to stage sets including minarets, domes, and crescent moons. Clothing designers like Yasmin Kidwai and Muzaffar Ali, and fashion houses like Dhaka's "Sufi Fashion" have successfully marketed a distinctive bourgeois, cosmopolitan, pop sufi look, featuring turbans, sherwanis, and "long, flowy" tunics that, in sartorial principle, at least, "transcend boundaries."[115] The putative transcendence of boundaries is key to the marketing of the pop sufi revival. However, as Peter Manuel points out, not all boundaries are so easily traversed: the upper reaches of Sufi chic are available only to a wealthy, cosmopolitan anglophone audience. To be sure, singing universalist pop sufi is far more lucrative than the world of shrines—by an order of magnitude or even two.[116] This is a large part of why it is offers such an attractive career path for so many singers, even non-Sufis and non-Muslims. But its ethical projects also cut across classes, offering a populist ethos of freedom, unity, and self-authorization that circulates on YouTube and Facebook no less than at designer fashion events. These projects have become so publicly salient, in fact, that praise and criticism of singing pop sufi often rings out in decidedly ethical terms. Most of its public contestation hinges not so much on aesthetic evaluation of tunes, timbres, grooves, or instrumentation, but on the forms of selfhood that the pop sufi voice announces and invites.

---

115. Tankha 2018; Manuel 2008.

116. Weston 2013. A qawwali party singing in a well-attended shrine might make a thousand rupees per night ($20) or less in nazrānā (donations from pilgrims). But for a ticketed urban stage show with a large sound system, even moderately well-paid groups can expect to be paid 20k–30k rupees ($500); big names like Kailash Kher might make several dozen times as much.

Many devout Sufis consider pop sufi song to be a pale, inauthentic *imitation* of qawwali. This line of critique holds that pop sufi is merely a "fake gesture" toward a domesticated Islamicate imaginary.[117] Indeed, many pop sufi singers themselves are critical of the term *sufi*—akin to the way that punks tend to decry the term *punk*. The cosmopolitan ethics of being "sufi" (a radically free individualism that transcends boundaries, categories, and social expectations) is at odds with "sufi" as a genre, an industry, or a social formation. Equally important is the range of substantive objections from actual Sufi brotherhoods, many of which apply to the growth of stage qawwali and recorded qawwali that long predate the current vogue.[118] Qawwals are often annoyed by the prevalence of sweet *filmi* voice in pop sufi song; a common distinction holds that qawwali should be sung from the chest (rather than from the throat, like *filmi*). Others criticize pop sufi performances in which the focus is on entertainment or elaborate orchestration on the grounds that it is distracting, disturbing, or misleading.[119] This contention often overlaps with sedimented moral proscriptions against women singing in public. The Madariyya foundation, for example, famously urged Sona Mohapatra to take down the music video for her pop sufi adaptation of Amir Khusrau's "Tori Surat" featuring dozens of women dancing to a pulsating electronic dance beat.[120] A related objection holds that the pop sufi craze contributes to the already dubious reputation of qawwali among orthodox Muslims. A more ontologically radical critique was offered to me once by a hereditary qawwal of the dargah of Moin-ud-din Chishti of Ajmer. We were watching a video of a pop sufi concert, when he turned to me and shook his head, saying: "He's singing *ali maula maula* and people are dancing. It's nothing." ("Nothing" as opposed to "they're doing a poor job of it.") No spiritual authority, no samā, no inner poetry revealed, no circuit of voice. Without this necessary relational scaffolding, in a *samā*-centered vocal ontology, merely singing pop sufi is, in practice, *nothing at all*.[121]

To its practitioners, however, pop sufi is certainly not nothing—neither an exact copy of orthodox Chishti practice nor a dilution, but a potent ethical cocktail in its own right. Practically speaking, to succeed at singing pop sufi requires a rather different set of skilled dispositions. Unlike qawwali, it does not require

---

117. Sangari in Manuel 2008, 392.

118. Qureshi 1999.

119. Viitamäki 2008, 78.

120. India Today Web Desk, 2018.

121. Rahaim 2019, 23–24.

the vocal endurance to sing at full volume for many hours at a stretch, late into the night, in the open air; but it does require careful microphone technique to maintain a glossy sonic perfection. Unlike qawwals, pop sufi singers do not need the relational skills to recognize and vocally sustain the visible signs of *wajd* in their listeners; but they do need to be able to recognize cues for section changes and to navigate the elaborate range of signals that enable working in a large ensemble, with a producer, in a studio.[122] They do not need to have a repertoire of canonical Farsi and Urdu poetic couplets ready on their tongue suitable for spontaneous insertion at just the right moment, but they do need to accurately memorize prearranged songs, singing freely over chord progressions undistracted by vocal harmonies. They don't need to recognize and pay proper respect to the complex dynamics of spiritual authority before them at a mahfil or shrine, but they do need to direct a convincingly personal performance to an invisible audience of notionally egalitarian strangers. While the "unity" sought in pop sufi may at first appear to find resonance with the egalitarian ethos of public dargah spaces, *samā* is by no means a performance of unity *among* participants.[123] The relational attunements of the qawwals do not produce a *unity* with their Chishti patrons, but a respectful rapport across a distance, between two irreducibly intertwined roles.[124] Perhaps most importantly, as Peter Manuel puts it, a successful Sufi singer must thoroughly acquire a "cosmopolitan" disposition that reaches out to the "modern urban bourgeoisie, whose sensibilities, shallow in some ways and sophisticated in others, are . . . different from those rooted

122. Qureshi 1994, 520; Ayyagari 2012.

123. This deployment of the pop sufi voice as a means of imagining political solidarities has a rather different texture from the long practical precedent of Chishti shrines welcoming non-Muslims, both as pilgrims and recipients of charity. Surely, among the vast press of pilgrims' bodies, where every head is piously covered, it is not always possible to distinguish Muslims from non-Muslims. In this sense, the very social space of the shrine might be understood to not only perform, but also metaphysically *affirm* a prior humanistic unity, extended metonymically to "Sufism" in general. And yet, there are clearly boundaries and barriers even in these open spaces. For example, the five-times-daily prayers are reserved for Muslims; the space of the room encasing Nizamuddin's tomb is reserved for men; and, of course, there are standards of differential comportment and decorum even during the qawwali sessions in the open courtyards.

124. See Levinas 2012.

in the shrine or the Punjabi village."[125] None of these dispositional skills comes "naturally," even to qawwals who make the leap into "Sufi." These skills afford a distinctive set of ethical, spiritual, and political aspirations quite distinct from the world of Chishti Sufism.

In this sense, pop sufi opens up a distinctive subject position. While qawwals singing for a samā or a shrine generally act as skilled "technicians of emotion,"[126] offering their virtuosity in service of devout pilgrims and trained Sufi listeners, pop sufi stars function as *artistes*. This is, in the first place, a product of certain practices of listening: whereas a Sufi listener is principally attuned to the poetry the qawwal delivers, a secular fan of pop sufi listens to an artist, savors the artist's expressions of the artist's own feelings, the artist's own personal realization. In an interview with Mukhtiyar Ali, for example, a photo shows him singing, with one hand in the air and his eyes gazing off into the distance, and captioned "in trance,"[127] blurring the traditional relational dyad between a spiritually elite listener in *wajd* and a qawwal in song. Qawwals, by contrast, may be treasured tradition bearers, rightly proud of their close association as with spiritual lineages, but they rarely serve as personal moral exemplars or spiritual guides. The pop Sufi artist, in contrast, tends to be principally concerned with self-expression, transcendence of externally imposed boundaries, and personal liberty—rather than devotion to a master, obedience to God, the perfection of character (*akhlāq*), or bringing the self (*nafs*) under the authority of divine will. This free, independent vocal subject position is a large part of the metaphysical allure of "Sufi." As singer Madan Gopal Singh put it to Peter Manuel, "People ask me why am I in Sufi music, and it's because it offers me enormous freedom, that no other kind of music gives me."[128] Muzaffar Ali likewise extols a musical "sense of oneness and unity . . . Sufism is a music of synthesis, where the liberation of music is really the essence."[129] Shireesh Thakur, an aspiring singer who left a corporate job to pursue *filmi* and pop sufi, once described to me his deep felt connection to "Kun Faya Kun," the superhit from the movie *Rockstar*: "at this point in my life, I really connect to this song. Because I really don't have anything . . . I had big jobs, big packages, multinational flight, travelling to different

---

125. Manuel 2008, 393.

126. Wolf 2014, 281 f.1.

127. Nagaraj 2010.

128. Manuel 2008, 392.

129. Singh 2018.

countries, working. I've left everything for the love of music." Accordingly, the characteristic vocal technique of pop sufi is not so much the sound of a qawwali party singing in unison, or in elaborate call-and-response, or the enunciation of esoteric poetry for elite listeners, but a single voice ringing out high and alone, free of any strophic or metrical boundaries. Nearly every blockbuster Bollywood film now has at least one moment of pop sufi spiritual revelation, featuring the high, lonesome sound of a single voice near the top of its range, shrouded in reverb, crying out wordlessly on a pure *ā*.

The figure of the pop sufi artiste is constituted through overlapping technological means: sensitive microphones and multitrack mixes that foreground the independent lead voice, staging and costuming that places the body of the artiste front and center, cameras and lighting that foreground their face (typically in an expressive attitude of searching or yearning) and eyes (typically closed in introspection or directed toward the distance, rather than attending to any particular listener).[130] In live performances, the audience is filled with anonymous, notionally equal listeners, not spiritually elite Sufis. To attend a concert in such a universalizing space, one needn't reach any particular stage of spiritual advancement, nor fulfill any particular decorum; one needs only to buy a ticket. Consider, for example, the 2011 performance of Rahat Fateh Ali Khan, a hereditary Pakistani qawwal (the nephew of Nusrat Fateh Ali Khan), on the reality TV show *Chhote Ustad: Do Deshon ki Ek Āwāz* (*Little Masters: One Voice of Two Nations*)—singing an abridged version of "Main Jahaan Rahoon," his hit from the film *Namastey London* (2007).[131] Most of the performance remains in a *filmi* disposition, crooning in the low-mid range of his voice. When he leaps into *buland* voice—the "Sufi" voice—the hostess, Deepika Padukone, is moved visibly to tears.[132] He brings the song to a triumphant conclusion, ending on a long, undulating melisma on the phrase *terī yād sāth hai*, sliding smoothly among the soaring glamour of a [*b*VI-*b*VII-I] harmonic cadence in the prearranged instrumental accompaniment. He nails it—it rings out gracefully and

130. See, for example, the opening scene of Sona Mohapatra's controversial video "Tori Surat," in which she strides alone across a meadow in slow motion, holding a microphone in her hand.

131. 2010. Rahat Fateh Ali Khan also served as a judge on *Chhote Ustaad*, along with Sonu Nigam.

132. Indeed, Deepika Padukone is easily prone to tears; there are several YouTube videos that focus on this.

settles on the tonic; without even taking a breath, he murmurs "thank you" into the microphone, inviting uproarious applause. Sonu Nigam calls out: "*kyā gānā gāyā*!" ("What a song you sang!") This performance, unlike samā, is all about the singer. He sings as an artiste, invites and acknowledges applause as an artiste, not as a qawwal in the service of Sufis. There is no space for him to respond to the effect he is having on his listeners. Even if he had wanted to repeat the line that had evoked *tasir* in a listener, as one would in samā, the fixed song arrangement could never afford such a spontaneous reaction to the moment.

Qawwals who (like Rahat Fateh Ali Khan himself) are familiar with both of these worlds are acutely aware of the profound difference in relational texture. Even in private mahfils held by wealthy (but non-spiritually elite) patrons, qawwals reach out to affect *particular* listeners in relationally constituted circuits of voice. And, as we saw in chapter 3, a mahfil-e samā requires a particularly virtuosic vocal and poetic attunement to one's listeners. Qawwal Sultan Nazan describes the practical differences between singing pop sufi on stage and singing in a mahfil-e samā both in terms of *andāz* (manner, comportment) and *adab* (etiquette). He emphasizes that a qawwal must sing to those who are sitting in this mahfil in particular:

> <On stage, you sing however you want. For the public, for the modern masses, it works. But inside a mahfil-e samā, *adab* is required . . . The *andāz* of the stage is different. In a mahfil-e samā, there is a great deal of *adab*. You must ritually wash yourself; sitting in front of the man who arranged the mahfil, the disciples, the saints, those who took initiation, pious people are sitting there. So we present a program in *their* circle, we recite for *this* mahfil-e samā.[133]>

Note that adab here is not some superficial "mannerism" or appearance set in contrast to a deep, invisible truth; *adab* is a virtue in and of itself that allows a space for *wajd*, or ecstasy, to happen. The manner of singing the poem, the conventional ritual gestures, the structures of authority that determine what is sung when, by whom, and who can listen—all of this makes wajd possible. The

---

133. *Stage mein jaise bhī gā lo. Ām public, yā ām modern se, chal jāte hai. Lekin mahfil-e samā ke andar adab zaruri hai . . . Stage kā andāz alag hai. Mahfil-e samā mein bahut adab ke sāth baiṭnā paḍtā hai bāwazū to sāhab-e qiblā ke sāmne baiṭhe rahate hain ahle murīd hazrāt baiṭe rahate khilāfat jo lie hue ķhalīfa log bhi baiṭe rahate. To unke darmiyāṃ meṃ hamko jo program pesh karnā aur usko mahfil-e samā jo ham paḍhte haiṃ.*

saints that founded Sufi orders and the living shaykhs that sustain them are, in principle, extraordinary beings, holding secret knowledge reserved for specially initiated insiders. Relationships between masters and disciples are precisely unequal; one seeks out a master and obeys them precisely because of the gulf in spiritual understanding and authority between them. Whichever path (*tariqa*) a student is on, it ascends through stages (*maqāmat*), producing distinct forms of authority, inviting particular forms of relational etiquette. Chishti institutional structure is marked by this fundamentally relational spiritual elitism.

For singers of pop sufi, the dynamic twoness of bounded relationality is effaced; the absolute oneness of unbounded irrelational freedom is paramount. Pop sufi encourages seekers to follow their *own* personal inclinations, heedless of authority, heedless of institutions, ultimately true to oneself regardless of how others respond. Pushkar Lele describes this tendency in one well-known star that has been absorbed into the Sufi revival, Parvathy Baul, a cosmopolitan Baul singer: "that kind of voice . . . 'I'm singing for myself and for my god. Not for your god, my god.' Self-sufficient, that kind of voice." Anuraag Dhoundeyal, pop sufi singer and composer, puts this irrelationality in explicitly metaphysical terms, linking personal authenticity to a lived metaphysics of unity and studied indifference to "the other":

> When it comes to . . . songs that are of a Sufi bent, I think the most important thing that one must have is authenticity. . . . And I feel that when you have that "one" sort of feeling, and that feeling of being honest to yourself, then I think everything falls into place. [But] when your intention is to impress the *other*, and to be someone who is liked by the other, or to compose something that will be more accepted by the others, that's when I think things start going downhill.

We see here an explicit ethical rejection of relationally singing to an *other* on the grounds that it limits the purity of unified, individual selfhood. This self-discovery and self-expression, like all practices, has its own pedagogies. It is deliberately cultivated. Anuraag co-directs a pop sufi-inflected personal training organization called The Looking Glass, which runs a workshop called "Songs of the Sufis." The motto of The Looking Glass is "peer within"—an apt pun. It refers both to the "peering within" of self-reflection (as in a looking glass) and to the figure of the *pīr*, a Sufi master. It's thus both an ethical injunction to look inside (peer within yourself) *and* a statement of where spiritual authority ultimately resides (the pīr is within yourself). At our first meeting, when I naively asked a psychologist at The Looking Glass which Sufi brotherhood they were affiliated with, she smiled politely. She said that their goal was to go *beyond* Sufi institutions, as sufism is "basically humanistic" (as opposed to Islamic). Their shows and workshops are explicitly billed as interactive experiences. In one such experience, Anuraag sings and plays guitar, encouraging a roomful of aspirants not just to listen, but to sing and dance along with one of the international anthems of pop sufi: "Dum a Dum Mast Qalandar." This egalitarian consumer-participant ethos is, needless to say, a radically different form of sociality than the *adab* that scaffolds a mahfil-e samā, where standing up at all is reserved for a specially authorized few, where singing along is prohibited, where the final spiritual authority rests with the shaykh. For pop sufi events, participation is not only allowed, but encouraged, as a form of ethically praiseworthy comportment, performing not a relational obligation to a spiritual authority, but uninhibitied personal freedom, distributed equally among consumers.[134]

The self-authorizing voice of pop sufi is sometimes deployed as a political rejoinder to modern Hindu-Muslim identity politics—often mapped onto the mutually constitutive religious nationalisms of India and Pakistan. Even classic poetic texts long predating current identity politics are often interpreted as celebrations of Hindu-Muslim unity. "*Chhaap Tilak Sab Cheeni*," for example, describes a glance from the poet's master, the Chishti saint Nizamuddin, that wipes the poet's forehead markings away (i.e., their worldly status)—which, in the current political climate, is widely read as an ecstatic transcendence of religious identity. The Looking Glass show "Sounds of the Sufis" narrates a history in which the participatory song of Sufis brings "oneness" to Hindus and Muslims (who, anachronistically, are constued to have been in quasi-nationalistic conflict over religious identity). Many pop sufi collaborations prominently feature singers from India and Pakistan collaborating, sometimes directly addressing the mending of this civilizational split, as on the 2010 reality TV series *Chhote Ustaad: Do Deshon Ki Ek Awaaz* ("Young Masters: The One Voice of Two Nations"). In *Chhote Ustaad*, teams of two children (one from India and one from Pakistan) competed in successive elimination rounds to win. The "one voice" of each team emerges in the space of this civic ritual competition, as a single "sufi" voice that, in principle, transcends religious and national borders. The characteristic sonorous dispositions and poetic canons of this emergent "sufi voice" are put in service of a politics verging on the ahistorical liberal humanism of "all lives matter." The

134. As Ali Hameed Almaas points out, there are Sufi metaphysical traditions that privilege a form of "essential" selfhood prior to egoic self-image (2000, 123–126).

vocally audible Hindu-Muslim harmony in the cosmopolitan Sufi world—what Manuel describes as one of several "islands" of communal harmony—thus performs a rejoinder to familiar narratives of Hindu-Muslim conflict.[135]

For many Hindus disenchanted with a Hindu nationalist movement that has staked an exclusive claim to bhakti devotion, pop sufi offers a venerable Hindustani spiritual path that seems to avoid majoritarian politics. In this way, it is much like the Kabir revival, with which it shares a great deal of metaphysical territory (and poetic repertoire).[136] Yet pop sufi is flexible enough to offer majoritarian political resonances as well. The leading Hindu nationalist party (BJP) has become a prominent patron in recent years, staging pop sufi concerts at many of their events.[137] Indeed, Hans Raj Hans, a pop sufi star, became a BJP member of parliament in 2019. The office of Prime Minister Narendra Modi released an official statement in 2015 asserting that "the ideology propounded by Sufi saints is an integral part of Indian ethos, and has contributed significantly to the creation of a pluralistic, multi-cultural society in India."[138] Modi himself was a featured speaker at the 2016 World Sufi Forum in New Delhi, where he spoke in glowing terms about the "spiritual love" of Sufism.[139] Though the party rarely campaigns among orthodox Sunnis or Deobandis, they do reach out strategically to Chishtis, often emphasizing a clear discursive distinction between Sufis and terrorists.[140]

The largest sponsors of pop sufi, though, remain multinational corporations. The affective power of a soaring solitary voice, crying out against boundaries, celebrating the struggle of individuals against social obligations, projects a cosmopolitan, free-market vision of the world.[141] A world in which "all is one," in which borders are meant to be transcended, in which spiritual salvation is located within each individual, invites not only a metaphysics of unity, and not only a politics of inclusion—but also a neoliberal economics. Boundaries, tariffs, and identitarian taste publics are the enemies of "global" capitalism; boundary crossing is the very essence of appropriative crossover marketing strategies.

---

135. Manuel 2008, 381.

136. Hess 2015; Virani 2016.

137. Manuel 2008, 383.

138. Press Information Bureau, 2015. See also Lipton 2011 on various geopolitical deployments of "sufi" ideology in the service of neoliberalism.

139. *Hindustan Times* 2016.

140. Pal 2019, "Performing Pluralism."

141. See Gershon 2011.

This strategy is quite explicit in corporate sponsorship of pop sufi music. *Coke Studio*—a TV show that curates pop sufi fusion projects between qawwals, folk musicians, and cosmopolitan electronic music producers (among others)—is the most spectacular example of this.[142] Wasim Basir, Coca-Cola India's director of integrated marketing communications, proclaims that *Coke Studio* "needed to capture the inclusive spirit of our brand." Aditya Swamy, the executive vice president of MTV India who conceived many of the early Coke "Sufi" collaborations, goes further: "*Coke Studio* celebrates the notion that music transcends language. It transcends everything."[143] This "transcendence" does not point to a radical metaphysical alterity, nor is it spiritual transcendence of worldly concerns. Rather, it is the transcendence of boundaries to connection and exchange. The pop sufi voice fits with an economic vision of free trade that transcends national borders, and it has long been central to the Coke brand, from the "Sign of Good Taste Everywhere" campaign of the 1960s (featuring nation-state after nation-state that loves the "universally right" taste of Coke) to the "I'd Like to Teach the World To Sing" campaign of the 1980s (featuring innumerable ethnically diverse bodies singing one song together, progressively zooming out from ethnically distinctive individual faces to a long shot of a unified, undifferentiated mass of bodies singing the jingle).

This is not to say that pop sufi is a "commercialization" of traditional shrine qawwali; the shrine has its own patterns of commerce. Qawwals attract devotees to a dargāh, sometimes in huge numbers (for example, in Thursday night sessions at Nizamuddin in Delhi, or the annual *urs* celebration of Moinuddin Chisti at Ajmer). Crowded stalls of merchants line the streets around shrines, and even into the periphery of the shrine courtyard itself, offering rosaries, scarves, and hats. Piles of fresh rose petals are purchased, brought inside the shrine, and deposited on the tomb of the saint; prayerful devotees then receive and chew a single petal from the pile. The world of Hindustani shrine qawwali is sustained by a vibrant, highly regulated world of face-to-face commerce. This includes elaborate patron-client relationships, sales of ritual items, and flows of cash between devotees, shrine officials, merchants, and professional qawwali parties. There is an elaborate *adab* involved in formally giving *nazrānā*, wherein money passes from devotee to "pick-up man" to spiritual authority to qawwal (see chapter 3). These visible flows of cash and goods changing hands is consubstantial in principle

142. Williams and Mahmood 2020.

143. Ryan 2012.

with the flow of *barakat* (blessings) through a shrine complex.[144] Even making small change, passing bills from hand to hand, are opportunities for participation in the flow of blessings, binding devotees together in a coherent economy.

The pop sufi voice, on the other hand, sounds out an entirely distinct world of commerce: unbounded, free, and, in principle, freely chosen. Its characteristic economic form consists of borderless, free-market exchanges between anonymous, notionally equal individuals, each choosing their own path. Whereas shrine commerce is maximally relational and visible, carried out publicly, and in cash whenever possible, pop sufi commerce is maximally irrelational and invisible. Buying a ticket for a pop sufi concert, downloading a pop sufi album, or reserving a seat for a "Sufi spirituality" workshop are unidirectional transactions from anonymous seller to anonymous buyer, not circulations of cash and barakat from hand to hand to hand. However many rupees are transferred, such an exchange begins and ends with the purchase. Pop sufi singers are often paid much more than qawwals, to be sure, but in any case they are ordinarily paid privately, invisibly, irrelationally, in a transaction shielded from the eyes of concertgoers. Like the pop sufi voice calling out a pure, wordless *ā*, it is a cry of unrestricted individual selfhood reverberating in an unbounded, undifferentiated field of unity.

Each of these crystallized dispositions, as we have seen, hinges not only on sound, but also on varieties of selfhood. Not all of these, as we have seen, are voices of individual selves; when individual selves do emerge as vocal subjects, they must be deliberately constructed and sustained. We will return to varieties of selfhood in chapter 6; chapter 5 turns to various techniques of vocal cultivation and their concomitant avenues of self-becoming.

144. Weston 2013, 154–157.

FIVE

Sādhanā

Vocal Striving

This chapter addresses *vocal striving*—deliberately working to change one's voice: to improve it, reshape it, or even, as suggested by the Hindi term *āvāz banānā*, to make it anew. The very idea of *making* one's voice, rather than simply finding it there waiting, like a fingerprint, complicates the usual figurations of voice as an expressive outpouring of the self or the sonic icon of a racialized national essence. We have seen that singing requires deeply entrained dispositions: the gaits and sonorities, poetic and temporal sensibilities, affective and relational attunements that make voices so powerful. These dispositions often appear automatic, natural, immediate, bolstering a sense of voice as an expression of a fixed, given, sovereign, individual interior life. But working on the voice—changing these dispositions—forces us to confront the difference between the (imperfect) voice one *has* and the (exemplary) voice that one *strives for*. As with learning to pronounce American r's late in life, or Arabic *ains*, vocal training denaturalizes one's own vocal disposition and provides an opening for pedagogies and coercion from others. It requires the vocal aspirant to move from a cultivated automaticity (in which a voice appears to be an effortless appendage of a self) to a mode of striving after a voice that is not yet one's own, producing a reflexive distance from one's "own" voice. For many singers, this striving is the very condition of an endless road, a journey in which one's voice is never fully complete. The term *sādhanā*, or ongoing striving, is often applied to this metaphysical figuration of vocal work, in which one proceeds without the expectation of fulfillment or final achievement.

We begin with two quick biographical sketches of singers who have worked to develop their voice in different directions, over the course of many years, in rather different circumstances.

Sharukh Shabab Niyazi grew up in Delhi. From a young age, he was groomed to become a Hindustani vocalist, trained by his father, Shabab Ahmed Khan (a disciple of Khadim Hussain Khan of Agra Gharana). Sharukh seasoned his sonority with sustained notes, developed kinetic agility with rapid scales, expanded his range high and low. Most importantly, his father taught him a foundational set of vocal dispositions: "what you have to do and where—when to take the voice high, when to take it low—the whole plan [*tarkīb*]." As in many hereditary vocal families, Sharukh's vocal sonority, power, and range were the foundation of his training, building a strong, bright, flexible voice in the first decade of his life. He became capable of *svar-jnan*, identifying notes by name, engraved in his mind through rigorous scalar patterns. Still, the vast traditional (*aslī*) knowledge of raga and repertoire on which he would build his career as a khyaliya was deferred until later. This was to come only after his voice had gone through its adolescent change and settled permanently on a pitch.

Sadly, this phase of his training never arrived. Just as Sharukh's voice was changing, his beloved father suddenly passed away. Sharukh thus never had a chance to learn traditional rāgas and compositions that would prepare him for a career as a performing classical singer. But his early preparations paid off nonetheless. Once his voice had settled stably in his mid-teens, it retained the remarkable strength and flexibility he had cultivated as a child. A kindly uncle, Ghulam Niyazi, on hearing Sharukh sing, invited him to sing in his professional qawwali party as a supporting singer. His voice was already *surīl* and agile and strong enough to project into the wide-open courtyards of Sufi shrines. Singing behind his uncle in the courtyard of the Nizamuddin shrine, his sharp memory, honed through years of disciplined practice, allowed him to quickly pick up dozens of songs by ear. Just as important, he acquired the subtle comportmental habits of *being* a qawwal that no amount of solitary practice could give him. Seated in a qawwali party behind his uncle, he acquired the relational craft of singing qawwali in a dargah. He learned the subtle art of "giving expressions" (ornaments, gestures, repetitions, salient citations) at the right moments to an assembly of devout listeners (see chapter 3). Rarely did his uncle sit him down and explicitly teach him the craft of the qawwal in formal lessons; he learned principally through hundreds of hours of watching and assimilating "on the job." Indeed, much of his education consisted of singing for hours in the atmosphere (*māhaul*) of a shrine, and building his own relationship with the saint interred therein: Hazrat Nizamuddin Auliya.

In his mid-twenties, Sharukh has been developing yet another vocal disposition: the art of recording Sufi songs in a studio (for example, a formidable cover of Kailash Kher's pop sufi hit "Teri Deewani"). He has cultivated the skill—so valuable in the current pop sufi economy—of singing both with the bold, open, buland voice of a qawwal, and the gentle, crooning, microphonic voice of a film singer. Mastering these twin dispositions, and the expressive comportment of a pop sufi singer, opens up a great many lucrative professional opportunities for a singer like Sharukh: for example, singing Sufi ghazals onstage at lavish weddings, where songs of mystical devotion and yearning read ambiguously as love songs.

Bindhumalini Narayanaswamy (sometimes listed professionally as "Bindhu Malini") has a far-reaching repertoire, ranging from Khusrau's devotional ghazals to khyal to the nirgun bhajans of Kabir. She has sung on several film soundtracks, winning a National Film Award for Best Female Playback Singer for Maayavi Manave in the Kannada film *Nathicharami* (2018). As a child, Bindhu grew up in Chennai in an educated Tamil Brahmin family, where her mother taught her to sing. She showed a great deal of early potential; she was giving concerts successfully in her teens, and even taking on students of her own. She had practiced Carnatic repertoire for hours each day, progressing along a well-worn vocal path: beginning from scalar patterns, moving through increasingly complex songs, and eventually reaching the rarefied territory of *manodharma*, the art of spontaneously improvising melody on the spot.

It is here, among the demands for spontaneous improvisation that are at the heart of raga music, that a conflict took shape in her early twenties. After years on this path, she faced, as she put it, "a roadblock." The problem was not notes; all her notes were in the right order and in tune.

But she felt an undeniable aversion to the rigorous discipline required of her. The repertoire was not the problem, nor even the character of her teachers—whom she continues to hold in high esteem. The problem was a particular vocal disposition. As she put it to me, her Carnatic training "put me through a lot of *rrr*." This wordless *rrr* became a recurring theme in her narrative, articulated entirely through clenching: of the back of the tongue to the roof of the mouth, of the velum, of the strap muscles in the neck. It is a caricature of the rigor, the strictness, the rigidity that, for her, undermined the freedom she wanted in her singing. She was faced with what she called a "Catch-22": the harder she worked on the disciplines of improvisation, the less free she felt. Bindhu faced a crisis: the training that she had received her whole life, training that had given her a highly acclaimed vocal disposition and even seemed to be promising a career as a concert singer of Carnatic music—this same training seemed to be inhibiting her improvisational freedom.

Around this time, Bindhu began listening seriously to Hindustani music. She was attracted to what she describes as the "dwelling," the patient, gentle exploration that she heard in Hindustani vocal music. So she decided to go north. In the summer of 2007, soon after her twenty-fifth birthday, she packed her bags and went to Calcutta to study with Abdul Rashid Khan, a venerable khyal singer. Bindhu was conscious, even then, that this could have been a form of escapism from a vocal challenge—but there was no easy escape from her training. She was initially, as she put it, "too anxious to not slip, so that hold is more tight," stuck in a disposition of "pushing" and "grabbing" and "gripping." Abdul Rashid Khan, too, could see the block in the road: the tense, rigorous attitude—the *rrr*—that she had brought with her. He identified a hard (*kaṭhor*) quality in her voice, like "a wall." At times her master worked directly to "chisel away" the wall, giving her more exercises to practice; at other times, he simply observed. Two years later, he invited her to tie the knot of a formal discipular bond (*gandabandhan*). Soon thereafter, in the middle of a lesson, she realized that she was suddenly able to sing a phrase that she had been struggling with smoothly, without the sense of holding. She attributes this shift to a shift in her relationship with her master: "He changed me as a person. Not by telling me anything, but just being who he is. And the way he allowed me to be with him." After years of "putting conscious effort, effort, effort, effort," she was able to release the grip, as she says, "when I forgot." She gradually found herself releasing the grip, relaxing into a new disposition of surrender—a dispositional shift no less difficult to achieve than speed or strength, and which requires its own form of striving.

In both of these cases, we see a process of vocal striving that is both volitional and guided, as it were, from the outside. As we see from Sharukh's story, his process of voicemaking—still unfolding, even now—has depended both on his own efforts (deliberate riyaz, imbibing qawwali repertoire, cultivating a *filmi* voice, seeking performance opportunities) and on his circumstances beyond his control (being born into a khāndān, his father's death, a public demand for pop sufi). Indeed, there is a great deal that Sharukh did not choose about his economic conditions of possibility—most importantly, the fact that he has been constrained by the need to earn money singing during a crucial formative moment in his career. For Bindhu, blessed with the financial means to choose a new vocal path, seeking and finding freedom has been at the center of her vocal practice. And yet, this freedom was achieved precisely by counter-volitional practices, relinquishing personal control over her voice: releasing a grip, letting go, surrendering to an elder master.

Bindhu and Sharukh are both extraordinary singers, and both, as of 2020, are working to build vocal careers for themselves. Both, too, have undergone significant periods of vocal work and reflection. But not all singers spend so much time consciously working on their own voice. A great deal of learning takes place "on the job," as it were, from being in the company of musicians, listening and watching closely, imbibing their dispositions.[1] Some, particularly those whose careers depend on a carefully framed "folk" or "Sufi" authenticity, speak proudly of singing with a "simple" (*sahaj*) voice, unblemished by the artificiality of deliberate riyaz—indeed, this often serves as the defining criterion of *lok-sangeet*. We saw in chapter 4 that the marketing of pop sufi tends to downplay the musical training of its stars, seeking and celebrating natural, soulful voices that bespeak a pure, unmediated selfhood (in contrast to the refined crooning of

1. See Weston 2013, 139 for what he calls "horizontal" or *birādarī* learning.

the *filmi* voices that dominated the public soundscapes of the first four decades of independence). At other end of the spectrum are classical vocalists—singers of khyal, dhrupad, thumri, and other raga-based genres—who speak at great length about the ascetic rigors of their vocal striving, their devotion to their master, the uniqueness of their path. To be sure, some people appear to be born with a genetic or spiritual predilection for a certain kind of singing. Reality TV is filled with extraordinary vocal prodigies who appear to be entirely self-taught, such as the national vocal hero now known as Sunny, who went from shining shoes to singing on *Indian Idol* (and who, according to one telling, was born moments after Nusrat Fateh Ali Khan's death and inherited his voice). And yet, as have seen in chapter 2, even the sonic "fingerprint" we recognize as vocal personhood owes its contours not only to a given anatomical or spiritual formation, but to a cultivated disposition. In any case, most singers, qawwals, ghazal singers, and pop sufi singers, however natural they sound in the moment of singing, have had to work for it over the course of many years.[2] Nearly every singer, moreover, has changed course at one time or another, deliberately learning a new vocal disposition. For many singers, this change occurs as a vocal crisis (physiological, spiritual, or both) that leads them to radically remake their vocal self.

The earliest stages of singing, in youth, come down to us in retrospect through cloudy lenses, inflected with all the nostalgia of childhood, the anxieties of family responsibility, and all the metaphysical weight borne by the question of hereditary authority. As with learning a language, the early years of vocal life (when the vocal cords are "soft") are particularly ripe for learning the kinetic dispositions of song. Those who are born into families of singers, surrounded by song before they can speak, are often given their first exercises at the age of three or four—or even earlier. I once asked Shafqat Ali Khan, son of legendary khyaliya Salamat Ali Khan, to describe his earliest memory of singing. He sat silently for a moment before saying, with some sadness, that he couldn't recall any early memories when he *wasn't* singing. Qawwals tend to have an early, intensive period of training, beginning their performing career as supporting singers in

---

2. Many famous playback singers had formal talim; for example, Mohammad Rafi learned from Abdul Wahid Khan, and Lata Mangeshkar learned from Amanat Ali Khan. It is not clear that this is true of all film singers, however; Alison Arnold points out that some of the earliest film singers (before the era of the specialist playback singers) came from a variety of backgrounds, some with classical training, some from theater, some with no training at all. (Arnold 1991, 48.)

a qawwali party around the time their voices change. Only later, if at all, do the most charismatic and effective qawwals learn to lead their own parties.[3] Other singers begin their formal training only in adulthood, having sung casually for their whole lives.

At a young age, some singers discover an inexplicable passion, or *shauq*, for singing. The great singer Bhimsen Joshi, for example, was compelled to run away from home to pursue singing because his parents were so strongly opposed to the idea. Others, like Namita Devidayal, without any instinctive *shauq* for singing, must be "dragged" into singing by their elders, developing their vocal passions only later.[4] And yet, *shauq* would also appear to be subject to cultivation like any other virtue of the heart. Qawwal Fareed Ayaz points out that in his family, when children sing out of *sur*, elders are careful not to discourage them: <"In order to fill up their hearts [*dil bharne ke liye*], we still praise them."[5]> Thus children are sometimes taught the boring abstractions of tāl cycles or note-names through story-songs or games. Another skill that sometimes appears to be inborn is *pakaḍ*[6] ("catching," or what is sometimes called in Hindi by the loan word "pick-up"), the ability to quickly assimilate by heart the melodic or poetic essence of what one hears. And yet, this skill, too, seems to improve with practice—teachers often complain that students who start training too late cannot remember anything without writing it down. But these inborn predelictions alone—whether suppressed or cultivated—are never sufficient; singing must be cultivated among others in a musical atmosphere.

The most well-known setting for this vocal cultivation is a long period of discipleship in which a master (*guru*, *ustād*) inculcates a range of vocal techniques in formal training (*tālīm*). This has long been the paradigmatic setting not only for classical vocalists, but also for courtesans and qawwals; most film singers have had some formal period of study as well. A range of vocal dispositions is taken in through bodily disciplines, and, by accompanying one's master in concert, the posture, gesture, and relational techniques of an exemplary singer are absorbed.[7]

---

3. See Weston 2013, 134–136.

4. Devidayal 2011, 7.

5. *Ham tārīf karte hai. Uskā dil bhar karne ke liye.*

6. Not to be confused with the *pakaḍ* of a rāga—the key phrases that make it identifiable and distinctive.

7. See Rahaim 2012, 107.

Striving after Another Voice: The Rīyāz-Tālīm *Complex*

Rīyāz (intensive solitary practice) and *tālīm* (receiving instruction from a master) are mutually dependent forms of vocal work. Riyaz is undertaken under the direction of a master (striving for the still-alien vocal abilities thereby offered), and talim proceeds on a foundation of riyaz that a student has already done (grounded in stable dispositional capacities already achieved). They thus form a tightly woven complex, corresponding to these phases of dispositional cultivation. Nearly every singer undertakes some amount of riyaz and talim, from playback singers to qawwals to classical vocalists to pop sufi stars.[8] Since independence, the drama of these forms of vocal striving have appeared widely in popular films (such as *Baiju Bawra*, *Man Pasand*, *Sur Sangam*, and *Katyar Kalzat Ghosli*), and there are now many detailed ethnographic studies of the rituals and institutions of master-disciple relationships that provide the relational scaffolding for vocal training.[9] Here, our principal concern is the processes by which riyaz and talim cultivate vocal dispositions. This training produces a wide variety of vocal sounds and dispositions, but in all cases, it requires a student to work for a voice that is not yet their own.

The most intense, focused techniques of vocal self-work in the Hindustani vocal ecumene are called riyaz. To gloss riyaz as "practice" doesn't quite do the trick. Riyaz consists of rigorous vocal exercises that challenge the current state of the voice, working toward establishing an unfamiliar vocal disposition firmly in the musicking body (for instrumentalists, riyaz consists of analogous exercises that train the wrists, arms, and fingers[10]). The changes that riyaz works

---

8. A typical period of talim-riyaz for a khyaliya or dhrupadiya is ten to twenty years; qawwals often move on to public performance after only five to ten years. It seems that in late-nineteenth-century Bombay, many courtesans would undergo basic training with an elder female mentor, and, by some reports, as few as three years of talīm in khyal with a male representative of a gharana before performing in public (Pradhan 2014, 35–36). Somewhere in the course of this talim, a student is acknowledged to be *taiyār*, ready for a public debut (Daniel Neuman 1990, 80; Dard Neuman 2004, 162). Aspiring film singers, too, typically require only a few years of talīm before moving on to recording careers.

9. Qureshi in Wolf 2009, 165; Daniel Neuman 1991; Dard Neuman 2004; Scott 1997; Magriel 2011.

10. Neuman 2004.

on one's voice could not possibly be achieved through theoretical study. No less than batting drills, these practices require what seems to be endless repetition: holding a tone steady, breath after breath, for an hour or more; skipping up and down scales hundreds of times; repeating abstract kinetic patterns long past the point of technical competence.

Nearly every world of Hindustani voice includes some amount of riyaz: qawwals, gawaiyyas, film singers, theater singers, and kirtankars, among others. The small fraction who go on to pursue raga music tend to have the longest and most arduous period of focused riyaz, typically ten to twenty years; many khyaliyas and dhrupadiyas continue daily riyaz until the end of their lives. For others, two to three years may suffice before moving on to more specialized training in *filmi* or bhajan, or ghazal. The folklore of riyaz ordinarily centers around extraordinary feats of asceticism undertaken by legendary singers. *Riyaz* is a term often used by Sufis in reference to techniques of breath, recitation, and attention that "engage the body, concentrate the mind, and purify the soul as part of the ethical transformation of self."[11] The nearly interchangeable synonym *sādhana* (often applied more broadly to include forms of striving beyond riyaz) also suggests yogic or devotional practices that grant extraordinary powers. As Vidya Rao puts it, thumri singers undergo years of riyaz "to arrive at not just *taiyari* (technical perfection) but *mizaj* (a state of mind, an attitude)."[12] The interminable repetition of phrases in riyaz, even without lexical reference, has much in common with the ongoing repetition of devotional formulas (*jap* or *zikr*) by Chishti Sufis and Krishna bhakts. If the hundredth repetition of *Rām* becomes different from its isolated utterance in a sentence, so too does riyaz transform a vocal disposition through repetition. Just as a Chishti Sufi might undertake *chillā* (a 40-day retreat dedicated to prayer), so too might a singer undertake a 40-day *chillā* filled with nothing but riyaz.[13] Stories abound of musicians waking to practice before the sun or tying their hair to the ceiling to remain awake late at night, secluding themselves from human contact, or even chemically extending their limits (taking *afīm* for the aches and pains of sitting for twelve hours

---

11. Flatt 2019, 198.

12. Rao 1990, WS-31.

13. Dard Neuman cautions against taking these analogies too far, going so far as to call riyaz "the non-spiritual quest," geared toward making the conscious unconscious, aptly contrasting the apparent parallels between spiritual pilgrimage and riyaz (2004, 225–229).

at a stretch, or *bhāng* for the crushing attentional tedium of repetition). These stories, even when embellished, serve a didactic function when told to students. They place a numinous ethical aura around the inevitable pains of riyaz, and they stress the devotion and perseverence required for vocal transformation. Aphorisms for impatient students abound. My own guru, L. K. Pandit, often will tell an ambitious student "*Dilli dūr ast*" (Delhi is [still] far)[14] when they ask for esoteric repertoire, to remind them that riyaz takes time, and to patiently reorient themselves to the task at hand. He sometimes recites Rahim's famous Braj couplet to me when I want to learn too many things too quickly, teasing me about my namesake who had attained so much more than I, and urging me to "water the roots," and focus on fundamentals:

> *Ekai sādhe sab sadhai sab sādhe sab jāy*
> *Rahim mūlahin sīncibo phūlai phalai aghāy*
>
> Strive for one thing and achieve it all; strive for it all and lose everything;
> Rahim says: Generously water the roots. The fruits and flowers will be fulfilled.

The couplet performatively reorients the disciple from systematic comprehension to focused practical striving, a stance central to riyaz. The grueling tenacity required for vocal riyaz—often extending to four or more hours a day, taking a voice to the very edge of its physical limits—this is not only a means to a technical end, but is widely considered a virtue in itself.[15] More to the point, the most intensive riyaz is characteristically *transformative*: it does not so much entrench one's current vocal disposition, but requires its ongoing *effacement* in favor of a voice that one does not yet have. Vocal joy, freedom, and magic will come later, if at all. First comes a period of work, frustration, and physical pain.

In the process, riyaz remakes the musicking body. The stamina and power of vocal muscles, no less than the heart, lungs, and biceps, must be gradually built up day by day. Sedentary students must endure weeks of aching muscles and nerve pain while their musculature adapts to the "body technique" of sitting

---

14. See Aquil 2016 for one account of the origin of this Persian idiom, now thoroughly absorbed into Hindustani, in a legend about Nizamuddin Auliya defending the propriety of *samā*.

15. Neuman 1991, 21.

cross-legged on the floor.[16] Namita Devidayal describes a long period of "pins and needles" in the soles of her feet as she began learning from Dhondhutai Kulkarni, relieved only periodically by "fidgeting and shifting" as she struggled to adapt to her teacher's requirements.[17] Indeed, as singers build a particular paramparic body from their various influences, they acquire stances that are suited for distinctive forms of kinetic action. Breathing, too, is reconfigured in riyaz; some teachers explicitly prescribe exercises in pranayama or zikr. Pushkar Lele, for example, once described for me a habitual energetic blockage in his throat region that opened only after many years of riyaz. As increasingly complex vocal routines are assimilated into the body, many singers report such shifts in subtle energy.

The earliest stages of riyaz focus on developing sonority. As we saw in chapter 2, *sur*—a luminous quality of tuneful intonational resonance—is one of the foundational vocal qualities in the Hindustani vocal ecumene. But this quality can be maddeningly elusive. Though some children seem to have a special knack for sur, everyone also has to work for it. *Surīlāpaṇ* (the disciplined vocal hexis of having-*sur*) is a hard-won vocal *guṇa*, achieved through years of striving. Sur requires the twin capabilities of aural discernment and tonal precision. It does not consist in producing a tone of any particular absolute frequency, but rather in luminously merging with accompanying instruments (typically tanpura, harmonium, and/or sarangi). The neurophysiological link between hearing and phonatory stability is well-studied,[18] even in non-singers, but cultivating sur requires extraordinarily subtle powers of discernment. Many singers are unable to hear that they are out of tune until their guru corrects them—the guru extends their own tonal acuity to their blissfully oblivious students.[19]

Once a singer does develop the capacity to discern the difference between right and wrong (*sur-īla* and *be-sur*), they begin a phase of extreme frustration: one becomes painfully aware that one is *be-sur* (out of sur) but is unable to correct it by force of will.

When I went through this period of struggle (belatedly, in my twenties), I confided in an older mentor, Mohan Darekar, who seemed (to my ears, at least) to have effortless, perfect sur. He nodded empathetically. He told me that in his

16. See Mauss 1973 [1934].

17. See Devidayal 2011, 36. On posture, see Rahaim 2012, 90.

18. Rathna Kumar, et al. 2013.

19. Deshpande 1989, 3.

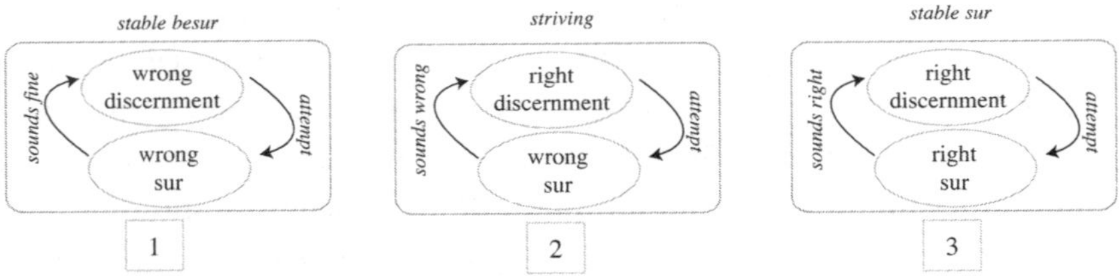

FIGURE 5.1 Developing sur

childhood, he too hungered for sur, wept after it, and stayed up all night working at it. He told me that this distress was a good sign: I had, at least, developed the capacity to hear when I was *be-sur*. In time, with years of riyaz, I passed through this phase. I cannot, however, claim to have developed perfect sur—indeed, perfection always seems to be just out of reach. Many singers insist that sur is always incomplete—recall Pushkar Lele's caution (chapter 2) that "we are never in the center" of the bull's eye. Simply noticing that a particular tone is too high is no more adequate for sur than noticing one's arrow flying above the target is adequate to achieve expert archery. Aiming vaguely up or down may get one close, but only sustained, repetitive practice can achieve sur. The practical methods for developing sur do not typically consist of willfully nudging one's pitch up or down (no one carries out arithmetical calculations of ideal Pythagorean ratios or cycles per second), but of extended, concerted repetition.

One foundational technique for developing sur is called *sā bharnā*[20] ("filling out" *sā*). This consists of singing the tonic, *sā* {1}, for an entire breath, over and over, blending it with the drone of the tanpura. Beginners are often required to do nothing else for hours at a stretch, far beyond the point when they are hitting the correct note. If this sounds simple, try it for just 60 seconds—as we saw in chapter 2, vocal utterances typically *move*; vocal stillness is a highly cultivated skill. This technique and the results, like sur itself, span both intonational precision and sonorous richness. Without the usual kinetic distractions of melody, the act of holding *sā* is revealed to be more than hitting a point in tonal space. A broad tonal tapestry rises to salience, marked by layered, shimmering overtones in dynamic play with the tone of the tanpura. V. H. Deshpande describes the thrill of insight that came to him after months of *sā bharnā* with Sureshbabu

20. *Bharnā* is a term unusually ripe with connotation, including fulfillment, becoming steeped in a substance, and satisfaction.

Mane: "not only did [my guru's] face glow with satisfaction, but I myself felt so thrilled with the sheer beauty of that one note that I felt the entire magic of music was contained in that one 'tonic.'"[21] The resonant spaces of the body arise to attention: the belly, chest, throat, and nose vividly become extensions of one's voice. Pooja Goswami even describes becoming aware of the resonance of *sā* in her knees. Mahesh Kale once described *sā bharnā* as a reflective practice of vocal presence that allows one to "feel the moment," to "soak it up."

For some aspiring qawwals, the first opportunities for performance require them to sustain a drone on *sā* while a soloist sings over it, without any instruments (often in the genres *soz* or *na'at*). Accordingly, many young qawwāls practice holding *sā* steady while another student sustains tones above it (see Fareed Ayaz's demonstration in chapter 2). The student must remain focused on the sound of the tanpura and join his voice with the fabric of its drone, resisting the temptation to join in unison with the other voice. For many aspiring khyaliyas, their first chance at vocal sangat in a mahfil will consist of supplying a high, sustained *sā* while their guru takes a breath.

Sā bharna is more than finding the correct pitch (in which case, you'd only have to find it once). It inculcates a dispositional complex of the steadiness of *thaharāv*, a lasting attunement to the richness of vocal sonority, and a temporal openness to long stretches of time. Ramanlal Mehta describes the transformative effect that it had on "Ghagghe" Khuda Bakhsh, an important nineteenth-century Agra gharana khyaliya who seems to have suffered a miserable childhood, born with a congenital voice defect into a family of great singers. But he found a sympathetic guru from another gharana—Natthan Pir Bakhsh of Gwalior:

> To rid his voice of its defects, Natthan Pir Bakhsh made Khudabakhsh [*sic*] practice sa [i.e., *sā*] for long periods of time. He made Khudabakhsh pluck only the sa strings of the tanpura, and match the tone as exactly as possible, for hours at a time. Khudabakhsh began his training with great devotion for his teacher in his heart and with great determination, and in the end succeeded in reaching his goals. All the faults in his voice disappeared and he was able to produce the notes perfectly with his voice. Khudabakhsh remained in Gwalior for a period of 12 years and studied music intensively with Natthan Pir Bakhsh. In that time, he gained great mastery over khyal. When he finally returned to

21. Deshpande 1989, 4.

Agra and sang for his family, everyone was . . . astonished by the vast improvement in his voice and music.[22]

A related technique is called *kharaj*—sustaining extremely low tones—to lend the voice weight and resonance, and to extend the range downward.[23] This is typically undertaken early in the morning, when the range tends to be lower, often proceeding step by step downwards from the fifth to the low tonic (the latter is often called *kharaj*). Most beginners cannot reach down to the low *sā* on their first try, but over the course of weeks, this lower range becomes increasingly stable and resonant, noticeably enriching the voice even later in the day. My own guru, L. K. Pandit, instructed me early on in my training with him to do 30–60 minutes of kharaj every day; when I called him from Minneapolis after three months of this practice, he reported with satisfaction that he could hear the *kharaj* in my speaking voice even over the phone. After a bout of laryngitis during which I had to abandon riyaz for a week, I recorded myself gradually building kharaj back into my voice over the course of eleven days. figure 5.2 shows kharaj gradually becoming longer, steadier, and louder.[24]

Kharaj imparts weight (*vazn*) to one's voice, producing a sonority that is heavy and resonant rather than light and sweet. But we have already seen (in chapter 2) that weightiness is not a universally desirable vocal disposition. Kharaj is practiced most rigorously by male qawwals, dhrupadiyas, and khyaliyas, and often deliberately avoided by singers developing a light disposition suitable for thumri, ghazal, or film song. But khyaliyas, too, acknowledge that kharaj has its dangers. Early in my training, one elder mentor cautioned me against doing kharaj from more than an hour each day, as it can lead a singer to "grip" each note in turn, cultivating sonorous depth at the expense of kinetic flexibility. There is a near-universal admonition against forcing one's range downward too quickly, and especially against continuing the practice if the voice itches or

---

22. Mehta 2017, 21–22. See also Dard Neuman's narrative analysis (2004, 148 and passim).

23. The word *ḳharaj* is generally regarded to be a dialectal pronunciation of *ṣadaj* (where the Sanskritic *ṣ* becomes *ḳh* in some dialects of Hindustani, as *ṛṣabh* becomes *riḳhabh*). Others consider it to refer to the "khar" of your throat, the bottom. See also Herbst 1997, 25 on sustaining low notes.

24. (Recorded on Zoom H1 at a distance of 9 inches, approximately 9:00 a.m. each day, September 6–16, 2019.)

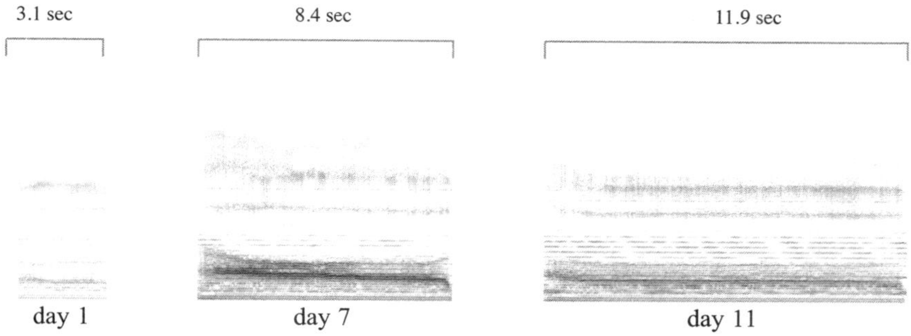

FIGURE 5.2 Re-development of kharaj over ten days of practice

becomes raspy.[25] All of these can put strain on the vocal mechanism, and even do permanent damage.

The usual technique for nudging the range upward is singing scales across progressively ascending octaves (i.e., *sā* to *sā*, *re* to *re*, *ga* to *ga*, and so on), carefully maintaining a constant sonority step by step. As we have seen in chapter 2, however, range is not merely a matter of squeaking out a pitch, but of maintaining flexible sonorous and kinetic possibilities. For qawwals, developing a high and open *buland* voice is essential to their power in singing unamplified in the wide-open spaces of shrines. They thus tend to have particularly rigorous techniques for expanding their usable range upwards, proceeding stepwise in octaves from their lowest notes to their highest. In ideal cases, many qawwals are able to move their tonic pitch upward significantly—most settle around F♯ (black three), and some get as high as Bb (black five). One common tendency that many young singers have is to close their voice when singing high up; a technique for counteracting this is to start low and open, and to proceed up a scale note by note, remaining conscious of its openness at every step.

Indeed, for khyaliyas and qawwals, openness is one of the key qualities cultivated in riyaz (see chapter 2). Teachers will often admonish their students to "*khul ke gāo*" (sing openly). But openness is a rather more complex thing than it may seem at first. There are ordinarily at least three points in the voice that can be opened through concerted riyaz. First, the mouth is trained to remain open, counteracting the usual tendency to close the mouth and obscure one's sonority during technically demanding kinetic action. This can be carried out through various techniques, including placing an almond between the molars

25. See Bhatkhande 1954, 50, and Mishra 2016.

in order to entrainment the mouth in a distinctive relaxed yet open disposition, or placing the fingers on the lower jaw or between to make palpably distinct the ordinarily subtle proprioception of opening or closing by a few millimeters. A second point of disciplined openness is the back of the tongue which, when elevated, blocks the vocal tract, producing a tone that sounds like the velar nasal /ŋ/, like the *ng* of *sing*. The usual instruction here is to relax the back of the tongue to allow it to lie flat. This openness is more difficult to achieve than openness of the jaw since the action all happens out of sight in the back of the mouth (producing the phoneme /ŋa/ can help to bring the movement of the back of the tongue into conscious awareness). In both cases, the usual vowel to be cultivated here is a wide open /a/, or *ākār*. A third point of openness is the nose, producing jivārī, a distinctive buzzing glowing sonority of nasal resonance. One way of training a student to sing *nāk se* (particularly important for Agra gayaki) is through a technique called *mukh band rīyāz* (closed-mouth riyaz). Here, the lips are sealed so that one is singing, as it were, through the nose, and a maximally resonant and buzzy /m/ is produced.[26] Once the student develops this /m/ into a bright hum, the mouth is slowly opened, producing an /a/ with bright jivārī. My guru taught me a diagnostic method of testing that the proper amount of jivārī has been produced: sustaining /a/ and alternately pinching the nose shut and releasing it, ensuring that a moderate but not a radical difference of sonority is produced by the nose.

The period of singing nothing but sā, focusing only on sonority, may stretch out for weeks or months. But once *sā* has been properly seasoned, the other six svaras come relatively quickly—there is ordinarily no commensurate period of months dedicated solely to any other note. Somehow, being rooted in *sā* ensures a dispositional *sur* that applies to the remaining svaras.

Once the dispositional foundation of sur is established, students ordinarily proceed to another phase of grueling, repetitive practice, working their way through scalar patterns (*palṭās, svaralankārs*). Written out, *palṭās* seem innocuous enough, suggesting a silent, cool, mathematical abstraction, as shown in figure 5.3:

But repeated dozens or hundreds of times, paltās take on a distinctly kinetic aspect, more like dance steps than coded sequences. Beginners often begin slowly, with focused attention to the *sur* of each swara. As the speed increases, one's attention shifts from *sur* to the cultivation of various vocal gaits (chapter

26. See also Scott 1997, 464.

```
SRG RGM GMP MPD PDN ...
123 234 345 456 567

SRGM RGMP GMPD MPDN ...
1234 2345 3456 4567

SGRG RMGM GPMP MDPD ...
1323 2434 3545 4656

SRSS RGRR GMGG MPMM ...
1211 2322 3433 4544
```

FIGURE 5.3 Paltas

2), repeated so many times that the gait itself becomes more or less automatic, and the student has only to ascend or descend in its characteristic cāl. Paltas sung in sargam also cultivate *svar-jnān*, the auditory capacity for discerning the named pitch-classes of sung tones (see chapter 3). Once these palte are established firmly in natural notes (shuddh svaras), some students proceed systematically through various scales (*ṭhāṭs*); for others, shuddh svaras provide an adequate foundation. Just as *sā bharna* prepares the voice for singing any svara in tune, *paltās* in shuddh svaras prepare the voice for moving freely in any scale. More importantly, it cultivates a disposition of confidence in the face of rigorous technical demands—one practices scales so that, as one often hears, one will not fear any raga. Developing this foundational confidence may take one year or twelve or more, depending on the guru, and forms an important dispositional bedrock for what is to come. Many singers, particularly those striving for a career in film song or ghazal, may then end their period of intensive riyaz and begin to focus on performance. For qawwals, khyaliyas, dhrupadiyas, and specialists in ghazal or thumri, the road is often considerably longer; they may begin to acquire competence in ragas and compositions, but it will be many years before they are *taiyār* (ready to perform).

For khyaliyas and qawwals in particular, preparing the voice for tāns (see chapter 2) requires a special repetitive riyaz. Students typically are given a small set of simple tāns to practice hundreds of times, with an emphasis on proper gait (see chapter 2). For example, in the development of distinct *dānās* (grains) so crucial to tāns in Agra and Gwalior gayaki, students are sometimes instructed to slap their right hand on their right thigh along with each pulse. This technique is wonderfully efficient, though it is not entirely clear *why* it works (one hint toward a more thorough sensorimotor explanation is the fact that alternating hands does not produce the same effect). I once saw a teacher shake his young student by the shoulders along with each pulse of a tān in order to develop deeper gamak. This, too, worked—after shaking him through the tān a dozen or so times, the teacher sat back and observed with satisfaction as the student sang on his own with the requisite gamak. (As with all talim, the victory was short-lived—the student was then told to practice it a hundred times on his own.)

Even in the acquisition of compositions, repetition is the principal technique. Students sing a composition, or even just a single seed phrase of a raga given by the master, over and over again, well past the point of being able to do it correctly, until it comes as easily as walking, without the need for reflective thought.[27] This practice—the pinnacle of tedium—seems to span gharanas and traditions and regions.[28] The term *tarāshnā* (used for sanding down or planing wood) is often used in relation to the voice as an object that the striving subject works on.

From the first practices of *sā bharnā* through the most elaborate repetitions of tāns, nearly all singers find the grinding redundancy of riyaz to be profoundly, soul-crushingly boring. To free oneself of the cognitive burden of counting repetitions, many singers use a string of prayer beads (a *mala* or a *tasbīh*), which is used for marking repetitions of zikr or jap. In addition to physical discomfort and fatigue, this may create an existential friction for ambitious singers who yearn to hurriedly acquire a dazzling repertoire. But this boredom is also productive, building an expanded sense of temporality and patience—passing through what Bakhar Hussein Khan called the "patience test" before moving on to sophisticated repertoire.[29] As Dard Neuman points out, this repetitive practice serves not only to aid memorization, not only to inculcate a personal humility, but also to establish the dispositional "body-knowledge" foundational for automatic vocal movement and improvisation.[30]

There are also limits to riyaz. As a student, one is subjected to didactic folklore about the old days, when great singers would practice for 16 hours a day, but it is also clear that, in practice, *too much* riyaz can do harm. While nearly all singers attribute their vocal prowess to tenacious riyaz, other singers' voices are said to have been damaged by relentless, forceful practice. The hoarseness, fatigue, and

---

27. Dard Neuman 2012, 440; Rahaim 2012, 57.

28. Ganesh 2006; Deodhar 1993, 90; Dard Neuman 2004, 188, and passim.

29. Scott 1997, 449.

30. Neuman 2012, 445.

trembling that now drive singers to biomedical, Ayurvedic, and yogic remedies are often attributed to excessive riyaz. Some teachers also claim that excessive riyaz can dull a singer's sensibilities. Rajan Mishra reports that his father, Hanuman Mishra, would limit he and his brother's riyaz to only three to four hours per day.[31] Vikas Kashalkar once advised me that an hour of intelligent riyaz could be more effective than ten hours of aimless riyaz. Dard Neuman convincingly diagnoses this widespread aversion to repetitive exercise as a characteristically rationalist drive for efficiency; and yet, as we will see, it would also appear that *chintan*, or reflection, can stand in a dialectical, rather than oppositional, relation to repetition.

Tālīm (instruction) is the relational complement of riyaz, unfolding "chest to chest" (*sīna ba sīna*) with master and disciple seated facing each other.[32] Talim certainly involves teaching canonical repertoire and ragas, but its essence is the cultivation of a stable gayaki: a distinctive vocal disposition. Talim is usually preceded by a preliminary phase—sometimes lasting months or even a full year after an aspirant is officially recognized as a disciple—dedicated to solitary riyaz exercises (*sa bharna, kharaj, palṭās*) prescribed and overseen by the master. During this period, the master may supervise from a distance; the student may carry out these exercises at their own home, or in some out-of-the-way space of the master's house while more advanced students receive talim downstairs.

The intensive, essentially relational phase of face-to-face talim begins once a disciple's voice is prepared (and their dedication is proven); many singers reserve the term *talim* for this period in particular. Ordinarily, talim proper proceeds in a call-and-echo pattern: the master sings an exemplary phrase, usually shorter than a breath, and the student echoes it back. When my master sings *ā*, I inhale, and *ā* forms on my tongue and lips before I even sing it, my own musicking body molding itself into a corporeal resonance of his sonority. When he springs upward in a bright tān to the *komal re* {♭2} above the tonic, holding it for a moment before whipping down to the *ga* {3}, I echo not only his sound, but also an entire routine of tension and release, impetus and stillness, enacted by the lips, tongue, throat, hands, and breath. I echo his calm dwelling on long tones, his

---

31. "[*Riyaz*] is not a laborious thing, that you are making a building, and carrying lots of weight on your head. The fragrance should be there." As Scott puts it, this fragrance is "a subtle thing, which can easily be destroyed by an overly forceful, laborious approach." (Scott 1997, 180.)

32. Qureshi in Wolf 2009.

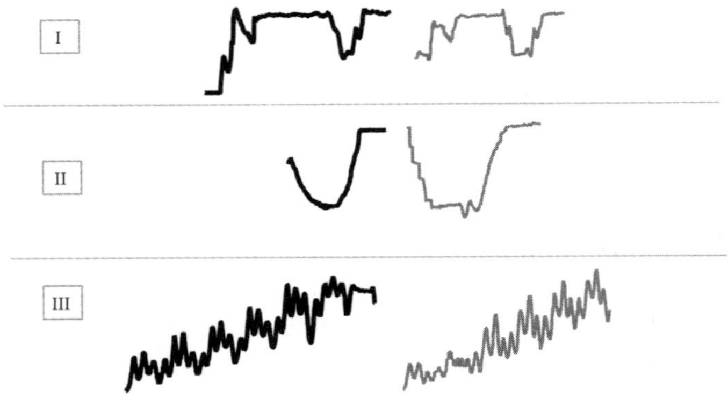

FIGURE 5.4 Tālīm echo

surprising turns that break from an established gait, his subtle temporal sense of when to remain in one space, and when to break out. I am learning to do as he does, not only mimicking individual moves, but also acquiring, slowly and imperfectly, a vocal disposition. Figure 5.4 shows pitch traces excerpted from talim I received from L. K. Pandit, in which he is giving a sequence of phrases in Rāg Puriya, each leading up to *ni* {7}. The exemplary phrases are thick and black; my echoes are printed lighter (see fig. 5.4).

It should be obvious even from the pitch traces that these echoes are imperfect. In phrase 1, my initial gamak is too shallow, and I overshoot on the ni. In phrase 2, Guruji's long, smooth glide (*mīṇḍ*) downwards over the octave is marred, in my echo, with several snags. Though my glide upwards is smoother, it is preceded by a quick *gamak* that was not there in the original, and I end up a bit shy of the high ni; the corrective scoop is concealed by my vibrato. In phrase 3, my gamaks are rougher and jerkier than Guruji's are, evincing not only imperfect execution, but also an imperfect gait.

These mimetic imperfections are an inevitable part of talim. One strives for, but never perfectly reproduces, the master's way of voice. Nonetheless, we keep going: the master gives a phrase, the disciple echoes imperfectly; the master gives another phrase, and so on. Part of the art of giving talim lies in knowing when to interrupt the flow to correct a student's distorted rendering, returning to the original given phrase, perhaps naming its svaras as signposts, repeating it until the student adequately grasps its essence, imparting to it, through repeated citation, a contingent solidity and textuality. Yet this ephemeral text-object dissolves again in the flow of spontaneous song, and master and disciple return to the shaping of a disposition. In some cases, the student hits a wall and can't find their way around. The master will often then prescribe a phrase, shorter than a breath, for repetitive practice—dozens or hundreds of times. At this point, talim pauses or ends, marked by a break in the relational flow of the lesson. The master may leave the room or pick up a newspaper; the student turns to solitary riyaz.

What the master offers, the student strives to catch in talim and eat in riyaz. L. K. Pandit often tells me to go eat (*khāo*) a composition that he has given me but that I have not yet fully taken in. As Chintan Upadhyay put it: "If anything comes from guruji's mouth I will grab it [and] put it into my belly. And there's a seed inside now that will grow a tree after three years." Alladiya Khan is said to have admonished Kesarbai on his deathbed for not having "emptied his belly" enough.[33] Catching, eating, growing a seed in the belly, learning "by heart"—one must take something exterior, foreign to the self, and assimilate it (however partially and contingently) into the musicking body.

Sometimes, the master will pause to explicitly guide the workings of the musicking body through imagery or direct corporeal realignment. Anuraag Dhoundeyal, for example, describes the elaborate vocal corporeality that Ramdesh Pande led him to: asking him to press on his incisors, and then feel his voice hitting the incisors from the other direction, to feel his stomach going in as he sang, even guiding him to sing more from the left or the right side of his body. My guru, L. K. Pandit, once pointed out a bad habit in my jaw—I was overenunciating my *tāns* by involuntarily "chewing" each of its grains. The dispositional remedy was for me to wedge an almond between my teeth to hold my jaw still, and to tap my thigh on each pulse. It felt awkward, at first, to be deprived of the sensorimotor action of the jaw, but the tapping somehow guided my tāns properly; after a week of daily "tapping" riyaz, the vocal defect was smoothed out. Qawwal Sultan Nazan describes a vivid image of the musicking body given to him by his ustad: the whole body is immersed in the ocean right up to the chin, so that waves are coming and going past one's throat; you then "apply the voice according to the waves,"[34] so that the voice is flowing and undulating with the effortless force.

Whether in echo-and-response, critical listening, or didactic advice, talim is an essentially relational activity. It implies both a giver and a receiver. But this is not to say that it is a collective, participatory, egalitarian enterprise. From the fine

33. Deodhar 1993, 228.

34. *Is laher ke mutabiq, āp uske sāth āvāz lagāte rahiye.*

motor control of the mouth and larynx to the posture one takes, the authority of the guru is paramount and unimpeachable. The master presents a challenge, by persistent contrary example, to the current dispositions of the musicking body. Talim is thus productively frustrating to the extent that it always undermines the habits one already has. These new dispositions offered by the teacher are, in turn, solidified in riyaz, the solitary exercises that fix these new ways of the voice as bodily hexis. In solitary riyaz, one may work with a recording—some singers even pride themselves on the irrelational purity of such an exercise—but this is a radically different undertaking. The very fabric of talim requires a foundational relational ethics for its sustenance: *shraddha* (faith in the master), *vinaya* (humility), and a mutual love and affection that makes hours of face-to-face striving possible.[35] Mahesh Kale described the foundational, asymmetrical magnetism of his relationship with Jitendra Abhisheki: "I used to be quite blinded and mesmerised by him. And I think that is—that magic is what drove most of the things for me. Because he used to say *sā bharo*, and as much as I would not *like* it, I used to *do* it—because it was his wish." Indeed, for better or worse, it is often hard to distinguish the technical skills imparted in talim from the personal being of the master. Singer Mira Banerjee once told Amie Masciewski about a time when her master, who had passed away many years before, came to her in a dream, teaching her the proper way to sing a set of tāns that she had wanted to sing that very night at a concert. As she awoke and her eyes opened, "I saw that the harkat [*movements*] of those tans gradually blended with his photo—I mean, they became one."[36] If the master's voice appears to be inseparable from their presence in such moments, talim is the format by which this voicely being becomes available, selectively, for assimilation by the disciple.

This assimilation requires discernment, not wholesale imbibing. The shishya must actively listen past the incidental, idiosyncratic features of the master's *sound* to discover a *voice* there. An elderly guru's hoarseness, for example, is not to be imitated; nor an incidental gurgle or crack, or a random wavering. Indeed, the indiscriminate adoption of these superficial features is often cited as a moral hazard of guru-shishya parampara—it tends to reproduce bad habits along with good, reproducing a voice like a recorder rather than a gayaki. When young Shailaja Pandit first got the opportunity to learn from Kirana gharana legend Hirabai Barodekar, she was so eagerly devoted to the task that she absorbed one

35. Deo 2011, 89.

36. Maciszewski 2001, 159.

of Hirabai's vocal idiosyncratic vocal habits: ending the open vowel ā with the diphthong āī. Shailaja only later became aware of having absorbed this habit, and, having discerned what to hear, corrected it. By the time the elder Hirabai had entered her last years, her range dropped and constricted, and her tone began to warble. But young Shailaja, after many years of intimate talim, had achieved an attunement with Hirabai's gayaki that allowed her to hear what her guru wanted to say to her, reproducing it in clear *sur*, an octave above:

> She will sing something, though it was not expressed very perfectly or anything. I will sing it: "is it like this?" She used to say *ho* ["yes"]. Then I repeat it . . . Our tuition, our thinking became so in tune with each other. . . . Due to being together for such a long period, I could feel her mind, what she *wants* to tell, now.

Shailaja was not, in other words, reproducing her guru's acoustical signal. A mature student does not try to replicate *sound*, but to adopt a *gayaki*, imbued with purposive action, available for uptake precisely by virtue of learned powers of discernment. With each breath, the student noetically constitutes a rich slurry of kinetics, sonority, and poetics as an exemplary vocal act.

Even at the height of a master's powers, each aspirant must exercise discernment. Each singer has a slightly different vocal apparatus, with slightly different capabilities, and thus each must discern what is to be taken on and what is to be rejected. Everyone seems to agree, for example, that students should find a range that suits their own voice, rather than imitating their guru's. Pushkar Lele describes choosing a "free-flowing" disposition over than the "strike of a hammer" disposition offered by his teacher:

> His way was to reach at the center of the note with a strike of hammer . . . I didn't want that heaviness. It's like putting weights on your voice . . . with a lot of depth and volume. So depth and volume versus speed and free-flowingness? I opted for free-flowingness.

As Qawwal Fareed Ayaz puts it, talim must be suited for an aspiring qawwal's vocal height [*ancī*], power [*sākh*], and depth [*gahrāī*]. This demand is particularly acute when a man teaches a woman, or vice versa, as the interval between male and female ranges typically requires the male to move their *sā* lower or the female to move their *sā* higher in order to sing at octaves or unisons. When Anwar Hussain Khan, for example, taught Kishori Amonkar, he is said to have advised her against his "aggressive" kinetic disposition, advising her instead to "follow [her] own voice and do it softly."[37] To the extent that a master merely hears their gifted proteges as a generic male or female voice, solidifying their sedimented vocal inclinations as a gendered bodily hexis, we would see here a crucial mechanism for crystallizing normatively gendered voices. Just as often, however, the ethnographic evidence seems to suggest that gurus pitch their teaching to the individual *sanskārs* of their students. For example, Gajananrao Joshi had famously learned Gwalior, Agra, and Jaipur gayaki from different gurus, and passed these on selectively to his students. L. K. Pandit reserves the rapid tāns of ṭappās for only certain students who "have that tān in their voice." At the same time, a student who learns from more than one guru—or even more than one exemplar—builds a paramparic body, both unconsciously and consciously, from the dispositions available in its world.[38]

This striving is never perfect; the mimetic art of vocally "becoming something else, of becoming other"[39] is never complete. For many singers, the "preparation for an unattainable perfection"[40] continues until the day they die, as a matter of maintenance, "like shining your shoes, or brushing your teeth."[41] No matter how ardently committed a disciple is, the disciple never *fully* comprehends the master. Master and student may go their separate ways, and indeed it is not uncommon for such a relationship to end badly (in a falling-out, a financial or legal dispute, even, tragically, in sexual assault). But talim never eventuates in any sort of graduation; master and student never become notionally equal.[42] The master-disciple relation never quite collapses into identity; one becomes a master only in relation to one's own disciple. The chain of transmission (*parampara, silsilā*) is a chain of relations, marked not by vocal completion but by vocal striving, always imperfect, always changing.

---

37. Deshpande 1979.

38. Rahaim 2012, 124–126.

39. Taussig 1993, 36.

40. Neuman 1990, 34.

41. Tiwari 2016.

42. One classically Levinasian way of saying this is that it preserves metaphysical *distance*. But this infinite metaphysical distance is different from the ontological distancing afforded by recordings, whereby a recorded voice becomes a comprehensible object. (See Levinas 2012 and Rahaim 2017, 185–187 for more.)

Immersion, Distancing, and Recorded Vocal Objects

We have seen that the repetitive exercises of riyaz serve to build immersive, unreflective vocal dispositions. Sonorities and gaits thus imprinted upon the musicking body may be called on effortlessly, without any faculty of conscious recall or deliberation. In the moment of spontaneous song, when all is going well, the voice seems to simply flow, breath by breath, in the circuit of voice between singer and listener. There isn't enough time to stop and think; to reflectively hesitate in the middle of a phrase—*was that ma or dha?*—is already to get stuck, pulled out of the relational flow. Shahrukh Niyazi once expressed this to me in the form of advice about the faculty of *dimāgh*—the discursive, analytic faculty of self typically located in the head: "Difficulty is all in the *dimāgh*. When confusion besets your mind, you can't sing . . . it is only the squabbling of the *dimāgh* [*dimāgh kā fitūr*] that can hold you back." It is indeed very difficult to examine one's own voice as an object *and* maintain the easy dispositional flow of singing at once. A range of aphorisms circulate that urge students to ground their singing in unreflective, imitative automaticity (*naql*) before exercising deliberative intellection (for example: "first imitation, then thinking" [*pahle naql phir aql*] and "genuineness is born from imitation" [*naql se asl paidā hotā hai*]).

And yet, we have also seen that this automaticity is not enough. Talim and riyaz require discernment as well as obedience. This ethical requirement is often mapped onto a human/animal binary: Vikas Kashalkar once admonished me for doing riyaz "like a donkey" (merely repeating what he had given me, without reflecting on what I was doing); as critic Rajan Parrikar puts it, with characteristic vitriol: "A musician with years of rigorous tālīm and not much else is little more than a well-trained dog." In the course of deliberate voice-making, vocal aspirants must occasionally step back from their own sounding voice, stopping to reflect on vocal action, as it were, from a distance. Singers often have to reconstitute a vocal habit as a vocal defect, so that the ready-to-hand voice (the voice as an unreflective appendage of oneself) suddenly arises as a puzzling object, present-to-hand like a broken hammer, in need of fixing. Thus, even the most authoritarian teachers will insist that vocal development requires a learned faculty of reflective analysis (sometimes called *chintan* or *zehn*). For a singer, *chintan* is the ability to regard one's own voice at a distance, as an object for contemplation and judgment. Sometimes this proceeds through *svar-jnan*, analyzing a phrase into discrete tones to generate new variations; sometimes it tunes into sonority, finding places where the voice opens or closes, brightens or dulls; at other times, it requires attention to where the poetics or kinetics of a phrase require a special touch. Vocal aspirants periodically reflect on what they are learning, deliberately choosing the voice they will strive after. Vocal self-work likewise requires a student to stand at a remove from their own vocal action, striving after a vocal comportment that is not yet their own. *Chintan* may also involve simply sitting and thinking reflexively about one's own voice. Bindhu describes a period of crisis in which she was thinking: "I was mentally like—there were too many questions, like what am I supposed to do, what is required out of me? Okay, yeah, so I can sing, does that mean it's my duty to do this? You know, there's too many struggles within."

In many cases, when changing course radically, a vocal aspirant must deliberately unlearn what has been trained into them by prior riyaz. Manjiri Asnare-Kelkar began learning from Madhusudan Kanetkar at age seventeen, after thirteen years of study. As she says, "within a month of starting lessons, I was totally lost. I had unlearnt what I knew earlier, and was struggling for a grip over what I was now being taught. One day, I broke down before Appa. He said that my learning would now begin since I realised I knew nothing. He was right. After that, my music sorted itself out quite fast."[43] Ragini Rainu once told me about the process of "cleansing" her voice when she started learning Sufiana Kalam from Bhajan Sopori, describing it as not only a new voice, but "a new world." Pushkar Lele describes a familiar sense of frustration in switching teachers and having to return to *sā bharnā* for six months, after sixteen years of training and concertizing. In Bindhu's case, her guru, Abdul Rashid Khan, told her that he had to break down the wall she had built in her voice, with a chisel, before she could start learning Hindustani music. Such a change of direction, in practice, is no beautiful process of self-discovery or innovation, but a frustrating return to vocal childhood, a state of dynamic limnality after an old voice is left behind, but before a new voice is settled upon. One must become distanced from the current sound of one's own voice before taking on another.

A mode of listening that hears vocal utterances as note sequences—*svar-jnan* (see chapter 3)—is one crucial technology of reflexive distancing. Though this distance discloses tone-objects for shared commentary, it does not yield a purely "objective," unmediated grasp of acoustical vibrations; rather, it affords a common *intersubjective* ground for vocal work. Even the fine movements of harkat are subject to this reflective distance and reconstruction. But this is a reflective

43. Raja 2009, 168–169.

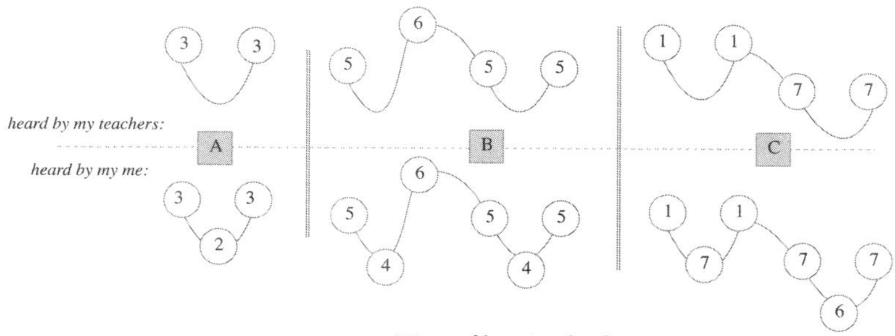

FIGURE 5.5 Ways of hearing harkat

discipline that must be learned. For example, in the first year of my training, the smooth motion of harkats registered to my keyboardic ear as extra notes rather than as motion. Figure 5.5 shows, in schematic form, this systematic pattern of mishearing. Note that, in each case, an identical melodic curve is given in the top and bottom rows; only the constitution of note-sequences is different.

Harkat B, which appears quite often on [5] and [1], was particularly puzzling for me. When my teachers insisted that I should be thinking of four equally spaced svaras [5655], I at first thought that they must have been mistaken. It was obvious to me that the pitch of their voice was dipping below the sruti of 5, and that the voice was zigging and zagging at an irregular speed. My mistake was in thinking as a keyboardist does, assigning a separate note-object (and thus a separate kinetic act) for each change of melodic direction. Thus I would find myself playing the lower reaches of these svaras on a virtual keyboard on my leg, with a separate finger articulation for [2] between the [3]s and [4] bewteen the [5]s.[44] But by trying to articulate the nadir of each swoop as a separate note, I was disturbing the kinetic continuity and rhythmic proportion of the harkats transmitted by my teachers. Learning to hear things as my teachers did—the conventional notation among vocalists—was not a matter of jettisoning analysis or svaras or rationality or music theory. On the contrary, the shared language—which disclosed a shared world of objects—enabled us to maneuver in a shared analytic world. This dialectal practice of listening was grounded both in a learned kinetic disposition (a round throat that gracefully swoops up to articulate each

44. This is, to be sure, exactly how a harmoniumist would have to articulate these harkats. Sitarists, for their part, have to articulate them from a lower fret, increasing the tension for the higher notes. What a vocalist would represent as {5655}, then, a sitarist must play from the {4} fret to accommodate the downward swoops up on each note.

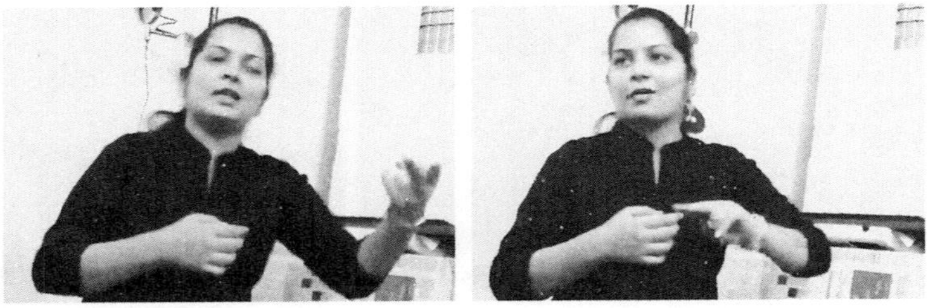

The line preceding it... Or after it...

FIGURE 5.6 Textualizing song

svara) *and* a reflective distance from the flow of singing, and thus an opportunity to deliberately change.

Another crucial technology for this vocal distancing is sound recordings, which allow repeated listening and the study of short audio segments—even shorter than breath—as objects. Digital recordings of vocal exemplars circulate widely among connoisseurs. They are hoarded, savored, transcribed, selectively shared, and emulated. Listening back on lesson recordings is a central part of nearly every student's training, allowing them to repeat and concretize and grasp anew the ephemeral phrases that flew past them in the course of a lesson. A film singer may play a single phrase over and over until they grasp a particularly elusive harkat; a khyaliya may puzzle over an elaborate tān on a single vowel. These moments require the student to listen at a distance from the voice of the exemplar, opening it up as an object for analysis. Aspiring playback singer Apoorva Gajjala described to me a method of studying a song by listening to a tape on which she dubs a single song over and over onto both sides of a blank cassette, immersing herself in an infinite loop. When a certain line of the song gives her trouble, she stops, rewinds, and repeats that section. But this line, when grasped in isolation, must then be integrated with the whole song: "I sing it with the whole song . . . when you sing that particular line, you get everything right; but when you sing it with the song, or the line preceding it or after it, you don't get it." While she spoke, Apoorva gesturally placed the lines on a virtual page extending in front of her body, showing a linear textual progression from top to bottom. Figure 5.6 shows this gestural stance.

This process of stitching these strophes together is a creative ontological act that discloses the song as a textual object for study, at a distance from the singer.

Then, through repetition, the separate text-object is absorbed into the heart, into an unreflective vocal disposition.

But this is not the only way to use a recording. In yet another mode of listening to a recording, a song is played all the way through, its voice emerging as a disposition to be inhabited rather than a text to be decoded. The student sings along, merging their voice with the exemplary voice of the recording, enacting a bodily listening in which, as Shikha Jhingan puts it, the musicking body is "immersed in the affective force-field of musicality."[45] Classic recordings that have been throughly absorbed like this offer not just textual canons, but dispositional repertoires for singing along with and absorbing into one's own musicking body. Calling these memories back is centrally a matter of inhabiting a vocal disposition.

Singers also record *themselves* for study and reflection. This allows the sound of their voice—which otherwise might appear to be a transparent, immediate organ of selfhood—to show up audibly as an aural object *for* conscious awareness, critical appraisal, and modification. Hearing one's voice played back for the first time, after the moment of singing, often sounds spookily different from hearing one's own voice conducted through the skull. (As one singer put it to me, "Is that *me*?") Though many singers were able to listen to gramophone records of themselves as early as the 1920s and '30s, and some singers made reel-to-reel tape recordings of talim in the '70s and '80s, it seems to have only been in the '90s, when cheap portable cassette recorders became widely available, that singers began recording their *own* practice sessions for further study. Indeed, Deepak Raja reports a case in which a singer who had not recorded his own voice for many years didn't recognize his own voice on a shiny new microphone—hearing it as "his" only when he heard it recorded on a 30-year-old microphone.[46] Now, with voice recorder apps available on every smartphone, lessons and riyaz are easily recorded, studied, and reflected on.

But techniques of vocal self-objectification for concerted improvement would seem to predate sound recording. Bade Ghulam Ali Khan, for example, is said to have practiced in front of a vast stone wall so that he could hear his own voice coming, as it were, from outside, rather than from his own head, allowing him to adjust it.[47] In a similar technique of reverberant reflection, Qawwal Sultan Nazan

---

45. Jhingan 2013, 101.

46. Raja 2016, 41:40.

47. Deodhar 1993, 249.

describes singing into a large clay pot to hear his own voice coming back at him. Another technology often used in service of detached *chintan* is the reflective surface of a mirror. Looking at one's own face while singing, one might notice a subtle scowl, grimace, or furrow forming in the lips, cheeks, or forehead, and these are much easier to correct visually than proprioceptively.[48] The mirror allows one's own vocal disposition (ordinarily an invisible stance for singing-*from*) to show up visibly as an object for conscious awareness and modification.[49]

Scientific Voice Culture and Other Vocal Authorities

In 1921, B. R. Deodhar (a disciple of leading khyaliya and music reformer V. D. Paluskar) stood in front of a mirror, bare-chested, and sang. He was in the studio of Giovanni Scrinzi (an Italian composer working in Bombay), who had recently accepted Deodhar into an experimental year-long course in Western music.[50] Scrinzi's diagnosis was a bit vague (Deodhar supposedly had a "throaty and wooden" voice), but the remedy had all the simplicity of Boyle's law: Deodhar must learn to "breathe scientifically."[51] This is why Deodhar had removed his shirt and stood in front of a mirror: so that they both could observe his chest as he breathed, trying to take air into "the lower broader portion of the lungs." Scrinzi also taught him a method of pronouncing (Italian) vowels, training him into a new corporeal awareness of his mouth: the soft palate, the hard palate, and "the hollow space inside the mouth" that allows vowels to sound "musical." This training went on twice a week for a year, and it seems to have had some success.[52] Though the exact practices enjoined upon Deodhar by Scrinzi are not recorded, it is clear that this method of voice culture, among other things, cultivates in its

---

48. The didactic aphorism *shuddh bani, shuddh mudra* (pure tone, pure expression) implies the facial calm cultivated by these reflexive means.

49. There is a long psychoanalytic tradition of analyzing a child's first encounter with their own image in a mirror as constitutive of the formation of self-identity (see Lacan 2006 [1949] for a classic statement).

50. Pradhan 2017.

51. Deodhar 1993, 58.

52. According to the secondhand testimony of master khyaliya Mogubai Kurdikar, his *sur* showed marked improvement even by the exacting standards of Jaipur gayaki—though there is no ready archive of his singing before his training to compare it to. (Deshpande 1989, 171–172.)

students a distinctive way of *hearing* sonority, leading to a near-universal feeling of dissatisfaction with what now shows up as "faulty vocal technique." Students in this tradition often express woeful, moralizing bafflement at the "artificial," "metallic," "wooden" tones of Hindustani vocalists, in contrast to the "denseness, depth, and fullness" that Scrinzi (and, with training, Deodhar) so relished in Italian opera singers of the 1920s. Prior to this Scrinzian aural discipline, of course, these voices had once sounded perfectly natural.

But Scrinzi's is not the only path. Many singers, in hopes of changing their voice, turn to varied, specialized techniques that appeal to the authority of scientific expertise (yogic, biomedical, Ayurvedic, phonetic, psychoanalytic, etc.). Their disciplines and techniques are called by various names: "Voice Science," "Western technique," "Nād Yoga," and so on. These universalizing practices of voice training are continuous with the practices of "voice culture" in the early twentieth-century anglophone world, and some of this training still is called by that name. Particularly in Bombay and other cities, a great many aspiring singers and actors invest heavily in expert guidance in hopes of quick improvement. Apoorva Gajjala, for example, recovered fully from trauma-induced unilateral paralytic dysphonia after several months of gentle breathing and vocal exercises prescribed by Dr. Sadhana Nayak, a well-regarded voice doctor in Bombay. Another of Dr. Nayak's patients, a successful stage singer, was able to recover from what appeared to be a career-ending voice injury through training in stretching and muscular relaxation (the patient shifted to English to mention that the relaxation exercises were "equivalent to meditation"). Khyaliya Pushkar Lele told me of a series of quasi-yogic humming exercises devised by voice trainer Mandar Karulkar which help to mitigate the "cracking" effects of a congenital (and theretofore intractable) phonatory gap that a laryngologist had earlier diagnosed.

Others attend group classes in music schools, progressing through a curriculum of repertoires, modal grammars, and techniques. In recent years, music schools offering training in *filmi* and "Western" vocal training have flourished, allowing students to study casually. Most cities have private music schools, such as the well-known chain of Gandharva Mahavidyalayas, that impart graded instruction in the repertoire and theory of raga music.[53] In general, schools offer group classes that focus on clearly transmitting song-objects rather than vocal dispositions. Their exams and certificates, ratifying various stages of fully accomplished completion, stand in stark contrast to the open-ended striving of

53. Alter 1999; Katz 2012; Upadhyay and Dalal 2016.

the riyaz-talim complex. The secrets that a master discloses to advanced disciples are, strictly speaking, esoteric—you can't learn to do *bol banāo* like Rasoolan Bai by studying a textbook, and that lends this gayaki a special aura. Opponents of schools can also point out, on a practical level, that every successful classical singer—even those who have had some schooling—has undergone an extensive period of riyaz and talim with a master.[54]

The relational format of these practices is radically different from the master-disciple relation. Where a relational dyad obtains, whether in a doctor's office or a yoga studio, it more often resembles therapist-client or doctor-patient. The relationship tends to be bounded and results-oriented, restricted to discrete lessons, usually lasting no longer than several months or a year. Even Deodhar, at the outset of his lessons with Scrinzi, notes in retrospect that his "instinct" (conditioned by the master-disciple model) had led him to "question how much a student could possibly learn in the space of one or two hours a week."[55] To be sure, these methods often do seem to succeed. But unlike the esoteric training offered in a master-disciple relation, all of these techniques of vocal engineering are understood to be universally efficacious, rooted in a totalizing biomedical or yogic model of voice, rather than the specific gayaki of a particular master, or the secret techniques of a particular lineage. These ways of knowing and shaping the body apply, in principle, to all voices, to produce what are construed as universally desirable results: efficiency, power, ease, health.

For many traditionalists, however, these schools, experts, and textbooks represent a distinctive ethical *lack*: a hollow shell of the ethical cultivation offered in talim, offering bare repertoire without the master-disciple bond, and without inculcating relational virtues like *shraddha*, humility, or love. Early music reformers conceived of schooling in nearly inverted ethical terms: as a way of freely imparting a national music without the authoritarian (and, as it would have seemed to modernizers, antiquated) baggage of master-disciple relations.[56] Schooling, then, is not principally a practical question of cultivating sounds and repertoires, but a field of ethical striving, hinging on the cultivation of contrasting forms of selfhood.

---

54. Many school-educated students *also* have a dedicated relationship with a master; indeed, this is institutionally required in a few university-level institutions like Sangeet Research Academy (Kolkata) and Lalit Kala Kendra (Pune).

55. Deodhar 1993, 53.

56. Bakhle 2005.

Filmi Voice and Mic-Fitting

Though the gentle crooning of *filmi* voice (see chapter 4) has come to be widely assimilated by millions of nurses and barbers, homemakers and clerks—the taken-for-granted amateur singing voice in cities and villages across the Hindustani ecumene, from Mountainview to Port of Spain to Calcutta—it still requires cultivation. Indeed, for singers trained in singing raga music bright and open, making the switch can often be challenging. Playback singer Chandana Dixit says that, contrary to what you might expect, in "the tender, soft voice, there's no way you can sing for an hour continuously." She herself was surprised by how difficult it was to move from raga music to *filmi* in her twenties; her sister used to make fun of her, teasing her for her "amazing ability" to make even the most playful *filmi* cabaret songs sound like rigorous, austere khyal. "When I actually tried to sing, whatever would come out would just start to sound like a confused voice because I would try to project it [like khyal]—because I hadn't really calmed myself down, prepared, listened." This period, which aspiring film singers like Chandana often refer to as "struggle," lasted for three years. For Chandana, as with many playback singers, the principal authority in the process of making *filmi* voice is not a guru, but a music director: a role in the film music world that spans composition, production, orchestral and electronic arrangement, and voice coaching. Gathering her courage, she cold-called one of the most famous music directors in Bollywood: Kalyanji (of the well-known music director duo Kalyanji-Anandji), who, much to her surprise, invited her to come and sing for him. Though quite different from talim, this relationship between a singer and a music director is nonetheless prolonged and quite crucial: "There's no way [I] could have learned any of this without actually being in Bombay and without being under the guiding hand of a music director." It entailed spending eight-hour days at Kalyanji's house, workshopping new songs, meeting with poets and choreographers and actors, sitting at the harmonium singing the same line in a dozen different ways. During this period, she had to "shrug off the whole baggage of classical" to build a reliable *filmi* voice. Whereas in classical you have to "get very calm, understand the rāg, establish your sā, think about how you're going to develop the rāg," for *filmi* gīt, the task is to "think like the hero," and place yourself in a dramatic situation—"you need to be an a very different place [to] bring those words to life." Kalyanji thus suggested that she stop singing khyal altogether in order to free herself dispositionally for playback singing. Under his tutelage, Chandana's voice shifted dramatically—and so did her own practices of listening. She began to hear her prior classical training as "aggressive," softening her "hard," open *ā* sound to a lighter, breathier, sweeter tone. She learned to apply vibrato, because singing into a microphone without it, the voice sounds "dead."

Meeta Pandit, trained from a young age in a household of hereditary khyaliyas, described the work she had to do to learn singing *ghazal* lightly into a microphone, in collaboration with a producer who was guiding her toward a light, intimate voice. She sang one take in the bright, open voice that she had mastered in singing Gwalior gayaki, but the producer said, "No, no, no, no. We don't want this voice." He coaxed her closer to the microphone—she indicated a distance of 1–2 inches—and instructed her to "just whisper." With headphones projecting the sound of her voice into her ears, she was at first sonically disoriented: "you can hear yourself—like you do [whispers *hā*] and you hear it." Once she mastered this voice—over the course of several recording projects—she was shocked at the result. It sounded so radically different from her usual voice that at first she thought it might be someone else. Lata Mangeshkar herself seems to have recorded while leaning on a railing to keep herself the proper distance from the microphone.[57] Anaar Desai-Stevens describes an explicit training in developing a "mic-fitting" voice at the Institute for Performing Arts in Mumbai. This is a voice *adapted* to the microphone. Some of this consisted in technical practice (for example, softening labial plosives so as not to impinge upon the diaphragm with a puff of air). But it also included training in suppressing certain kinds of movement (such as shaking the head)[58] that would vary the distance between the mouth and the mic.

Developing this voice, then, requires the development of an aural attunement to the amplification of the microphone. Voice, microphone, and monitors become linked as a prosthetic whole. Qawwals, film singers, and classical singers alike describe the painful process of learning mic technique, of early failures, of distortion, feedback, and disorientation. This often turns out to be profoundly vocally transformative. Indeed, many folkloric accounts of khyaliyas singing into a microphone for the first time include a motif of the singer rupturing the microphone with the power of their unsoftened voice. Just as certain styles of guitar solo are attuned to the dependable sustain and harmonic enhancement of overdrive, so too is a "mic-fitting" voice attuned to the requirements of a microphone.

But this is not only for the sake of acoustics. Equally important is a widely-

57. See *Lata Mangeshkar, A Musical Journey (Biography)*, available on YouTube.

58. Desai-Stevens, personal communication, email, 9/18/2019.

attested dispositional capacity for heartfelt attunement—a capacity now almost ubiquitously known with the English loan words *feel* or *emotion*. Sharukh Niyazi (a versatile qawwal who also sings pop sufi and and *filmi*) emphasizes that "you have to make feelings [*fīliñz banāne paṛte hai*]" in film songs. Aspiring film singer Shireesh Malhotra describes a method of close-mic singing in order to "bring some intense emotion in a slight whispering kind of sound . . . very close to the mic and whisper in the low notes so that you get the emotion right." Anaar Desai-Stevens describes a rigorous regime of cultivating *feel* at the Institute for Performing Arts, where feelingful, expressive singing is at the very center of vocal training. To be sure, students are taught the names of notes and raga theory, microphone technique, and the subtleties of recording to a backing track. But nearly all of the instruction seems to be directed ultimately toward opening students up to a depth of internal feeling that is, in principle at least, embodied and transmitted in performance. Feel is centrally a matter of the heart, but it is a whole-bodily disposition. During moments of maximum "feel," particularly in nostalgic evergreen songs of unfulfilled longing, singers often shut their eyes ("as if locating the feeling inside") or crinkle their brow: "one eyebrow slightly raised, the other slightly furrowed," not just passively yearning, but actively reaching for a note "just a little out of one's range."[59] Even when this learned depth of *feel* is maximally irrelational (singing alone in a soundproof recording booth, wearing headphones, reaching inside oneself for feeling), it is also potentially generative of feelings in listeners (see chapter 3). But, as these complex pedagogies attest, not all students are ready to dive into this depth of feeling right away; many students must be guided there gradually. Shy students are sometimes offered a sort of dispositional icebreaker: item numbers (bawdy provocative songs that share a performative heritage with the *mujras* of courtesans). Drawing on an easily imitable repertoire of expressive gesture, item numbers allow a singer to sing as someone *else*, and thus allow singers to get past the otherwise stubborn roadblock of trying to express oneself, and into the realm of *feel*.

More striking, though, is that this exploration of feelingful territory is somewhat more than acting a part. It is somehow personally transformative—in the words of one IPA teacher, "it totally changes them."[60] When Chandana Dixit began adapting her vocal disposition for playback singing in the 1990s, suddenly finding herself in the company of playback singers, she learned to carry herself differently,

59. Desai-Stevens 2018, 186.

60. Ibid., 183.

shedding the deferential humility that had so long been dispositionally encoded in her relation with her classical music gurus in favor of a more self-assured posture and bearing. This was a time of great change in the music industry, when live stage shows became major sources of revenue, and, as we saw in chapter 4, the liberalizing music industry began to welcome a wide range of newly formed, widely legible voices. Unlike the famously still and restrained live performances of Lata Mangeshkar, the stage shows demanded a new self-expressive ethos, in which the singer was expected to move expressively while singing. This also marked the beginning of the rise of "Western contemporary" singing, which demanded a distinction from *filmi* voice not only in tone, but also in subject position: the singer was now expected to be a sovereign expressive individual with a unique interior and—in this new ontology of vocal expression—an accordingly unique voice.

Making Western-Voice

We saw in chapter 4 that the appeal of Western-voice (in general, a voice disposed for the pop canon of the 1990s and Bollywood pop hits of the 2000s and 2010s) hinges largely on the distinctive ethical possibilities that it offers: individuality, independence, expressiveness. Of course, Hindustani Western-voice lessons involve technical training as well. Teachers of Western-voice often complain that students of raga music use too much nasal resonance, construing it as a sort of inappropriate crutch for producing a ringing brightness, and they encourage their students to close their velum in favor of other resonators. The frequent admonition to sing "from the core" is common enough to Hindustani and Western-voice training; more distinctive is the "head voice" that so many teachers help their students find. Producing "cut notes"—that is, notes cleanly separated from each other, without glides or *harkat*, requires some work, but not usually more than a few months.

Here, we digress for a moment to consider these "cut notes," the bogeyman of so many glib comparisons between Indian and Western music noted in chapter 4. Many teachers of Hindustani Western-voice do indeed begin by having their students unlearn their ordinary habits of phrasing by singing disconnected notes, but this is a brief, stripped-down phase of vocal striving, generating reflexivity, not a finished product. Indeed, early training in raga music also involves the production of cut notes: in learning sargam sequences, in learning palte, in singing isolated, extended tones. Turning a student's attention to a sequence of notes (*svar-jnān*) is a reflexive technique that produces a distance from one's

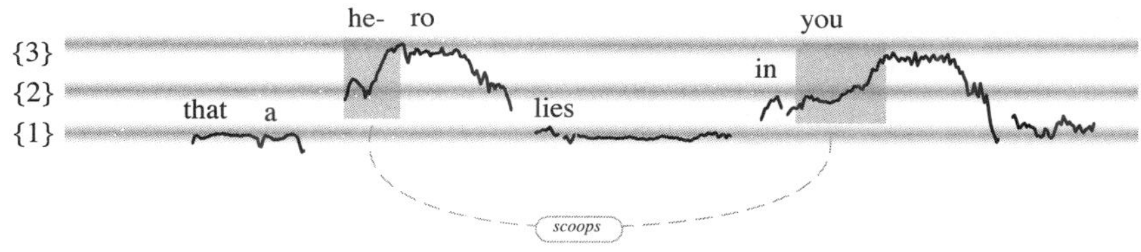

FIGURE 5.7 Scoops

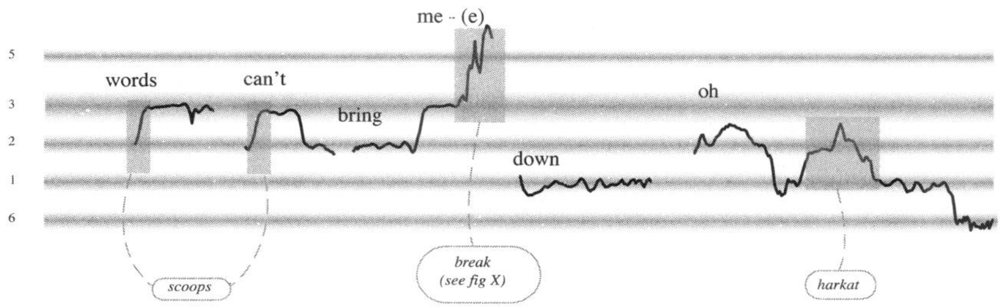

FIGURE 5.8 Western-voice harkat

own voice, for the development of a new vocal disposition. After all, Hindustani Western-voice rarely renders songs in utterly disconnected tones. It has its own repertoire of kinetic habits—sometimes called "ornaments" or "expressions," but most often the term *harkat* is applied to these as well. For example, *scooping* is a common expressive harkat in singing pop music. While vocalists in many traditions often begin a note low and correct it in the course of singing, the term *scooping* is usually reserved for expressively ornamenting a note (especially a third or fifth) by sliding up to it. In Hindustan, for the most part, this kind of harkat is used for songs that index R&B or pop expressivity. Figure 5.7 shows Nupur Joshi scooping up to the *ga* {3} in Mariah Carey's "Hero."

Figure 5.8 shows a pitch trace from a somewhat longer phrase, this time from Apoorva Gajjala's rendition of Christina Aguilera's "Beautiful," including two scoops, a break, and a *harkat* that would not be out of place in a ghazal.

The break on me-(e) not only slides up in pitch, but also breaks timbre briefly into a duller falsetto-like timbre,[61] as shown in figure 5.9.

61. This break is, according to Timothy Wise's rather more precise taxonomy, a "second species" yodel. See *Radical Musicology, Volume 2* (2007), "Yodel Species: A Typology of Falsetto Effects in Popular Music Vocal Styles."

FIGURE 5.9
Yodel spectrogram

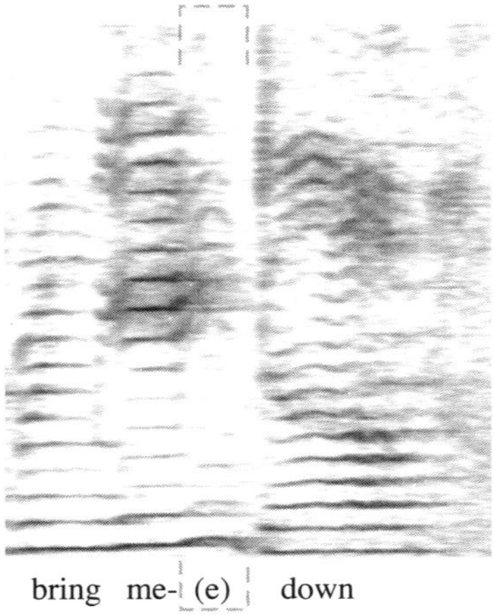

As with thumri or khyal, ornamenting too much may read as sappy; too little may read as dry.

When Ragini Rainu began taking lessons in "Western contemporary" voice with Bombay voice teacher (and Coke Studio star) Samantha Edwards in 2014, after years of singing Hindustani classical, *filmi*, and sufiana kalam, she hoped to expand her dispositional repertoire. When I first came to observe a lesson, Samantha was urging Ragini to "eliminate" the *harkats* that had become dispositionally inscribed in her voice, so that notes came out independently of each other. This is, of course, a far harder task than it seems. Ragini was working her way through exercises that cultivated this articulation, such as singing "ha ha ha ha" on the melody *sā re ga ma pa, pa, pa, pa, pa ma ga re sā* {12345, 5, 5, 5, 54321}. Figure 5.10 shows one of Ragini's attempts, followed by Samantha's correction:

Samantha's initial recommendation was to sing with "less air," and to "segregate and compartmentalize" the separate notes—a reflexive technique on the way to fluid motion.

As Samantha began fine-tuning Ragini's utterances at the level of phrases, returning the kinetic nuance to her singing, the focus of the lesson shifted to elocution and bearing. Sitting tall and upright at the piano, Samantha shifted her speaking range upwards somewhat, cheerfully instructing Ragini to sing *ha* "as though you were going to laugh *heartily*." Though this was an appeal to Ragini's affective spontaneity, it was clear that Samantha was listening for a very particular sort of laugh. She was not instructing Ragini to chortle or guffaw—this was no indistinct *heheheh*, but a posh *Ha! Ha! Ha!* Even her pronunciation of

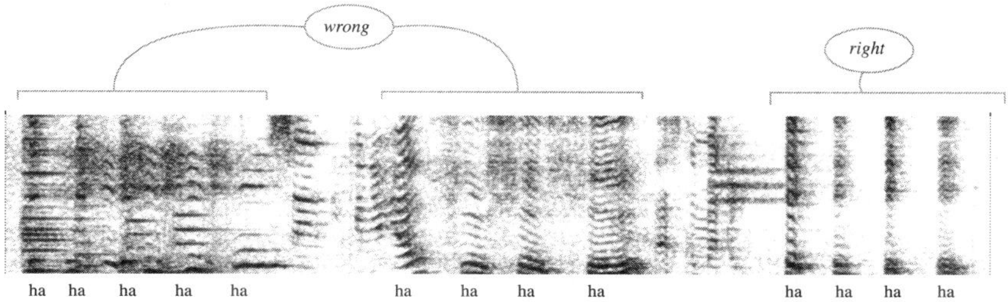

FIGURE 5.10 *Ha ha ha* lesson

heartily rang out in the pristine tones of high tea: the rhotic /ɹ̠ / absorbed into a soft, rounded /a/, the /t/ crisply enunciated. As Ragini took a deep breath and turned with all seriousness to the task at hand, Samantha encouraged her to *smile!*, shooting her a model smile of sparkling encouragement. So contagious was Samantha's polished cheerfulness that both Ragini and I found ourselves grinning in spite of ourselves. Ragini nailed it the very next time. But this was not, strictly speaking, simply a lesson in drawing-room voice culture. Later in the lesson, when Samantha coached Ragini through "What A Wonderful World," the kinetic habits she was inculcating rubbed against the comfortable, dispositionally entrenched harkats that Ragini had acquired for singing pop sufi. At one point, Ragini exclaimed, "I can't *think* Western!" But *thinking*—of "Western" tunes, generic traits, or rhythmic grammars—was not exactly what Samantha was after. Indeed, the lesson was mostly dedicated to exercises that built and rebuilt bodily dispositions and imaginative possibilities.

Among the reflective techniques employed by teachers of Hindustani-Western voice is the invocation of far-off lands. When a student is asked to imagine themselves in "a different country," this is not a rigorous sociological evocation of any particular nation-state, but rather a metaphysical "elsewhere" that pulls students out of their comfortable habits. Sometimes, like one configuration of "The West" itself, Western-voice seems to index post-industrial cities with vibrant nightlife and high salaries, populated by fair-skinned secular humanists, the sort of place ambitious IIT graduates imagine when they describe their bright future in a *foreign* country. But at other times, Hindustani Western-voice evokes a broader cosmopolitanism, founded on globalist discourses of humanism, economic liberalism, and political liberation. For example, the Bombay vocal academy Singing Express, founded by versatile singer Marianne D'Cruz Aiman, is envisioned as "a train that takes you through a journey across the world . . . to be as diverse as possible because that's what is needed in today's world." The lessons take place in an air-conditioned room with a well-loved piano and a gleaming, untouched bağlama saz in the corner, brought home from a recent tour in Istanbul. One class I visited was working on the hugely popular international gospel hit "Wahamba Nathi" ("You Walked with Us"), sung in Zulu language. Though everyone was singing in tune, the feel of the song wasn't coming properly, particularly the arcing, liquescent *ooh* that precedes the repeated utterance of "Wahamba Nathi." She called the class together into a circle, had them close their eyes, and led them through a powerful exercise in the vocal evocation of these distant imaginaries:

> The *oh* is a cry from the depths of your soul. It's a cry against injustice. I want you to imagine any picture of poverty that has really touched you, and then like *oh, I can't bear it.* Or injustice, and you're *soooo* much against it, vehemently opposed to that. Or seen some form of oppression, and the cry comes from the depths of your being saying *oh.* So I want you to just take a moment or two, don't worry about any new people who are here. Just close your eyes, and when you feel the cry coming out, just let it go, and let it be *oh.* Let it engage your soul, your body, your mind, everything you've gone through, and let it come out of your *self.* And let your voice just exude all of that energy and that emotion. When you feel it rising up, let it come out.

There followed thirty seconds of introspective silence. It was broken by a gut-wrenching *o*, somewhere from off to my left; then another, from across the room. Each student in turn unleashed a deep, resonant *o*. Upon opening their eyes and returning to the song, their voices were utterly transformed: louder, brighter, deeper. The vision that Marianne led her students to was not a rigorous sociological claim about any particular African political movement, but a successful exhortation to place their singing selves in a larger cosmos. She was not calling on them to imitate any particular motor routine, nor to learn Zulu (nor, crucially, to put their own bodies on the line in any particular struggle for racial justice) but to cultivate and vocally project a felt revulsion to an imaginatively constituted injustice. Her vocal technique, too, is conceived as a sort of remedy for vocal oppression, conceived as a radically free vocal idealism: "I believe the voice is capable of so much more than we allow it to do. You cannot straitjacket a voice. It can take any form that one chooses to give it." The central ethical vector of this vocal technique points toward a very particular cosmopolitan conception of freedom.

Devotion, Gifts, and Crises

Vocal transformation is not always the clear result of deliberate work. Huge shifts sometimes come all at once after a long plateau of effort, or even may seem to emerge on their own. At such moments, singers encounter their own voice not as a product of their own conscious volition, but as a mysterious gift from beyond themselves. The conventional term for this aspect of voice in Hindustani is a loan from English: *God-Gift*. Its formula is nearly identical among Hindus and Muslims; even resolutely non-theistic Kabir bhakts will cite "God-Gift." The first few times I heard singers refer to this, I dismissed it as a sort of conventional, performative humility. I have now come to take this seriously—not nessesarily as a theological report about the actual actions of a divine being, but as a way of opening a conceptual space for aspects of voice that are neither an expression of the self nor a result of self-work. The figure of the gift allows a ray of light into the otherwise closed dome of reflexive self-making implied by vocal practice. The substance of such a gift is often described as *rūh* (spirit), which enables a singer to evoke *tasir* as though through an agency outside of the individual self. Invoking "God-Gift" evokes an understanding of voice that goes beyond active work on an object, or a totalizing care of the self. It constitutes voice as something to some extent unpredictable even as we work at it.

Many vocalists have a vocal crisis in the middle of their careers that leaves them unable to sing. The silent recovery often leads them in a new direction marked by a spiritual, moral, and vocal rebirth. Gangubai Hangal, for example, went through a radical change of comportment after a bout of tonsillitis, shifting from a relatively higher, lighter voice, singing thumri, ghazal, and other songs cultivated in her courtesan lineage, to a thicker, deeper, more "masculine" voice, ranged a major third lower, principally suited for khyal.[62] Durgesh Upadhyay underwent a series of severe asthmatic attacks, which were cured, miraculously, by a period of intense vocal riyaz, and which, in his telling, catalyzed a spiritual "transformation of self."[63] Kumar Gandharva, a childhood prodigy who originally gained fame with his convincing mimicry of great singers, underwent a profound transformation of gayaki after a long bout with tuberculosis, during which he was unable to sing. During his recovery, he is said to have heard many wandering Nath Yogis singing Kabir; his inimitable post-crisis gayaki, with which

62. Masciewski 2001a, 4.

63. Upadhyay 2015.

he is now personally identified, emerged both from this influence and adapting his phrasing to a newly diminished lung capacity. Kishori Amonkar, one of the most influential khyal innovators of the twentieth century, followed a more or less orthodox track to success for the first few decades of her life, emerging as one of the rising stars of Jaipur gayaki, before her concert career was cut short when she lost her voice entirely in her mid-twenties. For two years, she held off singing while undergoing treatment with Sardeshmukh Maharaj, an Ayurvedic sage in Pune, giving her time to "to reflect on life and her music and crystallize the emergence of a new musical personality."[64] The crisis had striking dispositional results. She moved away from the orthodox Jaipur focus on phrases (*svara citra*), instead "surrendering" to each svara, "diving deep," pursuing "tonal purity," finding that this caused her "egoism . . . to wane." This transformation can be heard quite dramatically in her recordings.[65] Like Amir Khan, this crisis led to a renewed irrelational introspection, an inward-turned artistry often depicted in photographs where her eyes are closed and her ear is pressed against the tanpura. Unlike Amir Khan, this transformation has widely been construed as a turn to personal emotional expression. Deepak Raja goes as far as to call this a sort of "romanticism" in which "she smoothened the sharp edges of melody, and made them soft and silky. She shed the austere melodic practices of her seniors, and made her phrasing ornate and endearing."[66] It is this later post-crisis gayaki for which she is now best-known and loved; it has been at least as influential, especially among female khyaliyas, as has Amirkhani gayaki.

To work on one's voice, to receive a vocal gift, to undergo a vocal crisis—all of this reveals a distance between voice and self. One's voice, shielded from view but vividly evident, hovers between interiority and exteriority, between agent and patient. At times, in the moment of singing, this voice may indeed seem to be a direct expression of a sovereign, indivisible self. And yet vocal striving is characterized by a condition in which the voice one strives after is not exactly one's own.

---

64. Raja 2011.

65. Compare, for example, her early recordings of bhoop nat, shuddh nat, and jaijaivanti to her hour-long recording of Rageshri.

66. Raja 2011.

SIX
Ways Beyond

The previous chapters have explored traditions of relational vocal action, normatively situated among others, carefully cultivated, publicly sedimented and contested, charged with ethical and political valence. A figuration of dynamic *ways* of voice—dispositional, relational, striving, always *going* somewhere—contrasts sharply with the widespread tendency to figure the voice as an expressive outpouring of fixed, finished substance. In particular, it contrasts with two other commonsense figurations of voice: as the expression of an individual, and as the expression of a univocal collectivity.[1] I'll call these *individualist-expressivist* and *groupist-expressivist* figurations of voice.

Attention to relational vocal dynamism works against a commonsense *individualist-expressivist* figuration of voice, by which an ethically proper voice is normatively understood to express the interiority of a sovereign individual.[2] Of

1. See Ochoa Gautier 2014, 171–172 for a treatment of these figurations as mutually dependent, and Eidsheim 2019, 10–11 for a treatment of these figurations as mutually exclusive alternatives.

2. See Derrida 1967 [2011] on the vocal expression of interiority and Rahaim 2021 on alternatives. One classic account of the development of this intuitive sense of individuated selfhood is Charles Taylor's *Sources of the Self* (1989), including a history of "inner voice" as a crucial emblem of selfhood (see also Dolar 2006 on the inner guiding voice). Taylor's work provides a particularly strong model for the active formation of this sense of self in the long term, denaturalizing its apparently natural hegemony. However, as Taylor looks for "sources of the self" only in French, English, and German sources, he gives the impression that the formation of individuated selfhood is, in his

course, such a figuration makes intuitive sense in many ways. We recognize—or think we can—a beloved singer on the radio, or a beloved friend on the phone. As anthropologists and historians of voice have repeatedly have demonstrated, characteristic vocal settings often do function—rightly or wrongly—as indices of class, race, sect, sexuality, and way of life.[3] We routinely attempt to evaluate the moral character of strangers from their manner of speaking and singing, grounded in a sense that, as Simon Frith puts it, "we can hear someone's life in their voice"—even if the "life" thereby heard tends to be construed as a finished biography rather than an ongoing project.[4] We saw in chapter 4 that, for the past twenty years, on reality TV shows, in pop sufi and Bollywood, singers have been explicitly encouraged to discover and cultivate a personally unique voice.[5] Mod-

---

terms, an essentially "Western" feature of modernity. (See Appadurai [1990] for an alternative location of such "sources" in the New Testament.) Though I acknowledge the urge to ascribe the individualist figuration of voice a tidy colonial pedigree, I can't bring myself to sweepingly dismiss its Hindustani appearances as an imitation of a gleaming, fully formed "West." The "sources of the self" in the post-liberalization Hindustani ecumene rarely come from Rousseau, Locke, Kant, or even Freud; more often, they emerge from novel readings of Kabir and Nanak, Rumi and Bulleh Shah, Meera and Tuka and Rabindranath Tagore. No doubt these readings, in turn, are cosmopolitan in nature. Coleman Barks's English translation of Rumi, for example, circulates widely among anglophone readers. See Vajpayee 2012 for a virtuosic survey of Indic philosophical reflection on selfhood—both personal and political; see Novak 2013 on a model of cultural feedback that applies here.

3. Bourdieu 1991, 86; Fox 2004, Weidman 2006, Harkness 2014. See Eidsheim 2018 for a critique of these ascriptions as projections of taken-for-granted categories of difference.

4. Frith 1998, 185–186.

5. Desai-Stevens 2018; Kvetko 2005. The critical desideratum that a singer should find and express a unique voice has been occasionally and selectively applied to khyal singers since independence. (See Scott 1997, 53.) While there certainly was a mode of critique for unconscious imitation (for example, al-Ghazali's critique of the ta'alimites), it seems not to have applied to the leading khyaliyas and courtesans of the Mughal Empire. It has been a crucial frame for mass-market "Western" and pop sufi singers since the economic liberalization of the 1990s and has been enforced normatively by the critical regimes that dominate vocal reality TV. It has never, to my knowledge, applied to qawwals singing for samā or in dargāhs, nor to varkari kirtan or other participatory group song.

ern classical music critics, too, have evinced anxiety about the mimetic dangers of talim, expressed in a range of denigrative terms for students who sound just like their guru: parrot, carbon-copy, xerox, *amukh* (mouthless). Indeed, comportmental discipline is often construed as the pathological background against which an authentic, non-conformist, self-expressive voice stands out as ethically proper. The critical anxiety about the hegemonic ubiquity of Lata's voice derives precisely from this pathologicization of vocal imitation: a perilous disjuncture of inner self and outer voice, with all its illiberal implications. To hear someone's voice as *fake*, *derivative*, or *inauthentic* is to invoke a normative vocal ethics in which voice and individual self *ought* to be congruent. The correlative moral discourse of authenticity, originality, and self-expression requires that each singer excavate, cultivate, and express a unique voice.[6]

And yet, we have also seen that this individualist expression is only one of many possible configurations of voice and self. Film singers (whose voices are "picturized" onto another actor's body) train themselves to voice someone *else*'s interiority. Indeed, they are routinely praised precisely for the vocal malleability to give voice to many such characters. Such a singer must learn to bracket their own mood, and even their own personality, in order to voice someone *else*'s. (So thoroughly is the characterological center displaced from the playback singer that record companies have produced compilation albums of songs arranged by the actor on which songs were picturized, voiced by multiple singers.) In ritual situations, vocalists are generally expected to carry out their vocal labor without claiming the spotlight as artistes. A qawwal reciting mystical poetry for a gathering of Sufis may certainly be criticized for textual infidelity, insufficient *tasir*, or distracting fireworks—but their personal, inner feelings are not ordinarily at issue. A priest reciting mantras from the *Ṛg Veda* at a wedding is there as an exquisitely skilled celebrant, to enact ritual transformation, not to express his personal artistic vision. Among khyaliyas, a common formula of praise for a calm composure is to say that someone *else* seems to be singing—precisely the inverse of the individualist-expressive figuration.[7] One who has imbibed the paramparic body of a gharana gayaki may sound recognizably unique, but their voice is by no means entirely their own. Such a voice is not so much *in* a gharana, or *expressive of* a gharana (in a crude, groupist sense), but rather *belongs*

6. See Faubion 2011, 258.

7. See, for example, Hakim 1959, 10; Rahaim 2012, 126.

to a gharana.[8] This dispositional training is so thorough that many khyaliyas, dhrupadiyas, and qawwals (particularly cousins and siblings who have undergone near-identical talim) have sung in duets (Rajan-Sajan Mishra, Salamat-Nazakat Ali Khan, the Khan Bandhu, the Dagar Bandhu, the Nizami Bandhu, etc.), singing sometimes in blended unison, sometimes taking turns, even completing each other's phrases. They perform only as a pair, are invited for concerts as a pair, are cited as a pair—in fact, it is not uncommon for their students to refer to such a pair as "guru" in the singular, as a dual vocal subject.[9] For many *bhakti* singers, to sing is precisely to inhabit a special, devotional self. Many Krishna devotees in the Vallabhcharya tradition, for example, find their way through song into a sacred *lila* distinct from the ordinary world, removed from their usual worldly ties, in which they become a new devotionally consecrated self in relation to Krishna (his lover, his mother, his playmate, etc.).[10] Other bhakti singers embody the exemplary devotion of a poet-saint: a dedicated singer of Tukaram's songs, for example, may be called a "Tuka"; a singer of Mira's songs may be called a "Mirabai." The ambiguous personhood of a singer can even serve as a political resource, by which Tukaram is brought to life to hold forth on contemporary politics, or Mirabai's voice is brought to bear on daily struggles against oppression.[11] This non-personal ascription of moral type furthermore may be multivalent—"Mirabai," for example, is a term of abuse among Rajput men and of moral exemplarship and solidarity among subaltern women.[12] In a striking scene from Shabnam Virmani's documentary *Had Anahad*, Qawwal Fareed Ayaz sings as Kabir in the course of a Kabir bhajan, gesturing to himself while singing the word *faqīr* (in reference to the extraordinary spiritual accomplishment that Kabir himself proclaims). While shooting the scene, Shabnam (the director) took this gesture to be a kind of personal arrogance, as though Fareed

8. See also Basso 1996, 10, for an account of the moral burden of properly revoicing ancestral voices.

9. See Faubion 2011, 119 on vocal-ethical subjects that are non-individuals, and Marilyn Strathern's conception of dividual selfhood, opening the possibility of self-entities that are "split or paired with respect to another" (1988, 14).

10. Ho 2009; Wulff 1984. See Appadurai 1990 on praise. See also Mukhtiyar Ali's proclamation that he is a woman while singing (Nagaraj 2010), and Abida Parveen's proclamation that she is neither a man nor a woman while singing (Iqbal 2013).

11. Schultz 2013; Mukta 1997.

12. Mukta 1997, 2–3.

Sahab were claiming a high spiritual status for himself as an individual—taking for granted, that is, an expressive-individualist figuration of voice. But after she began singing Kabir herself, she saw things differently:

> When Fareed Ayaz is singing, he is not Fareed Ayaz. He is Kabir. He is living Kabir. He is living that truth. So when he [points to himself] he is pointing to Kabir. He is pointing to the Kabir in him. He is no longer pointing to Fareed Ayaz. You know? In that moment of performance, the truth of that poetry comes alive. It's like it's living in performance. And he is responding from that space. And then the spell is over; the performance is over. He is back to being Fareed Ayaz.

At other times, singing requires surrender to a transpersonal force precisely beyond the individual, allowing the musicking body to be moved.[13] The force is sometimes described as *rūh* (spirit), affording figurations of self, much like (and cognate with) the singer that is "moved by the spirit." In such a state, many singers describe surrendering, disappearing, or "singing from nothing." Pavan Naik once described a reorientation of self in singing qawwali at gatherings for samā, saying that the greatest tasir comes to listeners when he sings in a state of *fanā* (annihilation), in which he is no longer the author of his own voice: "Once you forget yourself, you realize that you are not singing; you are just acting. *Another one* is singing . . ." Sufi singer Ragini Rainu likewise describes operating from "a place of nothingness . . . to become a space of nothing so that He can operate." Chintan Upadhyay once described to me a state of irrelational absorption in a raga where the raga seems to sing itself: "Even if I want to, I can't stop. . . . I feel tired, I feel breathlessness, but I can't stop . . . I'm totally helpless. The raga itself wants to finish a few things." In other words, many of the profoundest vocal states require precisely a relinquishment of personal agency in favor of something Else.

Furthermore, as we have seen, in the midst of transformative vocal work, even the voice emerging from one's own throat can sound odd, distant, or even alien—it can feel as though it were someone *else*'s voice. As we saw in chapter 5, the time-honored method of *pahle naql phir aql* ("first imitation, then thinking," or "fake it till you make it") requires precisely that one start from a vocal self not yet fully achieved. The mimetic dimension of talim sometimes requires, as Michael Taussig puts it, a process of becoming other than what one is.[14] And

---

13. See also Racy 2004, 120 on *saltanah* and Rahaim 2012, 129 on immersion.

14. Taussig (1993, 33) tends to focus on the magical outcomes of a finished mimesis,

yet, one does not just set out to randomly become any old other. We have seen that the repertoire of possible vocal subject positions available to a particular subject at a particular time is varied but finite. Deliberately choosing between them (assuming one has the structural privilege to do so) is often an occasion for self-reflection and self-doubt. Moreover, for many singers, this mimetic process is never quite finished; the alterity of voice, the sense that it is not entirely one's own never entirely goes away. This is easy to forget, immersed in song, when singing feels as natural as walking. But in learning, in striving, singing-with others, in singing-to an empathetic listener, we remember: this voice belongs to more than just this one body.

This is not to say that singers never express themselves.[15] They certainly do, and it seems that they are under increasing pressure to do so. But there is nothing easy or natural about it. No less than vocal openness or sweetness, personal expressiveness must be cultivated assiduously. Finding oneself, looking inward to discovering one's "own" voice, suppressing the relational bonds which (in an individualist-expressive ethical regime) can only show up as fetters, requires the cultivation of a practiced irrelationality no less rigorous, in its own way, than the cultivation of *bhakti* or *nisbat*, kinetic or sonorous or poetic dispositions. One can be publicly called out for failing at it, one can receive formal corrective instruction, and one can *work* at it.[16] Khyaliya Rujul Pathak, for example, describes one such technique with great introspective clarity. She begins her daily riyaz by sustaining the mantra *auṃ* on *sā*, cultivating not only sonority, but also a unified personal selfhood: "You need to gather yourself up from different places, you need to get yourself back from being a mom and a wife and a full-time employee, and all of those things going on, I need to get all of the Rujuls back here—and just *within* myself." If this dispersal of relational roles (mom/wife/employee) is characteristic of a very particular social positioning, so too is its self-administered diagnosis (as a pathological fragmentation of a prior unity)[17] and its vocal therapeutics, which produces an autonomous, individuated, unified

---

rather than the unfinished striving that seems to me to be at the heart of the matter in talim. See also Lipsitz 1994, 56–66 for a profound consideration of the politics of taking on the voice of another.

15. On the shortcomings of the "expression theory" for accounting for raga music, see Saxena 2010, 8.

16. Desai-Stevens 2017, 110.

17. See Gershon 2011.

self. Such a project may well succeed in generating a coherence of selfhood, but it is a *project* nonetheless: a matter of ongoing *sādhanā*, not finished identity.[18]

An analytic of dynamic, relational vocal sociality likewise undermines a *groupist-expressivist* figuration, which hears voice as the natural outpouring of a large, univocal, irrelational collectivity of people.[19] The widespread folk sociology in which people are naturally organized into groups—"discrete, sharply differentiated, internally homogeneous and externally bounded"[20]—seems to call for the assignment of precisely one voice per group. Indeed, the model of voice as an immediate making-present of a self-identical collective interior has the same basic structure as individualist-expressivism: an unmediated projection of a prior interior selfhood, insulated from the influence of listening practices, from contestation, from social interplay with others.[21]

Vocal-racialisms that locate a distinctive voice "in the blood" of each race; nationalist desires for voices that exude the "real smell of Indian soil"[22] or "express the soul of the nation"[23]; cantometric construals of voice that discursively tether a vocal sound to a cultural essence[24]—these all are oriented toward a world quilted with coherent groups, each of which, like an individual, is assumed to have a single essential voice. Though this reflectionism sometimes passes for "social" analysis, it is peculiarly devoid of any social relations; each putatively unanimous group is characterized by eternally present, irrelational unity.[25] This groupism lives on in cultural-nationalist claims about a singular "voice of the people," visions of "the nation singing one song," and the construal of one singer or another as the voice of a nation. In India, such claims have been made on behalf of film singers (like Lata Mangeshkar), regional "folk" singers (like Mukhtiyar Ali), pop singers (like Kailash Kher), and even khyaliyas (like Bhimsen Joshi). In Egypt, the same is often claimed for Umm Kulthum or Abdel Halim Hafez; in France,

18. See Almaas 2000, 128–135, on the ongoing work of psychological individuation.

19. See also Gilroy 1993, 31 for a critique of a parallel expressivism that tends to frame black nationalist thought.

20. Brubaker 2002, 164.

21. See Rahaim 2020.

22. Ascribed to A. R. Rahman in Borkar 2007.

23. Bakhle 2005, 195.

24. Lomax in Cohen 2004, 267 and passim.

25. Cf. Guilbault 2014, 322.

for Charles Aznavour or Edith Piaf.[26] Though the particular claims vary widely, an invariant ontological template persists in each one: the voice of an exemplary individual singer is taken simultaneously to be the voice of a holistic collectivity.

And yet, vocal life rarely functions as the simple expression of a fixed collective interior. Instead, it typically serves as a field for the dynamic contestation of plural ethical or political possibilities. The soft, urbane tone cultivated so assiduously by Victorian voice culturists under the British Raj was not an expression of a prior, monolithic imperial culture, but a corrective pedagogy, directed precisely at an already-diverse vocal landscape of brash, loud, public voices—in London no less than Bombay. In fact, it was not until after the British quit India in 1947 that these vocal prescriptions flourished publicly, in the sweet, microphonic, widely beloved voices of Lata, Asha, Kishore, and Rafi. When Amir Khan adapted a similarly mellow disposition for khyal, his voice was welcomed not as a *reflection* of the world around him, but as a *remedy* for the widespread (and, for many critics, distressing) rushed temporality of modern Bombay and Calcutta. Pop sufi rose to popularity not as an *expression* of a unanimous "societal" agreement about antinomian spiritual freedom, secular individual sovereignty, or Islamic mysticism, but precisely during a widespread upsurge in Hindu nationalist power. For secular liberals, a soaring *ā* in *buland* voice may sound out as an emblem of pop sufi humanism against Hindu majoritarianism. But a rougher, breathier, more open disposition does not straightforwardly express a liberal, individualist ethos. It also acts as a *counter-voice*, sounding *against* another disposition, audible to vocal individualists as the very voice of hegemonic conformism: *filmi*. There surely are political movements that posit a univocal "voice of the people" and yoke it to majoritarian ends. But vocal resistance can also perform a kind of pluralism. The Shaheen Bagh demonstrations of early 2020, for example, did not constitute a finished expression of a rigid collectivity, but rather a dynamic contestation of sonic space, led by women, in which provisional political solidarities were formed, sustained, and undone over the course of a hundred days. The plurivocal performances therein did not constitute a substitute *revision* of a unified national voice, but a *rebuke* to univocal majoritarian nationalism in both form and content.

These ways of voice sound out contestations *between* ways of being, grounded precisely in a dynamic, churning ethical ferment. Hindustani vocal action takes

26. See also Skelchy 2019 on claims to the essential "Indonesianness" of popular singer Waldjinah's voice.

place, now more than ever, in a variegated ecumene of sedimented, mass-mediated vocal dispositions legible to various overlapping publics. These public crystallizations of voice (for all their durability across generations, for all their real, visceral, even hegemonic power) move across and between gender, caste, class, and religious formations. Though it's possible to trace rough cartographies of voice in retrospect, their territories are dynamic, shifting, fiercely contested, and never fully accomplished. This contestation occurs at various vocal sites, in various kinds of relational connection to listeners. The vocal "sociality" attested here thus is not the demographic magnitude of fully accomplished groups, but the dynamic, open-ended interplay of relationality: voices directed at listeners, trained by masters, modeled after exemplars, deriving their public ethical valence precisely from the mutual contestation between subject positions.

If a voice never quite succeeds in expressing a unanimous collectivity of millions of people, neither is it locked inside the fleshy outline of an isolated individual. As we saw in chapter 3, a circuit of voice not only *expresses* a mode of being; it also *produces* a mode of being-together. These forms of relational circuitry, brought to life among others, transforming a room into a vocal site, are also social practices of world-disclosure.[27] In this sense, they verge on practical ontology, disclosed by practices of listening, relationality, and infrastructures of amplification, staging, and broadcasting.[28] A way of voice includes not only the logic of its poetic content, and not only its lived ethics, but a lived physics as well, singing a world that can be sharply at odds with the world invoked by prosaic speech.[29] The voice of a trained qawwal situated in a *samā* evokes a cosmos studded with extraordinary prophets and saints at various stages of spiritual mastery, a world flowing with blessings and devotion and rigorously delineated rankings of status, animated by yearning for a transcendent Creator always just out of reach. The pop sufi voice, harnessed and focused by the infrastructures of Coke Studio, garbed in reverb, abstracted from hierarchies of spiritual status and broadcast equally to millions of notional equals, announces a radically different world: a place where boundaries and hierarchies are illusory projections on a prior unity, where spiritual authority resides inside the individual, where

27. Gad, et al. 2013. See also Riedel 2019 on atmosphere.

28. Rahaim 2019.

29. I borrow this tripartite formulation from Pierre Hadot's construal of philosophical traditions as practical ways of life—itself a critique of Michel Foucault's analytic privileging of ethics at the expense of physics and logic. (See Hadot 1995, 59.)

rugged heroes struggle against social obligation and restrictions. These worlds are typically diverse rather than monolithic, consisting of interwoven but distinct roles and subject positions. These are fields for mutual striving rather than accomplished identity.

To open one's mouth and be heard is already to step into just such a contested field. That these vocal formations can dissolve and coalesce on the scale of decades is evidence that these worlds are open-ended and unpredictable. That vocal sonority, so intimately connected to selfhood, is nonetheless malleable is a clue that formations of the self, too, are not always as rigid as they seem. Ways of voice, in this sense, are ways of dynamic relation, reaching far beyond any one body, far beyond any one state.

BIBLIOGRAPHY

Abbas, Shemeem Burney. 2002. *The Female Voice in Sufi Ritual: Devotional Practices of Pakistan and India*, 1st ed. Austin: University of Texas Press.

Abbate, Carolyn. 1996. *Unsung Voices: Opera and Musical Narrative in the Nineteenth Century*. Princeton, NJ: Princeton University Press.

Abe, Marié. 2018. *Resonances of Chindon-ya: Sounding Space and Sociality in Contemporary Japan*. Middletown, CT: Wesleyan University Press.

admin. 2015. "Ways To Improve Voice Production in Indian Classical Music." *Indian Classical Music and Raga - Surdemy* (blog). September 24, 2015. Accessed April 8, 2021 at https://surdemy.com/2015/09/24/ways-to-improve-voice-production.

AFP. 2016. "How Facebook Is Killing Lahore's Heera Mandi." Accessed April 8, 2021 at http://www.dawn.com/news/1279428.

Ajotikar, Rasika. 2019. "Music and the Politics of Caste and Gender: Women's Voices of Liberation in Western India." PhD Thesis, SOAS.

Alaghband-Zadeh, Chloë. 2015. "Sonic Performativity: Analysing Gender in North Indian Classical Vocal Music." *Ethnomusicology Forum* 24(3): 349–379.

———. 2012. "Formulas and the Building Blocks of Ṭhumrī Style—A Study in 'Improvised' Music." *Analytical Approaches to World Music*.

———. 2017. "Listening to North Indian Classical Music: How Embodied Ways of Listening Perform Imagined Histories and Social Class." *Ethnomusicology* 61(2): 207–233.

al-Ghazali. 2010. *The Alchemy of Happiness*. Translated by Claud Field. New York: Cosimo, Inc.

Ali, Ibrahim. N.d. "Amirkhani Khayal." Accessed April 23, 2019, at https://sites.google.com/site/amirkhanikhayal/14-effect-of-age-on-his-vocal-style.

Allen, W. H. 1847. "The Establishment of a Choir of Music at the Hindoo College." *Allen's Indian Mail and Register of Intelligence for British and Foreign India*.

alliance. 2016. "Interview with Warsi Brothers of Rampur." Accessed April 12, 2019, at https://alliancensut.com/2016/04/04/interview-with-warsi-brothers-of-rampur/.

Almaas, A. H. 2000. *The Pearl Beyond Price: Integration of Personality into Being; An Object Relations Approach.* Boston: Shambhala Publications.

Alter, A. B. 1999. "Institutional Music Education: Northern Area." In *Garland Encyclopedia of World Music: South Asia*, 442–448. New York: Garland.

Alter, Joseph S. 2004. *Yoga in Modern India: The Body Between Science and Philosophy.* Princeton, NJ: Princeton University Press.

Anjaria, Jonathan Shapiro, and Ulka Anjaria. 2020. "Mazaa: Rethinking Fun, Pleasure and Play in South Asia." *South Asia: Journal of South Asian Studies* 43(2): 232–242.

Appadurai, Arjun. N.d. "Empire of Ethics: Studying UK's Colonial Past through an Ethical Lens

Legitimises a Slippery Slope." Accessed April 8, 2021 at https://scroll.in/article/866242/empire-of-ethics-studying-uks-colonial-past-through-an-ethical-lens-legitimises-a-slippery-slope.

———. 1990. "Topographies of the Self: Praise and Emotion in Hindu India." In *Affecting Discourse: Anthropological Essays on Emotions and Social Life*, 92–112. Cambridge: Cambridge University Press.

———. 1996. *Modernity At Large: Cultural Dimensions of Globalization.* Minneapolis: University of Minnesota Press.

Aquil, Raziuddin. N.d. "Hazrat-i-Dehli: The Making of the Chishti Sufi Centre and the Stronghold of Islam." *Sahapedia.* Accessed March 11, 2020, at https://www.sahapedia.org/hazrat-i-dehli-the-making-of-the-chishti-sufi-centre-and-the-stronghold-of-islam.

Aristotle. 2009. *The Nicomachean Ethics.* Translated by David Ross and edited by Leslie Brown. New York: Oxford University Press.

Arnold, Alison. 1991. "Hindi Filmigit: On the History of Commercial Indian Popular Music." PhD Thesis, University of Illinois.

Ayyagari, Shalini. 2012. "Spaces Betwixt and Between: Musical Borderlands and the Manganiyar Musicians of Rajasthan." *Asian Music* 43(1): 3–33.

Bagchee, Sandeep. 1998. *Nād: Understanding Rāga Music.* Eeshwar.

Bailur, Chitra. 1955. "Music and Personality." *Lakshya Sangeet* 2(3).

Bakhle, Janaki. 2005. *Two Men and Music: Nationalism in the Making of an Indian Classical Tradition.* New York: Oxford University Press.

Banerjee, Nikhil. 1975. "Program Notes for a 'Music Conference to Raise Funds for a Mausoleum on the Grave of Amir Khan,' Amir Khan Sangeet Sangstha, Rabindra Sadan February 16, 1975, 5 PM."

Basso, Keith H. 1996. *Wisdom Sits in Places: Landscape and Language Among the Western Apache.* Albuquerque: University of New Mexico Press.

Basu, Sharmadip. 2011. "Tuning Modernity: Musical Knowledge and Subjectivities in Colonial India, c. 1780s–c. 1900." PhD Dissertation, Syracuse University.

Bauman, Richard, and Joel Sherzer. 1989. *Explorations in the Ethnography of Speaking*. Cambridge: Cambridge University Press.

Beaster-Jones, Jayson. 2015. *Bollywood Sounds: The Cosmopolitan Mediations of Hindi Film Song*. New York: Oxford University Press.

Becker, Judith. 2004. *Deep Listeners: Music, Emotion, and Trancing*. Bloomington: Indiana University Press.

Bellenoit, Hayden J. A. 2007. *Missionary Education and Empire in Late Colonial India, 1860–1920*. London: Pickering & Chatto.

Berger, Harris M. 2012. *Stance: Ideas about Emotion, Style, and Meaning for the Study of Expressive Culture*. Middletown, CT: Wesleyan University Press.

Bergeron, Katherine. 2010. *Voice Lessons: French Mélodie in the Belle Epoque*. New York: Oxford University Press.

Berlant, Lauren, and Michael Warner. 1998. "Sex in Public." *Critical Inquiry* 24(2): 547–566.

Bernier, François. 1826. *Travels in the Mogul Empire*. London: William Pickering.

Bertau, Marie-Cécile. 2008. "Voice: A Pathway to Consciousness as 'Social Contact to Oneself.'" *Integrative Physiological and Behavioral Science* 42(1): 92–113.

Bhagwat, Neela. 1992. *Krishnarao Shankar Pandit, a Doyen of Khayal*. Ann Arbor, MI: Popular Prakashan.

Bhatkhande, Vishnu Narayan. 1954. *Hindustani Sangeet Paddhati: Kramik Pustak Malika*. Hindi Edition. Vol. 1. Hathras, UP: Sangeet Karyalaya.

Bond, Brian. 2020. "A Heavy Rain Has Fallen Upon My People: Sindhi Sufi Poetry Performance, Emotion, and Islamic Knowledge in Kachchh, Gujarat." PhD Thesis, New York: City University of New York.

Bor, Joep. 2010. *Hindustani Music: Thirteenth to Twentieth Centuries*. Delhi: Manohar Publishers & Distributors.

Boral, R. C. 1956. "Soft Voice That Came of the Sore Throat." In *Indian Talkie 1931–'56: Silver Jubilee Souvenir*. Bombay: Film Federation of India.

Borkar, Pallavi. 2007. " 'DJs Have No Talent.' Kailash Kher." *Times of India*, July. Accessed April 8, 2021 at https://timesofindia.indiatimes.com/bangalore-times/DJs-have-no-talent-Kailash-Kher/articleshow/2211480.cms.

Born, Georgina. 2010. "For a Relational Musicology: Music and Interdisciplinarity, Beyond the Practice Turn." *Journal of the Royal Musical Association* 135(2): 205–243.

Bourdieu, Pierre. 1977. *Outline of a Theory of Practice*. Cambridge: Cambridge University Press.

———. 1991. *Language and Symbolic Power*. Cambridge: Harvard University Press.

———. 2000. *Pascalian Meditations*. Stanford: Stanford University Press.

Breckenridge, Carol A. 1989. "The Aesthetics and Politics of Colonial Collecting: India at World Fairs." *Comparative Studies in Society and History* 31(2): 195–216.

Brown, Katherine. 2006. "If Music Be the Food of Love: Masculinity and Eroticism in the Mughal Mehfil." In *Love in South Asia: A Cultural History*, edited by Francesca Orsini, 65. Cambridge: Cambridge University Press.

Brubaker, Rogers. 2002. "Ethnicity without Groups." *European Journal of Sociology / Archives Européennes de Sociologie / Europäisches Archiv Für Soziologie* 43(2): 163–189.

Buchanan, Donna A. 2007. *Balkan Popular Culture and the Ottoman Ecumene: Music, Image, and Regional Political Discourse*. Lanham, MD: Scarecrow Press.

Buckley, Jeff. N.d. "Nusrat." Accessed April 8, 2021 at https://www.liquidgnome.com/JeffBuckley/nusrat.html.

Busch, Allison. 2010. "Hidden in Plain View: Brajbhasha Poets at the Mughal Court." *Modern Asian Studies* 44(2): 267–309.

Butler, Judith. 1988. "Performative Acts and Gender Constitution: An Essay in Phenomenology and Feminist Theory." *Theatre Journal* 40(4): 519.

———. 2011. *Gender Trouble: Feminism and the Subversion of Identity*. London: Routledge.

Calvino, Italo. 2012. *Under the Jaguar Sun*. Boston: Houghton Mifflin Harcourt.

Capwell, Charles. 1986. *The Music of the Bauls of Bengal*. Kent: Kent State University Press.

Carter, Scott A. 2013. "Forging a Sound Citizenry: Voice Culture and the Embodiment of the Nation, 1880–1920." *The American Music Research Center Journal; Boulder* 22: 11–34, 81.

Caton, Steven C. 1990. *"Peaks of Yemen I Summon": Poetry as Cultural Practice in a North Yemeni Tribe*. Berkeley: University of California Press.

Cavarero, Adriana. 2005. *For More Than One Voice: Toward a Philosophy of Vocal Expression*. Stanford: Stanford University Press.

Chakrabarti, Sukanya. 2016. "Performing [as] Bauls Renegotiating 'Folk' Identities through the Lens of Performance." PhD Thesis, Stanford University.

Chaubey, S. K. 1958. *Musicians I Have Met*. Uttar Pradesh: Information Department.

Cobussen, Marcel, and Nanette Nielsen. 2016. *Music and Ethics*. London: Routledge.

Das, Veena. 2018. "Ethics, Self-Knowledge, and Life Taken as a Whole." *HAU: Journal of Ethnographic Theory* 8(3): 537–549.

Datta, Asoke Kumar, et al. 2017. *Signal Analysis of Hindustani Classical Music*. Springer.

Denning, Michael. 2015. *Noise Uprising: The Audiopolitics of a World Musical Revolution*. New York: Verso Books.

Deo, Aditi. 2011. "Alternative Windows into Tradition: Non-Hereditary Practices in Hindustani Khyal Music." PhD Thesis, Indiana University.

Deodhar, B. R. 1993. *Pillars of Hindustani Music*. Bombay: Popular Prakashan.

Derrida, Jacques. 2011. *Voice and Phenomenon: Introduction to the Problem of the Sign in Husserl's Phenomenology*. Evanston: Northwestern University Press.

Desai-Stevens, Anaar. 2017. "Singing Through the Screen: Indian Idol and the Cultural Politics of Aspiration in Post-Liberalization India." PhD Thesis, Cornell University.

Deshpande, Ashwini. 2004. "Lata Mangeshkar: The Singer and the Voice." *Economic and Political Weekly* 39(48): 5179–5184.

Deshpande, V. H. 1979a. *Ālāpinī*. Mauja.

———. 1979b. "Kishori Amonkar—Formative Years." *Economic Times*, June 3, 1979.

———. 1987. *Indian Musical Traditions: An Aesthetic Study of the Gharanas in Hindustani Music*. Popular Prakashan.

———. 1989. *Between Two Tanpuras*. Bombay: Popular Prakashan.

Deva, B. C. 1959. "The Vibrato in Indian Music." *Acustica* 9(3): 175–180.

Devidayal, Namita. 2011. *The Music Room*. Delhi: Random House India.

Deviprasadh, Rasiga. 2017. "Voice Culture for an 'Ideal Voice.'" *International Journal of Science and Research* 7(6): 1032–1034.

Dewan, Saba. 2019. *Tawaifnama*. Chennai: Westland Publications Private Limited.

Dhar, Sheila. 2001. *The Cooking of Music and Other Essays*. Delhi: Permanent Black.

Douglas, Susan Jeanne. 1999. *Listening in: Radio and the American Imagination, from Amos 'n' Andy and Edward R. Murrow to Wolfman Jack and Howard Stern*. New York: Times Books.

du Perron, Lalita. 2002. "'Ṭhumrī': A Discussion of the Female Voice of Hindustani Music." *Modern Asian Studies* 36(1): 173–193.

Durga, S. A. K. 1978. "Voice Culture - With Special Reference to South Indian Music." *Journal of the Indian Musicological Society; Baroda* 9(1): 5–136.

———. 2007. *Voice Culture: The Art of Voice Cultivation*. Delhi: B.R. Rhythms.

Dwyer, Rachel. 2000. *All You Want Is Money, All You Need Is Love: Sexuality and Romance in Modern India*. London: Cassell & Co.

Eidsheim, Nina. 2009. "Synthesizing Race: Towards an Analysis of the Performativity of Vocal Timbre." *TRANS - Revista Transcultural de Música - Transcultural Music Review* 13.

———. 2008. "Voice as a Technology of Selfhood: Towards an Analysis of Racialized Timbre and Vocal Performance." PhD Thesis, UC San Diego.

———. 2015. *Sensing Sound: Singing and Listening as Vibrational Practice*. Durham: Duke University Press.

———. 2018. *The Race of Sound: Listening, Timbre, and Vocality in African American Music*. Durham: Duke University Press.

Eisenlohr, Patrick. 2018. "Suggestions of Movement: Voice and Sonic Atmospheres in Mauritian Muslim Devotional Practices." *Cultural Anthropology* 33(1): 32–57.

Englund, Harri. 2015. "Multivocal morality: Narrative, sentiment, and Zambia's radio grandfathers." *Hau: Journal of Ethnographic Theory* 5(2): 251–273.

Ericsson, Anders. 1993. "The Role of Deliberate Practice in the Acquisition of Expert Performance." *Psychological Review* 100(3): 363–406.

Ettema, James S., and David Charles Whitney. 1994. *Audiencemaking: How the Media Create the Audience*. Thousand Oaks: Sage Publications.

Farrell, Gerry. 1999. *Indian Music and the West*. Oxford: Oxford University Press.

Faruqi, Shamsur Rahman, and Frances W. Pritchett. 1991. "Lyric Poetry in Urdu: The Ghazal." *Delos* 3(3–4): 7–12.

Fatone, Gina A., Martin Clayton, Laura Leante, and Matt Rahaim. 2011. "Imagery, Melody and Gesture in Cross-Cultural Perspective." In *New Perspectives on Music and Gesture*, edited by Anthony Gritten and Elaine King, 203–220. Farnham, Surrey: Ashgate.

Faubion, James D. 2011. *An Anthropology of Ethics*. Cambridge University Press.

Feldman, Martha, and Bonnie Gordon. 2006. *The Courtesan's Arts: Cross-Cultural Perspectives*. Oxford: Oxford University Press.

Feldman, Martha, et al. 2015. "Why Voice Now?" *Journal of the American Musicological Society* 68(3): 653–685.

Feldman, Martha, et al. 2019. *The Voice as Something More: Essays Toward Materiality*. Chicago: University of Chicago Press.

Finnegan, Ruth. 2014. *Communicating: The Multiple Modes of Human Communication*. London: Routledge.

Flatt, Emma J. 2019. *The Courts of the Deccan Sultanates: Living Well in the Persian Cosmopolis*. Cambridge: Cambridge University Press.

Foster, Robert J. 1991. "Making National Cultures in the Global Ecumene." *Annual Review of Anthropology* 20: 235–260.

Foucault, Michel. 2012a. *The History of Sexuality: An Introduction*. New York: Knopf Doubleday Publishing Group.

———. 2012b. *The History of Sexuality, Vol. 2: The Use of Pleasure*. New York: Knopf Doubleday Publishing Group.

———. 2012c. *The History of Sexuality, Vol. 3: The Care of the Self*. New York: Knopf Doubleday Publishing Group.

Fox, Aaron A. 2004. *Real Country: Music and Language in Working-Class Culture*. Durham: Duke University Press.

Frith, Simon. 1998. *Performing Rites: On the Value of Popular Music*. Cambridge: Harvard University Press.

Frykenberg, Robert Eric, and Alaine M. Low. 2003. *Christians and Missionaries in India: Cross-Cultural Communication Since 1500, with Special Reference to Caste, Conversion, and Colonialism*. Grand Rapids: Wm. B. Eerdmans Publishing.

Gad, C., C. B. Jensen, and B. R. Winthereik. 2013. "Practical Ontology. World(s) in STS and Anthropology." *NatureCulture* 67(January): 81–100.

Galton, Francis. 1869. *Hereditary Genius: An Inquiry Into Its Laws and Consequences*. New York: Macmillan.

Ganesh, Deepa. 2006. "A Life in Three Octaves." *Frontline* 23(4).

Ganguli, Kaustuv Kanti, and Amruta Vidwans. 2012. "Classification of Indian Classical Vocal Styles from Melodic Contours." *Proceedings of the 2nd Computational Music Workshop*.

Gay, Ross. 2019. *The Book of Delights: Essays*. Chapel Hill: Algonquin Books.

Geertz, Clifford. 1973a. *The Interpretation of Cultures*. New York: Basic Books.

———. 1973b. *The Interpretation of Cultures*. New York: Basic Books.

Gershon, Ilana. 2011. "'Neoliberal Agency.'" *Current Anthropology* 52(4): 537–555.

Geurts, Kathryn Linn. 2003. *Culture and the Senses: Bodily Ways of Knowing in an African Community*. Berkeley: University of California Press.

Gibb, Duncan. 1870. "'The Character of the Voice in the Nations of Asia and Africa, Contrasted with That of the Nations of Europe.'" In *Memoirs Read Before the Anthropological Society of London*, 244–259. London: Trübner and Company.

Gilligan, Carol. 1993. *In a Different Voice: Psychological Theory and Women's Development*. Cambridge: Harvard University Press.

Gilroy, Paul. 1993. *The Black Atlantic: Modernity and Double Consciousness*. Cambridge: Harvard University Press.

Godøy, Rolf Inge, et al. 2016. "Exploring Sound-Motion Similarity in Musical Experience." *Journal of New Music Research* 45(3): 210–222.

Gopal, Sangita, and Sujata Moorti, ed. 2008. *Global Bollywood: Travels of Hindi Song and Dance*. Minneapolis: University of Minnesota Press.

Green, Nile. 2004. "Geography, Empire and Sainthood in the Eighteenth-Century Muslim Deccan." *Bulletin of the School of Oriental and African Studies, University of London* 67(2): 207–225.

Gross, M. Melissa, Elizabeth A. Crane, and Barbara L. Fredrickson. 2012. "Effort-Shape and Kinematic Assessment of Bodily Expression of Emotion during Gait." *Human Movement Science* 31(1): 202–221.

Guilbault, Jocelyne. N.d. "Politics of Ethnomusicological Knowledge Production and Circulation." *Ethnomusicology* 58(2): 321–326.

Gupta, Charu. 2002. *Sexuality, Obscenity and Community: Women, Muslims, and the Hindu Public in Colonial India*. Berlin: Springer.

Gupta, Charu. 2005. *Sexuality, Obscenity, Community: Women, Muslims, and the Hindu Public in Colonial India*. Delhi: Permanent Black.

Habib, Irfan. 1997. *Akbar and His India*. Oxford: Oxford University Press.

Hadot, Pierre. 1995. *Philosophy as a Way of Life: Spiritual Exercises from Socrates to Foucault*. New York: Wiley.

Hahn, Tomie. 2007. *Sensational Knowledge: Embodying Culture Through Japanese Dance*. Middletown, CT: Wesleyan University Press.

Haldankar, Babanrao. 2001. *Aesthetics of Agra and Jaipur Traditions*. Mumbai: Popular Prakashan.

Hannerz, Ulf. 1989. "Notes on the Global Ecumene." *Public Culture* 1(2): 66–75.

Hansen, Kathryn. 1998. "Stri Bhumika: Female Impersonators and Actresses on the Parsi Stage." *Economic and Political Weekly* 33(35): 2291–2300.

Harkness, Nicholas. 2014. *Songs of Seoul: An Ethnography of Voice and Voicing in Christian South Korea*. Berkeley: University of California Press.

Harrison, Alexina Mackay. 1893. *Singing the Gospel Among Hindus and Gónds*. London: Hodder and Stoughton.

Hawley, John Stratton. 1984. "The Music in Faith and Morality." *Journal of the American Academy of Religion* 52(2).

———. 1987. *Saints and Virtues*. Berkeley University of California Press.

———. 2012. *Three Bhakti Voices: Mirabai, Surdas, and Kabir in Their Times and Ours*. Delhi: Oxford University Press India.

———. 2015. *A Storm of Songs*. Cambridge: Harvard University Press.

Hemani, Shumaila. 2011. *Representing Pakistan through Folk Music and Dance*. MA Thesis, University of Alberta.

Herbst, Edward. 1997. *Voices in Bali: Energies and Perceptions in Vocal Music and Dance Theater*. Hanover, NH: Wesleyan University Press.

Hess, Linda. 2015. *Bodies of Song: Kabir Oral Traditions and Performative Worlds in North India*. Oxford: Oxford University Press.

Hindustan Times. 2016. "Allah's 99 Names, Terror: What PM Modi Said at World Sufi Forum." *Hindustan Times*. Accessed April 8, 2021 at https://www.hindustantimes.com/india/from-99-names-of-allah-to-terrorism-top-10-quotes-of-pm-modi-s-speech/story-CGa4doolIuFYh2TxmdtY3J.html.

Hirschkind, Charles. 2006. *The Ethical Soundscape: Cassette Sermons and Islamic Counterpublics*. New York: Columbia University Press.

Ho, Meilu. 2013. "Connecting Histories: Liturgical Songs as Classical Compositions in Hindustānī Music." *Ethnomusicology* 57(2): 207–235.

Hobart, Angela, and Bruce Kapferer, eds. 2005. *Aesthetics in Performance: Formations of Symbolic Construction and Experience, First Edition*. New York: Berghahn Books.

Hoffman, Barbara G. 2001. *Griots at War: Conflict, Conciliation, and Caste in Mande*. Bloomington: Indiana University Press.

hooks, bell. 2004. *The Will to Change: Men, Masculinity, and Love*. New York: Simon and Schuster.

Huang, Pei-Ling. N.d. "Vocal Change as 'Nexus': Debating Authority and Interpreting Gendered Voice in a Sindhi Devotional Tradition."

Ihde, Don. (1976) 2012. *Listening and Voice: Phenomenologies of Sound, Second Edition*. Albany: SUNY Press.

India Today Web Desk. 2018. "Sona Mohapatra Threatened by Sufi Group over 'Vulgar' Music Video, Files Complaint." *India Today*. https://www.indiatoday.in/movies/celebrities/story/sona-mohapatra-threatened-sufi-group-music-video-complaint-1223878-2018-05-01.

Ingold, Tim. 1996. *Key Debates in Anthropology*. London: Psychology Press.

Iqbal, Nosheen. 2013. "Abida Parveen: 'I'm Not a Man or a Woman, I'm a Vehicle for Passion.'" *The Guardian*, July 8, 2013, sec. Culture.

James, William. 1950. *The Principles of Psychology*. New York: Dover Publications.

Jessen, Claus. 2012. *Temperature Regulation in Humans and Other Mammals*. Berlin: Springer Science & Business Media.

Jhingan, Shikha. N.d. "Lata Mangeshkar's Voice in the Age of Cassette Reproduction." *BioScope: South Asian Screen Studies* 4(2): 97–114.

———. 2009. "The Singer, the Star and the Chorus." In *Seminar* 598: 58–63.

Joshi, G. N. 1984. *Down Melody Lane*. Hyderabad: Orient Longman.

Kapcan, Deborah. 2009. "Learning to Listen: The Sound of Sufism in France." *World of Music* 51(2): 65–90.

Katz, Mark. 2004. *Capturing Sound: How Technology Has Changed Music*. Berkeley: University of California Press.

Katz, Max. 2017. *Lineage of Loss: Counternarratives of North Indian Music*. Middletown, CT: Wesleyan University Press.

Kaur, Inderjit N. 2016. "Multiple Authenticities in Motion: Styles and Stances in Sikh Sabad Kīrtan." *Yearbook for Traditional Music* 48: 71–93.

———. 2019. "A Multisensorial Affective Ecology of Sonic Worship: The Sikh Sacred Song Culture." *MUSICultures* 46(2): 109–133.

Keane, Webb. 2017. *Ethical Life: Its Natural and Social Histories*. Princeton: Princeton University Press.

Khan, Dargah Quli. 1989. *Muraqqa '-e-Delhi: The Mughal Capital in Muhammad Shah's Time*. Delhi: Deputy Publication.

Khan, Ghulam Haider. 2010. "Ustad Salamat Ali Khan." *The Friday Times* 22(48).

Khan, Hazrat Inayat. 1996. *The Mysticism of Sound and Music*. Boston: Shambhala.

Kimber, Marian Wilson. 2017. *The Elocutionists: Women, Music, and the Spoken Word*. Champaign: University of Illinois Press.

Kiranmayi, Indraganti. 2016. *Her Majestic Voice: South Indian Female Playback Singers and Stardom, 1945–1955*. Oxford: Oxford University Press.

Kosambi, Meera. 2017. *Gender, Culture, and Performance: Marathi Theatre and Cinema before Independence*. London: Routledge.

Kreiman, Jody, and Diana Sidtis. 2011. *Foundations of Voice Studies: An Interdisciplinary Approach to Voice Production and Perception*. New York: John Wiley & Sons.

Kunreuther, Laura. 2014. *Voicing Subjects: Public Intimacy and Mediation in Kathmandu*. Berkeley: Univ of California Press.

Kvetko, Peter. 2005. "Indipop: Producing Global Sounds and Local Meanings in Bombay." PhD Thesis, University of Texas at Austin.

Lacan, Jacques. 2006. *Ecrits: The First Complete Edition in English*. New York: W. W. Norton & Company.

Lacasse, Serge. 2010. "The Phonographic Voice: Paralinguistic Features and Phonographic Staging in Popular Music Singing." In *Recorded Music*. Cambridge: Cambridge University Press.

Ladd, D. Robert. 1996. *Intonational Phonology*. Cambridge: Cambridge University Press.

Laidlaw, James. 2000. "A Free Gift Makes No Friends." *The Journal of the Royal Anthropological Institute* 6(4): 617–634.

———. 2014. *The Subject of Virtue: An Anthropology of Ethics and Freedom*. Cambridge: Cambridge University Press.

Lambek, Michael. 2010. *Ordinary Ethics: Anthropology, Language, and Action*. New York: Fordham University Press.

Larkin, Brian. 2004. "Bandiri Music, Globalization, and Urban Experience in Nigeria." *Social Text 81*, 22(4): 91–112.

Lath, Mukund. N.d. "What Is Khyal? A Critique of Wade's Khyal: Creativity Within North India's Classical Music Tradition." *National Centre for the Performing Arts* 17(1): 1–11.

Lawrence, Bruce B. 1991. *Nizam Ad-Din Awliya: Morals for the Heart*. New York: Paulist Pr.

Lefebvre, Henri. 2004. *Rhythmanalysis: Space, Time and Everyday Life*. London: A&C Black.

Lelyveld, David. 1993. "Colonial Knowledge and the Fate of Hindustani." *Comparative Studies in Society and History* 35(4): 665–682.

———. 1994. "Upon the Subdominant: Administering Music on All-India Radio." *Social Text* 39: 111–127.

Levinas, Emmanuel. 2012. *Totality and Infinity: An Essay on Exteriority*. Berlin: Springer Science & Business Media.

Levy, Mark. 1982. *Intonation in North Indian Music: A Select Comparison of Theories with Contemporary Practice*. Delhi: Biblia Impex.

Lipsitz, George. 1994. *Dangerous Crossroads: Popular Music, Postmodernism, and the Poetics of Place*. London; New York: Verso.

Lipton, G. A. 2011. "Secular Sufism: Neoliberalism, Ethnoracism, and the Reformation of the Muslim Other." *The Muslim World* 101(3): 427–440.

Lomax, Alax. 2004. *Alan Lomax: Selected Writings, 1934-1997*. Ronald Cohen, editor. London: Routledge.

Lord, Albert Bates, Stephen Arthur Mitchell, and Gregory Nagy. 2000. *The Singer of Tales*. Cambridge: Harvard University Press.

Luhrmann, T. M. 2012. *When God Talks Back: Understanding the American Evangelical Relationship with God*. New York: Knopf Doubleday Publishing Group.

Lutgendorf, Philip. 1991. *The Life of a Text: Performing the Rāmcaritmānas of Tulsidas*. Berkeley: University of California Press.

Luthra, H. R. 1986. *Indian Broadcasting*. New Delhi: Publications Division Ministry of Information & Broadcasting.

Maciszewski, Amelia. 2001a. "Multiple Voices, Multiple Selves: Song Style and North Indian Women's Identity." *Asian Music* 32(2): 1–40.

———. 2001b. "Stories About Selves: Selected North Indian Women's Musical (Auto) Biographies." *The World of Music* 43(1): 139–172.

Macken, William, and Dylan Jones. 1995. "Functional Characteristics of the Inner Voice and the Inner Ear: Single or Double Agency?" *Journal of Experimental Psychology. Learning, Memory, and Cognition* 21 (April): 436–448.

Magriel, Nicolas. 2011. *Tālīm Aur Riyaz*. Accessed September 9, 2020 at http://www.growingintomusic.co.uk/the-growing-into-music-film.html.

Magriel, Nicolas, and Lalita du Perron. 2013. *The Songs of Ḵẖayāl*. Delhi: Manohar.

Mahmood, Saba. 2004. *Politics of Piety: The Islamic Revival and the Feminist Subject*. Princeton: Princeton University Press.

Majumdar, Neepa. 2010. *Wanted Cultured Ladies Only!: Female Stardom and Cinema in India, 1930s–1950s*. Champaign: University of Illinois Press.

Maṅgeśakara, Lata, and Nasreen Munni Kabir. 2009. *Lata Mangeshkar: In Her Own Voice*. New Delhi: Niyogi Books.

Manuel, Peter. 1988. "A Historical Survey of the Urdu G̱azal-Song in India." *Asian Music* 20(1): 93–113.

———. 1989. *Ṭhumrī in Historical and Stylistic Perspectives*. New Delhi: Motilal Banarsidass Publ.

———. 1992. "Popular Music and Media Culture in South Asia: Prefatory Considerations." *Asian Music* 24(1): 91–100.

———. 2015. "The Intermediate Sphere in North Indian Music Culture: Between and Beyond 'Folk' and 'Classical.'" *Ethnomusicology* 59(1): 82–115.

———. 1993. *Cassette Culture: Popular Music and Technology in North India*. Chicago: University of Chicago Press.

Martinez, José Luiz. 2001. *Semiosis in Hindustani Music*. New Delhi: Motilal Banarsidass Publ.

Martschukat, Jürgen. 2011. "'The Necessity for Better Bodies to Perpetuate Our Institutions, Insure a Higher Development of the Individual, and Advance the Conditions of the Race.' Physical Culture and the Formation of the Self in the Late Nineteenth and Early Twentieth Century USA." *Journal of Historical Sociology* 24(4): 472–493.

Mauss, Marcel. 1973. "Techniques of the Body." *Economy and Society* 2(1): 70–88.

McCracken, Allison. 1999. "'God's Gift to Us Girls': Crooning, Gender, and the Re-Creation of American Popular Song, 1928–1933." *American Music* 17(4): 365–395.

Meddegoda, Chinthaka P. 2018. "Oral Teaching Systems versus Ongoing Canonization in Hindustani Vocal Practice." *AEMR-EJ* 2: 53–64. Accessed February 17, 2020.

Mehta, Ramanlal. 2017. *Agra Gharana: Tradition, Musical Philosophy, and Repertoire*. CreateSpace Independent Publishing Platform.

Meizel, Katherine. 2020. *Multivocality: Singing on the Borders of Identity*. Oxford: Oxford University Press.

Menon, R. R. 1967. "K.L. Saigal: The Voice." *The Times of India (1861–Current); Mumbai, India*, June 11, 1967, sec. Magazine Page.

———. 1989. "Light Music Changes Scale." *Times of India*, May 8, 1989.

Menon, Raghavan. 2001. *The Musical Journey of Kumar Gandharva*. New Delhi: Vision Books.

Merleau-Ponty, Maurice. 2013. *Phenomenology of Perception*. London: Routledge.

Metcalf, Barbara Daly. 1984. *Moral Conduct and Authority: The Place of Adab in South Asian Islam*. Berkeley: University of California Press.

Michalak, Johannes, et al. 2009. "Embodiment of Sadness and Depression: Gait Patterns Associated with Dysphoric Mood." *Psychosomatic Medicine* 71(5): 580–587.

Miner, Allyn. 2004. *Sitar and Sarod in the 18th and 19th Centuries*. Motilal Banarsidass Publ.

Mintz, Sidney W. 1996. "Enduring Substances, Trying Theories: The Caribbean Region as Oikoumene." *The Journal of the Royal Anthropological Institute* 2(2): 289–311.

Mishra, Rajan & Sajan. 2016. *Kharaj Practice for a Deep, Resonant Voice*. Accessed September 12, 2019 at https://www.youtube.com/watch?v=wdxcwIiUYbk.

Mishra, Vijay. 2013. *Bollywood Cinema: Temples of Desire*. London: Routledge.

Misra, Susheela. 1981. *Great Masters of Hindustani Music*. New Delhi: Hem Publishers.

Morcom, Anna. 2007. *Hindi Film Songs and the Cinema*. Farnham: Ashgate Publishing, Ltd.

———. 2014. *Illicit Worlds of Indian Dance: Cultures of Exclusion*. London: Oxford University Press.

Mukherji, Kumar Prasad. 2006. *The Lost World of Hindustani Music*. New Delhi: Penguin India.

Mukta, Parita. 1997. *Upholding the Common Life: The Community of Mirabai*. Oxford: Oxford University Press.

Nadkarni, Mohan. 1986. "The Virtuoso: Krishna Rao Pandit." *The Illustrated Weekly of India*, October 5, 1986.

———. 1987. "Unhone Lokranjan Kī Sharton Se Samjhotā Nahin Kiyā." *Nai Duniya*, March 29, 1987.

———. 1999. *The Great Masters: Profiles in Hindustani Classical Vocal Music*. New Delhi: HarperCollins Publishers India.

Nagaraj, Preethi. 2010. "Mukhtiar Ali: I Am a Woman When I Sing." *Deccan Herald*, 2010.

Nair, Rajeev. 2007. *A Rasika's Journey through Hindustani Music*. New Delhi: Indialog Publications.

Nancy, Jean-Luc. 2007. *Listening*. New York: Fordham Univ Press.

Napier, John. 2007. "The Distribution of Authority in the Performance of North Indian Vocal Music." *Ethnomusicology Forum* 16(2): 271–301.

Narayan, Kirin. 2016. *Everyday Creativity: Singing Goddesses in the Himalayan Foothills.* Chicago: University of Chicago Press.

Neuman, Daniel M. 1990. *The Life of Music in North India: The Organization of an Artistic Tradition.* Reprint edition. Chicago: University of Chicago Press.

Neuman, Dard. 2012. "Pedagogy, Practice, and Embodied Creativity in Hindustani Music." *Ethnomusicology* 56 (September): 426–449.

Niranjana, Tejaswini. 2020. *Musicophilia in Mumbai: Performing Subjects & The Metropolitan Unconscious.* Durham: Duke University Press.

Nooshin, Laudan. 2016. *Music and the Play of Power in the Middle East, North Africa and Central Asia.* London: Routledge.

Novak, David. 2010. "Cosmopolitanism, Remediation, and the Ghost World of Bollywood." *Cultural Anthropology* 25(1): 40–72.

———. 2013. *Japanoise: Music at the Edge of Circulation.* Durham: Duke University Press.

Novetzke, Christian Lee. 2007. "Bhakti and Its Public." *International Journal of Hindu Studies* 11(3): 255–272.

Ochoa Gautier, Ana Maria. 2014. *Aurality: Listening and Knowledge in Nineteenth Century Colombia.* Durham: Duke University Press.

Ohala, Manjari. 1983. *Aspects of Hindi Phonology.* New Delhi: Motilal Banarsidass Publisher.

Okpewho, Isidore. 1992. *African Oral Literature: Backgrounds, Character, and Continuity.* Bloomington: Indiana University Press.

Oldenburg, Veena Talwar. 1990. "Lifestyle as Resistance: The Case of the Courtesans of Lucknow, India." *Feminist Studies* 16(2): 259–287.

Ollikala, Robert. 1996. "Concerning Begum Akhtar: 'Queen of Ghazal.'" PhD Thesis, University of Illinois.

Olwage, Grant. 2004. "The Class and Colour of Tone: An Essay on the Social History of Vocal Timbre." *Ethnomusicology Forum* 13(2).

Orsini, Francesca. 2006. *Love in South Asia: A Cultural History.* Cambridge: Cambridge University Press.

Padamsee, Alex. 2018. *The Return of the Mughal: Historical Fiction and Despotism in Colonial India, 1863–1908.* Berlin: Springer.

Pal, Felix. 2019. "Performing Pluralism: Why the BJP Wants Muslim Friends." *New Mandala.* Accessed April 8, 2021 at https://www.newmandala.org/performing-pluralism-why-the-bjp-wants-muslim-friends/.

Pandian, Anand. 2009. *Crooked Stalks: Cultivating Virtue in South India.* Durham: Duke University Press.

Pandian, Anand, and Daud Ali. 2010. *Ethical Life in South Asia*. Bloomington: Indiana University Press.

Pandya, Paritosh. 2005. "Beyond Swayambhu Gandhar: An Analysis of Perceived Tanpura Notes." *Ninad: The Journal of ITC Sangeet Research Academy* vol. 19, December 2005.

Parrikar, Rajan. 2001. "On Raga Bhatiyar." *Rajan Parrikar Music Archive* (blog). Accessed April 8, 2021 at https://www.parrikar.org/hindustani/bhatiyar/.

———. 2002. "Bhairavi (Part 1/2)." *Rajan Parrikar Music Archive* (blog). Accessed April 8, 2021 at https://www.parrikar.org/hindustani/bhairavi/.

Paschalidou, Panagiota-Styliani. 2017. "Effort in Gestural Interactions with Imaginary Objects in Hindustani Dhrupad Vocal Music." PhD Thesis, Durham University.

Pauwels, Heidi. 2017. *Mobilizing Krishna's World: The Writings of Prince Sāvant Singh of Kishangarh*. Seattle: University of Washington Press.

Pearson, Lara. 2013. "Gesture and the Sonic Event in Karnatak Music." *Empirical Musicology Review* 8(1): 2–14.

Pollock, Sheldon. 2016. *A Rasa Reader: Classical Indian Aesthetics*. New York: Columbia University Press.

Poolakkal, Vijay. 2014. *Remembering Mohammed Rafi*. United States: Lulu.

Potter, John, and Neil Sorrell. 2012. *A History of Singing*. Cambridge: Cambridge University Press.

Pradhan, Aneesh. 2004. "Perspectives on Performance Practice: Hindustani Music in Nineteenth and Twentieth Century Bombay (Mumbai)." *South Asia: Journal of South Asian Studies* 27(3): 339–358.

———. 2014. *Hindustani Music in Colonial Bombay*. Gurgaon: Three Essays Collective.

———. 2015. "Kesarbai Kerkar's Voice Was a Commanding Presence for Four Decades." Accessed April 8, 2021 at https://scroll.in/article/724481/kesarbai-kerkars-voice-was-a-commanding-presence-for-four-decades.

———. 2017. "Giovanni Scrinzi and B.R. Deodhar: An Intercultural Musical Dialogue in Colonial Bombay." Presented at "Presenting the Past: Mumbai University's Conference on the History of the City."

Prentiss, Karen Pechilis. 2000. *The Embodiment of Bhakti*. Oxford: Oxford University Press.

Press Information Bureau. 2015. "Delegation of Sufi Scholars Calls on PM." www.narendramodi.in. 2015.

Quinn, Jennifer Post. 1986. "Marathi and Konkani Speaking Women in Hindustani Music, 1880–1940." PhD Thesis, University of Minnesota.

Qureshi, Regula. 2006. "Female Agency and Patrilineal Constraints: Situating Courtesans in Twentieth-Century India." In *The Courtesan's Arts: Cross-Cultural Perspectives*, 312–331. Oxford; New York: Oxford University Press.

Qureshi, Regula Burckhardt. 1990. "Musical Gesture and Extra-Musical Meaning: Words

and Music in the Urdu Ghazal." *Journal of the American Musicological Society* 43(3): 457–497.
———. 1994. "Exploring Time Cross-Culturally: Ideology and Performance of Time in the Sufi Qawwālī." *The Journal of Musicology* 12(4): 491–528.
———. 1995. *Sufi Music of India and Pakistan: Sound, Context, and Meaning in Qawwali.* Chicago: University of Chicago Press.
———. 1999. "His Master's Voice? Exploring Qawwali and 'Gramophone Culture' in South Asia 1." *Popular Music* 18(1): 63–98.
———. 2001. "In Search of Begum Akhtar: Patriarchy, Poetry, and Twentieth-Century Indian Music." *The World of Music* 43(1): 97–137.
Racy, A. J. 2004. *Making Music in the Arab World: The Culture and Artistry of Tarab.* Cambridge: Cambridge University Press.
Radhakrishnan, Nandhu, Prakash Boominathan, Ronald Scherer, and Haidee Tan. 2008. "Rate of Change of F_0 in Performance Singing." *The Journal of the Acoustical Society of America* 123(5): 3379.
Rahaim, Matt, Srinivas Reddy, and Lars Christensen. 2014. "Authority, Critique, and Revision in the Sanskrit Music-Theoretic Tradition: Rereading the Svara-Mela-Kalānidhi." *Asian Music* 46(1): 39–77.
Rahaim, Matthew. 2013. *Musicking Bodies: Gesture and Voice in Hindustani Music.* Wesleyan University Press.
———. 2019a. "Object, Person, Machine, or What: Practical Ontologies of Voice." In *The Oxford Handbook of Voice Studies*, 19–34. Oxford: Oxford University Press.
———. 2019b. "Theories of Participation." In *Theory for Ethnomusicology*, edited by Harris Berger and Ruth Stone. London: Routledge.
———. 2021. "Not Just One, Not Just Now" in the *Oxford Handbook of the Phenomenology of Music Cultures.* Oxford: Oxford University Press. Online at https://www.oxfordhandbooks.com/view/10.1093/oxfordhb/ 9780190693879.001.0001/oxfordhb-9780190693879-e-2.
Rahman, M. 1987. "Host of New Playback Singers in the Reckoning." India Today. Accessed April 8, 2021 at https://www.indiatoday.in/magazine/society-the-arts/story/19871130-host-of-new-playback-singers-in-the-reckoning-799550-1987-11-30.
Rai, Alok. 2002. "The Persistence of Hindustani." *India International Centre Quarterly* 29(3/4): 70–79.
Raja, Deepak. 2009. *Khayal Vocalism: Continuity with Change.* 2009 edition. New Delhi: D.K. Print World Ltd.
———. 2011. "Kishori Amonkar: The Queen of Romanticism." *Deepak Raja's World of Hindustani Music* (blog). Accessed April 8, 2021 at http://swaratala.blogspot.com/2011/07/kishori-amonkar-queen-of-romanticism.html.
———. 2016. "Deepak Raja on Amplification, Recordings, and Hindustani Music: Bhat-

khande Memorial Lecture, Dadar Matunga Cultural Centre, October 22, 2016." Accessed April 8, 2021 at https://www.youtube.com/watch?v=zMsFwDoduZs.

Ram, Kalpana. 2011. "Being 'rasikas': The Affective Pleasures of Music and Dance Spectatorship and Nationhood in Indian Middle-Class Modernity." *The Journal of the Royal Anthropological Institute* 17: S159–S175.

Ranade, Ashok Damodar. 1984. *On Music and Musicians of Hindoostan*. New Delhi: Promilla.

Ranganathan, Sumitra. 2015. "Dwelling in My Voice: Tradition as Musical Judgment and Aesthetic Sense in North Indian Classical Dhrupad." PhD Thesis, University of California, Berkeley.

Rathna Kumar, S. B., Suhail Azeem, Abhishek Kumar Choudhary, and S. G. R. Prakash. 2013. "The Role of Auditory and Kinaesthetic Feedback Mechanisms on Phonatory Stability in Children." *Indian Journal of Otolaryngology and Head and Neck Surgery: Official Publication of the Association of Otolaryngologists of India* 65(Suppl 3): 562–568.

Report. 1925. "Report of the 4th All-India Music Conference." Lucknow: Taluqdar Press.

Revuluri, Sindhumathi. 2013. "Shifting the Gaze." *Journal of the American Musicological Society* 66(3): 848–852.

Riedel, Friedlind. 2015. "Music as atmosphere. Lines of becoming in congregational worship." *Lebenswelt: Aesthetics and Philosophy of Experience* 6: 80–111.

Riedel, Friedlind, and Juha Torvinen. 2019. *Music as Atmosphere: Collective Feelings and Affective Sounds*. London: Routledge.

Rommen, Timothy. 2007. *Mek Some Noise: Gospel Music and the Ethics of Style in Trinidad*. Berkeley: University of California Press.

Ross, Thomas W. 1993. "Forgotten Patterns: 'Mirkhand' and Amir Khan." *Asian Music* 24(2): 89–109.

Roy, Jeff. "From Jalsah to Jalsā: Music, Identity, and (Gender) Transitioning at a Hījṛā Rite of Initiation." *Ethnomusicology* 61(3): 389–418.

Roy, Robindra Lal. 1934. "Hindustani Ragas." *The Musical Quarterly* 20(3): 320–333.

Ryan, Ted. 2012. "Coke Studio Fuses Genres & Creates International Franchise." The Coca-Cola Company. 2012. Accessed April 8, 2021 at https://www.coca-colaindia.com/stories/music-transcends-everything-coke-studio-fuses-genres-and-cultures-creates-international-franchise.

Rydstrøm, Helle. 2003. *Embodying Morality: Growing Up in Rural Northern Vietnam*. Honolulu: University of Hawaii Press.

Saeed, Fouzia. 2015. *Taboo!: The Hidden Culture of a Red Light Area*. Made For Success Publishing.

Sahasrabuddhe, Veena, and Martin Clayton. 1999. *Khyal: Classical Singing of North India*. Booklet Accompanying Video Cassette. Ethno VC3. Milton Keynes: Open University.

Sanford, A. Whitney. 2009. *Singing Krishna: Sound Becomes Sight in Paramanand's Poetry*. Albany: SUNY Press.

Sanyal, Ritwik, and Richard Widdess. 2004. *Dhrupad: Tradition and Performance in Indian Music*. London: Ashgate.

Sathaye. 2010. "The Production of Unpleasurable *Rasas* in the Sanskrit Dramas of Ārya Kṣemīśvara." *Journal of the American Oriental Society* 130(3): 361–384.

Sathya Sai Baba. 2004. *A Compendium of the Teachings of Sri Sathya Sai Baba*. Bangalore: Sai Towers Publishing.

Satyasheel Deshpande. 2017. "Pandit Satyasheel Deshpande Pays Tribute to Kishoritai Amonkar." *Mumbai Mirror*, Accessed April 8, 2021 at https://mumbaimirror.indiatimes.com/mumbai/other/when-music-fell-silent/articleshow/58019052.cms.

Saxena, S. K. 1976. "Ustad A. Rahimuddin Khan Dagur." *Sangeet Natak* 39: 5–22.

Saxena, Sushil Kumar. 1974. "Ameer Khan: The Man and His Art." *Journal of the Sangeet Natak Akademi* 31: 5–12.

———. 2010. *Aesthetics: Approaches, Concepts and Problems*. 2010 ed. New Delhi: D.K. Printworld.

———. 2012. *The Winged Form: Aesthetical Essays on Hindustani Rhythm*. New Delhi: Sangeet Natak Akademi and D.K. Printworld.

Scarimbolo, Justin. 2014. Brahmans Beyond Nationalism, Muslims Beyond Dominance: A Hidden History of North Indian Classical Music's Hinduization. PhD Thesis, University of California, Santa Barbara.

Schofield, Katherine. 2016. "15. Learning to Taste the Emotions: The Mughal Rasika." In *Tellings and Texts: Music, Literature and Performance in North India*, edited by Francesca Orsini, 407–421. OBP Collection. Cambridge: Open Book Publishers.

Schofield, Katherine, and Francesca Orsini, eds. 2016. *Tellings and Texts: Music, Literature and Performance in North India*. OBP Collection. Cambridge: Open Book Publishers.

Schultz, Anna. 2002. "Hindu Nationalism, Music, and Embodiment in Marathi Rāshṭrīya Kīrtan." *Ethnomusicology* 46(2): 307–322.

———. 2013. *Singing a Hindu Nation: Marathi Devotional Performance and Nationalism*. New York: Oxford University Press.

———. 2014. "Bollywood Bhajans: Style as 'Air' in an Indian-Guyanese Twice-Migrant Community." *Ethnomusicology Forum* 23(3): 383–404.

Scott, J. Barton. 2014. "Unsaintly Virtue: Swami Dayananda Saraswati and Modern Hindu Hagiography." *The Journal of Hindu Studies* 7(3): 371–391.

Scott, Stan. 1997. "Power and Delight: Vocal Training in North Indian Classical Music." PhD Thesis, Wesleyan University.

Sen, Amartya. 2006. *The Argumentative Indian: Writings on Indian History, Culture and Identity*. New York: Macmillan.

Sengupta, Ranjan, et al. 1989. "Acoustic Comparison of Nasal and Non-Nasal Indian Classical Singing." *Journal of the Acoustical Society of India* 27(3–4): 285–289.

Sharma, Govind. 2017. *The Dev Anand Story*. Chennai: Notion Press.

Shringy, R. K. (trans.), and Dr. Prem Lata Sharma. 2007. *Sangitaratnakara Of Sarngadeva: Text and English Translation with Comments and Notes, New Delhi:* Munshiram Manoharlal Publishers Pvt. Limited.

Silver, Brian, and R. Arnold Burghardt. 1976. "On Becoming an Ustād: Six Life Sketches in the Evolution of a Gharānā." *Asian Music* 7(2): 27–58.

Singh, R. Raj. 2006. *Bhakti and Philosophy*. Lanham, MD: Lexington Books.

Singh, Veenu. 2018. "Merging the Modern with the Traditional: Muzaffar Ali Version 2.0." *Hindustan Times*, July 15, 2018.

Sinha, Juhi. 2016. "Begum Akhtar – 'Her Voice Was Flawed But That Was The Beauty Of It.'" *Kractivism*. Accessed April 8, 2021 at http://www.kractivist.org/begum-akhtar-her-voice-was-flawed-but-that-was-the-beauty-of-it/.

Skelchy, Russell P. 2019. "Voice, Age, and Islamic Practice in the Life of the Indonesian Keroncong Vocalist Waldjinah." *Ethnomusicology* 63(3): 445–469.

Slawek, Stephen. 1986. "Kirtan: A Study of the Sonic Manifestations of the Divine in the Popular Hindu Culture of Banāras." PhD Thesis, University of Illinois.

Slawek, Stephen M. 1988. "Popular Kīrtan in Benares: Some 'Great' Aspects of a Little Tradition." *Ethnomusicology* 32(2): 77–92.

Small, Christopher. 2012. *Musicking: The Meanings of Performing and Listening*. Middletown, CT: Wesleyan University Press.

Srivastava, Sanjay. 2004. "Voice, Gender and Space in Time of Five-Year Plans: The Idea of Lata Mangeshkar." *Economic and Political Weekly* 39(20): 2019–2028.

Srinivasan, Amrit. 2020. "Nepotism Is Key in Musical Gharanas Too. But Anger Only for Sushant Singh Rajput." Accessed April 8, 2021 at *ThePrint.In*. https://theprint.in/opinion/nepotism-is-key-in-musical-gharanas-too-but-anger-only-for-sushant-singh-rajput/472944/.

Stokes, Martin. 2010. *The Republic of Love: Cultural Intimacy in Turkish Popular Music*. Chicago: University of Chicago Press.

Strathern, Marilyn. 1988. *The Gender of the Gift: Problems with Women and Problems with Society in Melanesia*. Berkeley: University of California Press.

Subramanian, Lakshmi. 2005. "The Voice in Colonial and Post-Colonial India." *Economic and Political Weekly* 40(15): 1561–1562.

Sudnow, David. 1993. *Ways of the Hand: The Organization of Improvised Conduct*. Cambridge: The MIT Press.

Sundar, Pavitra. 2007. "Meri Awaaz Suno: Women, Vocality, and Nation in Hindi Cinema." *Meridians: Feminism, Race, Transnationalism* 8(1): 144–179.

Syring, David. 2009. "La Vida Matizada: Time Sense, Everyday Rhythms, and Globalized Ideas of Work." *Anthropology and Humanism* 34(2): 119–142.

Tankha, Madhur. 2018a. "On Garments That Embrace Sufism by Muzaffar Ali and Yasmin Kidwai." *The Hindu.* sec. Fashion. Accessed April 8, 2021 at https://www.thehindu.com/life-and-style/fashion/bringing-mysticism-into-mainstream/article23800931.ece.

Taussig, Michael T. 1993. *Mimesis and Alterity: A Particular History of the Senses.* London: Psychology Press.

Taylor, Charles. 1989. *Sources of the Self: The Making of the Modern Identity.* Cambridge: Harvard University Press.

Taylor, Timothy D. 2002. "Music and the Rise of Radio in 1920s America: Technological Imperialism, Socialization, and the Transformation of Intimacy." *Historical Journal of Film, Radio and Television* 22(4): 425–443.

Thatte, Arvind. 2010. *Sangeet Vimarsha: A Bouquet of Thoughts about the North Indian Classical Music.* Pune: Swanandi Prakashan.

Thomas, Rosie. 1985. "Indian Cinema: Pleasures and Popularity." *Screen* 26(3–4): 116–131.

Titze, Ingo R. 2001. "Acoustic Interpretation of Resonant Voice." *Journal of Voice* 15(4): 519–528.

Tiwari, Soumya. 2016. "I Don't like Hindi Film Songs: Begum Parveen Sultana." *Hindustan Times (Lucknow),* April 30, 2016.

Tomatis, Alfred, and Francis Keeping. 2005. *The Ear and the Voice.* Lanham, MD: Scarecrow Press.

Trivedi, Harish. 2004. "The Anxiety of Hindustani." In *The Yearbook of South Asian Languages and Linguistics,* edited by Rajendra Singh. Walter de Gruyter.

Turino, Thomas. 2003. "Are We Global Yet? Globalist Discourse, Cultural Formations and the Study of Zimbabwean Popular Music." *British Journal of Ethnomusicology* 12(2): 51–79.

Hornbostel, E. M. von. 1928. "African Negro Music." *Africa: Journal of the International African Institute* 1(1): 30–62.

Meer, Wim van der. 2014. "Audience Response and Expressive Pitch Inflections in a Live Recording of Legendary Singer Kesar Bai Kerkar." In *Expressiveness in Music Performance: Empirical Approaches across Styles and Cultures,* 170–184. Oxford: Oxford University Press.

Upadhyay, D. K., and A. K. Dalal. 2016. "Learners Perspectives on Music Training in Institutions of North India." *International Journal of Music Education* 35(4): 500–514.

Upadhyay, Dr. Durgesh. 2015. "Vocal Riyaz and Asthma - From Recovery to Transformation of 'Self.'" Accessed April 8, 2021 at https://doi.org/10.13140/RG.2.1.1284.4882.

Vaidyanathan, Ananth. 2010. "Voice Matters: My Experiences as a Music Voice Engineer."

Voice Matters (blog). Accessed April 8, 2021 at http://ananthvaidyanathan.blogspot.com/2010/01/my-experiences-as-music-voice-engineer.html.

Vajpeyi, Ananya. 2012. *Righteous Republic: The Political Foundations of Modern India*. Cambridge: Harvard University Press.

Van der Meer, W., and S. Rao. 2006. "What You Hear Isn't What You See: The Representation and Cognition of Fast Movements in Hindustani Music." In *Proceedings of the International Symposium Frontiers of Research on Speech and Music*, 12–20.

Vanita, Ruth. 2018. *Dancing with the Nation: Courtesans in Bombay Cinema*. New York: Bloomsbury Publishing USA.

Vergunst, Jo Lee, and Tim Ingold. 2016. *Ways of Walking: Ethnography and Practice on Foot*. London: Routledge.

Viitamäki, Mikko. 2008. "Text and Intensification of Its Impact in Chishti *Samā*." MA Thesis, University of Helsinki.

Virani, Vivek. 2016. "Find the True Country: Devotional Music and the Self in India's National Culture." PhD Thesis, UCLA.

Wade, Bonnie C. 1984. *Khyal: Creativity Within North India's Classical Music Tradition*. Cambridge: Cambridge University Press.

Waheed, Sarah. 2014. "Women of 'Ill Repute': Ethics and Urdu Literature in Colonial India." *Modern Asian Studies* 48(4): 986–1023.

Ware, Rudolph T. 2014. *The Walking Qur'an: Islamic Education, Embodied Knowledge, and History in West Africa*. Chapel Hill: University of North Carolina Press.

Waugh, Linda R., and C. H. van Schooneveld. 1980. *The Melody of Language*. Baltimore: University Park Press.

Weidman, Amanda. 2014. "Neoliberal Logics of Voice: Playback Singing and Public Femaleness in South India." *Culture, Theory and Critique* 55(2): 175–193.

———. 2016. "Circulating Voices: The Gendered Beginnings of Playback." *Working Papers of the Chicago Tamil Forum* 3: 47.

Weidman, Amanda J. 2006. *Singing the Classical, Voicing the Modern: The Postcolonial Politics of Music in South India*. Durham: Duke University Press.

Weston, Patrick. 2013. "Qawwals of Ajmer: Hereditary Musicians Making Connections at a Cultural Crossroads." PhD Thesis, University of Wisconsin, Madison.

Widdess, Richard. 1994a. "Festivals of Dhrupad in Northern India: New Contexts for an Ancient Art." *British Journal of Ethnomusicology* 3: 89–109.

———. 1994b. "Involving the Performers in Transcription and Analysis: A Collaborative Approach to Dhrupad." *Ethnomusicology* 38(1): 59–79.

Williams, Richard and Rafay Mahmood. 2020. "A Soundtrack for Reimagining Pakistan? Coke Studio, Memory and the Music Video." *Bioscope* 10(2): 111–128.

Williams, Tyler Walker. 2014. "Sacred Sounds and Sacred Books: A History of Writing in Hindi." PhD Thesis, Columbia University.

Wolf, Richard. 2009. *Theorizing the Local: Music, Practice, and Experience in South Asia and Beyond*. Oxford: Oxford University Press.

Wolf, Richard K. 2014. *The Voice in the Drum: Music, Language, and Emotion in Islamicate South Asia*. Champaign: University of Illinois Press.

Wulff, Donna Marie. 1984. *Drama as a Mode of Religious Realization: The Vidagdhamādhava of Rūpa Gosvāmī*. Chico, CA: Scholars Press.

Yahav, Amit S. 2018. *Feeling Time: Duration, the Novel, and Eighteenth-Century Sensibility*. Philadelphia: University of Pennsylvania Press.

Zahavi, Dan. 1999. *Self-Awareness and Alterity: A Phenomenological Investigation*. Evanston: Northwestern University Press.

Ziad, Homayra. 2007. "'I Transcend Myself Like a Melody': Khwajah Mir Dard and Music in Eighteenth-Century Delhi." *The Muslim World* 97(4): 548–570.

———. 2010. "Poetry, Music and the Muhammadi Path: How Khvajah Mir Dard Brought Three Worlds Together in Eighteenth-Century Delhi." *Journal of Islamic Studies* 21 (September): 345–376.

Zuberi, Irfan, and Natalie Sarrazin. 2017. "Evolution of a Ritual Musical Genre: The Adaptation of Qawwali in Contemporary Indian Film." In *Music in Contemporary Indian Film: Memory, Voice, Identity*, 162–175. London: Routledge.

INDEX

Page numbers in *italics* refer to figures

MUSIC / CULTURE

A series from Wesleyan University Press
Edited by Deborah Wong, Sherrie Tucker, and Jeremy Wallach
Originating editors: George Lipsitz, Susan McClary, and Robert Walser

The Music/Culture series has consistently reshaped and redirected music scholarship. Founded in 1993 by George Lipsitz, Susan McClary, and Robert Walser, the series features outstanding critical work on music. Unconstrained by disciplinary divides, the series addresses music and power through a range of times, places, and approaches. Music/Culture strives to integrate a variety of approaches to the study of music, linking analysis of musical significance to larger issues of power—what is permitted and forbidden, who is included and excluded, who speaks and who gets silenced. From ethnographic classics to cutting-edge studies, Music/Culture zeroes in on how musicians articulate social needs, conflicts, coalitions, and hope. Books in the series investigate the cultural work of music in urgent and sometimes experimental ways, from the radical fringe to the quotidian. Music/Culture asks deep and broad questions about music through the framework of the most restless and rigorous critical theory.

Marié Abe
Resonances of Chindon-ya: Sounding Space and Sociality in Contemporary Japan

Frances Aparicio
Listening to Salsa: Gender, Latin Popular Music, and Puerto Rican Cultures

Paul Austerlitz
Jazz Consciousness: Music, Race, and Humanity

Christina Baade and Kristin McGee
Beyoncé in the World: Making Meaning with Queen Bey in Troubled Times

Emma Baulch
Genre Publics: Popular Music, Technologies, and Class in Indonesia

Harris M. Berger
Metal, Rock, and Jazz: Perception and the Phenomenology of Musical Experience

Harris M. Berger
Stance: Ideas about Emotion, Style, and Meaning for the Study of Expressive Culture

Harris M. Berger and Giovanna P. Del Negro
Identity and Everyday Life: Essays in the Study of Folklore, Music, and Popular Culture

Franya J. Berkman
Monument Eternal: The Music of Alice Coltrane

Dick Blau, Angeliki Vellou Keil, and Charles Keil
Bright Balkan Morning: Romani Lives and the Power of Music in Greek Macedonia

Susan Boynton and Roe-Min Kok, editors
Musical Childhoods and the Cultures of Youth

James Buhler, Caryl Flinn, and David Neumeyer, editors
Music and Cinema

Thomas Burkhalter, Kay Dickinson, and Benjamin J. Harbert, editors
The Arab Avant-Garde: Music, Politics, Modernity

Patrick Burkart
Music and Cyberliberties

Julia Byl
Antiphonal Histories: Resonant Pasts in the Toba Batak Musical Present

Corinna Campbell
Parameters and Peripheries of Culture: Interpreting Maroon Music and Dance in Paramaribo, Suriname

Daniel Cavicchi
Listening and Longing: Music Lovers in the Age of Barnum

Susan D. Crafts, Daniel Cavicchi, Charles Keil, and the Music in Daily Life Project
My Music: Explorations of Music in Daily Life

Jim Cullen
Born in the USA: Bruce Springsteen and the American Tradition

Anne Danielsen
Presence and Pleasure: The Funk Grooves of James Brown and Parliament

Peter Doyle
Echo and Reverb: Fabricating Space in Popular Music Recording, 1900–1960

Ron Emoff
Recollecting from the Past: Musical Practice and Spirit Possession on the East Coast of Madagascar

Yayoi Uno Everett and Frederick Lau, editors
Locating East Asia in Western Art Music

Susan Fast and Kip Pegley, editors
Music, Politics, and Violence

Heidi Feldman
Black Rhythms of Peru: Reviving African Musical Heritage in the Black Pacific

Kai Fikentscher
"You Better Work!" Underground Dance Music in New York City

Ruth Finnegan
The Hidden Musicians: Music-Making in an English Town

Daniel Fischlin and Ajay Heble, editors
The Other Side of Nowhere: Jazz, Improvisation, and Communities in Dialogue

Wendy Fonarow
Empire of Dirt: The Aesthetics and Rituals of British "Indie" Music

Murray Forman
The 'Hood Comes First: Race, Space, and Place in Rap and Hip-Hop

Lisa Gilman
My Music, My War: The Listening Habits of U.S. Troops in Iraq and Afghanistan

Paul D. Greene and Thomas Porcello, editors
Wired for Sound: Engineering and Technologies in Sonic Cultures

Tomie Hahn
Sensational Knowledge: Embodying Culture through Japanese Dance

Edward Herbst
Voices in Bali: Energies and Perceptions i n Vocal Music and Dance Theater

Deborah Kapchan
Traveling Spirit Masters: Moroccan Gnawa Trance and Music in the Global Marketplace

Deborah Kapchan, editor
Theorizing Sound Writing

Max Katz
Lineage of Loss: Counternarratives of North Indian Music

Raymond Knapp
Symphonic Metamorphoses: Subjectivity and Alienation in Mahler's Re-Cycled Songs

Victoria Lindsay Levine and Dylan Robinson, editors
Music and Modernity among First Peoples of North America

Laura Lohman
Umm Kulthūm: Artistic Agency and the Shaping of an Arab Legend, 1967–2007

Preston Love
A Thousand Honey Creeks Later: My Life in Music from Basie to Motown—and Beyond

René T. A. Lysloff and Leslie C. Gay Jr., editors
Music and Technoculture

Ian MacMillen
Playing It Dangerously: Tambura Bands, Race, and Affective Block in Croatia and Its Intimates

Allan Marett
Songs, Dreamings, and Ghosts: The Wangga of North Australia

Ian Maxwell
Phat Beats, Dope Rhymes: Hip Hop Down Under Comin' Upper

Kristin A. McGee
Some Liked It Hot: Jazz Women in Film and Television, 1928–1959

Tracy McMullen
Haunthenticity: Musical Replay and the Fear of the Real

Rebecca S. Miller
Carriacou String Band Serenade: Performing Identity in the Eastern Caribbean

Tony Mitchell, editor
Global Noise: Rap and Hip-Hop Outside the USA

Christopher Moore and
Philip Purvis, editors
Music & Camp

Rachel Mundy
Animal Musicalities: Birds, Beasts, and Evolutionary Listening

Keith Negus
Popular Music in Theory: An Introduction

Johnny Otis
Upside Your Head: Rhythm and Blues on Central Avenue

Jeff Packman
Living from Music in Salvador: Professional Musicians and the Capital of Afro-Brazil

Kip Pegley
Coming to You Wherever You Are: MuchMusic, MTV, and Youth Identities

Jonathan Pieslak
Radicalism and Music: An Introduction to the Music Cultures of al-Qa'ida, Racist Skinheads, Christian-Affiliated Radicals, and Eco-Animal Rights Militants

Matthew Rahaim
Musicking Bodies: Gesture and Voice in Hindustani Music

Matthew Rahaim
Ways of Voice: Vocal Striving and Ethical Contestation in North India and Beyond

John Richardson
Singing Archaeology: Philip Glass's Akhnaten

Tricia Rose
Black Noise: Rap Music and Black Culture in Contemporary America

David Rothenberg and
Marta Ulvaeus, editors
The Book of Music and Nature: An Anthology of Sounds, Words, Thoughts

Nichole Rustin-Paschal
The Kind of Man I Am: Jazzmasculinity and the World of Charles Mingus Jr.

Marta Elena Savigliano
Angora Matta: Fatal Acts of North-South Translation

Joseph G. Schloss
Making Beats: The Art of Sample-Based Hip-Hop

Barry Shank
Dissonant Identities: The Rock 'n' Roll Scene in Austin, Texas

Jonathan Holt Shannon
Among the Jasmine Trees: Music and Modernity in Contemporary Syria

Daniel B. Sharp
Between Nostalgia and Apocalypse: Popular Music and the Staging of Brazil

Helena Simonett
Banda: Mexican Musical Life across Borders

Mark Slobin
Subcultural Sounds: Micromusics of the West

Mark Slobin, editor
Global Soundtracks: Worlds of Film Music

Tes Slominski
Trad Nation: Gender, Sexuality, and Race in Irish Traditional Music

Christopher Small
The Christopher Small Reader

Christopher Small
Music of the Common Tongue: Survival and Celebration in African American Music

Christopher Small
Music, Society, Education

Christopher Small
Musicking: The Meanings of Performing and Listening

Maria Sonevytsky
Wild Music: Sound and Sovereignty in Ukraine

Regina M. Sweeney
Singing Our Way to Victory: French Cultural Politics and Music during the Great War

Colin Symes
Setting the Record Straight: A Material History of Classical Recording

Steven Taylor
False Prophet: Field Notes from the Punk Underground

Paul Théberge
Any Sound You Can Imagine: Making Music/Consuming Technology

Sarah Thornton
Club Cultures: Music, Media, and Subcultural Capital

Michael E. Veal
Dub: Songscape and Shattered Songs in Jamaican Reggae

Michael E. Veal and E. Tammy Kim, editors
Punk Ethnography: Artists and Scholars Listen to Sublime Frequencies

Robert Walser
Running with the Devil: Power, Gender, and Madness in Heavy Metal Music

Dennis Waring
Manufacturing the Muse: Estey Organs and Consumer Culture in Victorian America

Lise A. Waxer
The City of Musical Memory: Salsa, Record Grooves, and Popular Culture in Cali, Colombia

Mina Yang
Planet Beethoven: Classical Music at the Turn of the Millennium

ABOUT THE AUTHOR

Matthew Rahaim is Professor of Ethnomusicology at the University of Minnesota. He is the author of *Musicking Bodies: Gesture and Voice in Hindustani Music* (2012). Recent essays include "Object, Person, Machine, or What: Practical Ontologies of Voice" (2019) and "Not Just One, Not Just Now: Voices in Relation" (2021.) He is also a Hindustani vocalist in the Gwalior tradition and a shagird of Laxman Krishnarao Pandit.